Lecture Notes in Computer Science 5713

Commenced Publication in 1973
Founding and Former Series Editors:
Gerhard Goos, Juris Hartmanis, and Jan van Leeuwen

W0193021

Andrew Butterfield (Ed.)

Unifying Theories of Programming

Second International Symposium, UTP 2008
Dublin, Ireland, September 8-10, 2008
Revised Selected Papers

 Springer

Volume Editor

Andrew Butterfield
University of Dublin, Trinity College, O'Reilly Institute
School of Computer Science and Statistics
Dublin 2, Ireland
E-mail: Andrew.Butterfield@cs.tcd.ie

Cover illustration: Andrew Butterfield, Ireland

Library of Congress Control Number: 2010930465

CR Subject Classification (1998): F.3, D.2, D.2.4, D.3, F.4.1, I.2.3

LNCS Sublibrary: SL 1 – Theoretical Computer Science and General Issues

ISSN   0302-9743
ISBN-10   3-642-14520-5 Springer Berlin Heidelberg New York
ISBN-13   978-3-642-14520-9 Springer Berlin Heidelberg New York

springer.com

© Springer-Verlag Berlin Heidelberg 2010
Printed in Germany

Typesetting: Camera-ready by author, data conversion by Scientific Publishing Services, Chennai, India
Printed on acid-free paper   06/3180

Preface

This book constitutes the thoroughly refereed proceedings of the Second International Symposium on Unifying Theories of Programming, UTP 2008, held at Trinity College, Dublin, Ireland, in September 2008.

This symposium followed on the success of the first held at Walworth Castle in 2006. Based on the pioneering work on unifying theories of programming of Tony Hoare, He Jifeng, and others, the aims of this symposium series are to continue to reaffirm the significance of the ongoing UTP project, to encourage efforts to advance it by providing a focus for the sharing of results by those already actively contributing, and to raise awareness of the benefits of such a unifying theoretical framework among the wider computer science and software engineering communities.

There were two invited talks, one of which appears here in full, the other in abstract form. We would like to warmly thank both Jifeng He and Ralph-Johann Back for their enthusiastic and engaged participation in this event.

There was a two-phase review process involved in assembling these proceedings. A pre-symposium full review process selected a number of papers for inclusion in these proceedings and for presentation at the symposium. The authors of the remaining papers were invited to present their work at the symposium as "work-in-progress" papers. Further work-in-progress papers were also solicited for the symposium from the formal methods community, with screening for relevance to the symposium's aims. After the symposium, having received feedback while presenting their papers, the work-in-progress authors were invited to submit expanded revised versions of their papers for inclusion in the proceedings, subject to a similar rigorous full-review process as for the earlier full papers. The 13 papers in this proceedings volume were chosen from a total of 20 submissions, of which 3 were rejected in the first review, presented as work-in-progress and then re-submitted for full review. All papers had at least three reviewers.

The symposium was organized using, and these proceedings assembled with the assistance of, EasyChair (www.easychair.org). I would like to thank them for being there, particularly at the finish!

May 2010

Andrew Butterfield

Conference Organization

Programme Committee

Bernhard Aichernig	Graz University of Technology
Andrew Butterfield	Trinity College Dublin (Chair)
Ana Cavalcanti	University of York
Yifeng Chen	University of Durham
Steve Dunne	University of Teesside
Colin Fidge	Queensland University of Technology
Jeremy Gibbons	University of Oxford
Lindsay Groves	Victoria University of Wellington
Ian Hayes	University of Queensland
Rick Hehner	University of Toronto
Martin Henson	University of Essex
Arthur Hughes	Trinity College Dublin
Zhiming Liu	United Nations University, Macau
David Naumann	Stevens Institute of Technology, New Jersey
Shengchao Qin	University of Durham
Augusto Sampaio	Universidade Federal de Pernambuco
Jim Woodcock	University of York
Huibiao Zhu	East China Normal University, Shanghai

Additional Reviewers

Brijesh Dongol	University of Queensland
Andreas Griesmayer	United Nations University, Macau
Albert Lai	York University
Sidney Nogueira	Universidade Federal de Pernambuco
Shuling Wang	Peking University, Beijing
Frank Zeyda	University of York

Local Organization

Andrew Butterfield
Paweł Gancarski
Arthur Hughes
Gillian Long

Sponsors

School of Computer Science and Statistics, Trinity College Dublin

Table of Contents

Refinement Calculus as a Theory of Contracts (Invited Paper)

Ralph-Johan Back

Abo Akademi University, Turku

Abstract. We describe a foundation for refinement calculus where programs and systems are described as contracts, carried out by a collection of interacting agents. The contract states explicitly what the agents are allowed to do, and who is to blame if things go wrong. A contract can be analyzed from the point of view of any participating agent or coalition of agents, to see what kind of goals the agents can achieve by following the contract. We give an intuitive overview of contracts in this setting, and then continue to describe the mathematical and logical foundations of the calculus. We show how contracts provide a unified framework for a number of seemingly different paradigms in computer science, such as concurrency, interactivity, games, temporal behavior vs input-output computation and high level system design.

A. Butterfield (Ed.): UTP 2008, LNCS 5713, p. 1, 2010.

Transaction Calculus
(Invited Paper)

Jifeng He*

Shanghai Key Laboratory of Trustworthy Computing
Software Engineering Institute
East China Normal University, China
jifeng@sei.ecnu.edu.cn

Abstract. Transaction-based services are increasingly being applied in solving many universal interoperability problems. Compensation is one typical feature for long-running transactions. This paper presents a design model for specifying the behaviour of compensable programs. The new model for handling exception and compensation is built as conservative extension of the standard relational model. The paper puts forward a mathematical framework for transactions where a transaction is treated as a mapping from its environment to compensable programs. We propose a transaction refinement calculus, and show that every transaction can be converted to a primitive one which simply consists of a forward activity and a compensation module.

1 Introduction

With the development of Internet technology, web services and web-based applications play an important role to information systems. The aim of web services is to achieve the universal interoperability between different web-based applications. Due to the provided interface, web services can be invoked across the Internet. In recent years, in order to develop web-based information systems and describe the infrastructure for carrying out business transactions, various business modelling languages have been introduced, such as XLANG, WSFL, BPEL4WS (BPEL) and StAC [7, 9, 16, 25].

Compensation is one typical feature for long-running transactions. Butler *et al.* investigated the compensation feature in the style of process algebra CSP [6–8]. StAC (Structured Activity Compensation) [6] is a business process modelling language, where compensation acts as one of its main features. Its operational semantics has also been studied in [7]. Further, Bruni *et al.* studied the transaction calculi for StAC programs in the form of Java API [4]. Qiu *et al.* carried a deep formal analysis of the fault behaviour for BPEL-like processes [23].

---

* This work is partially supported by the National Basic Research Program of China (No. 2005CB321904), the National High Technology Research and Development Program of China (No. 2007AA010302), the National Natural Science Foundation of China (No. 90718004) and Shanghai Leading Academic Discipline Project (No. B412).

A. Butterfield (Ed.): UTP 2008, LNCS 5713, pp. 2–21, 2010.

He *et al.* proposed a mathematical model for BPEL and explored its algebraic properties in [12].

The π-calculus has been applied in describing various compensable program models. Lucchi and Mazzara formalised the semantics of BPEL within the framework of the π-calculus [19]. Laneve and Zavattaro explored the application of the π-calculus in the formalisation of the compensable programs and the standard pattern of composition [17].

This paper is an attempt at taking a step forward to gain some perspectives on long-running transactions within the design calculus [15]. Our contributions include

- providing a conservative extension of the standard relational model to deal with fault handling and compensation
- establishing an algebraic system for exception handling and compensation.
- constructing a mathematical model for transactions and their combinators
- presenting a refinement calculus for transactions

The paper is organised as follows: Section 2 proposes an enriched design model for compensable programs where new healthiness conditions are introduced to identify such a subclass. We also show that this set of designs is closed under the conventional programming combinators. We provide a behavioural semantics for compensable programs, and present a set of new combinators in dealing with compensation and coordination. Section 4 is devoted to transaction combinators and their algebraic properties. The paper concludes with a short discussion.

2   An Enriched Design Model

In this section we work towards a precise characterisation of the class of *designs* [15] that can handle new programming features such as program failure, coordination and compensation.

A subclass of designs may be defined in a variety of ways. Sometimes it is done by a syntactic property. Sometimes the definition requires satisfaction of a particular collection of algebraic laws. In general, the most useful definitions are these that are given in many different forms, together with a proof that all of them are equivalent. This section will put forward additional healthiness conditions to capture such a subclass of designs. We leave their corresponding algebraic laws in Section 3.

2.1   Exception Handling

To handling exception requires a more explicit analysis of the phenomena of program execution. We therefore introduce into the alphabet of our designs a pair of Boolean variables *eflag* and *eflag'* to denote the relevant observations:

- *eflag* records the observation that the program is asked to start when the execution of its predecessor halts due to an exception.

– $eflag'$ records the observation that an exception occurs during the execution of the program.

The introduction of error states has implication for sequential composition: all the exception cases of program P are of course also the exception cases of $P;Q$. Rather than change the definition of sequential composition given in [15], we enforce these rules by means a healthiness condition: if the program Q is asked to start in an exception case of its predecessor, it leaves the state unchanged

$$(\mathbf{Req_1})\ Q\ =\ II \lhd eflag \rhd Q$$

when the design II adopts the following definition

$$II =_{df} true \vdash (s' = s)$$

where s denotes all the variables in the alphabet of Q.

A design is $\mathbf{Req_1}$-healthy if it satisfies the healthiness condition $\mathbf{Req_1}$. Define

$$\mathcal{H}_1(Q) =_{df} (II \lhd eflag \rhd Q)$$

Clearly $\mathcal{H}_1$ is idempotent. As a result, Q is $\mathbf{Req_1}$ healthy if and only if Q lies in the range of $\mathcal{H}_1$.

The following theorem indicates $\mathbf{Req_1}$-healthy designs are closed under conventional programming combinators.

Theorem 2.1

(1) $\mathcal{H}_1(P \sqcap Q)\ =\ \mathcal{H}_1(P) \sqcap \mathcal{H}_1(Q)$

(2) $\mathcal{H}_1(P \lhd b \rhd Q)\ =\ \mathcal{H}_1(P) \lhd b \rhd \mathcal{H}_1(Q)$

(3) $\mathcal{H}_1(P; \mathcal{H}_1(Q))\ =\ \mathcal{H}_1(P); \mathcal{H}_1(Q)$

2.2   Rollback

To equip a program with compensation mechanism, it is necessary to figure out the cases when the execution control has to rollback. By adopting the technique used in the exception handling model, we introduce a new logical variable $forward$ to describe the status of control flow of the execution of a program:

– $forward' = true$ indicates successful termination of the execution of the forward activity of a program. In this case, its successor will carry on with the initial state set up by the program.
– $forward' = false$ indicates it is required to undo the effect caused by the execution of the program. In this case, the corresponding compensation module will be invoked.

As a result, a program must keep idle when it is asked to start in a state where $forward = false$, i.e., it has to meet the following healthiness condition:

$$(\mathbf{Req_2})\ Q\ =\ II \lhd \neg forward \rhd Q$$

This condition can be identified by the idempotent mapping

$$\mathcal{H}_2(Q) \ =_{df} \ II \lhd \neg forward \rhd Q$$

in the sense that a program meets $\mathbf{Req}_2$ iff it is a fixed point of $\mathcal{H}_2$

We can characterize both $\mathbf{Req_1}$ and $\mathbf{Req_2}$ by composing $\mathcal{H}_1$ and $\mathcal{H}_2$. To ensure that their composition is an idempotent mapping we are going to show that

Theorem 2.2

$\mathcal{H}_2 \circ \mathcal{H}_1 \ = \ \mathcal{H}_1 \circ \mathcal{H}_2$

Proof. From the fact that

$$\mathcal{H}_1(\mathcal{H}_2(Q)) \ = \ II \lhd eflag \vee \neg foward \rhd Q \ = \ \mathcal{H}_2(\mathcal{H}_1(Q))$$

Define $\mathcal{H} \ =_{df} \ \mathcal{H}_1 \circ \mathcal{H}_2$.

Theorem 2.3

A design is healthy (i.e., it satisfies both $\mathbf{Req_1}$ and $\mathbf{Req_2}$) iff it lies in the range of $\mathcal{H}$.

The following theorem indicates that healthy designs are closed under the conventional programming combinators.

Theorem 2.4

(1) $\mathcal{H}(P \sqcap Q) \ = \ \mathcal{H}(P) \sqcap \mathcal{H}(Q)$

(2) $\mathcal{H}(P \lhd b \rhd Q) \ = \ \mathcal{H}(P) \lhd b \rhd \mathcal{H}(Q)$

(3) $\mathcal{H}(P; \mathcal{H}(Q)) \ = \ \mathcal{H}(P); \mathcal{H}(Q)$

In the following sections, we will confine ourselves to healthy designs only.

3   Programs

This section studies a simple programming language, which extends the Guarded Command Language [10] by adding coordination constructs. The syntax of the language is as follows:

$$
\begin{aligned}
P \ ::= \ &\text{skip} \mid \text{fail} \mid \text{throw} \mid \bot \mid x := e \mid \\
&P \sqcap P \mid P \lhd b \rhd P \mid P; P \mid b *_{\mathcal{H}} P \mid \\
&P \text{ else } P \mid P \text{ catch } P \mid P \text{ cpens } P \mid P \text{ or } P \mid P \text{ par } P
\end{aligned}
$$

In the following discussion, v will represent the program variables cited in the alphabet of the program.

3.1   Primitive Commands

The behaviour of the chaotic program $\bot$ is totally unpredictable

$$\bot \ =_{df} \ \mathcal{H}(\mathbf{true})$$

The execution of skip leaves program variables intact.

$$\text{skip} =_{df} \mathcal{H}(\textbf{success})$$

where **success** $=_{df}$ $true \vdash ((v' = v) \wedge forward' \wedge \neg eflag')$

The execution of fail rollbacks the control flow.

$$\text{fail} =_{df} \mathcal{H}(\textbf{rollback})$$

where **rollback** $=_{df}$ $true \vdash ((v' = v) \wedge \neg forward' \wedge \neg eflag')$

An exception case arises from the execution of throw

$$\text{throw} =_{df} \mathcal{H}(\textbf{error})$$

where **error** $=_{df}$ $true \vdash ((v' = v) \wedge eflag')$

3.2   Nondeterministic Choice and Sequential Composition

The nondeterministic choice and sequential composition have exactly the same meaning as the corresponding operators on the single predicates defined in [15].

$$P; Q =_{df} \exists m \bullet (P[m/s'] \wedge Q[m/s])$$

$$P \sqcap Q =_{df} P \vee Q$$

The change in the definition of $\perp$ and skip requires us to give a proof of the relevant laws.

Theorem 3.1

(1) $\text{skip}; P \ = \ P \ = \ P; \text{skip}$

(2) $\perp; P \ = \ \perp$

(3) $\perp \sqcap P \ = \ \perp$

Proof. Let $s = (v, forward, eflag)$.

(1) $\text{skip}; P$ {Theorem 2.4(3)}

$= \ \mathcal{H}(\textbf{success}; P)$ $\{\mathcal{H}(Q) \ = \ \mathcal{H}((forward \wedge \neg eflag)^{\top}; Q)\}$

$= \ \mathcal{H}((true \vdash (s' = s)); P)$ $\{(true \vdash (s' = s); D \ = \ D\}$

$= \ \mathcal{H}(P)$ $\{P$ is healthy$\}$

$= \ P$

Besides the laws presented in [15] for composition and nondeterministic choice, there are additional left zero laws for sequential composition.

Theorem 3.2

(1) $\text{throw}; P \ = \ \text{throw}$

(2) $\text{fail}; P \ = \text{fail}$

Proof

(1) $\textbf{throw}; P$ {Theorem 2.4(3)}

$= \mathcal{H}(\textbf{error}; P)$ {Def of **error**}

$= \mathcal{H}(\textbf{error}; (eflag)_\perp; P)$ {$P = \mathcal{H}(P)$}

$= \mathcal{H}(\textbf{error}; (eflag)_\perp; \mathcal{H}(P)[true/eflag])$ {Def of $\mathcal{H}$}

$= \mathcal{H}(\textbf{error}; (eflag)_\perp)$ {Def of **throw**}

$= \textbf{throw}$

3.3   Assignment

Successful execution of an assignment relies on the assumption that the expression will be successfully evaluated.

$$x := e \ =_{df} \ \textbf{skip}[e/x] \lhd \mathcal{D}(e) \rhd \textbf{throw}$$

where the boolean condition $\mathcal{D}(e)$ is true in just those circumstances in which e can be successfully evaluated [21]. For example we can define

$$\mathcal{D}(c) =_{df} true \ \text{ if } c \text{ is a constant}$$

$$\mathcal{D}(e_1 + e_2) =_{df} \mathcal{D}(e_1) \wedge \mathcal{D}(e_2)$$

$$\mathcal{D}(e_1/e_2) =_{df} \mathcal{D}(e_1) \wedge \mathcal{D}(e_2) \wedge e_2 \neq 0$$

$$\mathcal{D}(e_1 \lhd b \rhd e_2) =_{df} \mathcal{D}(b) \wedge (b \Rightarrow \mathcal{D}(e_1)) \wedge (\neg b \Rightarrow \mathcal{D}(e_2))$$

Notice that $\mathcal{D}(e)$ is always well-defined, i.e., $\mathcal{D}(\mathcal{D}(e)) = true$.

Definition 3.1

An assignment $x := e$ is *total* if the expression e is well-defined, i.e., $\mathcal{D}(e) = true$.

3.4   Conditional

The definition of conditional and iteration take the well-definedness of its Boolean test into account

$$P \lhd b \rhd Q \ =_{df} (\mathcal{D}(b) \wedge b \wedge P) \vee (\mathcal{D}(b) \wedge \neg b \wedge Q) \vee \neg \mathcal{D}(b) \wedge \textbf{throw}$$

$$b *_{\mathcal{H}} P \ =_{df} \ \mu_{\mathcal{H}} X \bullet (P; X) \lhd b \rhd \textbf{skip}$$

where $\mu_{\mathcal{H}} X \bullet F(X)$ stands for the weakest **Req**− healthy solution of the equation $X = F(X)$.

The alternation is defined in a similar way

$$\textbf{if}(b_1 \to P_1, .., b_n \to P_n)\textbf{fi} \ =_{df} \ \begin{pmatrix} \bigvee_i (\mathcal{D}(b) \wedge b_i \wedge P_i) \vee \\ \mathcal{D}(b) \wedge \neg b \wedge \perp \vee \\ \neg \mathcal{D}(b) \wedge \textbf{throw} \end{pmatrix}$$

where $b =_{df} \bigvee_i b_i$.

The following theorem illustrates how to convert a conditional into an alternation with well-defined boolean guards.

Theorem 3.3

$P \lhd b \rhd Q =$

if$((b \lhd \mathcal{D}(b) \rhd false) \rightarrow P, (\neg b \lhd \mathcal{D}(b) \rhd false) \rightarrow Q, \neg \mathcal{D}(b) \rightarrow \texttt{throw})$**fi**

A similar transformation can be applied to an assignment.

Theorem 3.4

$x := e = (x, y, .. z := (e, y, .., z) \lhd \mathcal{D}(e) \rhd (x, y, .., z)) \lhd \mathcal{D}(e) \rhd \texttt{throw}$

The previous theorems enable us to confine ourselves to well-defined expressions in later discussion. For total assignment, we are required to reestablish the following laws.

Theorem 3.5

(1) $(x := e; x := f(x)) = (x := f(e))$

(2) $x := e; (P \lhd b(x) \rhd Q) = (x := e; P) \lhd b(e) \rhd (x := e; Q)$

(3) $(x := e) \lhd b \rhd (x := f) = x := (e \lhd b \rhd f)$

(4) $(x := x) = \texttt{skip}$

The following laws for alternation are present in support of normal form reduction [13].

Theorem 3.6

Let $\underline{G}$ denote a list of alternatives, and $x := e$ a total assignment.

(1) **if**$(b_1 \rightarrow P_1, ... P_2, .. b_n \rightarrow P_n)$**fi** $=$ **if**$(b_{\pi(1)} \rightarrow P_{\pi(1)}, .., b_{\pi(n)} \rightarrow P_{\pi(n)})$**fi**

where π is an arbitrary permutation of $\{1, .., n\}$.

(2) **if**$(b \rightarrow$ **if**$(c_1 \rightarrow Q_1, .., c_n \rightarrow Q_n)$**fi**, $\underline{G})$**fi** $=$

  if$(b \wedge c_1 \rightarrow Q_1, .., b \wedge c_n \rightarrow Q_n, \underline{G})$**fi** provided that $\bigvee_k c_k = true$

(3) **if**$(b \rightarrow P, b \rightarrow Q, \underline{G})$**fi** $=$ **if**$(b \rightarrow (P \sqcap Q), \underline{G})$**fi**

(4) $(x := e);$ **if**$(b_1 \rightarrow P_1, .., b_n \rightarrow P_n)$**fi** $=$ **if**$(b_1[e/x] \rightarrow (x := e; P_1), ..., b_n[e/x] \rightarrow (x := e; P_n))$**fi**

(5) **if**$(b_1 \rightarrow P_1, .., b_n \rightarrow P_n)$**fi** $; Q =$ **if**$(b_1 \rightarrow (P_1; Q), .., b_n \rightarrow (P_n; Q))$**fi**

(6) **if**$(b_1 \rightarrow P_1, .., b_n \rightarrow P_n)$**fi** $\sqcap Q =$ **if**$(b_1 \rightarrow (P_1 \sqcap Q), .., b_n \rightarrow (P_n \sqcap Q)$**fi**

(7) **if**$(b_1 \rightarrow P_1, .., b_n \rightarrow P_n)$**fi** $\wedge Q =$ **if**$(b_1 \rightarrow (P_1 \wedge Q), .., b_n \rightarrow (P_n \wedge Q))$**fi**

provided that $\bigvee_k b_k = true$

(8) **if**$(false \rightarrow P, \underline{G})$**fi** $=$ **if**$(\underline{G})$**fi**

(9) **if**$(b_1 \rightarrow P_1, .., b_n \rightarrow P_n)$**fi** $=$ **if**$(b_1 \rightarrow P_1, .., b_n \rightarrow P_n, \neg \bigvee_i b_i \rightarrow \bot)$**fi**

(10) **if**$(true \rightarrow P)$**fi** $= P$

3.5   Error Handling

Let P and Q be programs. The notation P catch Q represents a program which runs P first. If its execution throws an exception case then Q is activated.

$$P \text{ catch } Q \ =_{df} \ \mathcal{H}(P; \phi(Q))$$

where $\phi(Q) \ =_{df} \ II \lhd \neg eflag \rhd Q[false, \, true/eflag, \, forward]$

Theorem 3.7

Let $x := e$ be a total assignment, and b a well-defined boolean expression, and $B \ =_{df} \ (forward \wedge \neg eflag)$.

(1) P catch $(Q$ catch $R) \ = \ (P$ catch $Q)$ catch R

(2) $(\text{throw catch } Q) \ = \ Q \ = \ (Q \text{ catch throw})$

(3) P catch $Q \ = \ P$ if $P \in \{\perp, \text{fail}, (x := e)\}$

(4) $(P; Q)$ catch $R \ = \ P; (Q \text{ catch } R)$ if $B^\top; P \ = \ B^\top; P; B_\perp$.

(5) $(P \lhd b \rhd Q)$ catch $R \ = \ (P \text{ catch } R) \lhd b \rhd (Q \text{ catch } R)$

(6) $(P \sqcap Q)$ catch $R \ = \ (P$ catch $R) \sqcap (Q$ catch $R)$

(7) P catch $(Q \sqcap R) \ = \ (P$ catch $Q) \sqcap (P$ catch $R)$

Proof

(4) *LHS*	{Def of catch}
$= \ \mathcal{H}(P; Q; \phi(R))$	$\{B^\top; P \ = \ B^\top; P; B_\perp\}$
$= \ \mathcal{H}(P; B_\perp; Q; \phi(R))$	{Def of $\mathcal{H}$}
$= \ \mathcal{H}(P; \mathcal{H}(Q; \phi(R)))$	{Theorem 2.4(3)}
$= \ \mathcal{H}(P); \mathcal{H}(Q; \phi(R)))$	{Def of catch}
$= \ RHS$	

3.6   Compensation

Let P and Q be programs. The program P cpens Q runs P first. If its execution fails, then Q is invoked as its compensation.

$$P \text{ cpens } Q \ =_{df} \ \mathcal{H}(P; \psi(Q))$$

where $\psi(Q) =_{df} (II \lhd forward \vee eflag \rhd Q[true/forward])$

Theorem 3.8

Let $x := e$ be a total assignment, and b a well-defined boolean expression, and $B \ =_{df} \ (forwaed \wedge \neg eflag)$.

(1) P cpens $(Q$ cpens $R)$ $=$ $(P$ cpens $Q)$ cpens R

(2) P cpens Q $=$ P if $P \in \{\texttt{throw}, \perp, (x := e)\}$

(3) $(\texttt{fail}\,\texttt{cpens}\,Q)$ $=$ Q $=$ $(Q\,\texttt{cpens}\,\texttt{fail})$

(4) $(P; Q)\,\texttt{cpens}\,R$ $=$ $P; (Q\,\texttt{cpens}\,R)$ if $B^\top; P$ $=$ $B^\top; P; B_\perp$.

(5) $(P \lhd b \rhd Q)\,\texttt{cpens}\,R$ $=$ $(P\,\texttt{cpens}\,R) \lhd b \rhd (Q\,\texttt{catch}\,R)$

(6) $(P \sqcap Q)\,\texttt{cpens}\,R$ $=$ $(P\,\texttt{cpens}\,R) \sqcap (Q\,\texttt{cpens}\,R)$

(7) $P\,\texttt{cpens}\,(Q \sqcap R)$ $=$ $(P\,\texttt{cpens}\,Q) \sqcap (P\,\texttt{cpens}\,R)$

Proof

$(1)\ RHS$ {Def of cpens}

$= \mathcal{H}(\mathcal{H}(P; \psi(Q)); \psi(R))$ {Def of $\mathcal{H}$}

$= \mathcal{H}(B^\top; \mathcal{H}(P; \psi(Q)); \psi(R))$ $\{Q \lhd false \rhd P = P\}$

$= \mathcal{H}(P; \psi(Q); \psi(R))$ $\{\psi(Q); \psi(R) = \psi(Q; \phi(R))\}$

$= \mathcal{H}(P; \psi(Q; \psi(R)))$ $\{\psi(Q) = \psi(\mathcal{H}(Q))\}$

$= \mathcal{H}(P; \psi(\mathcal{H}(Q; \psi(R))))$ {Def of cpens}

$= LHS$

3.7 Coordination

Let P and Q be programs. The program $P\,\texttt{else}\,Q$ behaves like P if its execution succeeds. Otherwise it behaves like Q.

$$P \texttt{ else } Q \ =_{df}\ (P; forward^\top) \vee (\exists t' \bullet P[false/forward'] \wedge Q)$$

where t denotes the vector variable $< ok, eflag, v >$.

Theorem 3.9

Let $x := e$ be a total assignment, and b a well-defined boolean expression.

(1) P else P $=$ P

(2) P else $(Q\,\texttt{else}\,R)$ $=$ $(P$ else $Q)$ else R

(3) P else Q $=$ P if $P \in \{\perp, (x := e), (x := e; \texttt{throw})\}$

(4) $(x := e;\ \texttt{fail})$ else Q $=$ Q

(5) $(P \lhd b \rhd Q)$ else R $=$ $(P\,\texttt{else}\,R) \lhd b \rhd (Q\,\texttt{else}\,R)$

(6) P else $(Q \lhd b \rhd R)$ $=$ $(P\,\texttt{else}\,Q) \lhd b \rhd (P\,\texttt{else}\,R)$

(7) $(P \sqcap Q)$ else R $=$ $(P$ else $R) \sqcap (Q$ else $R)$

(8) P else $(Q \sqcap R)$ $=$ $(P$ else $Q) \sqcap (P$ else $R)$

Proof

(1) LHS {Def of else}

$= P; forward^\top \vee \exists t' \bullet P[false/forward'] \wedge P$ {predicate calculus}

$= (\exists t' \bullet P[false/forward'] \vee \neg \exists t' \bullet P[false/forward'] \wedge \exists t' \bullet P[true/forward']) \wedge$

$\quad (P; forward^\top) \vee \exists t' \bullet P[false/forward'] \wedge P$ $\{forward^\top \vee II = II\}$

$= (\neg \exists t' \bullet P[false/forward'] \wedge \exists t' \bullet P[true/forward']) \wedge (P; forward^\top) \vee$

$\quad \exists t' \bullet P[false/forward'] \wedge P$ $\{P; II = P\}$

$= (\neg \exists t' \bullet P[false/forward'] \wedge \exists t' \bullet P[true/forward']) \wedge P \vee$

$\quad \exists t' \bullet P[false/forward'] \wedge P$ {predicate calculus}

$= (\exists t' \bullet P[true/forward'] \vee \exists t' P[false/forward']) \wedge P$ $\{\exists t', forward' \bullet P = true\}$

$= RHS$

The choice construct $P \,\mathrm{or}\, Q$ selects a successful one between P and Q. When both P and Q succeed, the choice is made nondeterministically.

$$P \text{ or } Q =_{df} (P \text{ else } Q) \sqcap (Q \text{ else } P)$$

Theorem 3.10

Let b be a well-defined boolean expression.

(1) $P \text{ or } P = P$

(2) $P \text{ or } Q = Q \text{ or } P$

(3) $(P \text{ or } Q) \text{ or } R = P \text{ or } (Q \text{ or } R)$

(4) $(P \triangleleft b \triangleright Q) \text{ or } R = (P \text{ or } R) \triangleleft b \triangleright (Q \text{ or } R)$

(5) $(P \sqcap Q) \text{ or } R = (P \text{ or } R) \sqcap (Q \text{ or } R)$

Proof

(1) From Theorem 3.9(1)

(2) From the symmetry of $\sqcap$

(3) From Theorem 3.9(2)

(4) From Theorem 3.9(7) and (8)

(5) From Theorem 3.9(9) and (10)

Let P and Q be programs with disjoint alphabet. The program $P \,\mathrm{par}\, Q$ runs P and Q in parallel. It succeeds only when both P and Q succeed. Its behaviour is described by the *parallel merge* construct defined in [15]:

$$P \text{ par } Q =_{df} (P \|_M Q)$$

where the parallel merge operator $\|_M$ is defined by

$$P \|_M Q =_{df} (P[0.m'/m'] \| Q[1.m'/m']); M(ok, 0.m, 1.m, m', ok')$$

where m represents the shared variables $forward$ and $eflag$ of P and Q, and $\|$ denotes the disjoint parallel operator

$$(b \vdash R) \| (c \vdash S) \ =_{df} \ (b \wedge c) \vdash (R \wedge S)$$

and the merge predicate M is defined by

$M =_{df}$

$$true \vdash \left(\begin{array}{l} (eflag' = 0.eflag1 \vee 1.eflag) \wedge \\ (\neg 0.eflag \wedge \neg 1.eflag) \Rightarrow (forward' = 0.forward1 \wedge 1.forward) \wedge \\ (v' = v) \end{array} \right)$$

Theorem 3.11

Let $x := e$ be a total assignment, and b a well-defined boolean expression.

(1) $(P \textbf{ par } Q) = (Q \textbf{ par } P)$

(2) $(P \textbf{ par } Q) \textbf{ par } R = P \textbf{ par } (Q \textbf{ par } R)$

(3) $\bot \textbf{ par } Q = \bot$

(4) $(P \triangleleft b \triangleright Q) \textbf{ par } R) = (P \textbf{ par } R) \triangleleft b \triangleright (Q \textbf{ par } R)$

(5) $(P \sqcap Q) \textbf{ par } R = (P \textbf{ par } R) \sqcap (Q \textbf{ par } R)$

(6) $(x := e; P) \textbf{ par } Q = (x := e); (P \textbf{ par } Q)$

(7) $\texttt{fail par throw} = \texttt{throw}$

(8) $\texttt{fail par fail} = \texttt{fail}$

(9) $\texttt{throw par throw} = \texttt{throw}$

(10) $\texttt{skip}_A \textbf{ par } Q = Q_{+A}$

$$(b \vdash R)_{+\{x, .., z\}} \ =_{df} \ b \vdash (R \wedge x = x' \wedge .. \wedge z' = z)$$

Proof

(1) and (2): From Theorem 7.2.10 of [15].

(3) From the fact that $(\bot \| Q) = \bot$ and $(\bot; M) = \bot$

(4) From Theorem 3.6(5) and the fact that

$$(P \triangleleft b \triangleright Q) \| R = (P \| R) \triangleleft b \triangleright (Q \| R)$$

(5) From the fact that $(P \sqcap Q) \| R = (P \| R) \sqcap (Q \| R)$

(6) From the fact that $(x := e; P) \| Q = (x := e); (P \| Q)$

4   Transaction

Let T be a transaction which consists of forward activity and compensation module, and let X be a program. We use the notation $T(X)$ denotes a program which runs the forward activity of T and X in sequel. If the execution of X fails, then the compensation module of T will be executed.

Definition 4.1 (Transaction Refinement)

Let U and V be transactions. U *refines* V (denoted by $U \sqsupseteq_T V$) if for all programs X, $U(X)$ is a refinement of $V(X)$

4.1   Primitive Transaction

Let A and C be programs. We use the notation $\mathcal{T}_C^A$ to represent a primitive transaction, where A and C represent its forward activity and compensation activity respectively. We assume that the compensation activity is not allowed to rollback, i.e.

$$C[true/forward] \;=\; C[true/forward]\,;(forward)_\bot$$

The behaviour of $\mathcal{T}_C^A(X)$ is defined by

$$\mathcal{T}_C^A(X) \;=_{df}\; A\,;(X \text{ cpens } (C;\texttt{fail}))\,;\textbf{end}\,flag$$

where $flag$ are the local variables introduced in A.

Theorem 4.1

Let v_1 and v_2 be local variables introduced by A_1 and A_2 respectively. $\mathcal{T}_{C1}^{A1} \sqsubseteq \mathcal{T}_{C2}^{A2}$ if there exists a total relation $\rho(v_1, v_2')$ such that

(1) $A_1 \sqsubseteq (A_2; \textbf{sim})$

(2) $(\textbf{sim}\,;\,C_1) \sqsubseteq (C_2; \textbf{sim})$

where $\textbf{sim} =_{df} (true \vdash \rho)$

Proof. $\mathcal{T}_{C_1}^{A_1}(X)$ {Condition (1)}

$\sqsubseteq \quad A_2; \textbf{sim};(X \text{ cpens } (C_1;\texttt{fail}));\textbf{end}\,v_1$ {Theorem 2.4(3) and 3.8(4)}

$= \quad A_2;(\textbf{sim};X) \text{ cpens } (C_1;\texttt{fail}));\textbf{end}\,v_1$ $\{v_1, v_2 \notin \alpha(X)\}$

$= \quad A_2;((X;\textbf{sim}) \text{ cpens } (C_1;\texttt{fail}));\textbf{end}\,v_1$ {Def of cpens}

$= \quad A_2; \mathcal{H}(X;(\textbf{sim} \lhd forward \lor eflag \rhd$

$\qquad (\textbf{sim};C_1[true,\,false/forward,\,eflag];\texttt{fail})));\textbf{end}\,v_1$ {Condition (2)}

$\sqsubseteq \quad A_2; \mathcal{H}(X;(\textbf{sim} \lhd forward \lor eflag \rhd$

$\qquad (C_2[true,\,false/forward,\,eflag];\textbf{sim};\texttt{fail})));\textbf{end}\,v_1$ $\{v_1, v_2 \notin \alpha(\texttt{fail})\}$

$= \quad A_2;(X \text{ cpens } (C_2;\texttt{fail}));\textbf{sim};\textbf{end}\,v_1$ $\{\textbf{sim};\textbf{end}\,v_1 = \textbf{end}\,v_2\}$

$= \quad \mathcal{T}_{C_2}^{A_2}(X)$

Theorem 4.2

(1) $\mathcal{T}_C^{A_1 \sqcap A_2}(X) \;=\; \mathcal{T}_C^{A_1}(X) \sqcap \mathcal{T}_C^{A_2}(X)$

(2) $\mathcal{T}_C^{A_1 \lhd b \rhd A_2}(X) \;=\; \mathcal{T}_C^{A_1}(X) \lhd b \rhd \mathcal{T}_C^{A_2}(X)$

(3) $\mathcal{T}_{C_1 \sqcap C_2}^A(X) \;=\; \mathcal{T}_{C_1}^A(X) \sqcap \mathcal{T}_{C_2}^A(X)$

Proof. From the definition of $\mathcal{T}_C^A$ and the disjunctivity of sequential composition. Define

$$\texttt{Skip} =_{df} \mathcal{T}_{\texttt{skip}}^{\texttt{skip}}$$

$$\texttt{Fail} =_{df} \mathcal{T}_C^{\texttt{fail}}$$

$$\texttt{Throw} =_{df} \mathcal{T}_C^{\texttt{throw}}$$

$$\texttt{Abort} =_{df} \mathcal{T}_C^{\perp}$$

Theorem 4.3

(1) $\texttt{Skip}(X) = X$

(2) $\texttt{Fail}(X) = \texttt{fail}$

(3) $\texttt{Throw}(X) = \texttt{throw}$

(4) $\texttt{Abort}(X) = \perp$ **Proof**

(1) $\texttt{Skip}(X)$	{Def of $\mathcal{T}_C^A$}
$= \texttt{skip}; (X \texttt{ cpens fail})$	{Theorem 3.8.(3)}
$= X$	
(2) $\texttt{Fail}(X)$	{Def of $\mathcal{T}_C^A$}
$= \texttt{fail}; (X \texttt{ cpens } C)$	{Theorem 3.2}
$= \texttt{fail}$	

4.2 Nondeterministic Choice

Let T and U be transactions. Their nondeterministic choice $T \sqcap U$ is defined by

$$(T \sqcap U)(X) =_{df} T(X) \sqcap U(X)$$

Theorem 4.4

(1) $T \sqcap T = T$

(2) $T \sqcap U = U \sqcap T$

(3) $(T \sqcap U) \sqcap V = T \sqcap (U \sqcap V)$

(4) $T \sqcap \texttt{Abort} = \texttt{Abort}$

Proof. (1), (2) and (3) follow from the fact the nondeterministic choice of designs is idempotent, symmetric and associative. (4) comes from Theorem 4.3(4).

Theorem 4.5 (Closure)

$\mathcal{T}_{C_1}^{A_1} \sqcap \mathcal{T}_{C_2}^{A_2} = \mathcal{T}_C^A$, where

$$A =_{df} (\textbf{var } flag := true \,;\, A_1) \sqcap (\textbf{var } flag := false \,;\, A_2)$$

$$C =_{df} (C_1 \lhd flag \rhd C_2)$$

and $flag$ is a fresh variable which does not appear in A_1, A_2, C_1 and C_2.

Proof. Let $P_1 =_{df} (\textbf{var } flag := true \,;\, A_1)$ and $P_2 =_{df} (\textbf{var } flag := false \,;\, A_2)$

$$\mathcal{T}_C^A(X) \qquad\qquad\qquad\qquad\qquad\qquad\qquad\qquad\quad \{\text{Theorem 4.2}\}$$

$$= \mathcal{T}_C^{P_1}(X) \sqcap \mathcal{T}_C^{P_2}(X)$$

$$\qquad\qquad\qquad\qquad \{(flag := true; X) = (flag := true; X; flag := true)\}$$

$$= \mathcal{T}_{flag:=true;C}^{P_1}(X) \sqcap \mathcal{T}_{flag:=false;C}^{P_2}(X) \qquad\qquad \{\text{Theorem 3.5}\}$$

$$= \mathcal{T}_{flag:=true;C_1}^{P_1}(X) \sqcap \mathcal{T}_{flag:=false;C_2}^{P_2}(X)$$

$$\qquad\qquad\qquad \{(flag := true; X) = (flag := true; X; flag := true)\}$$

$$= \mathcal{T}_{C_1}^{P_1}(X) \sqcap \mathcal{T}_{C_2}^{P_2}(X) \qquad \{(Q; \textbf{end } flag) = (\textbf{end } flag; Q) \text{ if } flag \notin \alpha(Q)\}$$

$$= \mathcal{T}_{C_1}^{P_1;\textbf{end } flag}(X) \sqcap \mathcal{T}_{C_2}^{P_2;\textbf{end } flag}(X)$$

$$\qquad\qquad\qquad\qquad\qquad \{\textbf{var } flag := true \,;\, \textbf{end } flag = \textbf{skip}\}$$

$$= \mathcal{T}_{C_1}^{A_1}(X) \sqcap \mathcal{T}_{C_2}^{A_2}(X)$$

4.3   Conditional

Let T and U be transactions. Their conditional choice $T \lhd b \rhd U$ is defined by

$$(T \lhd b \rhd U)(X) =_{df} T(X) \lhd b \rhd U(X)$$

Theorem 4.6

(1) $T \lhd b \rhd T = T$

(2) $T \lhd b \rhd U = U \lhd \neg b \rhd T$

(3) $(T \lhd b \rhd U) \lhd c \rhd V = T \lhd b \wedge c \rhd (U \lhd c \rhd V)$

(4) $T \lhd b \rhd (U \lhd c \rhd V) = (T \lhd b \rhd U) \lhd c \rhd (T \lhd b \rhd V)$

(5) $T \lhd true \rhd U = T$

(6) $T \sqcap (U \lhd b \rhd V) = (T \sqcap U) \lhd b \rhd (T \sqcap V)$

(7) $(T \sqcap U) \lhd b \rhd V = (T \lhd b \rhd V) \sqcap (U \lhd b \rhd V)$

Proof. From the corresponding laws of designs.

Theorem 4.7 (Closure)

$\mathcal{T}_{C_1}^{A_1} \lhd b \rhd \mathcal{T}_{C_2}^{A_2} = \mathcal{T}_C^A$, where

$$A =_{df} \textbf{var } flag := b \,;\, (A_1 \lhd b \rhd A_2)$$

$$C =_{df} (C_1 \lhd flag \rhd C_2)$$

Proof. Similar to Theorem 4.5.

4.4   Chain

Let T and U be transactions. The transaction $T >> U$ runs T and U in sequel:

$$(T >> U)(X) \; =_{df} \; T(U(X))$$

Theorem 4.8

(1) $(T >> U) >> V \; = \; T >> (U >> V)$

(2) $T >> \text{Skip} \; = \; T \; = \; \text{Skip} >> T$

(3) $\text{Throw} >> U \; = \; \text{Throw}$

(4) $\text{Fail} >> U \; = \; \text{Fail}$

(5) $(T \sqcap U) >> V \; = \; (T >> V) \sqcap (U >> V)$

(6) $(T \lhd b \rhd U) >> V \; = \; (T >> V) \lhd b \rhd (U >> V)$

(7) $T >> (U \sqcap V) \; = \; (T >> U) \sqcap (T >> V)$

Proof

(2) $(T >> \text{Skip})(X)$	{Def of $>>$}
$= T(\text{Skip}(X))$	{Theorem 4.3(1)}
$= T(X)$	{Theorem 4.3(1)}
$= \text{Skip}(T(X))$	{Def of $>>$}
$= (\text{Skip} >> T)(X)$	
(3) $(\text{Throw} >> U)(X)$	{Def of $>>$}
$= \text{Throw}(U(X))$	{Theorem 4.3(3)}
$= \text{throw}$	{Theorem 4.3(3)}
$= \text{Throw}(X)$	

Theorem 4.9 (Closure)

$\mathcal{T}_{C_1}^{A_1} >> \mathcal{T}_{C_2}^{A_2} \; = \; \mathcal{T}_C^A$, where

$$A =_{df} A_1; (A2 \, \text{cpens} \, (C_1; \text{fail}))$$

$$C =_{df} C_2; C_1$$

Proof. Let $\hat{C} =_{df} C; \text{fail}$.

$LHS(X)$	{Def of $>>$ and $\mathcal{T}_C^A$}
$= \mathcal{T}_{C_1}^{A_1}(A_2; (X \, \text{cpens} \, \hat{C}_2))$	{Def of $\mathcal{T}_C^A$}
$= A_1; ((A_2; (X \, \text{cpens} \, \hat{C}_2)) \, \text{cpens} \, \hat{C}_1)$	{Def of cpens}
$= A_1; \mathcal{H}(A_2; \mathcal{H}(X; \psi(\hat{C}_2)); \psi(\hat{C}_1))$	{$\lhd b \rhd$ $--$; distribution}

$$= A_1; \mathcal{H}(A_2; (\psi(\hat{C}_1) \triangleleft eflag \vee \neg forward \triangleright$$
$$(X; \psi(\hat{C}_2); \psi(\hat{C}_1)))) \qquad\qquad \{\psi(P; \psi(Q)) = \psi(P); \psi(Q)\}$$
$$\{\psi(P) = \psi(\mathcal{H}(P))\}$$
$$\{\text{and Theorem 3.8(4)}\}$$

$$= A_1; \mathcal{H}(A_2;$$

$$\mathbf{if} \begin{pmatrix} eflag \rightarrow II \\ \neg eflag \wedge \neg forward \rightarrow \\ \qquad \hat{C}_1[true,\ false/forward,\ eflag] \\ \neg eflag \wedge forward \rightarrow (X; \psi(C_2; \hat{C}_1)) \end{pmatrix} \mathbf{fi)} \qquad \{\text{Theorem 3.6(5)}\}$$

$$= A_1; \mathcal{H}(A_2;$$

$$\mathbf{if} \begin{pmatrix} eflag \rightarrow II \\ \neg eflag \wedge \neg forward \rightarrow \\ \qquad \hat{C}_1[true,\ false/forward,\ eflag] \\ \neg eflag \wedge forward \rightarrow II \end{pmatrix} \mathbf{fi;}$$

$$\mathcal{H}(X; \psi(C_2; \hat{C}_1))) \qquad\qquad \{\text{Def of } \psi \text{ and cpens}\}$$
$$= A_1; \mathcal{H}(A_2; \psi(C_1); (X\ \mathtt{cpens}\ (C_2; \hat{C}_1))) \qquad \{\text{Theorem 2.4(3)}\}$$
$$= A_1; \mathcal{H}(A_2; \psi(C_1)); (X\ \mathtt{cpens}\ (C_2; C_1; \mathtt{fail})) \qquad \{\text{Def of } \mathcal{T}_C^A\}$$
$$= RHS(X)$$

4.5 Else

Let T and U be transactions. The transaction T **else** U does U if T fails. From the closure property of transaction combinators we are only required to discuss the case where T and U are primitive transactions. In the following, we will use the notations $T.A$ and $T.C$ to represent the forward activity and compensation module of T.

$$T\ \mathbf{else}\ U\ =_{df}\ \mathcal{T}_C^A,\ \text{where}$$

$$A =_{df} \mathbf{var}\ flag;\ (flag := true; T.A)\ \mathtt{else}\ (flag := false; U.A)$$

$$C =_{df} (T.C \triangleleft flag \triangleright U.C)$$

Theorem 4.10

(1) T **else** $T = T$

(2) $(T$ **else** $U)$ **else** $V = T$ **else** $(U$ **else** $V)$

(3) Fail **else** $T = T$

(4) Skip **else** $U =$ Skip

(5) Abort **else** $U =$ **Abort**

(6) T **else** $(U \sqcap V) = (T$ **else** $U) \sqcap (T$ **else** $V)$

(7) $(T \sqcap U)$ **else** $V = (T \textbf{ else } U) \sqcap (U \textbf{ else } V)$

(8) $(T \lhd b \rhd U)$ **else** $V = (T \textbf{ else } U) \lhd b \rhd (U \textbf{ else } V)$

(9) T **else** $(U \lhd b \rhd V) = (T \textbf{ else } U) \lhd b \rhd (T \textbf{ else } V)$

Proof

(2) $LHS.A$ {Def of **else**}

$= (\textbf{var } flag1 := true; ((\textbf{var } flag2 := true; T.A) \texttt{ else }$

$(flag2 := false; U.A)) \texttt{ else } (flag1 := false; V.A)$ {Theorem 3.8(4)}

$= \textbf{var } flag1, flag2; (flag1, flag2 := true, true; T.A) \texttt{ else }$

$(flag1, flag2 := true, false; U.A) \texttt{ else }$

$(flag1, flag2 := false, false; V.A)$

$LHS.C$ {Def of **else**}

$= (T.C \lhd flag2 \rhd U.C) \lhd flag1 \rhd V.C$

In a similar way we obtain

$RHS.A$

$= (\textbf{var } flag3, flag4; (flag3 := true; T.A) \texttt{ else }$

$(flag3, flag4 := false, true; U.A) \texttt{ else }$

$(flag3, flag4 := false, false; V.A)$ Let

$RHS.C$

$= T.C \lhd flag3 \rhd (U.C \lhd flag4 \rhd V.C)$

$$\textbf{sim1} =_{df} (flag2 \Rightarrow flag1) \wedge (flag3' = (flag1 \wedge flag2)) \wedge$$
$$(flag4' = (flag1 \neq flag2))$$
$$\textbf{sim2} =_{df} (flag1' = (flag3 \vee flag4)) \wedge (flag2 = flag3)$$

We can show

$$(RHS.A \sqsubseteq (LHS.A; \textbf{sim1})) \quad \text{and} \quad ((\textbf{sim1}; RHS.C) \sqsubseteq (LHS.C; \textbf{sim1}))$$

and

$$(LHS.A \sqsubseteq (RHS.A; \textbf{sim2})) \quad \text{and} \quad ((\textbf{sim2}; LHS.C) \sqsubseteq (RHS.C; \textbf{sim2}))$$

The conclusion follows from Theorem 4.1.

4.6 Catch

Let T and U be transactions. T **catch** U fires T first. U will be invoked if T throws an exception case:

$$T \textbf{ catch } U \ =_{df} \ T_C^A, \text{ where}$$

$$A =_{df} (\textbf{var } flag := true \, ; \, T.A) \ \texttt{catch} \ (flag := false; U.A)$$

$$C =_{df} (T.C \lhd flag \rhd U.C)$$

Theorem 4.11

(1) $(T \textbf{ catch } U) \textbf{ catch } V \ = \ T \textbf{ catch } (U \textbf{ catch } V)$

(2) $\texttt{Throw catch } U \ = \ U$

(3) $\texttt{Skip catch } U \ = \ \texttt{Skip}$

(4) $\texttt{Abort catch } U \ = \ \texttt{Abort}$

(5) $T \textbf{ else } (U \sqcap V) \ = \ (T \textbf{ else } U) \sqcap (T \textbf{ else } V)$

(6) $(T \sqcap U) \textbf{ else } V \ = \ (T \textbf{ else } U) \sqcap (U \textbf{ else } V)$

(7) $(T \lhd b \rhd U) \textbf{ else } V \ = \ (T \textbf{ else } U) \lhd b \rhd (U \textbf{ else } V)$

4.7   Choice

Let T and U be transactions. The transaction $T \textbf{ or } U$ makes a deferred choice among T and U. When both succeed, the choice is made nondeterministically. It fails when both T and U fail.

$$T \textbf{ or } U \ =_{df} \ T_C^A, \text{ where}$$

$$A =_{df} (\textbf{var } flag := true \, ; \, T.A) \ \texttt{or} \ (\textbf{var } flag := false; U.A)$$

$$C =_{df} (T.C \lhd flag \rhd U.C)$$

Theorem 4.12

(1) $(T \textbf{ or } U) \ = \ (U \textbf{ or } T)$

(2) $(T \textbf{ or } U) \textbf{ or } V \ = \ T \textbf{ or } (U \textbf{ or } V)$

(3) $(T \textbf{ or } T) \ = \ T$

(4) $\texttt{Abort or } U \ = \ \texttt{Abort}$

(5) $(T_1 \sqcap T_2) \textbf{ or } U \ = \ (T_1 \textbf{ or } U) \sqcap (T_2 \textbf{ or } U)$

(6) $(T_1 \lhd b \rhd T_2) \textbf{ or } U \ = \ (T_1 \textbf{ or } U) \lhd b \rhd (T_2 \textbf{ or } U)$

4.8   Parallel

Let T and U be transactions without shared variables. The transaction $T \| U$ runs T and U in parallel, it succeeds only when both T and U do so.

$$T \textbf{ par } U \ =_{df} \ T_C^A, \text{ where}$$

$$A =_{df} (T.A \textbf{ par } U.A)$$

$$C =_{df} (T.C \textbf{ par } U.C)$$

Theorem 4.13

(1) $T \operatorname{par} U = U \operatorname{par} T$

(2) $T \operatorname{par} (U \operatorname{par} V) = (T \operatorname{par} U) \operatorname{par} V$

(3) $\texttt{Abort} \operatorname{par} U = \texttt{Abort}$

(4) $(T \sqcap U) \operatorname{par} V = (T \operatorname{par} V) \sqcap (U \operatorname{par} V)$

(5) $(T \triangleleft b \triangleright U) \operatorname{par} V = (T \operatorname{par} V) \triangleleft b \triangleright (U \operatorname{par} V)$

(6) $T \operatorname{par} \texttt{Skip} = T$

(7) $T \operatorname{par} \texttt{Chaos} = \texttt{Chaos}$

5   Conclusion

This paper presents a mathematical model for compensable programs and long-running transactions. We add new logical variables $eflag$ and $forward$ to the standard design model to deal with the features of exception and failures. As a result, we put forward new healthiness conditions $\mathbf{Req_1}$ and $\mathbf{Req_2}$ to characterise those designs which can be used to specify the dynamic behaviour of compensable programs. The notion of design matrix is introduced to describe the various types of outcome of a program.

A long-running transaction consists of forward activity and compensation module. It is defined as a mapping from the specification of its surrounding environment to the behaviour of a compensable program. This paper introduces a number of transaction combinators, and explores their properties. It is shown that the primitive transactions are *closed* under these combinators.

Acknowledgement

The ideas put forward in this paper have been inspired from the discussion with Tony Hoare, and the work of many earlier researchers.

References

1. Abadi, M., Gordon, A.D.: A calculus for cryptographic protocols: The spi calculus. Information and Computation 148(1), 1–70 (1999)
2. Alonso, G., Kuno, H., Casati, F., et al.: Web Services: Concepts, Architectures and Applications. Springer, Heidelberg (2003)
3. Bhargavan, K., et al.: A Semantics for Web Service Authentication. Theoretical Computer Science 340(1), 102–153 (2005)
4. Bruni, R., Montanari, H.C., Montannari, U.: Theoretical foundation for compensation in flow composition languages. In: Proc. POPL 2005, 32nd ACM SIGPLAN-SIGACT symposium on principle of programming languages, pp. 209–220. ACM, New York (2004)

5. Bruni, R., et al.: From Theory to Practice in Transactional Composition of Web Services. In: Bravetti, M., Kloul, L., Zavattaro, G. (eds.) EPEW/WS-EM 2005. LNCS, vol. 3670, pp. 272–286. Springer, Heidelberg (2005)
6. Bulter, M.J., Ferreria, C.: A process compensation language. In: Grieskamp, W., Santen, T., Stoddart, B. (eds.) IFM 2000. LNCS, vol. 1945, pp. 61–76. Springer, Heidelberg (2000)
7. Bulter, M.J., Ferreria, C.: An Operational Semantics for StAC: a Lanuage for Modelling Long-Running Business Transactions. In: De Nicola, R., Ferrari, G.-L., Meredith, G. (eds.) COORDINATION 2004. LNCS, vol. 2949, pp. 87–104. Springer, Heidelberg (2004)
8. Butler, M.J., Hoare, C.A.R., Ferreria, C.: A Trace Semantics for Long-Running Transactions. In: Abdallah, A.E., Jones, C.B., Sanders, J.W. (eds.) Communicating Sequential Processes. LNCS, vol. 3525, pp. 133–150. Springer, Heidelberg (2005)
9. Curbera, F., Goland, Y., Klein, J., et al.: Business Process Execution Language for Web Service (2003), http://www.siebei.com/bpel
10. Dijkstra, E.W.: A Discipline of Programming. Prentice Hall, Englewood Cliffs (1976)
11. Gordon, A.D., et al.: Validating a Web Service Security Abstraction by Typing. Formal Aspect of Computing 17(3), 277–318 (2005)
12. Jifeng, H., Huibiao, Z., Geguang, P.: A model for BPEL-like languages. Frontiers of Computer Science in China 1(1), 9–20 (2007)
13. Jifeng, H.: Modelling Compensation and Coordination. In: Proceedings of ISOLA 2008 (2008)
14. Hoare, C.A.R.: Communicating Sequential Language. Prentice-Hall, Englewood Cliffs (1985)
15. Hoare, C.A.R., Jifeng, H.: Unifying theories of programming. Prentice-Hall, Englewood Cliffs (1998)
16. Leymann, F.: Web Service Flow Language (WSFL1.0). IBM (2001)
17. Laneve, C., et al.: Web-pi at work. In: De Nicola, R., Sangiorgi, D. (eds.) TGC 2005. LNCS, vol. 3705, pp. 182–194. Springer, Heidelberg (2005)
18. Jing, L., Jifeng, H., Geguang, P.: Towards the Semantics for Web Services Choreography Description Language. In: Liu, Z., He, J. (eds.) ICFEM 2006. LNCS, vol. 4260, pp. 246–263. Springer, Heidelberg (2006)
19. Lucchi, R., Mazzara, M.: A Pi-calculus based semantics for WS-BPEL. Journal of Logic and Algebraic Programming (in press)
20. Milner, R.: Communication and Mobile System: the π-calculus. Cambridge University Press, Cambridge (1999)
21. Morris, J.M.: Non-deterministic expressions and predicate transformers. Information Processing Letters 61, 241–246 (1997)
22. Geguang, P., et al.: Theoretical Foundation of Scope-based Compensation Flow Language for Web Service. In: Ning, P., Qing, S., Li, N. (eds.) ICICS 2006. LNCS, vol. 4307, pp. 251–266. Springer, Heidelberg (2006)
23. Qiu, Z.Y., et al.: Semantics of BPEL4WS-Like Fault and Compensation Handling. In: Fitzgerald, J.S., Hayes, I.J., Tarlecki, A. (eds.) FM 2005. LNCS, vol. 3582, pp. 350–365. Springer, Heidelberg (2005)
24. Tarski, A.: A lattice-theoretical fixpoint theorem and its applications. Pacific Journal of Mathematics 5, 285–309 (1955)
25. Thatte, S.: XLANG: Web Service for Business Process Design. Microsoft (2001)

UTP and Temporal Logic Model Checking

Hugh Anderson[1], Gabriel Ciobanu[2], and Leo Freitas[3]

[1] Wellington Institute of Technology, New Zealand
[2] Romanian Academy, Institute of Computer Science, Romania
[3] University of York, Department of Computer Science, YO10 5DD, York, UK

Abstract. In this paper we give an additional perspective to the formal verification of programs through temporal logic model checking, which uses Hoare and He Unifying Theories of Programming (UTP). Our perspective emphasizes the use of UTP designs, an alphabetised relational calculus expressed as a pre/post condition pair of relations, to verify state or temporal assertions about programs. The temporal model checking relation is derived from a satisfaction relation between the model and its properties. The contribution of this paper is that it shows a UTP perspective to temporal logic model checking. The approach includes the notion of efficiency found in traditional model checkers, which reduced a state explosion problem through the use of efficient data structures.

Keywords: Symbolic model checking, unifying theories of programming.

1 Introduction

Unifying Theories of Programming (UTP) [16] develops a consistent theory of programming, based on an alphabetised relational calculus and strongly centered on refinement [1], which can be used to define a variety of programming paradigms. The book introduces the relational calculus, and uses it to develop concepts of program design, refinement of programs, and an algebra of programming. A UTP theory consists of an alphabet recording names representing possible observations of behaviour; a signature with the syntax of the language being given semantics; and a set of healthiness conditions determining the scope of the theory within the realm of relations. Specifications, designs, and implementations are all modelled as relations between initial and latter (*i.e.,* intermediate or final) observations of behaviour. Various paradigms can be linked using *Galois Connections*, hence giving a precise meaning when those paradigms are combined. In the UTP, the slogan is "programs are predicates", meaning that both specification, designs, as well as implementations are viewed as predicates with their scope restricted according to the corresponding set of healthiness conditions. As everything in the UTP is a predicate, refinement is simply universally closed reverse implication.

The work has been adopted by many researchers working in various areas of computing. It has been used to formally define the semantics of the programming/specification language *Circus* [25]. A series of other paradigms have also

A. Butterfield (Ed.): UTP 2008, LNCS 5713, pp. 22–41, 2010.

been formalised in the UTP: imperative, reactive, parallel, higher-order, and declarative [16,24]; object oriented[15,6,20,21]; pointers [10]; real time [22,20]; synchronous [3]; hardware [4]; angelic nondeterminism [7,9]; control laws [5]; mobility [23]; refinement model checking [13]; and so on.

The approach taken in the book is to formalise and characterize a class of relations useful for program development. One such class of relations is called a "**design**": a precondition-postcondition pair describing imperative features of specifications and programs. Another option is the *reactive process*, which has a basic failures-divergences semantics, and is used to represent concurrency and communication. Cavalcanti and Woodcock [8], present a theory of reactive designs, representing reactive processes as a (pre-postcondition) design.

In this paper, our motivation is to provide the development of a unifying theory, with an operational flavour, for model checking temporal logic formulae [11]. We link three components of model checking within UTP. Specifically, we outline how to express:

- models and states of the implementation which we are verifying;
- temporal properties that we wish to check;
- the *model checking* relation $\models$.

We take the view that a model may be derived directly from a UTP *design*, and that if a property is true for a particular UTP design, then it is also true for the related implementations (other UTP designs).

In temporal logic (or classic) model checking, the main goal is to specify properties as a *state* assertion or a *temporal* assertion, that can then be (somewhat) automatically discharged mechanically. It is not always fully automatic, since the business of modelling may need to be hand crafted. However, since it can find interesting counter-examples, it has become a quite popular verification technique, principally in the hardware community.

A traditional presentation of temporal logic model checking [11] centers around a finite state machine corresponding to a program, and data structures and algorithms to efficiently verify that the structure satisfies a temporal logic formula. By contrast, we show how to express state and temporal properties as a relation between observations over a model, and then derive a model checking relation between these properties and the model. In addition, the expectation we have of this approach is that any UTP design is already a model.

Work is currently being done in finding an adequate set of healthiness conditions, as well as a nice embedding of the theory presented here in the theory of UTP designs.

In the next Section, we briefly summarise the main concepts for the UTP. Section 3 presents basic notions from classical model checking. In Section 4, model checking is reformulated within the unifying theory framework, showing how model checking in UTP can be done using binary decision diagrams, closely following the approach used for symbolic model checking [18]. Finally we conclude with remarks about the links between traditional temporal logic model checking and our initial attempt to embedded it as a UTP theory.

2   Unifying Theories of Programming

The components of the unified theory are *alphabets*, *signatures* and *healthiness conditions*.

The *alphabet* is a set of names representing observations of behaviour made by the program. These names may include relations between program variables, and also between observational variables (*i.e.*, those related to some occurrence in the environment the program exists) not mentioned in the program text, such as:

- ok the program has started;
- ok' the program has terminated.

By convention, unprimed names indicate the initial observation of behaviour, whereas corresponding primed names indicate later observations, such as intermediate or final states.

The *signature* of a theory is a set of primitive operators and constants of the theory, and the syntax used for combining them. In UTP, one starts with the signature for the predicate calculus, and then extend it with new operators as needed. For example, in developing the concept of a *design* in the unifying theories, the connective $\vdash$ is introduced to indicate the relationship between a pair of predicates p (for *preconditions*) and q (for *postconditions*):

$$p \vdash q \;\hat{=}\; (\mathrm{ok} \wedge p) \Rightarrow (\mathrm{ok}' \wedge q)$$

Healthiness conditions are idempotent functions over predicates. They select sub-theories from a theory. For example, we may be able to specify all sorts of programs from a particular alphabet and signature, but we are only interested in programs that may be physically realized. For example, we can make no observations about a program that has not yet started running. This may be expressed as a healthiness condition for any observation o about a program:

$$o = (\mathrm{ok} \Rightarrow o)$$

This condition selects a sub-theory of all the possible programs, isolating those that are implementable if the healthiness condition is true.

2.1   Subtheories of Programming

We have already seen how the concept of a *design* is presented in UTP. Other programming concepts may also be easily represented. For example, the Hoare triple $\{p\} \, C \, \{q\}$ representing the relation between a precondition p, a code segment C and a postcondition q, is defined in UTP as a relation between three predicates p, C and q:

$$\{p\} \, C \, \{q\} \;\hat{=}\; [C \Rightarrow (p \Rightarrow q')]$$

The square brackets are a notational convenience, indicating that the enclosed expression is universally quantified over all variables in its alphabet.

Note that this definition for the Hoare-triple, like mostly everything in the UTP, can be reformulated as the refinement relation:

$$\{p\}\,C\,\{q\} \;\widehat{=}\; (p \Rightarrow q') \sqsubseteq C$$

That is, the program C satisfies the specification that the precondition p implies its postcondition q. Thus, the algebraic laws of Hoare logic can be nicely understood in terms of refinement. Similarly, the refinement calculus [1] can be embedded.

3   Traditional Temporal Logic Model Checking

Verification of programs may be viewed as the process of checking some property P against either the program itself, or a sufficiently detailed model $\mathcal{M}$ of it. For software in general, this is a hard problem, as the verification process may involve in-depth reasoning, perhaps requiring theorem provers to confirm parts of the verification.

The temporal logic model checking approach to verification [11,18] is to abstract out key elements of the program and then to verify just these elements. These key abstractions are binary predicates, and various techniques and structures have been developed to automatically and efficiently check the abstract elements against specified properties, once one has carefully hand-crafted a good model. As an example, we may be interested in checking that a certain program variable v has the value 0 at a certain stage of the execution of our program. In this case, the binary predicate $v = 0$ is checked against a representation (model) of the program which indicates how such binary predicates are transformed.

It is not immediately apparent how this model checking technique outlined above can be used to model-check the *execution* behaviour of programs. For example, how can we use the strategy to check for the *progress* of a program, or to establish if a section of code is ever executed? The solution to this is simple: we label each line of the program $(l_0, l_1, ..., l_n)$, and add to our variable state space a pseudo-variable **pc** for the *program counter* of the program. It ranges over the labels together with an undefined value $\perp$ (**pc** $\in \{l_0, l_1, ..., l_n, \perp\}$), and may be used and checked in exactly the same way as the other variables.

Given the underlying reliance on binary abstractions, it is no surprise that model checking is being used in the analysis of digital electronic circuits, but it has also proved effective in the software domain, particularly in the areas of protocol analysis, the behaviour of reactive systems, and for checking concurrent systems.

3.1   Traditional Notions of Model and State

It is difficult to find examples convincing enough to demonstrate a technique, but which are small enough to fully describe in a short paper. We choose to use as an example a simple mutual exclusion protocol in which two processes, P_1

and P_2 share six (boolean) variables, and co-operate to ensure mutually exclusive access to a critical section of code. A third process T_1 monitors the variables and changes a turn variable. The entire system is the parallel composition of these three processes, and is continuous (indicated by the trailing recursive call). Each line of code is considered to be atomic, and we use 1 to represent true, 0 to represent false.

```
P₁ = if idle₁ then (wait₁ := 1; idle₁ := 0) else
        if wait₁ ∧ idle₂ then (active₁ := 1; wait₁ := 0) else
           if wait₁ ∧ wait₂ ∧ ¬turn then (active₁ := 1; wait₁ := 0);
              if active₁ then (CritSect; idle₁ := 1; active₁ := 0);
P₂ = if idle₂ then (wait₂ := 1; idle₂ := 0) else
        if wait₂ ∧ idle₁ then (active₂ := 1; wait₂ := 0) else
           if wait₂ ∧ wait₁ ∧ turn then (active₂ := 1; wait₂ := 0);
              if active₂ then (CritSect; idle₂ := 1; active₂ := 0);
T₁ = if idle₁ ∧ wait₂ then turn := 1 else
        if idle₂ ∧ wait₁ then turn := 0;
System = (P₁ ‖ P₂ ‖ T₁); System;
```

The example is simple, but provides all the elements needed to demonstrate the mechanism of model checking UTP reactive processes. In this introduction, we give the protocol in pseudocode, but later in Section 4.1 it is reformulated in UTP.

We can represent a state s_i of this system as a valuation of the relevant variables. An initial state s_0 for the system is defined to be $(1, 0, 0, 1, 0, 0, 0)$ with S denoting the set of all states. Though there are 128 possible valuations of the relevant variables, given the specified starting state the system has only 16 *reachable* states. The states for this system are listed in Table 1.

Table 1. States for the complete system

State S	P_1 vars			P_2 vars			T_1 vars	Next state(s)
	idle$_1$	wait$_1$	active$_1$	idle$_2$	wait$_2$	active$_2$	turn	
s_0	1	0	0	1	0	0	0	s_1, s_2
s_1	0	1	0	1	0	0	0	s_3, s_5
s_2	1	0	0	0	1	0	0	s_4, s_5, s_6
s_3	0	0	1	1	0	0	0	s_0, s_7
s_4	1	0	0	0	0	1	0	s_0, s_8
s_5	0	1	0	0	1	0	0	s_7
s_6	1	0	0	0	1	0	1	s_9, s_{10}
s_7	0	0	1	0	1	0	0	s_2
s_8	0	1	0	0	0	1	0	s_1
s_9	0	1	0	0	1	0	1	s_{11}
s_{10}	1	0	0	0	0	1	1	s_{11}, s_{15}
s_{11}	0	1	0	0	0	1	1	s_{12}
s_{12}	0	1	0	1	0	0	1	s_1, s_9, s_{13}
s_{13}	0	0	1	1	0	0	1	s_{14}, s_{15}
s_{14}	0	0	1	0	1	0	1	s_6
s_{15}	1	0	0	1	0	0	1	s_6, s_{12}

We may also characterize this system using a Kripke structure/transition diagram as in Figure 1. The labels on the transitions relate to the line-numbers of the program, and the node annotations map each node to a set of properties that hold in the corresponding state.

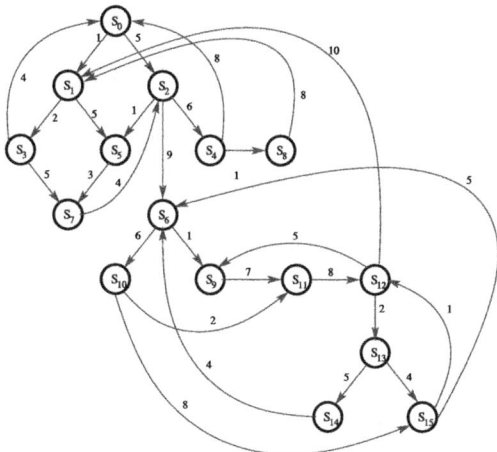

Fig. 1. State transition diagram

The representations are equivalent[1], but the next representation has provided the basis for the mechanisms used in model checking software. In this representation, the transition relation is expressed (using short names for the variables) as the following predicate m:

$$
\begin{aligned}
m = \quad & (i_1 \wedge w_1' \wedge \overline{i_1'}) \vee (w_1 \wedge i_2 \wedge a_1' \wedge \overline{w_1'}) \vee (w_1 \wedge w_2 \wedge \overline{t} \wedge a_1' \wedge \overline{w_1'}) \vee (a_1 \wedge i_1' \wedge \overline{a_1'}) \\
& \vee (i_2 \wedge w_2' \wedge \overline{i_2'}) \vee (w_2 \wedge i_1 \wedge a_2' \wedge \overline{w_2'}) \vee (w_2 \wedge w_1 \wedge t \wedge a_2' \wedge \overline{w_2'}) \vee (a_2 \wedge i_2' \wedge \overline{a_2'}) \\
& \vee (i_1 \wedge w_2 \wedge t') \vee (i_2 \wedge w_1 \wedge \overline{t'})
\end{aligned}
$$

The predicate has been ordered to correlate with the original program. The first and seond lines correspond to P_1 and P_2 and the third to T_1.

Any such predicate may also be encoded as a binary decision tree (BDT), in which the levels denote the different variables, and paths through the tree represent valuations of the transition relation. The BDT for the running example is too large to show, as it would have 16384 leaves. Instead we will consider the smaller predicate t using the variables $(x,\ y,\ z,\ x',\ y'$ and $z')$ and given in disjunctive normal form:

$$
\begin{aligned}
t = \ & (x \wedge \bar{y} \wedge \bar{z} \wedge x' \wedge \bar{y}' \wedge z') \\
& \vee (x \wedge \bar{y} \wedge z \wedge \bar{x}' \wedge y' \wedge z') \\
& \vee (\bar{x} \wedge y \wedge z \wedge \bar{x}' \wedge \bar{y}' \wedge \bar{z}') \\
& \vee (\bar{x} \wedge \bar{y} \wedge \bar{z} \wedge x' \wedge \bar{y}' \wedge z')
\end{aligned}
$$

---

[1] Throughout this paper "m" (model) will be used to refer to *this* particular transition relation, which is used as a running example.

Starting at the top of the tree, we take the left path for $\bar{x}$ and the right path for x. In general we take the left path for a **false** component, and the right path for a **true** component. In this diagram, the valid transitions are highlighted by the darker lines. There is one darker line for each of the four components of t. All other paths represent invalid transitions.

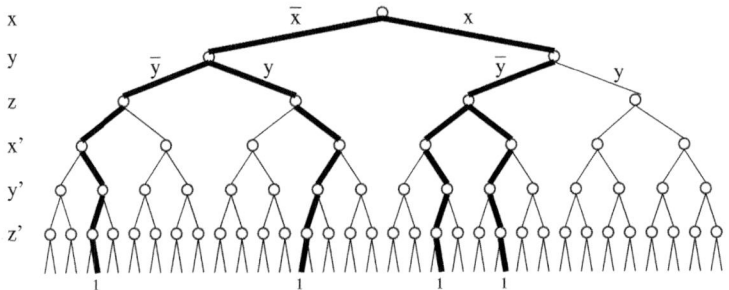

Fig. 2. Binary decision tree for the predicate

Note that if we reorder the variables, we get a different decision tree, but this new tree still represents a transition relation. The relation is independent of the order of the variables.

The binary decision tree does not scale well, but there are optimizations that may be done. A key optimization makes use of the likelihood that the tree is often sparse. We can remove any parts of the decision tree that do not contribute to the transition relation. This can be seen by considering the evaluation of $x \wedge y \wedge z \wedge \bar{x} \wedge \bar{y} \wedge \bar{z}$. If we begin to evaluate this by considering x and y, then we can cut short the further evaluation of the predicate, as all other possible valuations will be **false**. The resultant tree has only 18 nodes after removing the non-contributing ones. An optimization to exploit repetition on BDTs is given by the use of Reduced Ordered Binary Decision Diagrams (ROBDDs) to efficiently represent the relation [2]. The ROBDDs provide a canonical form for the BDTs.

In summary, with the traditional presentation, a model is a finite state transition system $\mathcal{M} = (S, \mathcal{R}, V)$, where S represents a finite set of states, $\mathcal{R}$ represents a transition relation between the states, and V is a valuation function defining the truth values for each state.

3.2   Specification of Properties

We now consider how to express the desired properties of the model. In model checking terms, this is the *specification*. Specifications are given as state and temporal formulae in modal logics such as Computation Tree Logic (CTL) and Linear Temporal Logic (LTL). These temporal logics are propositional languages with modal operators and quantifiers related to time, and each is a sub-logic of CTL*; CTL* in turn is a sublogic of the μ-Calculus [14].

A CTL formula may either be a *state* formula or a *path* formula. A *state* formula is one which is true in a particular state, whereas a *path* formula is one which is true along a particular computation path.

There are several different notations used to express CTL expressions, however each notation expresses the same concept. For example in CTL, the path quantifiers ∀ (all computation paths) and ∃ (at least one computation path) are also found as the letters **A** and **E**. In addition, the path operators ◊ (at some future time) and □ (at all future times) are also found as the letters **F** and **G**. The operators **X** (in the next state), **U** (one property holds until another holds) and **R** (the dual of **U**) complete the set.

The CTL expressions are used to express properties of state transition diagrams that have been unfolded. If we unfold the diagram shown in Figure 1, we get an infinite *tree* of computations as seen in Figure 3.

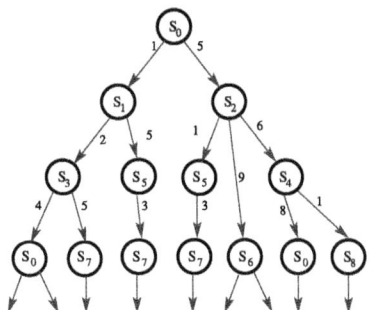

Fig. 3. An unfolded state transition diagram

CTL expressions require every temporal operator to be preceded by a quantifier. Since there are five temporal operators, and two quantifiers, we have ten base expression types, but all of these may be expressed in terms of just three expressions:

- **EX** p : For one computation path, property p holds in the next state;
- **EG** p : For one computation path, property p holds at every state;
- **E**[p **U** q] : For one computation path, property p holds until q holds.

For example, we can express:

- **A**[p **U** q] : For all computation paths, property p holds until q holds;
- **AG** p : For all computation paths, property p holds in every state;
- **AF** p : For all computation paths, property p will eventually hold.

in the following way:

$$\mathbf{A}[p\ \mathbf{U}\ q] = \neg\mathbf{E}[\neg q\ \mathbf{U}\ (\neg p \wedge \neg q)] \wedge \neg\mathbf{EG}\ \neg q$$
$$\mathbf{AG}\ p = \neg\mathbf{E}[\mathbf{true}\ \mathbf{U}\ \neg p]$$
$$\mathbf{AF}\ p = \mathbf{A}[\mathbf{true}\ \mathbf{U}\ p]$$

3.3   Model Checking of Properties

Model checking is commonly expressed as a ternary relation ($\models$):

$$\mathcal{M}, s_n \models P$$

The relation is true when the property P holds in state s_n for a given model $\mathcal{M}$. The relation is normally defined inductively, with a set of interlocking rules for state and path formulae.

A labelling algorithm operating on the Kripke diagram representation may then be used to establish the set of states satisfying the relation. However, this approach is not particularly efficient, in terms of the size of the structure used.

A more efficient technique relies on representing the relation as a ROBDD, and constructing a checking procedure for the CTL. The checking procedure returns a ROBDD structure which represents the states that satisfy the formula. This technique is efficient as operations on ROBDDs are relatively efficient [2].

4   Model Checking in UTP

In the UTP theory of model checking explored here, we begin by defining the notions of *model* and *state*, and the *property* to be checked for that model. We follow the same path travelled in the previous section, with Section 4.1 mirroring Section 3.1 and so on. We show how UTP designs may be used to create an appropriate model, and work through the same model used in Section 3.

A major difference in the UTP model checking approach is that the checking is performed using a transition relation derived directly from a UTP design.

4.1   UTP Notions of Model and State

In this section, the model is derived directly from a UTP *design*. A UTP design expresses the relation between a pair of predicates representing the preconditions (assumptions) and postconditions (commitments) for a program. This relation is expressed as a predicate with unprimed state variables representing key observations over the program before the program starts, and primed variables standing for the values when the program terminates.

Since a UTP design is already expressed as a predicate it is relatively easy to derive the transition relation m of Section 3.1.

If we consider our example, we might express[2] it in UTP terms as the parallel composition of three components:

$$P_1 \cong \text{true} \vdash (i_1 \wedge w_1' \wedge \overline{i_1'}) \vee (w_1 \wedge i_2 \wedge a_1' \wedge \overline{w_1'}) \vee (w_1 \wedge w_2 \wedge \overline{t} \wedge a_1' \wedge \overline{w_1'}) \vee (a_1 \wedge i_1' \wedge \overline{a_1'})$$

$$P_2 \cong \text{true} \vdash (i_2 \wedge w_2' \wedge \overline{i_2'}) \vee (w_2 \wedge i_1 \wedge a_2' \wedge \overline{w_2'}) \vee (w_2 \wedge w_1 \wedge t \wedge a_2' \wedge \overline{w_2'}) \vee (a_2 \wedge i_2' \wedge \overline{a_2'})$$

$$T_1 \cong \text{true} \vdash (i_1 \wedge w_2 \wedge t') \vee (i_2 \wedge w_1 \wedge \overline{t'})$$

$$\text{Xform} \cong P_1 \parallel P_2 \parallel T_1$$

---

[2] This might later be refined to an implementation: $P_1 \cong (w_1 := 1; i_1 := 0) \triangleleft i_1 \triangleright \dots$.

Since the output alphabets of each of the components are disjoint, the parallel composition of the components is easy to compute from the pre and postconditions, and we get:

$$\text{Xform} \; \hat{=} \; \text{true} \vdash \begin{aligned} & (i_1 \wedge w_1' \wedge \overline{i_1'}) \vee (w_1 \wedge i_2 \wedge a_1' \wedge \overline{w_1'}) \vee (w_1 \wedge w_2 \wedge \overline{t} \wedge a_1' \wedge \overline{w_1'}) \vee (a_1 \wedge i_1' \wedge \overline{a_1'}) \\ & \vee (i_2 \wedge w_2' \wedge \overline{i_2'}) \vee (w_2 \wedge i_1 \wedge a_2' \wedge \overline{w_2'}) \vee (w_2 \wedge w_1 \wedge t \wedge a_2' \wedge \overline{w_2'}) \vee (a_2 \wedge i_2' \wedge \overline{a_2'}) \\ & \vee (i_1 \wedge w_2 \wedge t') \vee (i_2 \wedge w_1 \wedge \overline{t'}) \end{aligned}$$

This corresponds to the transition system for the system, and expresses a transformer which, when given values for i, w, a and t, returns the new primed values. However, we are more interested in the sequence of states when our system runs continuously, and so we define a recursive design which mimics the system precisely:

$$\text{System} \; \hat{=} \; \text{Xform}; \text{System}$$

We can view this design in an operational sense as a predicate transformer, transforming an observation consistent with the assumptions of the design, into a new observation consistent with the commitments of the design. If we begin with an initial observation over the state variables matching state s_0 from Section 3, then the Xform asserts that the commitment will be either s_1 or s_2. Operationally, we could view this as a transition from s_0 to s_1, or s_0 to s_2.

In the following presentation, the set S of program states represents a set of valuations of all observations of the process. Formally speaking, we start with an alphabet A of observation variables. In our case $A = \{i_1, w_1, a_1, i_2, w_2, a_2, t\}$. These observation variables are evaluated according to a valuation function $v : A \to \{\text{true, false}\}$. We use $\overline{t}$ to express that $v(t) = \text{false}$, and t for $v(t) = \text{true}$.

An observation $o \in O$ is a conjunction of valuations over the alphabet A. The observations w_1 or $\overline{w_1} \wedge t$, are examples of observations that may be made about the system. The observation $\overline{w_1} \wedge t$ is sometimes written as $\overline{w_1}t$ for short, and so we may write expressions such as $\overline{w_1}t \wedge \overline{w_2}a_2t$, or $(o \wedge s_0) = o$, where o is an observation, and s_0 is a state. The set of observations is larger than the set of states. Each state is an observation, but there are observations that are not states. Later in this presentation, when we consider a relation consisting of pairs of observations, this is a more general, and larger set than a transition relation which is a set of pairs of states.

The set S of states is given by all possible valuations over all observation variables. We write individual states in S as s_n or in shorthand as a string of observation values. In our case, $S = \{i_1\overline{w_1a_1}i_2\overline{w_2a_2}t, \ldots, i_1\overline{w_1a_1}i_2w_2a_2\overline{t}\}$.

We can (informally) derive the transition relation for the system by applying the Xform to the initial state s_0, collecting the original and transformed state variables as a transition, and repeating with the new transformed variables until no new transitions are returned. The transition relation is expressed as a set of pairs of states in the usual way:

$$\text{Trans} = \{(s_0, s_1), (s_0, s_2), \ldots, (s_{15}, s_6), (s_{15}, s_{12})\}$$

This *set-of-pairs* notation will be re-used when we define model checking in UTP.

In addition, if we retain the ordering of the observation variables, and con-catenate the first and second elements, with the second elements primed as they stand for observations after the program executes, then we can re-express the transition relation as:

$$m = \{(s_0, s_1), \ldots\}$$
$$= \{i_1 \overline{w_1 a_1} i_2 \overline{w_2 a_2} t i_1' w_1' \overline{a_1'} i_2' \overline{w_2' a_2'} t', \ldots\}$$

This representation mirrors exactly the binary decision tree (BDT) structure which we used to represent predicates. This *set-of-strings* notation will be used in Section 4.4 where we define model checking using ROBDD representations for UTP.

4.2   Specification of Properties in UTP

This section outlines how the properties in Section 3.2 may be expressed in UTP. In UTP terms, a property P is an expression whose elements are observations, and whose connectives are simple state ones ($\wedge$, $\vee$ and $\neg$) or the more complex temporal ones (**G**, **X** and **U**).

For example, we may be interested in the property "x will be true until $\bar{y}$". This property would be written as $x \ \mathbf{U} \ \bar{y}$.

4.3   Model Checking in UTP

We begin with the general structure of our presentation of UTP model checking. The model checking relation is expressed as a ternary relation $\models$ between a design, a state and the property to be checked.

For state formulæ in UTP, the atomic components are observations, and we use only the non-temporal connectives $\wedge$, $\vee$ and $\neg$. Given a transition relation $r \in \mathcal{R}$ for the design $\mathcal{D}$, the model checking relation $\mathcal{D}, s \models P$ for a property $P \in \mathcal{P}$ in state s is defined by

$$\mathcal{D}, s \models P \ \widehat{=} \ (\mathbf{map}(r, s) \blacktriangleleft \mathbf{satmap}(r, P)) \neq \emptyset$$

Informally, we check that the state s belongs to the set of "satisfied pairs". We have not of course defined **map**, $\blacktriangleleft$ or **satmap**, and these definitions follow.

The function $\mathbf{map} : 2^{\mathcal{R}} \times S \rightarrow 2^{\mathcal{R}}$ (where $2^{\mathcal{R}}$ is the set of all subsets of $\mathcal{R}$) takes as arguments a transition relation r and a state s and returns a subrelation in which each element has the state s as a first component of the transition relation pair:

$$\mathbf{map}(r, s) \ \widehat{=} \ \{(s_1, s_2) \in r \mid s_1 = s\}$$

The function $\mathbf{tmap} : 2^{\mathcal{R}} \times O \rightarrow 2^{\mathcal{R}}$ takes as arguments a transition relation r and an observation o and returns a subrelation of r in which the observation o is "included" in the first component of the transition relation pair:

$$\mathbf{tmap}(r, o) \ \widehat{=} \ \{(s_1, s_2) \in r \mid (o \wedge s_1) = o\}$$

In this definition $(o \wedge s_1) = o$ expresses the fact that the observation o is part of the conjunction provided by s_1. This is why we use the phrase "o is included in the first component". For instance,

$$\mathbf{tmap}(\mathrm{Trans}, a_1 w_2 t) = \{(\overline{i_1 w_1 a_1 \overline{i_2} w_2 \overline{a_2}} t, i_1 w_1 a_1 i_2 w_2 \overline{a_2} t)\}$$
$$= \{(s_{14}, s_6)\}$$

The function $\mathbf{fmap} : 2^{\mathcal{R}} \times O \to 2^{\mathcal{R}}$ takes a transition relation r and an observation o and returns a subrelation of the complement $\bar{r}$ of r, in which the observation o is included in the first component of the transition relation pair:

$$\mathbf{fmap}(r, o) \,\hat{=}\, \{(s_1, s_2) \in \bar{r} \mid (o \wedge s_1) = o\}$$

Note that $\mathbf{fmap}$ could also be done using set minus.

Given two pairs of observations $o = (o_1, o_2)$, and $o' = (o'_1, o'_2)$, we define

$$o \lhd o' \,\hat{=}\, ((o_1 \wedge o'_1) = o_1) \wedge ((o_2 \wedge o'_2) = o_2)$$

We now define a matching function $\blacktriangleleft : 2^{\mathcal{O} \times \mathcal{O}} \times 2^{\mathcal{O} \times \mathcal{O}} \to 2^{\mathcal{O} \times \mathcal{O}}$ which takes two sets of pairs of observations and returns a subset of the second one. The sets of pairs of observations may be used to express transition relations, in which the observations correspond exactly to the states. Given two such relations r_1 and r_2, we define

$$r_1 \blacktriangleleft r_2 \,\hat{=}\, \{o \in r_2 \mid \exists o' \in r_1 : o' \lhd o\}$$

For example:

$$\{(a_2 t, a_2 t)\} \blacktriangleleft \mathrm{Trans} = \{(i_1 \overline{w_1 a_1 i_2 w_2} a_2 t, \overline{i_1} w_1 \overline{a_1 i_2 w_2} a_2 t)\}$$
$$= \{(s_{10}, s_{11})\}$$

We observe that the first pair of r_1 matches the second pair of r_2, and that the second pair of r_1 also matches the second pair of r_2. As a final result, we get the second pair of r_2.

State Formulae in UTP. We go on to show how to express state formulae in UTP. When model checking a UTP design, a property P is given as a CTL formula. For state formulae in UTP, the atomic components are observations, and we use only the non-temporal connectives $\wedge$, $\vee$ and $\neg$.

Given arbitrary properties $p, q \in \mathcal{P}$, and a transition relation $r \in \mathcal{R}$ for the design $\mathcal{D}$, we define a satisfaction mapping function $\mathbf{satmap} : 2^{\mathcal{R}} \times \mathcal{P} \to 2^{\mathcal{R}}$ by:

$$\mathbf{satmap}(r, p) \,\hat{=}\, \mathbf{tmap}(r, p) \blacktriangleleft r$$
$$\mathbf{satmap}(r, \neg p) \,\hat{=}\, \mathbf{fmap}(r, p) \blacktriangleleft r$$
$$\mathbf{satmap}(r, p \wedge q) \,\hat{=}\, \mathbf{tmap}(r, p) \blacktriangleleft r \,\cap\, \mathbf{tmap}(r, q) \blacktriangleleft r$$
$$\mathbf{satmap}(r, p \vee q) \,\hat{=}\, \mathbf{tmap}(r, p) \blacktriangleleft r \,\cup\, \mathbf{tmap}(r, q) \blacktriangleleft r$$

This function returns a set of "satisfied pairs", a subset of r satisfying the property.

As a worked example of some checks on our design, let us try to see which states satisfy $a_1 \wedge t$ using the approach. We can calculate the satisfaction mapping function:

$$\mathbf{satmap}(m, a_1 \wedge t) \mathrel{\hat=} \mathbf{tmap}(m, a_1) \blacktriangleleft m \cap \mathbf{tmap}(m, t) \blacktriangleleft m$$
$$= \{(s_3, s_0), (s_3, s_7), (s_7, s_2), (s_{13}, s_{14}), (s_{13}, s_{15}), (s_{14}, s_6)\}$$
$$\cap \{(s_6, s_9), (s_6, s_{10}), \dots, (s_{14}, s_6), (s_{15}, s_6), (s_{15}, s_{12})\}$$
$$= \{(s_{13}, s_{14}), (s_{13}, s_{15}), (s_{14}, s_6)\}$$

Now, for each of the states there is a corresponding set of mapping functions:

$$\mathbf{map}(m, s_0) = \{(s_0, s_1), (s_0, s_2)\}$$
$$\dots = \dots$$
$$\mathbf{map}(m, s_{14}) = \{(s_{14}, s_6)\}$$
$$\mathbf{map}(m, s_{15}) = \{(s_{15}, s_6), (s_{15}, s_{12})\}$$

We can now calculate the model checking relation in each state:

$$\mathcal{D}, s_0 \models a_1 \wedge t = (\mathbf{map}(m, s_0) \blacktriangleleft \mathbf{satmap}(m, a_1 \wedge t)) \neq \emptyset = \mathbf{false}$$
$$\dots = \dots$$
$$\mathcal{D}, s_{14} \models a_1 \wedge t = (\mathbf{map}(m, s_{14}) \blacktriangleleft \mathbf{satmap}(m, a_1 \wedge t)) \neq \emptyset = \mathbf{true}$$
$$\mathcal{D}, s_{15} \models a_1 \wedge t = (\mathbf{map}(m, s_{15}) \blacktriangleleft \mathbf{satmap}(m, a_1 \wedge t)) \neq \emptyset = \mathbf{false}$$

This may be confirmed by examining Table 1, and noting which states have both a_1 and t.

Temporal Formulae in UTP. For temporal formulae in UTP, we use the temporal connectives **EX**, **EG** and **EU**. We begin with a pair of temporal functions (F, P) forming a Galois connection, and representing *future*[3] and *past* respectively. Karger and Hoare [17] demonstrate how these functions may be used to express temporal relations. The interested reader is also directed to the section on Galois connections in the UTP book [16]. F_r represents the *future* function for the transition relation r, which returns a relation r' with r in its immediate future. Using the running example of transition relation m, we have that

$$F_m(\{(s_8, s_1)\}) = \{(s_4, s_8)\}$$
$$F_m(\{(s_5, s_7)\}) = \{(s_1, s_5), (s_2, s_5)\}$$

It is easy to understand the two examples by examining Figure 1.

---

[3] Note that this function F is not to be confused with the CTL future operator **F**. The font is different for each.

P_{rq} represents the *past* function for the relation r, which returns a relation r' with r in its past, and which satisfies **EX** q. Using the running example of transition relation m, and using the observation $q = w_1 \wedge i_2$ we have that

$$P_{mq}(m) = \{(s_4, s_8)\}$$

Once again it is easy to understand the example by examining Figure 1. The results of the P_{mq} function consist of the transition leading from state s_4 to s_8. If we take the *next* transition, the observation q will be true.

The CTL temporal connectives may be characterized as the fixed point of the temporal functions F_r and P_{rq} [18]. We define the following two fixpoint operators:

$$F^{\Diamond}(X) \mathrel{\widehat{=}} (\nu Y \bullet X \sqcap F(Y))$$
$$P^{\Box}(X) \mathrel{\widehat{=}} (\mu Y \bullet X \sqcup P(Y))$$

Note that we use the $\Diamond$ and $\Box$ symbols to highlight the function iterators. Given properties $p, q \in \mathcal{P}$, and a transition relation $r \in \mathcal{R}$ for a design $\mathcal{D}$, we can define the satisfaction mapping function **satmap** for CTL *temporal* formulae by induction. For a start, let us express a satisfaction function for the required temporal formulae of Section 3.2 in terms of the temporal functions and their fixpoints:

$$\mathbf{satmap}(r, \mathbf{EX}\ p) \mathrel{\widehat{=}} F_r(\mathbf{satmap}(r, p))$$
$$\mathbf{satmap}(r, \mathbf{EG}\ p) \mathrel{\widehat{=}} F_r^{\Diamond}(\mathbf{satmap}(r, p))\,\{r\}$$
$$\mathbf{satmap}(r, \mathbf{E}[p\ \mathbf{U}\ q]) \mathrel{\widehat{=}} P_{rq}^{\Box}(\mathbf{satmap}(r, p))\,\emptyset$$

The satisfaction function for the **EG** p temporal formula uses the *future* function iterator $F_r^{\Diamond}$, the greatest fixed point of F_r. The satisfaction function for the $\mathbf{E}[p\ \mathbf{U}\ q]$ temporal formula uses the *past* function iterator $P_{rq}^{\Box}$, the least fixed point of P_{rq}. These functions provide a high-level description of the satisfaction function for the temporal formulae, but not many clues in how to implement the functions. A lower level description, closer to our approach, requires an appropriate function **backstep** to implement the core of the F_r function:

$$\mathbf{backstep}(r, s) \mathrel{\widehat{=}} \{(s_1, s_2) \in r \mid \forall a \in s : a = s_2\}$$

The function **backstep** : $2^{\mathcal{R}} \times 2^S \to 2^{\mathcal{R}}$ takes a transition relation r together with a set of states, and returns a subrelation of r in which each pair has its second element drawn from the set of states. We can view this as a backwards step in the transition relation. If we have a set of states s which satisfy a property, then we can take a backwards step, and determine the transitions leading to those states. The iterator $P_{rq}^{\Box}$ may be expressed without requiring a new function.

Proposition 1. *The satisfaction function for our temporal formulae may be expressed in terms of the lower-level operators in the following way:*

$$\mathbf{satmap}(r, \mathbf{EX}\ p) \equiv \{(s_1, s_2) \in r \mid \mathbf{satmap}(\mathbf{backstep}(r, s_1), p) \neq \emptyset\}$$

$$\mathbf{satmap}(r, \mathbf{EG}\ p) \equiv \mathbf{satmap}(r, p)\ \cap\ \mathbf{satmap}(r, \mathbf{EX}\ \mathbf{EG}\ p)$$
$$\equiv \bigcap_i (\lambda y.(\mathbf{satmap}(r, p)\ \cap\ \mathbf{satmap}(y, \mathbf{EX}\ p)))^i\ \{r\}$$

$$\mathbf{satmap}(r, \mathbf{E}[p\ \mathbf{U}\ q])$$
$$\equiv \mathbf{satmap}(r, q)\ \cup\ (\mathbf{satmap}(r, p)\ \cap\ \mathbf{satmap}(r, \mathbf{EX}\ \mathbf{E}[p\ \mathbf{U}\ q]))$$
$$\equiv \bigcup_i (\lambda y.(\mathbf{satmap}(r, q)\ \cup\ (\mathbf{satmap}(r, p) \cap \mathbf{satmap}(y, \mathbf{EX}\ q))))^i\ \emptyset$$

Proof. We provide here the intuition behind the technical details of the proof. Firstly, the $\mathbf{satmap}(r, \mathbf{EX}\ p)$ function definition just given returns those transitions from the transition relation which lead to a state in which the property p holds. Secondly, the intuition behind the $\mathbf{satmap}(r, \mathbf{EG}\ p)$ function definition is that it returns those transitions from the transition relation which always involve a state in which the property p holds. This is done by iteration, starting from the entire transition relation until we reach the greatest fixed point. Finally, the intuition behind the $\mathbf{satmap}(r, \mathbf{E}[p\ \mathbf{U}\ q])$ function definition is that it returns those transitions from the transition relation which have p holding until the property q holds. Again, this is done by iteration, starting from an empty transition relation until we reach the least fixed point.   □

As an example to check a temporal formula against our model, we calculate which states satisfy $\mathbf{EG}\ \neg(a_1 a_2)$. This expresses the idea that a_1 and a_2 cannot both be true at the same time, which is an essential requirement for the mutual exclusion algorithm. We begin by calculating the function $\mathbf{satmap}(\mathrm{Trans}, \mathbf{EG}\ \neg(a_1 a_2))$.

$$\mathbf{satmap}(\mathrm{Trans}, \mathbf{EG}\ \neg(a_1 a_2)) \cong F_{\mathrm{Trans}}^{\Diamond}(\mathbf{satmap}(\mathrm{Trans}, \mathbf{EG}\ \neg(a_1 a_2)))\ \{\mathrm{Trans}\}$$
$$\equiv \bigcap_i (\lambda y.(\mathbf{satmap}(\mathrm{Trans}, \neg(a_1 a_2)) \cap \mathbf{satmap}(y, \mathbf{EX}\ \neg(a_1 a_2))))^i\{\mathrm{Trans}\}$$
$$= (\mathrm{Trans} \cap \mathbf{satmap}(\mathrm{Trans}, \mathbf{EX}\ \neg(a_1 a_2))) \cap \ldots$$
$$= \mathrm{Trans} \cap (\mathrm{Trans} \cap \mathbf{satmap}(\mathrm{Trans}, \mathbf{EX}\ \neg(a_1 a_2))) \cap \ldots$$
$$= \mathrm{Trans}$$

We can then calculate the model checking relation:

$$\mathcal{D}, s_0 \models \mathbf{EG}\ \neg(a_1 a_2) = \mathbf{map}(\mathrm{Trans}, s_0) \blacktriangleleft \mathbf{satmap}(\mathrm{Trans}, \mathbf{EG}\ \neg(a_1 a_2)) \neq \emptyset$$
$$= \mathbf{true}$$

This may be confirmed by examining the table in Section 4.1.

4.4   Model Checking with ROBDDs

Our presentations of transition relations, state and properties do not rely on any particular ordering of the variables, but it is easy to extend the approach by imposing a discipline on the representation of the model and state. This discipline does not amount to a healthiness condition for the theory. It does not produce a subtheory: the UTP theory of model checking is equivalent to the UTP theory of ROBDD-style model checking.

The discipline is imposed by using strings to represent observations, states and transition relations. Each element in the string corresponds to an observation, and must occur in a specific order. By using corresponding $\mathbf{map}_{\mathrm{BD}}$ and $\mathbf{tmap}_{\mathrm{BD}}$ functions, and with a new matching relation $\blacktriangleleft_{\mathrm{BD}}$ operating over strings, we can closely follow the structures and algorithms used for symbolic model checking. We include this section to emphasize the simpler and more elegant and program-oriented approach in UTP.

We begin with the definition of the model checking relation $\models_{\mathrm{BD}}$. Given a transition relation $r \in \mathcal{R}$ for the design $\mathcal{D}$, the ROBDD model checking relation $\mathcal{D}, s_n \models_{\mathrm{BD}} P$ for property $P \in \mathcal{P}$ in state s_n is defined by

$$\mathcal{D}, s_n \models_{\mathrm{BD}} P \,\widehat{=}\, (\mathbf{map}_{\mathrm{BD}}(r, s_n) \,\blacktriangleleft_{\mathrm{BD}}\, \mathbf{satmap}_{\mathrm{BD}}(r, P)) \neq \emptyset$$

The presentation in this section is necessarily brief, and we appeal to the use of analogy rather than redefining at length all the new functions. Each function or operator works in an analogous way to those in Section 4.3, except that they now operate over strings and sets of strings, rather than over observations, pairs of observations, and sets of pairs of observations. For example, in Section 4.3 we might refer to the observation $a_1 a_2$ meaning $a_1 \wedge a_2$, but here we refer to the string "$a_1 a_2$" in which the order of the elements of the string is relevant. This *ordering* becomes important when trying to characterize the behaviour of ROBDD model checkers.

We now define properties of a binary decision tree structure used to represent predicates. This structure is defined in such a way as to allow for BDT as well as ROBDD representations of functions. A binary diagram $B = (V, E)$ is a rooted, directed, acyclic graph with vertices V and edges E satisfying

i) Vertices are of two types: either <u>node</u> or <u>leaf</u>;
ii) Each vertex is labelled with the strings that lead to it;
iii) Leaf vertices have as an attribute a value $\mathbf{T}$ or $\mathbf{F}$ (**true** or **false**).

We term any connected set of edges that begin at the root and terminate in a leaf as a path. The valuation of a path is given by the attribute at the leaf. Such a binary diagram is shown in Figure 4. The labelling language consists of strings defined over an alphabet A whose elements are ordered.

We define a function $\mathbf{map}_{\mathrm{BD}}$ over labelled vertices of a binary diagram representing the transition relation r, which returns the set of maps that pass through the vertex. The $\mathbf{tmap}_{\mathrm{BD}}$ of the vertex $l_i \in V$ is a function which returns the set of paths that pass through the labelled vertex and terminate with a $\mathbf{T}$-leaf. The $\mathbf{fmap}_{\mathrm{BD}}$ of the vertex $l_i \in V$ is a function which returns the set of paths that pass through the labelled vertex and terminate with an $\mathbf{F}$-leaf.

According to the binary diagram B in Figure 4:

$$\mathbf{map}_{\mathrm{BD}}(\mathrm{B}, l_5) = \{\bar{i}w\bar{a}, \bar{i}wa\}$$
$$\mathbf{tmap}_{\mathrm{BD}}(\mathrm{B}, l_7) = \emptyset$$
$$\mathbf{fmap}_{\mathrm{BD}}(\mathrm{B}, l_3) = \{i\bar{w}\bar{a}, iw\bar{a}, iwa\}$$

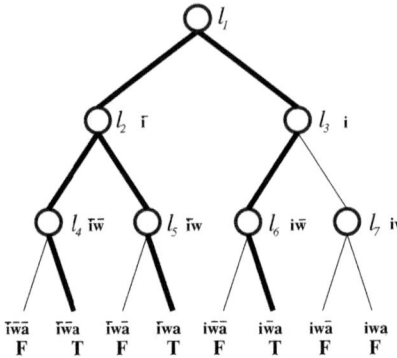

Fig. 4. Labelling of binary diagram B

Since the strings are all ordered, we say that a label m_1 is *included* in m_2 if each non-null element of m_1 is found in m_2. Note that this inclusion relation just allows us to check if one of the strings is contained within another, considering possible gaps. We use this inclusion relation to define the function $\blacktriangleleft_{\mathrm{BD}}$ which returns a set of labels from one set which are inclusive of labels in the other set. For example:

$$\{ia\} \blacktriangleleft_{\mathrm{BD}} \{\bar{i}wa, i\bar{w}a, \bar{i}\bar{w}\bar{a}\} = \{i\bar{w}a\}$$
$$\{ia, \bar{w}a\} \blacktriangleleft_{\mathrm{BD}} \{iwa, i\bar{w}a, \bar{i}\bar{w}\bar{a}\} = \{iwa, i\bar{w}a\}$$

In the first example, the string ia is only included in the middle label, so we return the middle label. In the second example, the string ia is included in the first two labels, and $\bar{w}a$ is included in the middle label, so we return the first two labels.

These functions may now be directly used for similar definitions for **satmap** as those given previously:

$$\mathbf{satmap}_{\mathrm{BD}}(r, p) \mathrel{\hat{=}} \mathbf{tmap}_{\mathrm{BD}}(r, p) \blacktriangleleft_{\mathrm{BD}} r$$
$$\mathbf{satmap}_{\mathrm{BD}}(r, \neg p) \mathrel{\hat{=}} \mathbf{fmap}_{\mathrm{BD}}(r, p) \blacktriangleleft_{\mathrm{BD}} r$$
$$\mathbf{satmap}_{\mathrm{BD}}(r, p \wedge q) \mathrel{\hat{=}} \mathbf{tmap}_{\mathrm{BD}}(r, p) \blacktriangleleft_{\mathrm{BD}} r \cap \mathbf{tmap}_{\mathrm{BD}}(r, q) \blacktriangleleft_{\mathrm{BD}} r$$
$$\mathbf{satmap}_{\mathrm{BD}}(r, p \vee q) \mathrel{\hat{=}} \mathbf{tmap}_{\mathrm{BD}}(r, p) \blacktriangleleft_{\mathrm{BD}} r \cup \mathbf{tmap}_{\mathrm{BD}}(r, q) \blacktriangleleft_{\mathrm{BD}} r$$
$$\mathbf{satmap}_{\mathrm{BD}}(r, \mathbf{EX}\ p) \mathrel{\hat{=}} F_r(\mathbf{satmap}_{\mathrm{BD}}(r, p))$$
$$\mathbf{satmap}_{\mathrm{BD}}(r, \mathbf{EG}\ p) \mathrel{\hat{=}} F_r^{\Diamond}(\mathbf{satmap}_{\mathrm{BD}}(r, p))\ \{r\}$$
$$\mathbf{satmap}_{\mathrm{BD}}(r, \mathbf{E}[p\ \mathbf{U}\ q]) \mathrel{\hat{=}} P_{rq}^{\Box}(\mathbf{satmap}_{\mathrm{BD}}(r, p))\ \emptyset$$

In this specification of $\models_{\mathrm{BD}}$, the interpretation is different from that in Section 4.3. In particular, the operations over the binary diagram structure closely follow the operations used in traditional symbolic model checking using BDDs.

5 Conclusion

Reactive systems provide an appealing abstraction for real-time and embedded systems. Such systems are now found in nearly every facet of life, and their correctness has become critical. Four principal approaches are considered for the correctness of reactive systems: simulation, testing, deductive verification and model checking. In the case of complex reactive systems, simulation and testing are widely used, but these techniques cover only a limited set of possible behaviours. Deductive verification employs the use of axioms and proof rules to verify the correctness of the system, and is rarely used. Model checking differs from these verification methods in being fully algorithmic and of low computational complexity. Model checking employs an exhaustive search of the state space of the system in order to determine if a specification is true or not. Since it has been shown to be cost-efficient, model checking can be adopted as a efficient procedure for the quality assurance of reactive systems.

Model checking is being used routinely to design and debug reactive systems, usually by using specific algorithms for model checking, automata-theoretic approaches and linear temporal logic [19]. In [12], the checking algorithms are enhanced by taking into account the abstractions that are involved in the design of the program model/abstract semantics, and new reachability analysis and abstract testing techniques are proposed. In this paper we describe model checking of reactive processes with a simple set-based description of the models and states of a reactive process, as well as of the properties that we wish to verify. This emphasizes the mathematical properties of model checking, and a model checking relation is derived from a satisfaction relation between the model and its properties.

The unified theory of programming provides a basis for the presentation of programming topics, unifying a wide range of diverse notations and concepts for program development, in a single coherent notation. The approach taken here adds to the development of verification for reactive processes within the theory. A specific advantage of the model checking formalism presented in this paper is that there is a direct relation between the UTP reactive process and its model.

We have presented our encoding of reactive process verification for UTP along the lines of the traditional model checking paradigm. UTP reactive processes are structured around predicates representing intermediate observations. These predicates provide an appropriate basis for creating the transition relation needed for model checking, and we have shown how to automatically generate this transition relation.

We have deliberately structured the presentation with an implementation in mind. At an abstract level we compactly characterize the temporal operators using function iterators, but in addition we have re-expressed them in an implementable fashion. More technical results could be established, but at this stage we emphasize the conceptual approach, introducing a starting platform for further theoretical and practical steps.

References

1. Back, R.-J., von Wright, J.: Refinement Calculus, A Systematic Introduction. Springer, Heidelberg (1998)
2. Bryant, R.E.: Graph-based algorithms for Boolean function manipulation. IEEE Transactions on Computers C-35(8), 677–691 (1986)
3. Butterfield, A., Sherif, A., Woodcock, J.: Slotted-Circus. In: Davies, J., Gibbons, J. (eds.) IFM 2007. LNCS, vol. 4591, pp. 75–97. Springer, Heidelberg (2007)
4. Butterfield, A., Woodcock, J.: A "Hardware Compiler" Semantics for Handel-C. Electronic Notes on Theoretical Computer Science 161, 73–90 (2006)
5. Cavalcanti, A., Clayton, P., O'Halloran, C.: Control Law Diagrams in Circus. In: Fitzgerald, J.S., Hayes, I.J., Tarlecki, A. (eds.) FM 2005. LNCS, vol. 3582, pp. 253–268. Springer, Heidelberg (2005)
6. Cavalcanti, A., Sampaio, A., Woodcock, J.: Unifying Classes and Processes. Software and System Modeling 4(3), 277–296 (2005)
7. Cavalcanti, A., Woodcock, J.: Angelic Nondeterminism and Unifying Theories of Programming. Electr. Notes on Theoretical Computer Science 137(2), 45–66 (2005)
8. Cavalcanti, A., Woodcock, J.: A Tutorial Introduction to CSP in Unifying Theories of Programming. In: Cavalcanti, A., Sampaio, A., Woodcock, J. (eds.) PSSE 2004. LNCS, vol. 3167, pp. 220–268. Springer, Heidelberg (2006)
9. Cavalcanti, A., Woodcock, J., Dunne, S.: Angelic Nondeterminism in the Unifying Theories of Programming. Formal Aspects of Computing 18(3), 288–307 (2006)
10. Cavalcanti, A., Harwood, W., Woodcock, J.: Pointers and Records in the Unifying Theories of Programming. In: Dunne, S., Stoddart, B. (eds.) UTP 2006. LNCS, vol. 4010, pp. 200–216. Springer, Heidelberg (2006)
11. Clarke, E.M., Grumberg, O., Peled, D.A.: Model Checking. MIT Press, Cambridge (1999)
12. Cousot, P., Cousot, R.: Software Analysis and Model Checking, pp. 37–56. Springer, Heidelberg (2002)
13. Freitas, L.: Model Checking Circus. Ph.D. thesis. Department of Computer Science, University of York (2005)
14. Goldblatt, R.: Modal Logics of Programs. Research Report 94-146, Victoria University of Wellington (1994)
15. He, J., Liu, Z., Li, X.: rCOS: A refinement calculus of object systems. Theoretical Computer Science 365, 109–142 (2006)
16. Hoare, C.A.R., He, J.: Unifying Theories of Programming. Prentice-Hall, Englewood Cliffs (1998)
17. von Karger, B., Hoare, C.A.R.: Sequential calculus. Information Processing Letters 53(3), 123–130 (1995)
18. McMillan, K.L.: Symbolic Model Checking: An Approach to the State Explosion Problem. PhD thesis, School of Computer Science, Carnegie Mellon University (1992)
19. Merz, S.: Model Checking Techniques for the Analysis of Reactive Systems. Synthese, 173–201 (2002)
20. Qin, S., Dong, J.-S., Chin, W.-N.: A Semantic Foundation for TCOZ in Unifying Theories of Programming. In: Araki, K., Gnesi, S., Mandrioli, D. (eds.) FME 2003. LNCS, vol. 2805, pp. 321–340. Springer, Heidelberg (2003)
21. Santos, T.L.V.L., Cavalcanti, A., Sampaio, A.: Object-Orientation in the UTP. In: Dunne, S., Stoddart, B. (eds.) UTP 2006. LNCS, vol. 4010, pp. 18–37. Springer, Heidelberg (2006)

22. Sherif, A., He, J.: Towards a Time Model for Circus. In: George, C.W., Miao, H. (eds.) ICFEM 2002. LNCS, vol. 2495, pp. 613–624. Springer, Heidelberg (2002)
23. Tang, X., Woodcock, J.: Travelling Processes. In: Kozen, D. (ed.) MPC 2004. LNCS, vol. 3125, pp. 381–399. Springer, Heidelberg (2004)
24. Woodcock, J.: Unifying Theories of Parallel Programming. In: Logic and Algebra for Engineering Software. IOS Press, Amsterdam (2002)
25. Woodcock, J., Cavalcanti, A.: The Semantics of Circus. In: Bert, D., P. Bowen, J., C. Henson, M., Robinson, K. (eds.) B 2002 and ZB 2002. LNCS, vol. 2272, pp. 184–203. Springer, Heidelberg (2002)

A Note on Traces Refinement and the *conf* Relation in the Unifying Theories of Programming

Ana Cavalcanti[1] and Marie-Claude Gaudel[2]

[1] University of York, Department of Computer Science
York YO10 5DD, UK
[2] LRI, Université de Paris-Sud and CNRS
Orsay 91405, France

Abstract. There is a close relation between the failures-divergences and the UTP models of CSP, but they are not equivalent. For example, miracles are not available in the failures-divergences model; the UTP theory is richer and can be used to give semantics to data-rich process algebras like *Circus*. Previously, we have defined functions that calculate the failures-divergences model of a CSP process characterised by a UTP relation. In this note, we use these functions to calculate the UTP characterisations of traces refinement and of the *conf* relation that is widely used in testing. In addition, we prove that the combination of traces refinement and *conf* corresponds to refinement of processes in *Circus*. This result is the basis for a formal testing technique based on *Circus*; as usual in testing, we restrict ourselves to divergence-free processes.

1 Introduction

Formal specifications have been widely explored as a starting point for software testing; the works reported in [8,11,3,4,2,14] give a few examples. In our own previous work [5], we have instantiated Gaudel's long-standing theory of formal testing [12] to CSP [19]. We now face the challenge of a richer language: *Circus* [6], which combines CSP with Z [20] and Morgan's refinement calculus [17] to provide a notation that supports refinement of reactive systems with state.

The *Circus* semantic model [18] is based on the UTP [13]; a *Circus* process is characterised by a relation in a restriction of the UTP theory for CSP. In this model, we can define, for example, the application of CSP constructs like external choice to processes that involve operations on a local state. We can also accommodate miraculous specifications from Morgan's refinement calculus.

In previous work, to study the relationship between the UTP and the canonical failures-divergences model of CSP, we have defined functions that calculate the failures-divergences model of a UTP relation that characterises a CSP process [7]. The UTP theory for CSP is richer than the failures-divergences model. In addition, refinement in the UTP is in close correspondence with failures-divergences refinement, but the other two main refinement relations that support compositional and stepwise reasoning in CSP, namely traces and failures refinement, have not been studied in the UTP.

A. Butterfield (Ed.): UTP 2008, LNCS 5713, pp. 42–61, 2010.
© Springer-Verlag Berlin Heidelberg 2010

Traces refinement is useful for reasoning about safety properties of a process; it ensures that the implementation does not engage in any interactions with the environment that are not allowed by the specification. Failures refinement, on the other hand, is used for reasoning about liveness: the interactions in which an implementation has to be prepared to engage.

Our interest is in a testing technique based on *Circus* specifications; our long-term goal is to provide automated support for test generation with the objective of verifying that a system under test implements a *Circus* specification correctly. In other words, we are interested in testing for refinement using *Circus*.

It is usual for testing techniques to assume that the specification and the system under test are divergence free. In addition, testing for trace inclusion and for reduction of deadlock is typically carried out separately to simplify the individual tests. Trace inclusion is, of course, traces refinement in the context of CSP, and reduction of deadlock, is captured by a relation usually called *conf* (for conformance). For CSP, we have proved that traces refinement and *conf*, together, are equivalent to failures-divergences refinement for divergence-free processes.

For *Circus*, we follow a similar approach, but there is no accepted definition of traces refinement and *conf* in the UTP. In this note, we calculate definitions for these relations, and prove that their combination corresponds to refinement of divergence-free *Circus* processes. Our calculations are based on functions that map UTP relations to components of the failures-divergences model. A perhaps surprising result is that the combination of traces refinement and *conf* do not correspond to the refinement relation in the UTP, but to refinement when state components are encapsulated; this is the notion of process refinement in *Circus*.

In the next section, we discuss the requirements and assumptions that are common to testing techniques based on process algebra. Afterwards, in Section 3, we give a brief and informal presentation of our process algebra of choice: *Circus*. Sections 4, 5, and 6 present our main results: the calculations of UTP characterisations of traces refinement and *conf*, and a proof that, together, they correspond to process refinement. Finally, in Section 7, we summarise our results and discuss our plans for future work. An appendix presents a few lemmas used in the proofs of our main theorems.

2   Process-Algebra Based Formal Testing

In this section we briefly recall some basic principles of specification-based testing.

In testing, an executable system, called the *system under test (SUT)* is given as a black-box. We can only observe the behavior of the *SUT* on any chosen input, or input sequence, and then decide whether it is acceptable or not with respect to some description of its intended behavior.

Given a formal specification *SP* and an *SUT*, any testing activity is, explicitly or not, based on a satisfaction relation: *SUT sat SP*. Since the *SUT* is a black-box, the testing process consists in using the specification *SP* to construct a set of tests, such that the *SUT* passes them if, and only if, it satisfies *SP*.

The tests are derived from the specification on the basis of the satisfaction relation, and often on the basis of some additional knowledge of the SUT and of its operational environment called *testability hypothesis*. Such test sets are called *exhaustive* in [12] or *complete* by other authors [4].

In the case of specifications based on some process algebra, tests are processes built on the same alphabet of events as the specification (possibly enriched by some special symbols). The execution of a given test consists in running it and the SUT in parallel. This can be done under the assumption (testability hypothesis) that the SUT behaves as some unknown, maybe infinite, transition system.

This testability hypothesis builds a bridge between the notions of satisfaction, (as introduced above, between a system and a specification) and refinement between two models: a specification model and an implementation model. Refinement has the advantage of being formalisable and well studied, while satisfaction is less easily formalisable, since it relates a model and a system.

The verdict about the success or not of a test execution depends on the observations that can be made, and it is based on the satisfaction relation. Most testing methods based on process algebras consider that two kinds of observations are possible: external events, and deadlock (that is, refusal of some external events). Deadlock is observed via time-out mechanisms: it is assumed that if the SUT does not react after a given time limit, it is blocked.

Divergences raise problems of observability; generally, it is not possible to distinguish a divergent from a deadlocked system using testing. So, most methods assume that the SUT is divergence free. This is equivalent to identifying divergence with deadlock in the unknown models of the systems under test; most authors, including us in [5], circumvent the problem of observability in this way. If the SUT is divergent, the divergence is detected as a (probably forbidden) deadlock and reported as such by the verdict of the tests.

Exhaustive test sets are often infinite, or too large to be used in practice. They are, however, used as references for selecting finite, practical, test subsets according to a variety of criteria, such as additional hypotheses on the SUT [2], coverage of the specification [8,14], or test purposes [10].

3   Circus

A *Circus* program is a sequence of paragraphs just like in Z, but we can declare channels and processes. A system is specified in *Circus* as a process: it encapsulates a state, and exhibits some behaviour. Figure 1 gives a small example: the specification of a fresh identifier generator; it has four paragraphs. The first paragraph declares a given set *ID* containing all valid identifiers. The second and third paragraphs declare a few channels: *req* is used to request a fresh identifier, which is output by the system using the channel *out*; and the channel *ret* is used to return an identifier that is no longer required. The type of a channel determines the values that it can communicate; in the case of *req*, the absence of a type declaration indicates that it is used only for synchronisation.

[*ID*]

channel *req*

channel *ret*, *out* : *ID*

process *FIG* $\widehat{=}$ **begin**

    state $S == [\, idS : \mathbb{P}\, ID \,]$

    Init $\widehat{=}$ *idS* := $\emptyset$

    ┌─ *Out* ────────────────────────────────
    │ ΔS
    │ $v!$: *ID*
    ├────────────────────────────────
    │ $v! \notin idS$
    │ $idS' = idS \cup \{v!\}$
    └────────────────────────────────

    ┌─ *Remove* ────────────────────────────────
    │ ΔS
    │ $x?$: *ID*
    ├────────────────────────────────
    │ $idS' = idS \setminus \{x?\}$
    └────────────────────────────────

    • *Init* ;
      var v : *ID* • ($\mu\, X$ • (*req* $\rightarrow$ *Out* ; *out!v* $\rightarrow$ *Skip* $\square$ *ret?x* $\rightarrow$ *Remove*) ; X)

end

Fig. 1. Simple *Circus* specification: fresh identifier generator

The process *FIG* specifies the system; it is a basic process defined as a sequence of process paragraphs that specify its state and behaviour. The state is defined using a (horizontal) Z schema; in our example it contains just one component: the set *idS* of identifiers currently in use.

The behaviour of a process is given by a main action at the end of its specification. In our example, first of all, it uses the action *Init* to initialise the state: it assigns the empty set to *idS*. Afterwards, a local variable v is declared, and a recursion is used to define that *FIG* repeatedly offers to its environment the choice of requesting or returning an identifier. After a request via a synchronisation on *req*, the action *Out*, which is specified by a Z schema, is used to define the value of v to be that of any unused identifier, which is then recorded in *idS*. The value of v is output via the channel *out*. If, on the other hand, an identifier x is returned via *ret*, then the action *Remove* is used to update the state.

As shown in our small example, an action can be defined using a combination of Z, CSP, and imperative programming constructs. It can be a data operation specified in Z, or an assignment for example. It can also be *Skip*, the action that terminates immediately, without interacting with the environment, or *Stop*, the action that deadlocks. More interestingly, an action can interact with the environment via channels that can be used for input and output of values. Process algebra constructs like parallelism and external choice can be used to combine actions that involve both communications and data operations.

In addition, processes can also be combined using CSP operators. For example, we can combine *FIG* in parallel with another process that uses it to provide identifiers for new employees, for instance. In this case, the channels *req*, *ret*, and *out* are likely to be internal to the system, and can be hidden like in CSP.

Actions are modelled as predicates of a restriction of the UTP theory for CSP, in which the state components and local variables in scope, and their dashed counterparts, are part of the alphabet, in addition to the extra variables *ok*, *wt*, *tr*, and *ref*, and their dashed counterparts. Action refinement is characterised by reverse implication just like in the UTP. Process refinement, on the other hand, is characterised by refinement of the main actions, with the state components taken as local variables. This follows from the fact that the state of a process is encapsulated, and its behaviour is given by the main action.

In the sequel, we calculate a characterisation of traces refinement and *conf* for the UTP theory for CSP, and, therefore, for *Circus* actions and processes. We also establish that, jointly, they are equivalent to process refinement.

4   Traces Refinement

In the *Circus*, or CSP, theory of the UTP, the boolean variable *ok* records whether or not a process is in a divergent state (of another process that has already started). If the state is not divergent, that is, if *ok* holds, then *wt*, also a boolean observational variable, determines whether the previous process is waiting for interaction or has terminated. The sequence of events *tr* gives the history of interactions of the previous process, and finally, *ref* gives a set of events in which it may refuse to engage. Similarly, the dashed variables ok', wt', tr' and ref' give similar information about the current process.

A number of healthiness conditions characterise first reactive processes in general, and then those that are in the CSP theory. The *Circus* theory has an extra healthiness condition. Here we use the healthiness conditions **R2** and **CSP4**, which we describe below. A complete discussion can be found in [18].

The healthiness condition **R2** requires that an action does not rely on the history of interactions that passed before its activation, that is, *tr*, and restricts only the new events to be recorded since the last observation, that is, $tr' - tr$. It has two different formulations; we use the one shown below.

$$\textbf{R2}(A) \;\; \widehat{=} \;\; A[\langle\rangle, tr' - tr/tr, tr']$$

This requires that the action A is not changed if tr is taken to be the empty sequence, and tr' to be just the new events arising from the execution of A. The condition **CSP4** requires that *Skip* is a right-unit for sequence.

$$\textbf{CSP4}(A) \;\; \widehat{=} \;\; A\,;\mathit{Skip}$$

In more intuitive terms, $CSP4$ requires that, on termination or divergence, the value of ref' is irrelevant. The following lemma [7] makes this clear; for completeness its proof is presented in the appendix, along with the proof of all other lemmas used in this paper.

Lemma 1

$$A \, ; Skip = (\exists \, ref' \bullet A) \land ok' \land \neg \, wt' \ \lor \ A \land ok' \land wt' \ \lor \ (A \land \neg \, ok') \, ; tr \leq tr'$$

This result shows that, if $A = A \, ; Skip$, then if A has terminated without diverging, the value of ref' is not relevant. If A has not terminated, then the value of ref' is as defined by A itself. Finally, if it diverges, then the only guarantee is that the trace is extended; the value of the other variables is irrelevant.

We define $A^n \stackrel{\frown}{=} ok \land \neg \, wt \land A \land ok'$ as the predicate that gives the behaviour of the action A when its preceding action has not diverged and has terminated, and when A itself does not lead to divergence. This is the normal behaviour of A; behaviour in other situations is defined by healthiness conditions. The terminating, non-diverging behaviour of A is $A^t \stackrel{\frown}{=} A^n \land ok' \land \neg \, wt'$, and finally, the diverging behaviour of A is $A^d \stackrel{\frown}{=} ok \land \neg \, wt \land A \land \neg \, ok'$. We define that an action A is divergence free if, and only if, $[\neg \, A^d]$.

The function *traces* defined below [7] gives the set of traces of a *Circus* action defined as a UTP predicate A. This gives a traces model to A compatible with that adopted in the failures-divergences model of CSP.

As already said, the behaviour of the action itself is that prescribed when ok and $\neg \, wt$. The behaviour in the other cases is determined by healthiness conditions of the UTP theory. For example, in the presence of divergence, that is, when $\neg \, ok$, every action can only guarantee that the trace is only extended, so that past history is not modified. This behaviour is not recorded by $traces(A)$.

$$traces(A) = \{ \, tr' - tr \mid A^n \, \} \cup \{ \, (tr' - tr) \frown \langle \checkmark \rangle \mid A^t \, \}$$

As mentioned above, tr records the history of interactions before the start of the action; tr' carries this history forward. Therefore, the traces in $traces(A)$ are sequences $tr' - tr$ obtained by removing from tr' its prefix tr. In addition, if $tr' - tr$ leads to termination, then $traces(A)$ also includes $(tr' - tr) \frown \langle \checkmark \rangle$, since $\checkmark$ is used in the failures-divergences model to signal termination.

The properties of $traces(A)$ depend on those of A. Since the UTP actions do not satisfy all healthiness conditions imposed on the failures-divergences model, there are sets of traces that do not correspond to any of those of a CSP process. For example, $\boldsymbol{R}(true \vdash tr' = tr \frown \langle \, a, b \, \rangle \land \neg \, wt')$ is an action that engages in the events a and b and then terminates. Its behaviour does not allow for the traces $\langle \rangle$ and $\langle \, a \, \rangle$, so its set of traces does not include the empty trace and is not prefix closed as required in the failures-divergences model.

The divergent behaviour of a UTP action in the theory of CSP processes does not enforce $\neg \, ok'$; the healthiness condition $CSP2$ enforces exactly that, whenever $\neg \, ok'$ is possible, so is ok'. This means that no process is required to diverge, and that one of the possible behaviours of a divergent process is not to diverge or even terminate. For example, the behaviour of the divergent process *Chaos*, when *ok* and $\neg$ *wt* hold, is given simply by $tr \leq tr'$. This means that *traces*(*Chaos*), for example, includes every possible trace. This is in contradiction with the traces model of CSP, where the process that diverges immediately is identified with *Stop* in the traces model [19]; its only trace is the empty trace.

In this work, however, since we are interested only in divergence-free actions, this is not an issue. In [7], we have actually introduced the set $traces_\perp(A)$, which is defined as follows to include all traces that lead to divergence.

$$traces_\perp(A) = traces(A) \cup divergences(A)$$
$$divergences(A) = \{\, tr' - tr \mid A^d \,\}$$

For **CSP2** reactive actions A, the sets $traces(A)$ and $traces_\perp(A)$ are the same, because the traces that lead to divergence may also lead to non-divergence, and so are included in $traces(A)$. Since divergence-free actions are **CSP2**, and in any case we are interested in (models of) *Circus* actions and processes, which are **CSP2**, it is adequate for us to use $traces(A)$ in our work. In addition, for divergence-free actions A, the set $traces(A)$ is that in the traces model of CSP, which is also the set $traces_\perp(A)$ defined in the failures-divergences model.

Here, using the connection between the UTP theory and the CSP traces model defined by *traces*, we now calculate a characterisation for traces refinement in the UTP for divergence-free actions. Refinement in the UTP is defined for predicates on the same alphabet. In the case of traces refinement, it is defined for CSP processes, and so, for *Circus* actions in particular, but there is no need to assume that the programming variables in their alphabets are the same. In what follows, we consider actions A_1 and A_2, whose alphabets include the lists v_1 and v_2 of undashed variables. Both v_1 and v_2 include *ok*, *wt*, *tr*, and *ref*, but also possibly different (lists of) variables x_1 and x_2 representing state components.

The proof of the theorem below, and of the others in the sequel, use a few lemmas stated and proved in the appendix; in particular, the next theorem uses Lemma 2. We use $[\,A\,]$ as an abbreviation for a universal quantification over all variables v_1, v_1', v_2, and v_2'. As expected, for a list of variables v, the list v' contains the corresponding dashed variables.

Theorem 1

$$A_1 \sqsubseteq_T A_2 \Leftrightarrow [A_2^n \Rightarrow (\exists\, w_1, w_1' \bullet A_1^n) \wedge (\neg\, wt' \Rightarrow \exists\, w_1, w_1' \bullet A_1^t)]$$

where the variable list $v_1 = w_1, tr$, *and provided* A_1 *and* A_2 *are divergence free.*

Proof

$A_1 \sqsubseteq_T A_2$

$\Leftrightarrow traces(A_2) \subseteq traces(A_1)$ [definition of traces refinement]

$\Leftrightarrow \{\, tr' - tr \mid A_2^n \,\} \cup \{\, (tr' - tr)^\frown \langle \checkmark \rangle \mid A_2^t \,\}$ [definition of *traces*]
$\quad \subseteq \{\, tr' - tr \mid A_1^n \,\} \cup \{\, (tr' - tr)^\frown \langle \checkmark \rangle \mid A_1^t \,\}$

$$\Leftrightarrow \{\, tr' - tr \mid A_2^n \,\} \subseteq \{\, tr' - tr \mid A_1^n \,\} \wedge \{\, tr' - tr \mid A_2^t \,\} \subseteq \{\, tr' - tr \mid A_1^t \,\}$$

$$[\text{property of sets and } \checkmark \text{ not in the range of } tr \text{ or } tr']$$

$$\Leftrightarrow \left(\begin{array}{l} (\forall\, t \bullet (\exists\, v_2, v_2' \bullet A_2^n \wedge t = tr' - tr) \Rightarrow (\exists\, v_1, v_1' \bullet A_1^n \wedge t = tr' - tr)) \wedge \\ (\forall\, t \bullet (\exists\, v_2, v_2' \bullet A_2^t \wedge t = tr' - tr) \Rightarrow (\exists\, v_1, v_1' \bullet A_1^t \wedge t = tr' - tr)) \end{array} \right)$$

$$[\text{property of sets}]$$

$$\Leftrightarrow \left(\forall\, t, v_2, v_2' \mid t = tr' - tr \wedge A_2^n \bullet \left(\begin{array}{l} (\exists\, v_1, v_1' \bullet A_1^n \wedge t = tr' - tr) \wedge \\ (\neg\, wt' \Rightarrow \exists\, v_1, v_1' \bullet A_1^t \wedge t = tr' - tr) \end{array} \right) \right)$$

$$[\text{predicate calculus, and definitions of } A_2^t \text{ and } A_2^n]$$

$$\Leftrightarrow \left(\forall\, t, v_2, v_2' \mid t = tr' - tr \wedge A_2^n \bullet \left(\begin{array}{l} (\exists\, w_1, w_1' \bullet A_1^n[\langle\,\rangle, t/tr, tr']) \wedge \\ (\neg\, wt' \Rightarrow \exists\, w_1, w_1' \bullet A_1^t[\langle\,\rangle, t/tr, tr']) \end{array} \right) \right)$$

$$[\text{Lemma 2}]$$

$$\Leftrightarrow \left(\forall\, v_2, v_2' \bullet A_2^n \Rightarrow \left(\begin{array}{l} (\exists\, w_1, w_1' \bullet A_1^n[\langle\,\rangle, tr' - tr/tr, tr']) \wedge \\ (\neg\, wt' \Rightarrow \exists\, w_1, w_1' \bullet A_1^t[\langle\,\rangle, tr' - tr/tr, tr']) \end{array} \right) \right)$$

$$[\text{predicate calculus}]$$

$$\Leftrightarrow \forall\, v_2, v_2' \bullet A_2^n \Rightarrow (\exists\, w_1, w_1' \bullet A_1^n) \wedge (\neg\, wt' \Rightarrow \exists\, w_1, w_1' \bullet A_1^t) \qquad [R2]$$

$$\Leftrightarrow [A_2^n \Rightarrow (\exists\, w_1, w_1' \bullet A_1^n) \wedge (\neg\, wt' \Rightarrow \exists\, w_1, w_1' \bullet A_1^t)] \qquad [\text{predicate calculus}]$$

$$\square$$

In words, this characterisation of traces refinement establishes that if t is a trace of A_2, then it is a trace of A_1, and if it leads to termination for A_2, then it also leads to termination for A_1.

We observe that, if a trace is not terminating for A_2, then it may or may not be terminating for A_1. If it is not terminating for A_2 because A_2 deadlocks, but it is terminating for A_1, we have a situation in which termination is refined by deadlock. Indeed, in the simplest case, we observe that *Skip* is refined by *Stop*; in fact, *Stop* is the most refined CSP process according to the traces refinement relation. If, on the other hand, a trace is not terminating for A_2 because it proceeds to carry out further interactions, but A_1 terminates, for the extension of the trace, the required property for traces refinement does not hold.

5   The *conf* Relation

The well-studied satisfaction relation [4] called *conf*, for conformance relation, can be defined in terms of failures. A failure of a process P is a pair (t, X), where t is a trace of P, and X is a set of events in which it may refuse to engage after performing the events in t (in the order determined by t).

The *conf* relation is defined for divergence-free processes. The function defined below gives the set of failures of a divergence-free action A.

$$
\begin{aligned}
failures(A) = \ & \{\, ((tr' - tr), ref') \mid A^n \,\} \cup \\
& \{\, ((tr' - tr), ref' \cup \{\,\checkmark\,\}) \mid A^n \wedge wt' \,\} \cup \\
& \{\, ((tr' - tr) \frown \langle\,\checkmark\,\rangle, ref') \mid A^t \,\} \cup \\
& \{\, ((tr' - tr) \frown \langle\,\checkmark\,\rangle, ref' \cup \{\,\checkmark\,\}) \mid A^t \,\}
\end{aligned}
$$

In a state that is not terminating, for every refusal set ref', there is an extra set $ref' \cup \{\,\checkmark\,\}$. This is because $\checkmark$ is not part of the UTP model and is not considered in the definition of ref', just as it is not considered in the definition of tr'. As before, for a terminating state, the extra trace $(tr' - tr) \frown \langle\,\checkmark\,\rangle$ is recorded. Finally, after termination, $\checkmark$ is also refused, and so $ref' \cup \{\,\checkmark\,\}$ is included.

For actions A_1 and A_2, *conf* can be defined as follows.

$$
A_2 \; conf \; A_1 \; \widehat{=} \; \forall t : traces(A_1) \cap traces(A_2) \bullet Ref(A_2, t) \subseteq Ref(A_1, t)
$$
$$
\text{where } Ref(A, t) \; \widehat{=} \; \{\, X \mid (t, X) \in failures(A) \,\}
$$

The above definition of $Ref(A, t)$ is compatible with the definition of $refusals(P)$ in CSP, for the process P/t [19, pages 94,197]. Intuitively, the action A_2 conforms to another action A_1 if, and only if, whenever A_2 performs a trace of events that is also possible for A_1, it does not refuse more events than A_1. In other words, deadlock is reduced or maintained after common traces.

The following theorem gives a characterisation of *conf* for the UTP. It is a relation between divergence-free actions.

Theorem 2

$$
A_2 \; conf \; A_1 \Leftrightarrow \left[(\exists\, w_1, w_1' \bullet A_1^n) \wedge A_2^n \Rightarrow \left(\begin{array}{l} (\exists\, k_1, k_1', ref \bullet A_1^n) \wedge \\ (wt' \Rightarrow \exists\, k_1, k_1', ref \bullet A_1^n \wedge wt') \end{array} \right) \right]
$$

where $v_1 = w_1, tr$, *and* $w_1 = k_1, ref$, *and* A_1 *and* A_2 *are divergence free.*

Proof

$A_2 \; conf \; A_1$

$\Leftrightarrow \forall t : traces(A_1) \cap traces(A_2) \bullet Ref(A_2, t) \subseteq Ref(A_1, t)$ [definition of *conf*]

$$
\Leftrightarrow \left(\left(\left(\forall\, v_2, v_2' \bullet \left(\begin{array}{l} \forall t : traces(A_1) \cap traces(A_2) \bullet \\ \left(\begin{array}{l} A_2^n \wedge t = tr' - tr \Rightarrow \\ \quad \exists\, u_1, u_1', ref \bullet A_1^n \wedge t = tr' - tr \end{array} \right) \wedge \\ \left(\begin{array}{l} A_2^n \wedge t = tr' - tr \wedge wt' \Rightarrow \\ \quad \exists\, u_1, u_1', ref \bullet A_1^n \wedge t = tr' - tr \wedge wt' \end{array} \right) \wedge \\ \left(\begin{array}{l} A_2^t \wedge t = (tr' - tr) \frown \langle\checkmark\rangle \Rightarrow \\ \quad \exists\, u_1, u_1', ref \bullet A_1^t \wedge t = (tr' - tr) \frown \langle\checkmark\rangle \end{array} \right) \end{array} \right) \right) \right) \right)
$$

[Lemma 3]

$$\Leftrightarrow \forall t \bullet \left(\begin{array}{l} \left(\begin{array}{l} (\exists\, v_1, v_1' \bullet A_1^n \wedge (t = tr' - tr \vee \neg\, wt' \wedge t = (tr' - tr) \,\widehat{}\, \langle \checkmark \rangle)) \wedge \\ (\exists\, v_2, v_2' \bullet A_2^n \wedge (t = tr' - tr \vee \neg\, wt' \wedge t = (tr' - tr) \,\widehat{}\, \langle \checkmark \rangle)) \end{array} \right) \\ \Rightarrow \\ \left(\forall v_2, v_2' \bullet \left(\begin{array}{l} \left(\begin{array}{l} A_2^n \wedge t = tr' - tr \Rightarrow \\ \quad \exists\, u_1, u_1', ref \bullet A_1^n \wedge t = tr' - tr \end{array} \right) \wedge \\ \left(\begin{array}{l} A_2^n \wedge t = tr' - tr \wedge wt' \Rightarrow \\ \quad \exists\, u_1, u_1', ref \bullet A_1^n \wedge t = tr' - tr \wedge wt' \end{array} \right) \wedge \\ \left(\begin{array}{l} A_2^t \wedge t = (tr' - tr) \,\widehat{}\, \langle \checkmark \rangle \Rightarrow \\ \quad \exists\, u_1, u_1', ref \bullet A_1^t \wedge t = (tr' - tr) \,\widehat{}\, \langle \checkmark \rangle \end{array} \right) \end{array} \right) \right) \end{array} \right)$$

[definition of *traces* and property of sets]

$$\Leftrightarrow \forall t \bullet \left(\begin{array}{l} \left(\begin{array}{l} (\exists\, v_1, v_1' \bullet A_1^n \wedge t = tr' - tr) \wedge (\exists\, v_2, v_2' \bullet A_2^n \wedge t = tr' - tr) \vee \\ \left(\begin{array}{l} (\exists\, v_1, v_1' \bullet A_1^t \wedge t = (tr' - tr) \,\widehat{}\, \langle \checkmark \rangle) \wedge \\ (\exists\, v_2, v_2' \bullet A_2^t \wedge t = (tr' - tr) \,\widehat{}\, \langle \checkmark \rangle) \end{array} \right) \end{array} \right) \\ \Rightarrow \\ \left(\forall v_2, v_2' \bullet \left(\begin{array}{l} \left(\begin{array}{l} A_2^n \wedge t = tr' - tr \Rightarrow \\ \quad \exists\, u_1, u_1', ref \bullet A_1^n \wedge t = tr' - tr \end{array} \right) \wedge \\ \left(\begin{array}{l} A_2^n \wedge t = tr' - tr \wedge wt' \Rightarrow \\ \quad \exists\, u_1, u_1', ref \bullet A_1^n \wedge t = tr' - tr \wedge wt' \end{array} \right) \wedge \\ \left(\begin{array}{l} A_2^t \wedge t = (tr' - tr) \,\widehat{}\, \langle \checkmark \rangle \Rightarrow \\ \quad \exists\, u_1, u_1', ref \bullet A_1^t \wedge t = (tr' - tr) \,\widehat{}\, \langle \checkmark \rangle \end{array} \right) \end{array} \right) \right) \end{array} \right)$$

[predicate calculus]

$$\Leftrightarrow \left(\begin{array}{l} \left(\begin{array}{l} \forall t, v_2, v_2' \bullet \\ (\exists\, v_1, v_1' \bullet A_1^n \wedge t = tr' - tr) \\ \Rightarrow \\ \left(\begin{array}{l} (\exists\, v_2, v_2' \bullet A_2^n \wedge t = tr' - tr) \Rightarrow \\ \left(\begin{array}{l} \left(\begin{array}{l} A_2^n \wedge t = tr' - tr \Rightarrow \\ \quad \exists\, u_1, u_1', ref \bullet A_1^n \wedge t = tr' - tr \end{array} \right) \wedge \\ \left(\begin{array}{l} A_2^n \wedge t = tr' - tr \wedge wt' \Rightarrow \\ \quad \exists\, u_1, u_1', ref \bullet A_1^n \wedge t = tr' - tr \wedge wt' \end{array} \right) \wedge \\ \left(\begin{array}{l} A_2^t \wedge t = (tr' - tr) \,\widehat{}\, \langle \checkmark \rangle \Rightarrow \\ \quad \exists\, u_1, u_1', ref \bullet A_1^t \wedge t = (tr' - tr) \,\widehat{}\, \langle \checkmark \rangle \end{array} \right) \end{array} \right) \end{array} \right) \end{array} \right) \wedge \\ \left(\begin{array}{l} \forall t, v_2, v_2' \bullet \\ (\exists\, v_1, v_1' \bullet A_1^t \wedge t = (tr' - tr) \,\widehat{}\, \langle \checkmark \rangle) \wedge \\ \Rightarrow \\ \left(\begin{array}{l} (\exists\, v_2, v_2' \bullet A_2^t \wedge t = (tr' - tr) \,\widehat{}\, \langle \checkmark \rangle) \Rightarrow \\ \left(\begin{array}{l} \left(\begin{array}{l} A_2^n \wedge t = tr' - tr \Rightarrow \\ \quad \exists\, u_1, u_1', ref \bullet A_1^n \wedge t = tr' - tr \end{array} \right) \wedge \\ \left(\begin{array}{l} A_2^n \wedge t = tr' - tr \wedge wt' \Rightarrow \\ \quad \exists\, u_1, u_1', ref \bullet A_1^n \wedge t = tr' - tr \wedge wt' \end{array} \right) \wedge \\ \left(\begin{array}{l} A_2^t \wedge t = (tr' - tr) \,\widehat{}\, \langle \checkmark \rangle \Rightarrow \\ \quad \exists\, u_1, u_1', ref \bullet A_1^t \wedge t = (tr' - tr) \,\widehat{}\, \langle \checkmark \rangle \end{array} \right) \end{array} \right) \end{array} \right) \end{array} \right) \end{array} \right)$$

[predicate calculus]

$$\Leftrightarrow \left(\begin{array}{l} \left(\forall\, t, v_2, v_2' \bullet \left(\begin{array}{l} (\exists\, v_1, v_1' \bullet A_1^n \wedge t = tr' - tr) \wedge A_2^n \wedge t = tr' - tr \\ \Rightarrow \\ \left(\begin{array}{l} (\exists\, u_1, u_1', ref \bullet A_1^n \wedge t = tr' - tr) \wedge \\ (wt' \Rightarrow \exists\, u_1, u_1', ref \bullet A_1^n \wedge t = tr' - tr \wedge wt') \end{array} \right) \end{array} \right) \wedge \\ \left(\forall\, t, v_2, v_2' \bullet \left(\begin{array}{l} (\exists\, v_1, v_1' \bullet A_1^n \wedge \neg\, wt' \wedge t = (tr' - tr) ^\frown \langle\checkmark\rangle) \wedge \\ A_2^n \wedge \neg\, wt' \wedge t = (tr' - tr) ^\frown \langle\checkmark\rangle \\ \Rightarrow \\ (\exists\, u_1, u_1', ref \bullet A_1^n \wedge \neg\, wt' \wedge t = (tr' - tr) ^\frown \langle\checkmark\rangle) \end{array} \right) \right) \end{array} \right)$$

[predicate calculus]

$$\Leftrightarrow \left(\begin{array}{l} \left(\forall\, v_2, v_2' \bullet (\exists\, w_1, w_1' \bullet A_1^n) \wedge A_2^n \Rightarrow \left(\begin{array}{l} (\exists\, k_1, k_1', ref \bullet A_1^n) \wedge \\ (wt' \Rightarrow \exists\, k_1, k_1', ref \bullet A_1^n \wedge wt') \end{array} \right) \right) \wedge \\ (\forall\, v_2, v_2' \bullet (\exists\, w_1, w_1' \bullet A_1^t) \wedge A_2^t \Rightarrow \exists\, k_1, k_1', ref \bullet A_1^t) \end{array} \right)$$

[Lemma 2, R2, $v_1 = w_1$, tr and $v_1 = k_1, tr, ref$]

$$\Leftrightarrow \left(\begin{array}{l} \left(\forall\, v_2, v_2' \bullet (\exists\, w_1, w_1' \bullet A_1^n) \wedge A_2^n \Rightarrow \left(\begin{array}{l} (\exists\, k_1, k_1', ref \bullet A_1^n) \wedge \\ (wt' \Rightarrow \exists\, k_1, k_1', ref \bullet A_1^n \wedge wt') \end{array} \right) \right) \wedge \\ (\forall\, v_2, v_2' \bullet (\exists\, k_1, k_1', ref \bullet A_1^t) \wedge A_2^t \Rightarrow \exists\, k_1, k_1', ref \bullet A_1^t) \end{array} \right)$$

[Lemma 4]

$$\Leftrightarrow \left[(\exists\, w_1, w_1' \bullet A_1^n) \wedge A_2^n \Rightarrow \left(\begin{array}{l} (\exists\, k_1, k_1', ref \bullet A_1^n) \wedge \\ (wt' \Rightarrow (\exists\, k_1, k_1', ref \bullet A_1^n \wedge wt')) \end{array} \right) \right]$$

[predicate calculus]

□

This establishes that, if a trace of A_2 is also a trace of A_1, with any refusal, then (1) it must be possible for A_1 to have that trace with the same refusal; and (2) if the trace leads to an intermediate state of A_2, then it should also lead to an intermediate state of A_1 (with the same refusal). If it leads to a terminating state of A_2, then A_1 may or may not terminate, but must have the same refusals. This stresses the fact that *Skip conf Stop*, but not *Stop conf Skip*, a fact that is perhaps not so obvious in the original definition.

6   Process Refinement

Refinement of *Circus* processes is defined as shown below, where we consider two processes P_1 and P_2 whose (lists of) states components are x_1 and x_2, and whose main actions are A_1 and A_2; for simplicity, we omit types.

$$P_1 \sqsubseteq_P P_2 \mathrel{\hat{=}} (\mathbf{var}\ x_1 \bullet A_1) \sqsubseteq (\mathbf{var}\, x_2 \bullet A_2)$$

The variable blocks make the state components local to the actions. Precisely, the UTP model of a *Circus* variable block is defined as follows.

$$(\mathbf{var}\ x \bullet A) \mathrel{\hat{=}} (\exists\, x, x' \bullet A)$$

In the definition of process refinement, the alphabets of the actions (**var** $x_1 \bullet A_1$) and (**var** $x_2 \bullet A_2$) are the same; it includes no programming variables. The refinement relation between actions is the standard UTP relation.

Below, we establish that process refinement can be characterised in terms of traces refinement and *conf*. This establishes that we can determine refinement just by examining the traces and refusals of a process. We do not need information about its internal state, to which an observer has no access.

As already mentioned, in our previous work, we have established that traces refinement and *conf* correspond to failures-divergences refinement in CSP. Here, we show that they do not establish refinement in the richer model of *Circus* processes in the UTP. Instead, it corresponds to processes refinement; this clarifies the role of data in testing for traces inclusion and deadlock reduction.

Theorem 3. *Provided P_1 and P_2 are divergence-free Circus processes with main actions A_1 and A_2, we can characterise refinement as follows.*

$$P_1 \sqsubseteq_P P_2 \Leftrightarrow A_1 \sqsubseteq_T A_2 \wedge A_2 \ conf \ A_1$$

Proof

$A_1 \sqsubseteq_T A_2 \wedge A_2 \ conf \ A_1$

$$\Leftrightarrow \left(\begin{array}{l} [A_2^n \Rightarrow (\exists w_1, w_1' \bullet A_1^n) \wedge (\neg \ wt' \Rightarrow \exists w_1, w_1' \bullet A_1^t)] \wedge \\ \left[(\exists w_1, w_1' \bullet A_1^n) \wedge A_2^n \Rightarrow \left(\begin{array}{l} (\exists k_1, k_1', ref \bullet A_1^n) \wedge \\ (wt' \Rightarrow \exists k_1, k_1', ref \bullet A_1^n \wedge wt') \end{array} \right) \right] \end{array} \right)$$

[Theorems 1 and 2]

$$\Leftrightarrow \left[\begin{array}{l} (A_2^n \Rightarrow (\exists w_1, w_1' \bullet A_1^n) \wedge (\neg \ wt' \Rightarrow \exists w_1, w_1' \bullet A_1^t)) \wedge \\ \left((\exists w_1, w_1' \bullet A_1^n) \wedge A_2^n \Rightarrow \left(\begin{array}{l} (\exists k_1, k_1', ref \bullet A_1^n) \wedge \\ (wt' \Rightarrow \exists k_1, k_1', ref \bullet A_1^n \wedge wt') \end{array} \right) \right) \end{array} \right]$$

[predicate calculus]

$$\Leftrightarrow \left[\begin{array}{l} (A_2^n \Rightarrow (\exists w_1, w_1' \bullet A_1^n) \wedge (\neg \ wt' \Rightarrow \exists w_1, w_1' \bullet A_1^t)) \wedge \\ \left(\left((\exists w_1, w_1' \bullet A_1^n) \Rightarrow \left(\begin{array}{l} (\exists k_1, k_1', ref \bullet A_1^n) \wedge \\ (wt' \Rightarrow \exists k_1, k_1', ref \bullet A_1^n \wedge wt') \end{array} \right) \right) \vee \\ (A_2^n \Rightarrow ((\exists k_1, k_1', ref \bullet A_1^n) \wedge (wt' \Rightarrow \exists k_1, k_1', ref \bullet A_1^n \wedge wt'))) \end{array} \right) \end{array} \right]$$

[predicate calculus]

$$\Leftrightarrow \left[\begin{array}{l} \left(\begin{array}{l} (A_2^n \Rightarrow (\exists w_1, w_1' \bullet A_1^n) \wedge (\neg \ wt' \Rightarrow \exists w_1, w_1' \bullet A_1^t)) \wedge \\ \left((\exists w_1, w_1' \bullet A_1^n) \Rightarrow \left(\begin{array}{l} (\exists k_1, k_1', ref \bullet A_1^n) \wedge \\ (wt' \Rightarrow \exists k_1, k_1', ref \bullet A_1^n \wedge wt') \end{array} \right) \right) \end{array} \right) \vee \\ \left(A_2^n \Rightarrow \left(\begin{array}{l} (\exists k_1, k_1', ref \bullet A_1^n) \wedge \\ (\neg \ wt' \Rightarrow \exists w_1, w_1' \bullet A_1^t) \wedge \\ (wt' \Rightarrow \exists k_1, k_1', ref \bullet A_1^n \wedge wt') \end{array} \right) \right) \end{array} \right]$$

[predicate calculus]

$$\Leftrightarrow \left[\begin{pmatrix} \begin{pmatrix} (A_2^n \Rightarrow \exists\, w_1, w_1' \bullet A_1^n) \wedge (A_2^n \Rightarrow (\neg\, wt' \Rightarrow \exists\, w_1, w_1' \bullet A_1^t)) \wedge \\ (\exists\, w_1, w_1' \bullet A_1^n) \Rightarrow \begin{pmatrix} (\exists\, k_1, k_1', ref \bullet A_1^n) \wedge \\ (wt' \Rightarrow \exists\, k_1, k_1', ref \bullet A_1^n \wedge wt') \end{pmatrix} \end{pmatrix} \vee \\ A_2^n \Rightarrow \begin{pmatrix} (\exists\, k_1, k_1', ref \bullet A_1^n) \wedge \\ (\neg\, wt' \Rightarrow \exists\, w_1, w_1' \bullet A_1^t) \wedge \\ (wt' \Rightarrow \exists\, k_1, k_1', ref \bullet A_1^n \wedge wt') \end{pmatrix} \end{pmatrix}\right]$$

[predicate calculus]

$$\Leftrightarrow \left[\begin{pmatrix} \begin{pmatrix} (A_2^n \vee (\exists\, w_1, w_1' \bullet A_1^n)) \Rightarrow \begin{pmatrix} (\exists\, k_1, k_1', ref \bullet A_1^n) \wedge \\ (wt' \Rightarrow \exists\, k_1, k_1', ref \bullet A_1^n \wedge wt') \end{pmatrix} \end{pmatrix} \wedge \\ (A_2^n \Rightarrow (\neg\, wt' \Rightarrow \exists\, w_1, w_1' \bullet A_1^t)) \end{pmatrix} \vee \\ A_2^n \Rightarrow \begin{pmatrix} (\exists\, k_1, k_1', ref \bullet A_1^n) \wedge \\ (\neg\, wt' \Rightarrow \exists\, w_1, w_1' \bullet A_1^t) \wedge \\ (wt' \Rightarrow \exists\, k_1, k_1', ref \bullet A_1^n \wedge wt') \end{pmatrix} \right]$$

[predicate calculus]

$$\Leftrightarrow \left[\left(A_2^n \Rightarrow \begin{pmatrix} (\exists\, k_1, k_1', ref \bullet A_1^n) \wedge \\ (\neg\, wt' \Rightarrow \exists\, w_1, w_1' \bullet A_1^t) \\ (wt' \Rightarrow \exists\, k_1, k_1', ref \bullet A_1^n \wedge wt') \end{pmatrix}\right)\right]$$

[predicate calculus]

$$\Leftrightarrow \left[\left(A_2^n \Rightarrow \begin{pmatrix} (\exists\, k_1, k_1', ref \bullet A_1^n) \wedge \\ (\neg\, wt' \Rightarrow \exists\, w_1, ok', ref', x' \bullet A_1^n[false/wt']) \\ (wt' \Rightarrow \exists\, k_1, ok', x' \bullet A_1^n[true/wt']) \end{pmatrix}\right)\right]$$

[one-point rule]

$$\Leftrightarrow \left[\left(A_2^n \Rightarrow \begin{pmatrix} (\exists\, k_1, k_1', ref \bullet A_1^n) \wedge \\ (\neg\, wt' \Rightarrow \exists\, w_1, ok', ref', x' \bullet A_1^n) \\ (wt' \Rightarrow \exists\, k_1, ok', x' \bullet A_1^n) \end{pmatrix}\right)\right]$$

[predicate calculus]

$$\Leftrightarrow \left[\left(A_2^n \Rightarrow \begin{pmatrix} (\exists\, k_1, k_1', ref \bullet A_1^n) \wedge \\ (\neg\, wt' \Rightarrow \exists\, x_1, x_1' \bullet A_1^n) \\ (wt' \Rightarrow \exists\, x_1, x_1' \bullet A_1^n) \end{pmatrix}\right)\right]$$

[ok, wt, ref, ok', and ref' are not free in $\neg\, wt'$ and wt']

$$\Leftrightarrow [A_2^n \Rightarrow (\exists\, k_1, k_1', ref \bullet A_1^n) \wedge (\exists\, x_1, x_1' \bullet A_1^n)] \qquad \text{[predicate calculus]}$$

$$\Leftrightarrow [A_2^n \Rightarrow (\exists\, x_1, x_1' \bullet A_1^n)] \qquad \text{[predicate calculus]}$$

$$\Leftrightarrow [(\exists\, x_2, x_2' \bullet A_2^n) \Rightarrow (\exists\, x_1, x_1' \bullet A_1^n)] \qquad \text{[x_2 and x_1 are not free in A_1]}$$

$$\Leftrightarrow P_1 \sqsubseteq_P P_2 \qquad \text{[definition of process refinement]}$$

$$\square$$

Actions do not represent systems in *Circus*. Their effects on state are visible, and refinement is only defined for actions on the same state. Therefore, an account of system testing based on *Circus* needs to rely on process refinement. This does not mean, however, that data does not play a part in a testing technique based on *Circus*; we further discuss this issue in the next section.

7   Conclusions

In this paper we have established the foundation of a testing theory for *Circus*, by calculating definitions for traces refinement and *conf* and proving that, together, they characterise process refinement. We are now in a position to consider how the standard techniques of test generation to establish traces refinement and conformance can be applied to the state-rich operational semantics of *Circus*.

Formalisation of testing techniques in the UTP has also been considered in [1]. That work is concerned with fault-based testing using mutations; it goes well beyond what we present here, in that it already provides test-case generation techniques. It is not, however, concerned with testing for refinement in state-rich reactive languages. The formalisation is conducted in the theory of designs for total correctness of sequential imperative programs.

A predicative account of traces refinement is also presented in [9]. In that work, traces refinement is defined for abstract data types, and characterised using simulation relations. It is also observed that *conf* cannot be treated in the same way, because it is not a preorder.

We have already defined exhaustive test sets for CSP processes in [5]. For *Circus*, the operational semantics is defined symbolically, with events referring to values that are constrained by the state and local variable definitions and by the data operations. It supports the integration of model checking and theorem proving techniques in reasoning about *Circus* processes and actions. For testing, the symbolic operational semantics provides guidance for the coverage of traces (by giving structure to the set of traces of an action) and, therefore, for the construction of tests to establish both traces refinement and *conf*.

In the case of CSP, values are part of event names, and are treated indistinctively. For example, $c.0$, $c.1$, and so on, are just event names. In the case of *Circus*, symbolic traces like $\langle c.w_0, d.w_1 \rangle$, for instance, represent collections of traces; this example, in particular, defines a family of traces that record a communication over a channel c followed by a communication over a channel d, of values w_0 and w_1. The symbolic representation and the constraints that w_0 and w_1 are required to satisfy give us an indication of how to produce test data to achieve acceptable coverage of the collection of traces.

These constraints are raised by the local state of the processes, and by its data operations. Therefore, even though testing for process refinement does not require observation of internal state, the valid traces reflect restrictions that arise from the state operations. It is in our immediate plans to adapt to *Circus* the test generation strategy based on a combination of IOLTS (Input-Output Labelled Transition Systems) and algebraic specifications provided in [16,15]. We will formalise the proposed technique based on the results presented here.

Traces refinement and *conf* also have value as tools for reasoning about safety and liveness properties of actions; we are yet to explored this aspect of the UTP theory. For traces refinement, further work on healthiness conditions are necessary to allow a closer correspondence with the CSP traces model. Algebraic laws of traces refinement and *conf* is also an interesting topic for future work.

Acknowledgments

We are grateful to the Royal Society of London, who support our collaboration through an International Joint Project. We have discussed this work with Jim Woodcock, and are grateful for his comments.

References

1. Aichernig, B., Jifeng, H.: Mutation testing in UTP. Formal Aspects of Computing (2008)
2. Bernot, G., Gaudel, M.-C., Marre, B.: Software Testing Based on Formal Specifications: A theory and a tool. Software Engineering Journal 6(6), 387–405 (1991)
3. Bougé, L., Choquet, N., Fribourg, L., Gaudel, M.-C.: Test set generation from algebraic specifications using logic programming. Journal of Systems and Software 6(4), 343–360 (1986)
4. Brinksma, E.: A theory for the derivation of tests. In: Protocol Specification, testing and Verification VIII, pp. 63–74. North-Holland, Amsterdam (1988)
5. Cavalcanti, A.L.C., Gaudel, M.-C.: Testing for Refinement in CSP. In: Butler, M., Hinchey, M.G., Larrondo-Petrie, M.M. (eds.) ICFEM 2007. LNCS, vol. 4789, pp. 151–170. Springer, Heidelberg (2007)
6. Cavalcanti, A.L.C., Sampaio, A.C.A., Woodcock, J.C.P.: A Refinement Strategy for Circus. Formal Aspects of Computing 15(2-3), 146–181 (2003)
7. Cavalcanti, A.L.C., Woodcock, J.C.P.: A Tutorial Introduction to CSP in Unifying Theories of Programming. In: Cavalcanti, A., Sampaio, A., Woodcock, J. (eds.) PSSE 2004. LNCS, vol. 3167, pp. 220–268. Springer, Heidelberg (2006)
8. Chow, T.S.: Testing Software Design Modeled by Finite-State Machines. IEEE Transactions on Software Engineering SE-4(3), 178–187 (1978)
9. Derrick, J., Boiten, E.: More Relational Concurrent Refinement: Traces and Partial Relations. In: REFINE Workshop. Electronic Notes in Theoretical Computer Science. Elsevier, Amsterdam (2008)
10. Fernandez, J.-C., Jard, C., Jéron, T., Viho, G.: An Experiment in Automatic Generation of Conformance Test Suites for Protocols with Verification Technology. Science of Computer Programming 29, 123–146 (1997)
11. Gannon, J., McMullin, P., Hamlet, R.: Data abstraction implementation, specification and testing. ACM Transactions on Programming Languages and Systems 3(3), 211–223 (1981)
12. Gaudel, M.-C.: Testing can be formal, too. In: Mosses, P.D., Schwartzbach, M.I., Nielsen, M. (eds.) CAAP 1995, FASE 1995, and TAPSOFT 1995. LNCS, vol. 915, pp. 82–96. Springer, Heidelberg (1995)
13. Hoare, C.A.R., Jifeng, H.: Unifying Theories of Programming. Prentice-Hall, Englewood Cliffs (1998)
14. Lee, D., Yannakakis, M.: Principles and methods of testing finite state machines - A survey. Proceedings of the IEEE 84, 1090–1126 (1996)
15. Lestiennes, G.: Contributions au test de logiciel basé sur des spécifications formelles. PhD thesis, Université de Paris-Sud (2005)
16. Lestiennes, G., Gaudel, M.-C.: Testing processes from formal specifications with inputs, outputs, and datatypes. In: IEEE International Symposium on Software Reliability Engineering, pp. 3–14 (2002)

17. Morgan, C.C.: Programming from Specifications, 2nd edn. Prentice-Hall, Englewood Cliffs (1994)
18. Oliveira, M.V.M., Cavalcanti, A.L.C., Woodcock, J.C.P.: A UTP Semantics for *Circus*. Formal Aspects of Computing, online first (2007)
19. Roscoe, A.W.: The Theory and Practice of Concurrency. Prentice-Hall Series in Computer Science. Prentice-Hall, Englewood Cliffs (1998)
20. Woodcock, J.C.P., Davies, J.: Using Z—Specification, Refinement, and Proof. Prentice-Hall, Englewood Cliffs (1996)

A   Some Lemmas

Lemma 1

$$A \,; Skip = (\exists\, ref' \bullet A) \wedge ok' \wedge \neg\, wt' \ \vee\ A \wedge ok' \wedge wt' \ \vee\ (A \wedge \neg\, ok') \,; tr \leq tr'$$

Proof. We take v to be a list of the undashed variables in the alphabet of A, including ok, wt, tr, ref, and programming variables x.

$A \,; Skip$

$= \exists\, v_0 \bullet A[v_0/v'] \wedge \boldsymbol{R}(true \vdash tr' = tr \wedge \neg\, wt' \wedge x' = x)[v_0/v]$

　　　　[definition of sequence and *Skip* (as a reactive design [18])]

$$= \left(\exists\, v_0 \bullet \left(\begin{array}{l} A[v_0/v'] \wedge \\ (wt_0 \wedge ((\neg\, ok_0 \wedge tr_0 \leq tr') \vee \boldsymbol{I\!I}[v_0/v])) \vee \\ (\neg\, wt_0 \wedge (ok_0 \Rightarrow ok' \wedge tr' = tr_0 \wedge \neg\, wt' \wedge x' = x_0) \wedge tr_0 \leq tr') \end{array} \right) \right)$$

　　　　[definition of $\boldsymbol{R}$ and property of substitution]

$$= \left(\exists\, v_0 \bullet \left(\begin{array}{l} A[v_0/v'] \wedge wt_0 \wedge \neg\, ok_0 \wedge tr_0 \leq tr' \ \vee \\ A[v_0/v'] \wedge wt_0 \wedge ok' \wedge \boldsymbol{I\!I}[v_0/v] \ \vee \\ A[v_0/v'] \wedge \neg\, wt_0 \wedge \neg\, ok_0 \wedge tr_0 \leq tr' \ \vee \\ A[v_0/v'] \wedge \neg\, wt_0 \wedge ok_0 \wedge ok' \wedge tr' = tr_0 \wedge \neg\, wt' \wedge x' = x_0 \end{array} \right) \right)$$

　　　　[predicate calculus]

$$= \left(\exists\, v_0 \bullet \left(\begin{array}{l} A[v_0/v'] \wedge \neg\, ok_0 \wedge tr_0 \leq tr' \ \vee \\ A[v_0/v'] \wedge wt_0 \wedge ok_0 \wedge ok' \wedge \boldsymbol{I\!I}[v_0/v] \ \vee \\ A[v_0/v'] \wedge \neg\, wt_0 \wedge ok_0 \wedge ok' \wedge tr' = tr_0 \wedge \neg\, wt' \wedge x' = x_0 \end{array} \right) \right)$$

　　　　[predicate calculus]

$$= \left(\begin{array}{l} (\exists\, v_0 \bullet A[v_0/v'] \wedge \neg\, ok_0 \wedge tr_0 \leq tr') \ \vee \\ (\exists\, v_0 \bullet A[v_0/v'] \wedge wt_0 \wedge ok_0 \wedge \boldsymbol{I\!I}[v_0/v]) \ \vee \\ (\exists\, v_0 \bullet A[v_0/v'] \wedge \neg\, wt_0 \wedge ok_0 \wedge ok' \wedge tr' = tr_0 \wedge \neg\, wt' \wedge x' = x_0) \end{array} \right)$$

　　　　[predicate calculus]

$$= \left(\begin{array}{l} (A \wedge \neg\, ok'); (tr \leq tr') \ \vee \\ A \wedge wt' \wedge ok' \ \vee \\ (\exists\, ref' \bullet A) \wedge \neg\, wt' \wedge ok') \end{array} \right)$$
　　　　[definition of sequence and one-point rule]

□

Lemma 2

$$(\exists\, tr, tr' \bullet A \wedge t = tr' - tr) = A[\langle\,\rangle, t/tr, tr']$$

*provided A is **R2**-healthy.*

Proof

$\exists\, tr, tr' \bullet A \wedge t = tr' - tr$

$= \exists\, tr_1, tr_1' \bullet A[tr_1, tr_1'/tr, tr'] \wedge t = tr_1' - tr_1$ [predicate calculus]

$= \exists\, tr_1, tr_1' \bullet A[\langle\,\rangle, tr' - tr/tr, tr'][tr_1, tr_1'/tr, tr'] \wedge t = tr_1' - tr_1$ [**R2**]

$= \exists\, tr_1, tr_1' \bullet A[\langle\,\rangle, tr_1' - tr_1/tr, tr'] \wedge t = tr_1' - tr_1$ [property of substitution]

$= \exists\, tr_1, tr_1' \bullet A[\langle\,\rangle, t/tr, tr'] \wedge t = tr_1' - tr_1$ [property of equality]

$= A[\langle\,\rangle, t/tr, tr'] \wedge \exists\, tr_1, tr_1' \bullet t = tr_1' - tr_1$ [predicate calculus]

$= A[\langle\,\rangle, t/tr, tr']$ [property of sequences]

$\square$

Lemma 3

$$Ref(A_2, t) \subseteq Ref(A_1, t) \Leftrightarrow$$
$$\begin{bmatrix} (A_2^n \wedge t = tr' - tr \Rightarrow \exists\, u_1, u_1', ref \bullet A_1^n \wedge t = tr' - tr) \wedge \\ (A_2^n \wedge t = tr' - tr \wedge wt' \Rightarrow \exists\, u_1, u_1', ref \bullet A_1^n \wedge t = tr' - tr \wedge wt') \wedge \\ (A_2^t \wedge t = (tr' - tr)^\frown\langle\checkmark\rangle \Rightarrow \exists\, u_1, u_1', ref \bullet A_1^t \wedge t = (tr' - tr)^\frown\langle\checkmark\rangle) \end{bmatrix}$$

Proof

$Ref(A_2, t) \subseteq Ref(A_1, t)$

$\Leftrightarrow \{X \mid (t, X) \in failures(A_2)\} \subseteq \{X \mid (t, X) \in failures(A_1)\}$
       [definition of $Ref(A, t)$]

$$\Leftrightarrow \left(\left\{ X \mid (t, X) \in \begin{pmatrix} \{\,((tr' - tr), ref') \mid A_2^n \,\} \cup \\ \{\,((tr' - tr), ref' \cup \{\checkmark\}) \mid A_2^n \wedge wt'\,\} \cup \\ \{\,((tr' - tr)^\frown\langle\checkmark\rangle, ref') \mid A_2^t \,\} \cup \\ \{\,((tr' - tr)^\frown\langle\checkmark\rangle, ref' \cup \{\checkmark\}) \mid A_2^t \,\} \end{pmatrix} \right\} \right.$$
$$\left. \subseteq \left\{ X \mid (t, X) \in \begin{pmatrix} \{\,((tr' - tr), ref') \mid A_1^n \,\} \cup \\ \{\,((tr' - tr), ref' \cup \{\checkmark\}) \mid A_1^n \wedge wt'\,\} \cup \\ \{\,((tr' - tr)^\frown\langle\checkmark\rangle, ref') \mid A_1^t \,\} \cup \\ \{\,((tr' - tr)^\frown\langle\checkmark\rangle, ref' \cup \{\checkmark\}) \mid A_1^t \,\} \end{pmatrix} \right\} \right)$$

       [definition of *failures* and property of sets]

$$\Leftrightarrow \left(\forall X \bullet \left(\begin{array}{l} \left(\exists\, v_2, v_2' \bullet \left(\begin{array}{l} A_2^n \,\wedge \\ \left(\begin{array}{l} t = tr' - tr \,\wedge\, X = ref' \,\vee \\ t = tr' - tr \,\wedge\, wt' \,\wedge\, X = ref' \cup \{\checkmark\} \,\vee \\ \neg\, wt' \,\wedge\, t = (tr' - tr) ^\frown \langle \checkmark \rangle \,\wedge\, X = ref' \,\vee \\ \neg\, wt' \,\wedge\, t = (tr' - tr) ^\frown \langle \checkmark \rangle \,\wedge\, X = ref' \cup \{\checkmark\} \end{array} \right) \end{array} \right) \right) \\ \Rightarrow \\ \left(\exists\, v_1, v_1' \bullet \left(\begin{array}{l} A_1^n \,\wedge \\ \left(\begin{array}{l} t = tr' - tr \,\wedge\, X = ref' \,\vee \\ t = tr' - tr \,\wedge\, wt' \,\wedge\, X = ref' \cup \{\checkmark\} \,\vee \\ \neg\, wt' \,\wedge\, t = (tr' - tr) ^\frown \langle \checkmark \rangle \,\wedge\, X = ref' \,\vee \\ \neg\, wt' \,\wedge\, t = (tr' - tr) ^\frown \langle \checkmark \rangle \,\wedge\, X = ref' \cup \{\checkmark\} \end{array} \right) \end{array} \right) \right) \end{array} \right) \right)$$

[predicate calculus]

$$\Leftrightarrow \left(\forall X, v_2, v_2' \bullet \left(\begin{array}{l} \left(A_2^n \,\wedge\, \left(\begin{array}{l} t = tr' - tr \,\wedge\, X = ref' \,\vee \\ t = tr' - tr \,\wedge\, wt' \,\wedge\, X = ref' \cup \{\checkmark\} \,\vee \\ \neg\, wt' \,\wedge\, t = (tr' - tr) ^\frown \langle \checkmark \rangle \,\wedge\, X = ref' \,\vee \\ \neg\, wt' \,\wedge\, t = (tr' - tr) ^\frown \langle \checkmark \rangle \,\wedge\, X = ref' \cup \{\checkmark\} \end{array} \right) \right) \\ \Rightarrow \\ \left(\exists\, v_1, v_1' \bullet \left(\begin{array}{l} A_1^n \,\wedge \\ \left(\begin{array}{l} t = tr' - tr \,\wedge\, X = ref' \,\vee \\ t = tr' - tr \,\wedge\, wt' \,\wedge\, X = ref' \cup \{\checkmark\} \,\vee \\ \neg\, wt' \,\wedge\, t = (tr' - tr) ^\frown \langle \checkmark \rangle \,\wedge\, X = ref' \,\vee \\ \neg\, wt' \,\wedge\, t = (tr' - tr) ^\frown \langle \checkmark \rangle \,\wedge\, X = ref' \cup \{\checkmark\} \end{array} \right) \end{array} \right) \right) \end{array} \right) \right)$$

[predicate calculus]

$$\Leftrightarrow \left(\forall\, v_2, v_2' \bullet \left(\begin{array}{l} \left(\begin{array}{l} A_2^n \,\wedge\, t = tr' - tr \Rightarrow \\ \exists\, u_1, u_1', ref, refX \bullet \\ \left(\begin{array}{l} A_1^n[refX / ref'] \,\wedge \\ \left(\begin{array}{l} t = tr' - tr \,\wedge\, ref' = refX \,\vee \\ \neg\, wt' \,\wedge\, t = (tr' - tr) ^\frown \langle \checkmark \rangle \,\wedge\, ref' = refX \end{array} \right) \end{array} \right) \end{array} \right) \wedge \\ \left(\begin{array}{l} A_2^n \,\wedge\, t = tr' - tr \,\wedge\, wt' \Rightarrow \\ \exists\, u_1, u_1', ref, refX \bullet \\ \left(\begin{array}{l} A_1^n[refX / ref'] \,\wedge \\ \left(\begin{array}{l} t = tr' - tr \,\wedge\, wt' \,\wedge\, ref' = refX \,\vee \\ \neg\, wt' \,\wedge\, t = (tr' - tr) ^\frown \langle \checkmark \rangle \,\wedge\, ref' = refX \end{array} \right) \end{array} \right) \end{array} \right) \wedge \\ \left(\begin{array}{l} A_2^n \,\wedge\, \neg\, wt' \,\wedge\, t = (tr' - tr) ^\frown \langle \checkmark \rangle \Rightarrow \\ \exists\, u_1, u_1', ref, refX \bullet \\ \left(\begin{array}{l} A_1^n[refX / ref'] \,\wedge \\ \left(\begin{array}{l} t = tr' - tr \,\wedge\, ref' = refX \,\vee \\ \neg\, wt' \,\wedge\, t = (tr' - tr) ^\frown \langle \checkmark \rangle \,\wedge\, ref' = refX \end{array} \right) \end{array} \right) \end{array} \right) \wedge \\ \left(\begin{array}{l} A_2^n \,\wedge\, \neg\, wt' \,\wedge\, t = (tr' - tr) ^\frown \langle \checkmark \rangle \Rightarrow \\ \exists\, u_1, u_1', ref, refX \bullet \\ \left(\begin{array}{l} A_1^n[refX / ref'] \,\wedge \\ \left(\begin{array}{l} t = tr' - tr \,\wedge\, wt' \,\wedge\, ref' = refX \,\vee \\ \neg\, wt' \,\wedge\, t = (tr' - tr) ^\frown \langle \checkmark \rangle \,\wedge\, ref' = refX \end{array} \right) \end{array} \right) \end{array} \right) \end{array} \right) \right)$$

[predicate calculus, $v_1 = u_1, ref$, and $\checkmark$ is not ref']

$$\Leftrightarrow \left(\left(\left(\begin{array}{l} \forall\, v_2, v_2' \bullet \\ \left(\begin{array}{l} \left(\begin{array}{l} A_2^n \wedge t = tr' - tr \Rightarrow \\ \left(\begin{array}{l} \exists\, u_1, u_1', \mathit{ref}, \mathit{refX} \bullet \\ \left(\begin{array}{l} A_1^n[\mathit{refX}/\mathit{ref}'] \wedge \\ \left(\begin{array}{l} t = tr' - tr \wedge \mathit{ref}' = \mathit{refX} \vee \\ \neg\, wt' \wedge t = (tr' - tr) \,\widehat{}\, \langle\checkmark\rangle \wedge \mathit{ref}' = \mathit{refX} \end{array} \right) \end{array} \right) \end{array} \right) \\ \left(\begin{array}{l} A_2^n \wedge t = tr' - tr \wedge wt' \Rightarrow \\ \left(\begin{array}{l} \exists\, u_1, u_1', \mathit{ref}, \mathit{refX} \bullet \\ \left(\begin{array}{l} A_1^n[\mathit{refX}/\mathit{ref}'] \wedge \\ \left(\begin{array}{l} t = tr' - tr \wedge wt' \wedge \mathit{ref}' = \mathit{refX} \vee \\ \neg\, wt' \wedge t = (tr' - tr) \,\widehat{}\, \langle\checkmark\rangle \wedge \mathit{ref}' = \mathit{refX} \end{array} \right) \end{array} \right) \end{array} \right) \\ \left(\begin{array}{l} A_2^n \wedge \neg\, wt' \wedge t = (tr' - tr) \,\widehat{}\, \langle\checkmark\rangle \Rightarrow \\ \left(\begin{array}{l} \exists\, u_1, u_1', \mathit{ref}, \mathit{refX} \bullet \\ \left(\begin{array}{l} A_1^n[\mathit{refX}/\mathit{ref}'] \wedge \\ \left(\begin{array}{l} t = tr' - tr \wedge wt' \wedge \mathit{ref}' = \mathit{refX} \vee \\ \neg\, wt' \wedge t = (tr' - tr) \,\widehat{}\, \langle\checkmark\rangle \wedge \mathit{ref}' = \mathit{refX} \end{array} \right) \end{array} \right) \end{array} \right) \end{array} \right) \end{array} \begin{array}{l} \wedge \\ \\ \\ \wedge \end{array} \right) \right) \right)$$

$$\hfill \text{[predicate calculus]}$$

$$\Leftrightarrow \left(\forall\, v_2, v_2' \bullet \left(\begin{array}{l} \left(A_2^n \wedge t = tr' - tr \Rightarrow \exists\, u_1, u_1', \mathit{ref} \bullet A_1^n \wedge t = tr' - tr \right) \wedge \\ \left(\begin{array}{l} A_2^n \wedge t = tr' - tr \wedge wt' \Rightarrow \\ \exists\, u_1, u_1', \mathit{ref} \bullet A_1^n \wedge t = tr' - tr \wedge wt' \end{array} \right) \wedge \\ \left(\begin{array}{l} A_2^n \wedge \neg\, wt' \wedge t = (tr' - tr) \,\widehat{}\, \langle\checkmark\rangle \Rightarrow \\ \exists\, u_1, u_1', \mathit{ref} \bullet A_1^n \wedge \neg\, wt' \wedge t = (tr' - tr) \,\widehat{}\, \langle\checkmark\rangle \end{array} \right) \end{array} \right) \right)$$

$$\hfill \text{[predicate calculus]}$$

$$\Leftrightarrow \left[\begin{array}{l} (A_2^n \wedge t = tr' - tr \Rightarrow \exists\, u_1, u_1', \mathit{ref} \bullet A_1^n \wedge t = tr' - tr) \wedge \\ (A_2^n \wedge t = tr' - tr \wedge wt' \Rightarrow \exists\, u_1, u_1', \mathit{ref} \bullet A_1^n \wedge t = tr' - tr \wedge wt') \wedge \\ (A_2^t \wedge t = (tr' - tr) \,\widehat{}\, \langle\checkmark\rangle \Rightarrow \exists\, u_1, u_1', \mathit{ref} \bullet A_1^t \wedge t = (tr' - tr) \,\widehat{}\, \langle\checkmark\rangle) \end{array} \right]$$

$$\hfill \text{[definition of } A_2^t \text{ and } A_1^t]$$

$$\hfill \square$$

Lemma 4

$$(\exists\, \mathit{ref}' \bullet A^t) = A^t$$

*provided A is **CSP4**-healthy.*

Proof

$(\exists\, \mathit{ref}' \bullet A^t)$

$= ok \wedge \neg\, wt \wedge (\exists\, \mathit{ref}' \bullet A) \wedge ok' \wedge \neg\, wt'$ \hfill [definition of A^t]

$= ok \wedge \neg\, wt \wedge (\exists\, \mathit{ref}' \bullet ((\exists\, \mathit{ref}' \bullet A) \vee ((A \wedge \neg\, ok');\ tr \leq tr'))) \wedge ok' \wedge \neg\, wt'$

$$\hfill \text{[Lemma 1]}$$

$$= ok \wedge \neg\, wt \wedge ((\exists\, ref' \bullet A) \vee ((A \wedge \neg\, ok');\ tr \le tr')) \wedge ok' \wedge \neg\, wt'$$
$$[ref' \text{ is not free in } (\exists\, ref' \bullet A) \vee ((A \wedge \neg\, ok');\ tr \le tr')]$$

$$= ok \wedge \neg\, wt \wedge A \wedge ok' \wedge \neg\, wt' \qquad\qquad\qquad\qquad [\text{Lemma } 1]$$

$$= A^t \qquad\qquad\qquad\qquad\qquad\qquad\qquad\qquad\qquad [\text{definition of } A^t]$$

$$\square$$

Reasoning about Loops in Total and General Correctness

Steve E. Dunne[1], Ian J. Hayes[2], and Andy J. Galloway[3]

[1] School of Computing
University of Teesside, Middlesbrough, UK
`s.e.dunne@tees.ac.uk`
[2] School of Information Technology and Electrical Engineering
University of Queensland, Brisbane, Australia
[3] Department of Computer Science
University of York, York, UK

Abstract. We introduce a calculus for reasoning about programs in total correctness which blends UTP designs with von Wright's notion of
a demonic refinement algebra. We demonstrate its utility in verifying
the familiar loop-invariant rule for refining a total-correctness specification by a while loop. Total correctness equates non-termination with
completely chaotic behaviour, with the consequence that any situation
which admits non-termination must also admit arbitrary terminating
behaviour. General correctness is more discriminating in allowing non-
termination to be specified together with more particular terminating
behaviour. We therefore introduce an analogous calculus for reasoning
about programs in general correctness which blends UTP prescriptions
with a demonic refinement algebra. We formulate a loop-invariant rule
for refining a general-correctness specification by a while loop, and we
use our general-correctness calculus to verify the new rule.

1   Introduction

In this paper we introduce a calculus for reasoning about programs in total correctness which blends UTP designs [15] with von Wright's notion of a demonic
refinement algebra [27]. We demonstrate the utility of such a calculus in verifying succinctly the familiar loop-invariant rule for refining a total-correctness
specification by a while loop. The rule itself is by no means new, but we believe
that both our formulation of it and —even more particularly— our algebraic
style of its verification are of interest.

Total correctness equates non-termination with completely chaotic behaviour,
with the consequence that any situation which admits non-termination must
also admit arbitrary terminating behaviour. In contrast, general correctness is
more discriminating in allowing non-termination to be specified together with
more particular terminating behaviour, or even without any allowed terminating
behaviour at all. We introduce an analogous calculus for reasoning about programs in general correctness which blends UTP prescriptions [9] with a demonic

A. Butterfield (Ed.): UTP 2008, LNCS 5713, pp. 62–81, 2010.

refinement algebra. We formulate a loop-invariant rule for refining a general-correctness specification by a while loop —the first time, as far as we are aware, that this has been done. We then use our general-correctness calculus to verify the new rule, whose significance is that it completes our general-correctness refinement calculus by allowing us to verify the refinement of a UTP prescription all the way to an actual implementation in executable code.

The rest of the paper is organised as follows. After disposing of certain necessary preliminary issues in Section 2, in Section 3 we develop our total-correctness calculus, then in Section 4 we formulate and prove our version of the classical total-correctness variant-invariant while-loop refinement rule. In Section 5 we develop a corresponding general-correctness calculus based on UTP prescriptions instead of designs, and in Section 6 we formulate and verify our new general-correctness while-loop refinement rule, and illustrate its application on a small example refinement. We conclude Section 6 by deriving an interesting subsidiary general-correctness while-loop refinement rule.

2 Preliminaries

Here we clarify the symbolic conventions we employ throughout the rest of the paper, and we also give a brief historical summary of program algebras.

2.1 Systematic Decoration

We note here a typographical convention that we adopt throughout the paper, namely the systematic dash-decoration of variables and metavariables which is usual in UTP. So if b, for example, represents a condition on the plain (*i.e.* undashed) variables of a program's before-state, then b' represents the corresponding condition on the dashed variables of that program's after-state.

2.2 Logical Notation

We use $\Rightarrow$ only as the *material implication* connective between propositions in our relational term language. On the other hand, we use $\Rrightarrow$ and its typographical inverse $\Lleftarrow$ in rules and proofs to signify logical entailment between factual assertions *about* relations. Similarly, we use $\equiv$ to assert mutual logical entailment in both directions. However, we employ the ordinary equality symbol $=$ to assert equivalence between individual computation-denoting relations such as UTP designs and prescriptions, because this is more natural when treating such entities algebraically.

Although we use $\wedge$ as the conjunction connective between propositions in our relational term language, we also employ it in rules and proofs to conjoin factual assertions *about* relations. Its latter use is always distinguished by generous white spacing around it.

2.3   About Refinement in UTP

The most important single unifying feature of UTP is that refinement is always modelled simply by universally quantified reverse logical implication. In this paper we encounter refinement in three separate semantic contexts: namely, partial correctness, total correctness and general correctness. In each case refinement is denoted by the same symbol $\sqsubseteq$ because this always signifies universally quantified reverse logical implication. All that varies between the three contexts is the family of alphabetised relations being related by $\sqsubseteq$. In the case of partial correctness, the relations concerned are just the binary relations on the alphabet $\{v, v'\}$ where v is the list of program state variables. In the case of total correctness, the relations concerned are designs, which, as we shall see, are a family of binary relations over the alphabet $\{v, ok, v', ok'\}$[1] which are characterised by certain healthiness conditions. Similarly, in the case of general correctness the relations concerned are prescriptions, which are another family of binary relations over the same alphabet $\{v, ok, v', ok'\}$ characterised by different healthiness conditions. In any appearance of $\sqsubseteq$ in a formula within the ensuing text its operands there will enable us to determine whether it signifies partial-, total- or general-correctness refinement in that particular case.

2.4   Precedence

We adopt the conventional order of precedence for the binding powers of our propositional connectives: namely (in descending order), negation $\neg$, conjunction $\wedge$, disjunction $\vee$, material implication $\Rightarrow$ and material bi-implication $\Leftrightarrow$. These all precede our design constructor $\vdash$ and prescription constructor $\Vdash$, which in turn precede the equality operator $=$ and refinement operator $\sqsubseteq$ between computation-denoting relations such as designs and prescriptions. These in turn precede our widely-spaced conjunction " $\wedge$ " between factual assertions about relations. Lowest in precedence we have our logical entailment metasymbols $\Rightarrow$, $\Leftarrow$ and $\equiv$. In our program algebra sequential composition, denoted by " ; " or more usually by simple juxtaposition, has a higher precedence than nondeterministic choice $\sqcap$. Where we believe it improves readability, especially in designs and prescriptions, we sometimes use parentheses even when they are superfluous in the light of these precedence rules.

2.5   History of Program Algebras

Kleene Algebras (KA) were developed first by Conway [5] and later by Kozen [18] in response to the American mathematician Stephen Kleene's challenge to find a complete axiomatisation of regular expressions. As well as binary operators representing choice, sequence, etc, KA has a postfix unary operator "$*$" (star) to represent finite repetition. More recently, KA was extended by Kozen

---

[1] ok' and ok are auxiliary boolean variables introduced to record the observation of termination respectively of the current program and of its sequential predecessor.

[19,20], who added tests to provide "Kleene Algebra with Tests" (KAT) for reasoning about programs in partial correctness. Subsequently von Wright [26,27] developed a variation of KAT called Demonic Refinement Algebra (DRA), intended as a framework for reasoning about programs in total correctness, in which he introduces a second unary postfix operator ω (omega) to represent arbitrary (*i.e.* finite or infinite) repetition. To accommodate the latter he discards the right-zero axiom of KAT. As von Wright points out, DRA is in many ways similar to Cohen's omega algebra [4], save that the latter, being a conservative extension of KAT, requires finite and infinite executions to be reasoned about separately. From DRA von Wright has gone on to develop General Refinement Algebra (GRA), so called because it incorporates a second choice operator to model angelic as well as demonic nondeterminism, but this is beyond the scope of our work here. In particular, the "General" in von Wright's GRA is not to be confused with with the semantics of general correctness which we address in this paper.

3   A Total-Correctness Program Calculus

Our program calculus models conjunctive programs, *i.e.* those which may exhibit demonic but not angelic nondeterminism. The basic statements of our calculus are H3-healthy UTP designs [15]. Let v be the list of state variables of the state space and ok be an additional auxiliary boolean variable which when initially true (ok) signifies that, its predecessor having terminated, the present computation has started, and when finally true (ok') signifies the present computation has itself subsequently terminated. Then a design is an alphabetised relation over an alphabet $\{v, ok, v', ok'\}$ which is expressible in the form

$$ok \wedge p \Rightarrow ok' \wedge q$$

where p and q are subsidiary predicates respectively over v and $\{v, v'\}$. We abbreviate the above to $p \vdash q$, which can be informally interpreted as

> If the program starts in circumstances satisfying p, it will terminate in a state satisfying q.

The design $p \vdash q$ is semantically equivalent, for example, to the Morgan specification statement [23]

$$v : [p, q]$$

or the B Abstract Machine Notation (AMN) [1] substitution

PRE p THEN ANY v' WHERE q THEN $v := v'$ END END

In particular, for convenience the following designs have their own special representations:

skip	$=_{\text{def}}$	$\text{true} \vdash v' = v$	
abort	$=_{\text{def}}$	$\text{false} \vdash \text{true}$	
magic	$=_{\text{def}}$	$\text{true} \vdash \text{false}$	
$[p]$	$=_{\text{def}}$	$\text{true} \vdash p \wedge v' = v$	guard
$\{p\}$	$=_{\text{def}}$	$p \vdash v' = v$	assertion

Our operational intuitions about these primitive statements are as follows:

- skip terminates without changing the state;
- abort is completely chaotic and may even fail to terminate;
- magic behaves everywhere miraculously;
- The guard statement $[p]$ behaves like skip from states where p holds, while from states where p doesn't hold it behaves miraculously. We note that magic could equivalently be expressed as $[\text{false}]$.
- The assertion statement $\{p\}$ also behaves like skip from states where p holds, but from states where p doesn't hold it behaves like abort. We note that abort could equivalently be expressed as $\{\text{false}\}$.

Our program calculus has the following binary operators:

nondeterministic choice $s \sqcap t$

sequential composition $s\,;t$

We usually omit the " ; " in a sequential composition when no confusion arises, relying instead on simple juxtaposition. Thus we write, for example, simply $s\,t$ instead of $s\,;t$. We give sequential composition a higher precedence than $\sqcap$. The familiar *conditional* construct can be expressed in terms of our primitive constructs as

if b then s else t end $=_{\text{def}}$ $[b]\,s \sqcap [\neg\,b]\,t$

As we have seen, in UTP each conjunctive program is modelled predicatively as an alphabetised binary relation between undashed before-state and dashed after-state variables which is "design-healthy", *i.e.* semantically equivalent to one in the form of a design. In particular $\sqcap$ is modelled by disjunction and sequential composition by alphabetised relational composition. Designs enjoy the following algebraic properties:

$s \sqcap t$	$=$	$t \sqcap s$	commutativity
$(s \sqcap t) \sqcap v$	$=$	$s \sqcap (t \sqcap v)$	associativity
$s \sqcap s$	$=$	s	idempotence
$s \sqcap \text{magic}$	$= \quad s \quad =$	$\text{magic} \sqcap s$	unit of choice
$s \sqcap \text{abort}$	$= \quad \text{abort} \quad =$	$\text{abort} \sqcap s$	zero of choice
$(s\,t)\,v$	$=$	$s\,(t\,v)$	associativity
$s\,\text{skip}$	$= \quad s \quad =$	$\text{skip}\,s$	unit of composition
$\text{abort}\,s$	$=$	abort	left zero of composition
$\text{magic}\,s$	$=$	magic	left zero of composition

$$(s \sqcap t)v \;=\; sv \sqcap tv \qquad\qquad\qquad \text{distributivity}$$
$$s(t \sqcap v) \;=\; st \sqcap sv \qquad\qquad\qquad \text{distributivity}$$

In addition we make use of the following specific properties of UTP designs, where a, b, c and p are simple conditions, $i.e.$ predicates over the undashed state variables, and q is an alphabetised binary relation, $i.e.$ a predicate relating before-states represented by undashed variables to after-states represented by dashed variables:

$$(p \vdash q)\,[b] \;=\; p \vdash q \wedge b' \tag{1}$$
$$\{b\}\,(p \vdash q) \;=\; p \wedge b \vdash q \tag{2}$$

The relationship between the refinement ordering on programs and nondeterministic choice is expressed by the following property:

$$s \sqsubseteq t \quad\equiv\quad s = s \sqcap t \tag{3}$$

The associativity, commutativity and idempotence of $\sqcap$ respectively guarantee that $\sqsubseteq$ is transitive, antisymmetric and reflexive, so ensuring that it is a partial order. Its bottom is abort and its top is magic:

$$\text{abort} \;\sqsubseteq\; s \;\sqsubseteq\; \text{magic} \tag{4}$$

It is easy to show that $\sqcap$ is a meet operator for $\sqsubseteq$:

$$(s \sqsubseteq t) \;\wedge\; (s \sqsubseteq u) \quad\equiv\quad s \sqsubseteq t \sqcap u \tag{5}$$

Composition and $\sqcap$ are monotonic with respect to $\sqsubseteq$, and the following refinement properties of designs are easily verified:

$$p \vdash p' \;\sqsubseteq\; \text{skip} \tag{6}$$
$$a \vdash c' \;\sqsubseteq\; (a \vdash b')\,(b \vdash c') \tag{7}$$

This equality follows from the previous two properties and the monotonicity of composition with respect to $\sqsubseteq$:

$$(p \vdash p')\,(p \vdash p') \;=\; p \vdash p' \tag{8}$$

This trading rule captures the duality between assertions and guards:

$$\{p\}s \;\sqsubseteq\; t \quad\equiv\quad s \sqsubseteq [p]t \tag{9}$$

This rule captures the equivalence between two ways of expressing that a given program s is always guaranteed to terminate:

$$\text{magic} \;\sqsubseteq\; s\,\text{magic} \quad\equiv\quad \text{true} \vdash \text{true} \;\sqsubseteq\; s \tag{10}$$

The set of conjunctive programs over the state space spanned by state variable(s) v forms a complete lattice with respect to $\sqsubseteq$.

3.1 Fixed-Point Definitions in Total Correctness

We define the following unary operators as fixed points with respect to $\sqsubseteq$, where ν_{ref} and μ_{ref} denote respectively greatest fixed point and least fixed point:

$$s^* \quad =_{\text{def}} \quad \nu_{\text{ref}}\, x \,.\, s\,x \,\sqcap\, \text{skip} \qquad\qquad \text{weak iteration} \qquad (11)$$

$$s^\infty \quad =_{\text{def}} \quad \mu_{\text{ref}}\, x \,.\, s\,x \qquad\qquad\qquad \text{infinite repetition} \qquad (12)$$

$$s^\omega \quad =_{\text{def}} \quad \mu_{\text{ref}}\, x \,.\, s\,x \,\sqcap\, \text{skip} \qquad\qquad \text{strong iteration} \qquad (13)$$

The Knaster-Tarski theorem [25] guarantees that the above fixed-point definitions are sound. We give these three unary operators a higher precedence than either sequential composition or $\sqcap$. Our operational intuition of them is as follows:

- s^* signifies zero or finitely more repetitions of s;
- s^∞ signifies infinite repetition of s;
- s^ω signifies arbitrary general (*i.e.* zero, finite or infinite) repetition of s.

The $*$, ∞ and ω operators are themselves monotonic with respect to $\sqsubseteq$. They are related by the property [21, Lemma 13]

$$s^\omega \;=\; s^* \sqcap s^\infty \qquad\qquad (14)$$

The $*$, ∞ and ω operators enjoy the following standard pre- and post-fixpoint induction properties respectively of greatest and least fixed points *cf* [15, Laws 2.6L1 and 2.7L1]:

$$t \;\sqsubseteq\; s\,t \sqcap \text{skip} \qquad \Rightarrow \qquad t \;\sqsubseteq\; s^* \qquad\qquad (15)$$

$$s\,t \;\sqsubseteq\; t \qquad\qquad \Rightarrow \qquad s^\infty \;\sqsubseteq\; t \qquad\qquad (16)$$

$$s\,t \sqcap \text{skip} \;\sqsubseteq\; t \qquad \Rightarrow \qquad s^\omega \;\sqsubseteq\; t \qquad\qquad (17)$$

The following property is a consequence of the definition of s^*, see [3, Lemma 21.2]:

$$s^*\,t \quad = \quad \nu_{\text{ref}}\, x \,.\, s\,x \sqcap t \qquad\qquad (18)$$

3.2 Well-Foundedness in Total Correctness

We describe a program s as *well-founded* if its infinite repetition is everywhere miraculous: that is, $s^\infty = \text{magic}$. Also, if p is a condition on the state we describe a program s as *well-founded on* p if its infinite repetition is miraculous from all states which satisfy p: that is, if $[p]\,s^\infty = \text{magic}$. Note that $[p]\,s^\infty$ is not the same as $([p]\,s)^\infty$, so saying s is well-founded on p is not the same as saying $[p]\,s$ is well-founded.

4   Loop Refinement in Total Correctness

Before we can formulate any loop refinement rule we must determine the formal meaning of the loop construct in question. The appropriate way to do so is to interpret the construct concerned as a recursive expression obtained by "unfolding" it, whose meaning is then taken as a least fixed-point with respect to total-correctness refinement. In this way, we define our while loop as follows:

$$\mathsf{while}\ b\ \mathsf{do}\ s\ \mathsf{end} \quad =_{\mathsf{def}} \quad \mu_{\mathsf{ref}}\ x\ .\ \mathsf{if}\ b\ \mathsf{then}\ s\,x\ \mathsf{else}\ \mathsf{skip}\ \mathsf{end}$$

Such a while-loop turns out to be closely related to strong-iteration. This is exposed by the following equality [3, Lemma 21.8]:

$$\mathsf{while}\ b\ \mathsf{do}\ s\ \mathsf{end} \quad = \quad ([\,b\,]\,s)^{\omega}\,[\neg\,b\,] \tag{19}$$

4.1   A Total-Correctness Loop-Refinement Rule

Identifying an invariant condition and a variant expression by which to demonstrate that a particular while loop refines a given abstract specification is a familiar and long-established technique in formal development. There are numerous presentations of such a technique: among the very first must be those of Floyd [12] expressed using flowcharts and of Hoare [14] —the latter in partial correctness only, while more recent ones include those in [23,17,1]. In our calculus the technique can be expressed succinctly by the following rule:

$$p\ \vdash\ p'\wedge\neg\,b' \quad \sqsubseteq \quad \mathsf{while}\ b\ \mathsf{do}\ s\ \mathsf{end} \qquad\qquad \text{TC Loop}$$
provided
1. $p\ \vdash\ p'\ \sqsubseteq\ [\,b\,]\,s$
2. $[\,b\,]\,s$ is well-founded on p.

Proviso 1 requires that, under the assumption of the loop guard b, the loop body, s, preserves the loop invariant p; its purpose is to ensure that if and when the loop terminates the resulting final state will satisfy p. Proviso 2 requires that infinite repetition of s under the assumption of b is impossible starting from a state which satisfies p; its purpose is to guarantee termination from any starting state which satisfies the loop invariant p.

There is no explicit notion of a variant in this formulation of the rule. However, a standard technique for demonstrating well-foundedness of a computation is to formulate a variant expression, *i.e.* a natural-number-valued or similar well-founded-domain-valued expression over the state space which is strictly decreased by that computation. Our formulation of the rule therefore neatly separates our twin concerns of correctness and termination. We verify the rule by the following reasoning in our total-correctness calculus.

Proof:

$$p\vdash p'\wedge\neg\,b' \quad \sqsubseteq \quad \mathsf{while}\ b\ \mathsf{do}\ s\ \mathsf{end}$$
$$\Longleftarrow \qquad \{\ (1),\ (19)\ \}$$

$$(p \vdash p')\,[\neg\, b] \;\sqsubseteq\; ([\,b\,]\,s)^\omega\,[\neg\, b]$$

$\Longleftarrow$ { monotonicity of seq comp wrt $\sqsubseteq$ }

$$p \vdash p' \;\sqsubseteq\; ([\,b\,]\,s)^\omega$$

$\equiv$ { (14) }

$$p \vdash p' \;\sqsubseteq\; ([\,b\,]\,s)^* \;\sqcap\; ([\,b\,]\,s)^\infty$$

$\equiv$ { (2) }

$$\{p\}\,(p \vdash p') \;\sqsubseteq\; ([\,b\,]\,s)^* \;\sqcap\; ([\,b\,]\,s)^\infty$$

$\equiv$ { (9) }

$$p \vdash p' \;\sqsubseteq\; [p]\,(([\,b\,]\,s)^* \;\sqcap\; ([\,b\,]\,s)^\infty)$$

$\equiv$ { distributivity }

$$p \vdash p' \;\sqsubseteq\; [p]\,([\,b\,]\,s)^* \;\sqcap\; [p]\,([\,b\,]\,s)^\infty$$

$\equiv$ { Proviso 2 }

$$p \vdash p' \;\sqsubseteq\; [p]\,([\,b\,]\,s)^* \;\sqcap\; \mathsf{magic}$$

$\equiv$ { magic is unit of $\sqcap$ }

$$p \vdash p' \;\sqsubseteq\; [p]\,([\,b\,]\,s)^*$$

$\equiv$ { (9) }

$$\{p\}\,(p \vdash p') \;\sqsubseteq\; ([\,b\,]\,s)^*$$

$\equiv$ { (2) }

$$p \vdash p' \;\sqsubseteq\; ([\,b\,]\,s)^*$$

$\Longleftarrow$ { (15) }

$$p \vdash p' \;\sqsubseteq\; [\,b\,]\,s\,(p \vdash p') \;\sqcap\; \mathsf{skip}$$

$\equiv$ { (5), (6) }

$$p \vdash p' \;\sqsubseteq\; [\,b\,]\,s\,(p \vdash p')$$

$\equiv$ { (8) }

$$(p \vdash p')\,(p \vdash p') \;\sqsubseteq\; [\,b\,]\,s\,(p \vdash p')$$

$\Longleftarrow$ { monotonicity of seq comp wrt $\sqsubseteq$ }

$$p \vdash p' \;\sqsubseteq\; [\,b\,]\,s \qquad\qquad \{\ \text{Proviso 1}\ \} \qquad\qquad \square$$

So much for total correctness. In the next sections we move on to consider general correctness.

5   A General-Correctness Program Calculus

Whereas the total-correctness semantics of programs is captured in predicate-transformer terms by the weakest-precondition (wp) transformer alone, for general correctness the weakest-liberal-precondition (wlp) transformer is also required [7,16,24]. In [9] prescriptions were introduced as the general-correctness counterparts of Hoare and He's total-correctness designs, and their properties have since been further explored in [6] and [13]. Let v be the list of state variables of the state space and ok be an additional auxiliary boolean variable with the same interpretation as that already described in Section 3 for designs. Then a prescription is an alphabetised relation over (v, ok, v', ok') whose predicate can be expressed in the form

$$(ok \wedge p \Rightarrow ok') \wedge (ok' \Rightarrow q \wedge ok)$$

where p and q are subsidiary predicates not referring to ok or ok'. We abbreviate this as $p \Vdash q$. If p is simply a *condition* — *i.e.* it constrains only the undashed state variables v — then we call $p \Vdash q$ a *normal* prescription. From here on we only consider normal prescriptions. Intuitively, we can then interpret $p \Vdash q$ operationally as follows:

> If the computation starts from an initial state satisfying p it must inevitably terminate; moreover, if it terminates —whether inevitably from an initial state satisfying p or just fortuitously from any other— then q will be satisfied, and the computation must certainly have started.

General-correctness specifications are more expressive than total-correctness ones because among other things they can express non-termination requirements as well as termination requirements. For example, the extreme prescription false $\Vdash$ false describes a computation which can start from any initial state but must then never terminate. Our general-correctness calculus like our earlier total-correctness one models conjunctive programs. Its basic statements are prescriptions. In particular, for convenience the following prescriptions have these special representations, where v is the list of all state variables and p is a predicate on the state:

skip	$=_{\text{def}}$	true $\Vdash v' = v$	
abort	$=_{\text{def}}$	false $\Vdash$ true	
magic	$=_{\text{def}}$	true $\Vdash$ false	
$[p]$	$=_{\text{def}}$	true $\Vdash p \wedge v' = v$	guard
$\{p\}$	$=_{\text{def}}$	$p \Vdash v' = v$	assertion
loop	$=_{\text{def}}$	false $\Vdash$ false	

Our operational intuitions about the first five of these primitive statements are the same as before. The last one loop is particular to general correctness and represents an infinite loop which never terminates. Our new calculus has the same binary operators $\sqcap$ and "; " modelling nondeterministic choice and sequential composition, all of whose algebraic properties are the same as before, and its conditional construct is defined in the same way. We define our refinement ordering $\sqsubseteq$ exactly as in total correctness. Properties (4), giving us the bottom and top of our $\sqsubseteq$ ordering, and (9), our trading rule for guards and assertions, remain the same in general correctness as in total correctness. We make use of the following properties of UTP prescriptions, which are the direct counterparts of those we saw earlier for designs:

$$(p \Vdash q) ; [b] = p \Vdash q \wedge b' \tag{20}$$

$$\{b\} \; ; \; (p \Vdash q) \quad = \quad p \wedge b \Vdash q \tag{21}$$

$$a \Vdash c' \quad \sqsubseteq \quad (a \Vdash b') \; ; \; (b \Vdash c') \tag{22}$$

5.1   Splitting a Prescription

A general-correctness specification can be projected without loss of information into its total-correctness and partial-correctness components. We adopt a subscripting convention that, if u denotes a general-correctness specification, we write u_{par} and u_{tot} to denote respectively its partial-correctness and total-correctness components. In terms of prescriptions, the prescription $p \Vdash q$ can be projected into its total-correctness and partial-correctness components as follows:

$$(p \Vdash q)_{tot} \quad =_{def} \quad p \vdash q$$

$$(p \Vdash q)_{par} \quad =_{def} \quad q$$

The following equivalence relates refinement of prescriptions in general correctness to refinement of designs in total correctness and relations in partial correctness:

$$p \Vdash q \sqsubseteq u \quad \equiv \quad (p \vdash true \sqsubseteq u_{tot}) \wedge (q \sqsubseteq u_{par}) \tag{23}$$

It can easily be verified by unpacking the prescription and designs into their underlying predicative forms and interpreting $\sqsubseteq$ as reverse implication.

5.2   Fixed-Point Definitions in General Correctness

We introduce a different ordering with respect to which we make our fixed-point definitions in general correctness, namely the Egli-Milner approximation ordering $\leq_{em}$. This has long been recognised as the appropriate ordering for the interpretation of recursions in general correctness [24]. We define it as follows:

$$s \leq_{em} t \quad =_{def} \quad (s_{tot} \sqsubseteq t_{tot}) \wedge (t_{par} \sqsubseteq s_{par}) \tag{24}$$

Expressing this equivalently in terms of prescriptions we have

$$p_1 \Vdash q_1 \leq_{em} p_2 \Vdash q_2 \quad \equiv \quad [q_1 \Rightarrow q_2] \wedge [p_1 \Rightarrow p_2] \wedge [p_1 \Rightarrow (q_1 \Leftrightarrow q_2)] \tag{25}$$

where the square brackets [...] on the right-hand side denote universal quantification over the alphabet of variables. The set of conjunctive programs over the state space spanned by state variable(s) v forms a complete partial order (cpo) with respect to $\leq_{em}$. The bottom of the $\leq_{em}$ ordering is loop, but we note that $\leq_{em}$ has no overall top, because any everywhere-terminating program is maximal. Our composition and $\sqcap$ operators are monotonic with respect to $\leq_{em}$. We define the following unary operators as least fixed points with respect to $\leq_{em}$:

$$s^{\infty} \quad =_{def} \quad \mu_{em} \, x \, . \, s \, x \qquad \qquad \text{infinite repetition}$$

$$s^{\omega} \quad =_{def} \quad \mu_{em} \, x \, . \, s \, x \sqcap skip \qquad \text{strong iteration}$$

Because $\leq_{em}$ induces a cpo rather than a complete lattice we need the generalisation of Tarski's fixed-point theorem given in [24] to ensure that the above definitions are sound. Our operational intuitions of them remain the same as before, namely that

- s^∞ signifies infinite repetition of s;
- s^ω signifies arbitrary general (*i.e.* finite or infinite) repetition of s.

However, these operational interpretations must be made in the context of general correctness rather than total correctness. This means, for example, than skip^∞ is loop rather than abort as it would be in total correctness. Our use of the Egli-Milner ordering $\leq_{em}$ rather than the refinement ordering $\sqsubseteq$ in the formal definitions of these fixed points reflects this.

Our ∞ and ω operators here also again enjoy the standard post-fixpoint induction property of least fixed points, although the ordering in question is now $\leq_{em}$ rather than $\sqsubseteq$:

$$s\,t \;\leq_{em}\; t \qquad\qquad \Rightarrow \qquad s^\infty \;\leq_{em}\; t \qquad\qquad (26)$$

$$s\,t \;\sqcap\; \text{skip} \;\leq_{em}\; t \qquad \Rightarrow \qquad s^\omega \;\leq_{em}\; t \qquad\qquad (27)$$

5.3 Well-Foundedness in General Correctness

For general correctness we again describe a program s as *well-founded* if its infinite repetition is everywhere miraculous: that is, $s^\infty = \text{magic}$. Also, if p is a condition on the state we describe a program s as *well-founded on p* if its infinite repetition is miraculous from all states which satisfy p: that is, $[p]\,s^\infty = \text{magic}$. In fact, a general-correctness program is well-founded exactly when its projection in total correctness is well-founded, so there is no need in practice to distinguish well-foundedness in general correctness from that in total correctness.

5.4 Partitioning the Egli-Milner Ordering

Let $E(x)$ be any expression in our general-correctness calculus built using any of its primitive statements and its binary operators of $\sqcap$ and ";" as well as the variable x denoting any general-correctness computation. Then $\lambda x.E(x)$ is monotonic with respect to $\leq_{em}$ and therefore has a well-defined $\leq_{em}$-least fixed point $\mu_{em}\,x.E(x)$. Moreover, the definition in (24) of the Egli-Milner ordering ensures that a sufficient condition for a general-correctness computation u to be such a fixed point is that $u_{tot} = \mu_{ref}\,x.E(x)$ and $u_{par} = \nu_{ref}\,x.E(x)$. That is to say, we have that

$$u_{tot} = \mu_{ref}\,x.E(x) \;\wedge\; u_{par} = \nu_{ref}\,x.E(x) \qquad \Rightarrow \qquad u = \mu_{em}\,x.E(x) \qquad (28)$$

If we now apply property (28) above to the case where $E(x)$ is $([\,b\,]\,s\,x \sqcap \text{skip})$ and apply the definitions of strong and weak iteration, we obtain

$$u_{tot} = ([\,b\,]\,s)^\omega \;\wedge\; u_{par} = ([\,b\,]\,s)^* \qquad \Rightarrow \qquad u = ([\,b\,]\,s)^\omega \qquad (29)$$

Notice that because u_{tot} is a total-correctness computation the first occurrence of $([b] s)^\omega$ in (29) above is interpreted in total correctness, whereas its second occurrence is interpreted in general correctness because u is a general-correctness computation.

6   Loop Refinement in General Correctness

As in the case of total correctness, in general correctness we again interpret a while loop by "unfolding" it, and its meaning is then again taken as a least fixed-point, although "least" now means least with respect to the Egli-Milner ordering $\leq_{em}$:

$$\text{while } b \text{ do } s \text{ end} \quad =_{def} \quad \mu_{em} \, x \, . \text{ if } b \text{ then } s\,x \text{ else skip end}$$

Again our while-loop turns out to be intimately related to our strong-iteration construct via the following equality, which is analogous to property (19) for the total-correctness case:

$$\text{while } b \text{ do } s \text{ end} \quad = \quad ([b] s)^\omega \, [\neg \, b] \tag{30}$$

We must remember, though, that both the while loop and the strong iteration in (30) have different meanings from their total-correctness counterparts in (19), because they are defined with respect to $\leq_{em}$ rather than $\sqsubseteq$. Nevertheless property (30) can be proved in a similar manner to (19) in [3, Lemma 21.8]. This requires only that the Fusion Theorem cited in the associated [3, Lemma 21.2] is replaced by the Transfer Lemma[2] of [2].

6.1   A General-Correctness Loop-Refinement Rule

One might reasonably ask why we need a new loop-refinement rule for general correctness at all. After all, can we not simply translate the existing total-correctness rule directly into a general-correctness setting? Indeed we can, giving us the following rule:

$$p \Vdash (p \Rightarrow p' \wedge \neg \, b') \quad \sqsubseteq \quad \text{while } b \text{ do } s \text{ end}$$

provided
1. $(p \Rightarrow p') \sqsubseteq [b] s$
2. $[b] s$ is well-founded on p.

However, such a rule is inadequate for proving any refinements involving required non-termination. The simplest of these, remembering that loop is the prescription false $\Vdash$ false, would be

---

[2] The proof also relies on the fact that the relevant "transfer" function used in [3, Lemma 21.2], namely $(\lambda X . X ; T)$, is continuous with respect to $\leq_{em}$. Fortunately, this *is* so, because, as observed in [24], sequential composition is indeed continuous with respect to $\leq_{em}$ in its left argument.

$$\text{false} \Vdash \text{false} \quad \sqsubseteq \quad \text{while true do skip end}$$

Any putative general-correctness loop-refinement rule that cannot be applied to verify even so simple a refinement as this is hardly worth our consideration at all. We therefore propose instead the following general-correctness while-loop refinement rule:

$$p \Vdash (j \Rightarrow j' \wedge \neg\, b') \quad \sqsubseteq \quad \text{while } b \text{ do } s \text{ end} \qquad\qquad \textsf{GC Loop 1}$$

provided

1. $(j \Rightarrow j') \sqsubseteq [b]s$
2. $[b]s$ is well-founded on p.

We note that Proviso 1 involves only partial-correctness refinement because the relation $j \Rightarrow j'$ on its left-hand side is simply a before-after relation on the state space. As far as we are aware no such practical general-correctness loop refinement rule has been formulated before. An interesting feature of the rule is that the loop invariant j is entirely separate from the termination precondition p. We verify the rule by the following reasoning in our general-correctness calculus.

Proof:

$$p \Vdash (j \Rightarrow j' \wedge \neg\, b') \quad \sqsubseteq \quad \text{while } b \text{ do } s \text{ end}$$

$\equiv \qquad \{\ (30)\ \}$

$$p \Vdash (j \Rightarrow j' \wedge \neg\, b') \quad \sqsubseteq \quad ([b]s)^\omega [\neg\, b]$$

$\Lleftarrow \qquad \{\ \text{relax postcondition}\ \}$

$$p \Vdash (j \Rightarrow j') \wedge \neg\, b' \quad \sqsubseteq \quad ([b]s)^\omega [\neg\, b]$$

$\equiv \qquad \{\ (20)\ \}$

$$(p \Vdash j \Rightarrow j')[\neg\, b] \quad \sqsubseteq \quad ([b]s)^\omega [\neg\, b]$$

$\Lleftarrow \qquad \{\ \text{monotonicity of seq comp wrt } \sqsubseteq\ \}$

$$p \Vdash (j \Rightarrow j') \quad \sqsubseteq \quad ([b]s)^\omega$$

$\Lleftarrow \qquad \{\ (23)\ \}$

$$p \vdash \text{true} \sqsubseteq ([b]s)^\omega \quad \wedge \quad (j \Rightarrow j') \sqsubseteq (([b]s)^\omega)_{\textsf{par}}$$

$\equiv \qquad \{\ (29)\ \}$

$$p \vdash \text{true} \sqsubseteq ([b]s)^\omega \quad \wedge \quad (j \Rightarrow j') \sqsubseteq ([b]s)^* \qquad\qquad \textsf{A}$$

We now prove each of the two conjuncts of A above separately. First, we prove the right-hand conjunct:

$$(j \Rightarrow j') \sqsubseteq ([b]s)^*$$

$\Lleftarrow \qquad \{\ (15)\ \}$

$$(j \Rightarrow j') \sqsubseteq [b]s(j \Rightarrow j') \sqcap \text{skip}$$

$\Lleftarrow \qquad \{\ j \Rightarrow j' \sqsubseteq \text{skip}\ \}$

$$(j \Rightarrow j') \sqsubseteq [b]s(j \Rightarrow j')$$

$\equiv \qquad \{\ (j \Rightarrow j')(j \Rightarrow j') = (j \Rightarrow j')\ \}$

$$(j \Rightarrow j')(j \Rightarrow j') \sqsubseteq [b]s(j \Rightarrow j')$$

$\Lleftarrow \qquad \{\ \text{monotonicity of seq comp wrt } \sqsubseteq\ \}$

$$(j \Rightarrow j') \sqsubseteq [b]s \qquad \{ \text{ Proviso 1 } \}$$

Secondly, we prove the left-hand conjunct of A:

$$p \vdash \text{true} \quad \sqsubseteq \quad ([b]s)^\omega$$

$\equiv \quad \{ (14) \}$

$$p \vdash \text{true} \quad \sqsubseteq \quad ([b]s)^* \sqcap ([b]s)^\infty$$

$\equiv \quad \{ (2), \text{ noting that } p \vdash \text{true is } p \wedge \text{true} \vdash \text{true} \}$

$$\{p\}(\text{true} \vdash \text{true}) \quad \sqsubseteq \quad ([b]s)^* \sqcap ([b]s)^\infty$$

$\equiv \quad \{ (9) \}$

$$\text{true} \vdash \text{true} \quad \sqsubseteq \quad [p](([b]s)^* \sqcap ([b]s)^\infty)$$

$\equiv \quad \{ \text{ distributivity } \}$

$$\text{true} \vdash \text{true} \quad \sqsubseteq \quad [p]([b]s)^* \sqcap [p]([b]s)^\infty$$

$\equiv \quad \{ \text{ Proviso 2 } \}$

$$\text{true} \vdash \text{true} \quad \sqsubseteq \quad [p]([b]s)^* \sqcap \text{magic}$$

$\equiv \quad \{ \text{ magic is unit of } \sqcap \}$

$$\text{true} \vdash \text{true} \quad \sqsubseteq \quad [p]([b]s)^*$$

$\equiv \quad \{ (10) \}$

$$\text{magic} \quad \sqsubseteq \quad [p]([b]s)^* \text{magic}$$

$\equiv \quad \{ (9) \}$

$$\{p\} \text{magic} \quad \sqsubseteq \quad ([b]s)^* \text{magic}$$

$\equiv \quad \{ (18) \}$

$$\{p\} \text{magic} \quad \sqsubseteq \quad \nu_{\text{ref}} x \cdot [b]s\,x \sqcap \text{magic}$$

$\equiv \quad \{ \text{ magic is unit of } \sqcap \}$

$$\{p\} \text{magic} \quad \sqsubseteq \quad \nu_{\text{ref}} x \cdot [b]s\,x$$

$\Longleftarrow \quad \{ \mu f \sqsubseteq \nu f, \text{ transitivity of } \sqsubseteq \}$

$$\{p\} \text{magic} \quad \sqsubseteq \quad \mu_{\text{ref}} x \cdot [b]s\,x$$

$\equiv \quad \{ (12) \}$

$$\{p\} \text{magic} \quad \sqsubseteq \quad ([b]s)^\infty$$

$\equiv \quad \{ (9) \}$

$$\text{magic} \quad \sqsubseteq \quad [p]([b]s)^\infty$$

$\equiv \quad \{ (4) \}$

$$[p]([b]s)^\infty \quad = \quad \text{magic} \qquad \{ \text{ Proviso 2 } \} \qquad \square$$

6.2   An Application of the General-Correctness Loop Rule

Concert. In previous works such as [11,8,10] Dunne *et al.* have already described combining two general-correctness computations "in concert" under a termination pact by which the overall result, if any, of their parallel executions on separate copies of the state space is determined entirely by whichever of them happens to terminate first. Such a concert operator # can be simply defined in terms of prescriptions by

$$(p_1 \Vdash q_1) \quad \# \quad (p_2 \Vdash q_2) \quad =_{\text{def}} \quad (p_1 \vee p_2) \Vdash (q_1 \vee q_2) \tag{31}$$

What may at first sight seem surprising about the definition of concert here in (31) is that the preconditions of the two prescriptions on the left-hand side appear in the right-hand prescription to have lost their particular association with their respective postconditions. This is indeed so, and reflects the fact that even if the concerted execution takes place from an initial state where only, say, its first component $p_1 \Vdash q_1$ is guaranteed to terminate, it is still possible that its other component $p_2 \Vdash q_2$ will terminate first entirely fortuitously. In such a case the result delivered by $p_2 \Vdash q_2$ must under general correctness still satisfy q_2 despite its termination being fortuitous rather than guaranteed. This is in contrast to the analogous situation in total correctness where the result delivered by any fortuitous termination of a design $p \vdash q$ from an initial state outside its precondition p is unconstrained by its postcondition q.

Our concert operator $\#$ is both well-defined (because $p \Vdash q$ is a canonical form for prescriptions[3]) and monotonic on the refinement ordering $\sqsubseteq$ on prescriptions.

An example refinement using concert. To illustrate the use of our concert operator $\#$ we consider an impoverished computing environment in which values can be tested only for equality (or inequality) with zero, and where variables can only be modified by incrementing or decrementing by one. In such an austere environment even something as simple as setting an integer variable to zero, as specified by the prescription $\text{true} \Vdash x' = 0$, poses a considerable programming challenge. However, rising to that challenge we observe that

$$\text{true} \Vdash x' = 0$$
$$= \quad \{ \text{ integer property } \}$$
$$(x \le 0 \vee x \ge 0) \Vdash x' = 0$$
$$= \quad \{ \text{ defn of } \# \}$$
$$(x \le 0 \Vdash x' = 0) \quad \# \quad (x \ge 0 \Vdash x' = 0)$$

Interestingly, the two concerted specifications above can each be implemented by a while loop within our austere computing environment. Intuitively

$$x \le 0 \Vdash x' = 0 \quad \sqsubseteq \quad \text{while } x \ne 0 \text{ do } x := x + 1 \text{ end} \qquad (32)$$
$$x \ge 0 \Vdash x' = 0 \quad \sqsubseteq \quad \text{while } x \ne 0 \text{ do } x := x - 1 \text{ end} \qquad (33)$$

This means that we can fulfil our original requirement to set x to zero within the constraints imposed by our impoverished computing environment by executing the two loops above in concert on separate copies of the state space. But how do we verify these putative refinements (32) and (33) formally? In the case of (32) we do so by applying GC Loop 1 with p as $x \le 0$, j as true, b as $x \ne 0$ and s as $x := x + 1$. This gives us an obligation to discharge the provisos

    1. $(\text{true} \Rightarrow \text{true}) \sqsubseteq [x \ne 0] \, x := x + 1$

---

[3] That is to say, two prescriptions $p_1 \Vdash q_1$ and $p_2 \Vdash q_2$ are equal if and only if $p_1 = p_2$ and $q_1 = q_2$, as shown in [9].

and

2. $[x \neq 0]\, x := x + 1$ is well-founded on $x \leq 0$,

which are both trivial. In the case of (33), on the other hand, we again apply GC Loop 1 but this time with p as $x \geq 0$, j as true, b as $x \neq 0$ and s as $x := x - 1$. This then gives us an obligation to discharge the provisos

1. $(\text{true} \Rightarrow \text{true})$ $\sqsubseteq$ $[x \neq 0]\, x := x - 1$

and

2. $[x \neq 0]\, x := x - 1$ is well-founded on $x \geq 0$,

which again are both trivial.

What the example shows. We would stress that the purpose of the above example is not the refinement *per se*, which is —in operational terms at least— obviously quite trivial. Rather, it lies in the refinement's formal verification. This is simply not possible within the confines of total correctness. Only with our new general-correctness loop-refinement rule GC Loop 1 can we establish the refinement's correctness. The point of the example is therefore to illustrate the necessity of such a rule in verifying even such "obvious" refinements.

6.3   Another General-Correctness Loop Rule

We can derive more specialised general-correctness loop rules from our primary rule GC Loop 1. For example if we simply re-write it with $\neg\, j$ replacing j we obtain this version of the rule:

$p \Vdash (\neg\, j \Rightarrow \neg\, j' \wedge \neg\, b')$ $\sqsubseteq$ while b do s end   GC Loop 1a

provided

1. $(\neg\, j \Rightarrow \neg\, j')$ $\sqsubseteq$ $[b]\, s$
2. $[b]\, s$ is well-founded on p.

Now combining GC Loop 1 and GC Loop 1a we obtain this further version:

$p \Vdash (j \Leftrightarrow j') \wedge \neg\, b'$ $\sqsubseteq$ while b do s end   GC Loop 1b

provided

1. $(j \Leftrightarrow j')$ $\sqsubseteq$ $[b]\, s$
2. $[b]\, s$ is well-founded on p.

If we then strengthen our provisos with the requirement that $\neg\, j \Rightarrow b$, from which it follows immediately that $\neg\, j' \Rightarrow b'$, we can then further simplify the postcondition of the prescription on the left-hand side of GC Loop 1b to obtain the following rule:

$p \Vdash j \wedge \neg\, b'$ $\sqsubseteq$ while b do s end   GC Loop 2

provided

1. $\neg\, j \Rightarrow b$
2. $(j \Leftrightarrow j')$ $\sqsubseteq$ $[b]\, s$
3. $[b]\, s$ is well-founded on p.

In the next subsection we illustrate the use of this rule by applying it to verify another "intuitively obvious" general-correctness refinement.

6.4 An Application of the GC Loop 2 Rule

A prescription of the particular form $p \Vdash (p \wedge q)$, where as usual p is a condition on the the initial state v and q is a binary relation on $\{v, v'\}$, has a commitment which demands that the initial state of any execution which terminates must have satisfied p. It therefore has the following interesting operational interpretation:

> From any initial state which satisfies p the program must terminate in a final state which satisfies q, whereas from any other initial state the program **must not terminate**.

From our operational intuition it therefore seems obvious that the while loop

$$\textsf{while } x \neq 0 \textsf{ do } x := x - 1 \textsf{ end}$$

which we saw earlier will terminate in a final state with $x = 0$ when started from any initial state where $x \geq 0$, whereas it will fail to terminate from any other initial state. In other words, it implements the prescription

$$x \geq 0 \Vdash (x \geq 0 \wedge x' = 0).$$

Yet our GC Loop 1 rule cannot be applied directly to verify such a refinement because the above prescription doesn't match the form $p \Vdash (j \Rightarrow j' \wedge \neg b')$. On the other hand, by setting p and j both to $x \geq 0$ and b to $x \neq 0$ it does match the form $p \Vdash j \wedge \neg b'$ of our GC Loop 2 rule. Moreover, all three of this rule's provisos, namely

1. $\neg (x \geq 0) \Rightarrow x \neq 0$,
2. $(x \geq 0 \Leftrightarrow x' \geq 0) \sqsubseteq [x \neq 0] x := x - 1$

and

3. $[x \neq 0] x := x - 1$ is well-founded on $x \geq 0$,

are then satisfied. Hence we can apply GC Loop 2 to verify this implementation.

7 Conclusion

We have presented a calculus for reasoning about programs in total correctness, and demonstrated its utility in verifying succinctly the familiar loop-invariant rule for refining a specification in total correctness by a while loop. We have also presented an analogous calculus for reasoning about programs in general correctness, which we then used to verify our new loop-invariant rule for refining a specification in general correctness by a while loop. We believe our verification proofs of our rules demonstrate that our algebraically-inspired calculi provide an apt framework for reasoning about such rules.

Finally, it is perhaps worth noting that we are not the only ones to have espoused an algebraic style in reasoning about general correctness. In [22], for example, Möller and Struth apply a notably abstract algebraic approach to reasoning about wp and wlp. It would certainly be interesting to explore further the relationship of their work to ours.

Acknowledgements

We are grateful to Walter Guttmann for feedback on the work-in-progress extended abstract which preceded this paper, to Roland Backhouse for directing us to Apt and Plotkin's Transfer Lemma in [2], and to the referees of the original review draft of this paper whose insightful comments we have endeavoured to address in this final version. The second author's research was supported by Australian Research Council (ARC) Discovery Grant DP0558408, *Analysing and generating fault-tolerant real-time systems* and the EPSRC-funded Trustworthy Ambient Systems (TrAmS) Platform Project.

References

1. Abrial, J.-R.: The B-Book: Assigning Programs to Meanings. Cambridge University Press, Cambridge (1996)
2. Apt, K.R., Plotkin, G.D.: Countable nondeterminism and random assignment. Journal of the ACM 33(4), 724–767 (1986)
3. Back, R.-J., von Wright, J.: Refinement Calculus: A Systematic Introduction. Springer, New York (1998)
4. Cohen, E.: Separation and reduction. In: Backhouse, R., Oliveira, J.N. (eds.) MPC 2000. LNCS, vol. 1837, pp. 45–59. Springer, Heidelberg (2000)
5. Conway, J.H.: Regular Algebra and Finite Machines. Chapman Hall, Boca Raton (1971)
6. Deutsch, M., Henson, M.C.: A relational investigation of UTP designs and prescriptions. In: Dunne, S.E., Stoddart, W.J. (eds.) UTP 2006. LNCS, vol. 4010, pp. 101–122. Springer, Heidelberg (2006)
7. Dijkstra, E.W., Scholten, C.S.: Predicate Calculus and Program Semantics. Springer, Heidelberg (1990)
8. Dunne, S.E.: Abstract commands: a uniform notation for specifications and implementations. In: Fidge, C.J. (ed.) Computing: The Australasian Theory Symposium 2001. Electronic Notes in Theoretical Computer Science, vol. 42. Elsevier, Amsterdam (2001), http://www.elsevier.nl/locate/entcs
9. Dunne, S.E.: Recasting Hoare and He's unifying theory of programs in the context of general correctness. In: Butterfield, A., Strong, G., Pahl, C. (eds.) Proceedings of the 5th Irish Workshop in Formal Methods, IWFM 2001, Workshops in Computing. British Computer Society (2001), http://ewic.bcs.org/conferences/2001/5thformal/papers
10. Dunne, S.E.: Junctive compositions of specifications in Total and General Correctness. In: Derrick, J., Boiten, E., Woodcock, J.C.P., von Wright, J. (eds.) Refine 2002: The BCS FACS Refinement Workshop. Electronic Notes in Theoretical Computer Science, vol. 70(3). Elsevier Science BV (2002), http://www.elsevier.nl/locate/entcs
11. Dunne, S.E., Stoddart, W.J., Galloway, A.J.: Specification and refinement in general correctness. In: Evans, A., Duke, D., Clark, A. (eds.) Proceedings of the 3rd Northern Formal Methods Workshop. BCS Electronic Workshops in Computing (1998), http://www.ewic.org.uk/ewic/workshop/view.cfm/NFM-98
12. Floyd, R.W.: Assigning meanings to programs. In: Proceedings of Symposia in Applied Mathematics, vol. 19, pp. 19–32 (1967)

13. Guttmann, W., Möller, B.: Modal design algebra. In: Dunne, S.E., Stoddart, W.J. (eds.) UTP 2006. LNCS, vol. 4010, pp. 236–256. Springer, Heidelberg (2006)
14. Hoare, C.A.R.: An axiomatic basis for computer programming. Communications of the ACM 12, 576–583 (1969)
15. Hoare, C.A.R., Jifeng, H.: Unifying Theories of Programming. Prentice-Hall, Englewood Cliffs (1998)
16. Jacobs, D., Gries, D.: General correctness: a unification of partial and total correctness. Acta Informatica 22, 67–83 (1985)
17. Jones, C.B.: Systematic Software Development Using VDM, 2nd edn. Prentice-Hall, Englewood Cliffs (1990)
18. Kozen, D.: A completeness theorem for Kleene algebras and the algebra of regular events. Information and Computation 110, 366–390 (1994)
19. Kozen, D.: Kleene algebra with tests. ACM Transactions on Programming Languages and Systems 19, 427–443 (1999)
20. Kozen, D.: On Kleene algebras and closed semirings. In: Rovan, B. (ed.) MFCS 1990. LNCS, vol. 452, pp. 26–47. Springer, Heidelberg (2000)
21. Meinicke, L., Hayes, I.J.: Algebraic reasoning for probabilistic action systems and while-loops. Acta Informatica 45(5), 321–382 (2008)
22. Möller, B., Struth, G.: wp is wlp. In: Düntsch, I., MacCaull, W., Winter, M. (eds.) RelMiCS 2005. LNCS, vol. 3929, pp. 855–874. Springer, Heidelberg (2006)
23. Morgan, C.C.: Programming from Specifications, 2nd edn. Prentice Hall International, Englewood Cliffs (1994)
24. Nelson, G.: A generalisation of Dijkstra's calculus. ACM Transactions on Programmg Languages and Systems 11(4) (1989)
25. Tarski, A.: A lattice-theoretical fixpoint theorem and its applications. Pacific Journal of Mathematics 5(2), 285–309 (1955)
26. von Wright, J.: From Kleene algebra to refinement algebra. In: Möller, B., Boiten, E. (eds.) MPC 2002. LNCS, vol. 2386, pp. 233–262. Springer, Heidelberg (2002)
27. von Wright, J.: Towards a refinement algebra. Science of Computer Programming 51, 23–45 (2004)

Lazy UTP

Walter Guttmann

Institut für Programmiermethodik und Compilerbau
Universität Ulm, 89069 Ulm, Germany
walter.guttmann@uni-ulm.de

Abstract. We integrate non-strict computations into the Unifying Theories of Programming. After showing that this is not possible with designs, we develop a new relational model representing undefinedness independently of non-termination. The relations satisfy additional healthiness conditions that model dependence in computations in an elegant algebraic form using partial orders. Programs can be executed according to the principle of lazy evaluation, otherwise known from functional programming languages. We extend the theory to support infinite data structures and give examples to show their use in programs.

1 Introduction

Our goal is to extend the Unifying Theories of Programming (UTP) by non-strict computations. Consider the statement $P =_{\text{def}} (x_1, x_2 := 1/0, 2)$ that simultaneously assigns an undefined value to x_1 and 2 to x_2. In UTP and most conventional languages its execution fails, but we want undefined expressions to remain harmless if their value is not needed. This is standard in functional programming languages with lazy evaluation like Haskell [25], Clean [26] and Miranda [37]. Yet also in an imperative language the equation $P \; ; (x_1 := x_2) = (x_1, x_2 := 2, 2)$ can be reasonable since the value of x_1 after the execution of P is never used. This is confirmed by the following Haskell program that implements $P \; ; (x_1 := x_2)$ in monadic style:

```
import Data.IORef;
main = do r <- newIORef (div 1 0 , 2)
          modifyIORef r (\(x1,x2) -> (x2,x2))
          x <- readIORef r
          print x
```

It prints (2,2) terminating successfully, but would abort if (x2,x2) was changed to (x1,x1). With non-strict computations available, programs can be expressed more freely since less attention has to be paid to avoid non-termination. For example, in functional programming languages they enable the use of infinite data structures. They too are not supported by UTP so far.

Regarding the statement P again, we have to address that UTP models undefinedness as non-termination [15, page 78]. In particular, $P = (\text{false} \vdash \text{true})$ holds, hence P is the never terminating program (the solution of the recursive

A. Butterfield (Ed.): UTP 2008, LNCS 5713, pp. 82–101, 2010.
© Springer-Verlag Berlin Heidelberg 2010

specification $X = X$). In consequence there is no distinction between undefinedness of individual variables; actually $P = (x_1, x_2 := 2, \frac{1}{0})$ holds. Moreover, computations are strict in the sense that $P \,;\, (x_1 := x_2)$ is again the endless loop.

In some contexts such a uniform treatment of non-termination and undefinedness is not appropriate. UTP's point of view is that of the specifier who does not care whether a program loops indefinitely or aborts due to an error, since in both cases it does not fulfil its objective. We can, however, argue for a differentiation between finite and infinite failure. From the users' point of view, errors can actually be observed about executions of programs whereas non-termination cannot. From the programmers' and language designers' point of view, errors might be recovered from, for example, by exception handling. From the theorists' point of view, error detection is semidecidable in contrast to *non*-termination which is not semidecidable. We therefore strive for a theory that separates undefinedness and non-termination. It is then manifest to regard variables individually to obtain an even finer distinction.

As explained in Section 2, UTP's designs are not adequate to support non-strict computations. Let us therefore describe our new approach. As usual, we represent undefinedness of individual variables by adding a special value $\perp$ to their ranges. We add another special element ∞ to distinguish non-termination from undefinedness. The difficulty is to choose the relations and operations (that model computations) such that, on the one hand, they handle these special values correctly and, on the other hand, they are continuous. The latter is required to iteratively approximate the solutions to recursive equations, which corresponds to the evaluation of recursion in practice. Furthermore, key constructs such as composition and choice should retain their familiar relational meaning to obtain nice algebraic properties. We solve this problem by introducing a partial order on the ranges of variables and states, and forming the closure of relations with respect to this order.

Section 3 gives the relational basics. A compendium of relations modelling the programming constructs known from UTP is presented in Section 4. We identify several healthiness conditions they satisfy, starting with isotony and the left and right unit laws. In Section 5 we derive further properties, namely finite branching, continuity and totality. We thus obtain a theory similar to that of designs, but describing non-strict computations, able to yield defined results in spite of undefined inputs. Moreover, it is sufficient to execute only those parts of a program necessary to calculate the final results, which can improve efficiency.

Our framework can also be applied to programs with infinite data structures. Several examples constructing and modifying infinite lists are discussed in Section 6. We also show how to express in our framework the class of fold- and unfold-computations on (finite and infinite) lists. They are well-known in functional programming languages and include such operations as *map* and *filter*, the building blocks of list comprehensions.

With lazy execution comes the need to consider dependences between individual computations. Such dependences also play a role in optimising program transformations like those performed in compilers. Their structure is investigated in Section 7. Starting from the observation that non-strict computations with defined results cannot depend on undefined inputs, we derive two additional healthiness conditions. Using another partial order we develop an equivalent, algebraically elegant form of these properties. All our programming constructs satisfy them, but they are also applicable to relations modelling new constructs.

In short, the contributions of this paper are an extension of UTP by non-strict computations, appropriate healthiness conditions and infinite data structures.

This paper uses material obtained as a part of the author's PhD thesis [11]. A condensed account of that part is given in [12]. Substantial extensions of the present paper include the connections to UTP, a theory extended to more general orders, and programs using infinite data structures. Proofs of our results can be adapted from [11] to the present, more general setting (although some claims are considerably harder to show).

2   Designs

We have seen the need to separate undefinedness from non-termination. Already modelling non-termination, UTP's designs are obvious candidates for a modified treatment of undefinedness. In this section we show that although such an extension is possible, it leads to a fundamental problem. The conclusion is that designs cannot adequately model non-strict computations. In Section 3 we therefore introduce the relational foundations of an alternative model which is used in the remainder of this paper.

Before we investigate designs, and for further reference, recall that the healthiness conditions H1–H4 of UTP are equivalent to the following four algebraic restrictions with respect to sequential composition:

H1a. $\mathbb{I}_\mathrm{D} \; ; R = R$ H3. $R = R \; ; \mathbb{I}_\mathrm{D}$

H1b. $\mathbb{O}_\mathrm{D} \; ; R = \mathbb{O}_\mathrm{D}$ H4. $\mathbb{O}_\mathrm{D} = R \; ; \mathbb{O}_\mathrm{D}$

The skip design $\mathbb{I}_\mathrm{D} = (true \vdash \vec{x} = \vec{x}')$ should be left- and right-neutral and the design $\mathbb{O}_\mathrm{D} = (false \vdash true)$ should be left- and right-absorbing. The design $\mathbb{O}_\mathrm{D}$ is also denoted $true$ by [15] which is correct but confusing in the following discussion. We intend to explain in detail why the law H1b is incompatible with non-strictness; the reader who takes this for granted may jump to Section 3.

Consider the design $(P \vdash Q)$ where the precondition P represents the terminating states, while Q represents the possible transitions starting in those states. Let us focus on the type of the relation Q between program states. Assume for the sake of exposition that the program has two variables x_1 and x_2 ranging over the natural numbers $\mathbb{N}$. A state then is an element of $\mathbb{N}^2 =_{\mathrm{def}} \mathbb{N} \times \mathbb{N}$, and the transition relation Q is an element of $\mathbb{N}^2 \leftrightarrow \mathbb{N}^2$. No provisions are made to represent variables with undefined values. Indeed, there is no reason to, since undefinedness is modelled as non-termination in the component P of designs.

To separate undefinedness from non-termination we have to provide means to represent undefined values in the transition relation Q of designs. This is achieved by modifying the set of states in either of two ways. Both start by extending the range of each variable to $\mathbb{N} \cup \{\bot\}$, where the special element $\bot$ represents the undefined value.

The first approach uses the smash product of both variable ranges $\mathbb{N}^2 \cup \{\bot\}$ as the set of states. A transition relation then is an element of $(\mathbb{N}^2 \cup \{\bot\}) \leftrightarrow (\mathbb{N}^2 \cup \{\bot\})$. In this case $\bot$ models undefinedness of the state as a whole but not of its constituents, the individual variables.

To achieve the latter, we instead take the Cartesian product $(\mathbb{N} \cup \{\bot\})^2$ as the set of states (the problem we exhibit below remains also with the smash product). Thus undefined and defined variables may coexist as exemplified by

$$(x_1, x_2 := \tfrac{1}{0}, 2) \, ; \, (x_1 := x_2)$$
$$= \{((x_1, x_2), (x_1', x_2')) \mid x_1' = \bot \wedge x_2' = 2\} \, ; \, \{((x_1, x_2), (x_1', x_2')) \mid x_1' = x_2 \wedge x_2' = x_2\}$$
$$= \{((x_1, x_2), (x_1', x_2')) \mid x_1' = 2 \wedge x_2' = 2\}$$
$$= (x_1, x_2 := 2, 2) \, .$$

Note that the assignment here is regarded as a plain transition relation, not as a design, because termination is not treated yet. The special element $\bot$ represents that x_1 has been assigned an expression with undefined value. However, this first assignment to x_1 has no effect since its value is never used but immediately overwritten. It is not even necessary to evaluate the corresponding right hand side. Unaffected by these considerations is the value of x_2.

The transition relations, now elements of $(\mathbb{N} \cup \{\bot\})^2 \leftrightarrow (\mathbb{N} \cup \{\bot\})^2$, are built into designs to deal with non-termination. For the following argument, we redefine the assignment as the design

$$(x_1, x_2 := e_1, e_2) =_{\text{def}} (true \vdash x_1' = e_1 \wedge x_2' = e_2) \, ,$$

reflecting the fact that an assignment always terminates as opposed to the original assignment of UTP. To complete the separation of undefinedness and non-termination, also conditional statements would have to be redefined, since their conditions are expressions and can have undefined values, too. We leave out this definition, because it does not affect the following two facts. First,

$$(x_1 := \tfrac{1}{0}) \, ; \, (x_1, x_2 := 2, 3) = (true \vdash x_1' = \bot \wedge x_2' = x_2) \, ; \, (true \vdash x_1' = 2 \wedge x_2' = 3)$$
$$= (true \vdash x_1' = 2 \wedge x_2' = 3) = (x_1, x_2 := 2, 3) \, ,$$

using the composition formula of designs. The undefined value of x_1 has no effect, which is just what we expect from a non-strict computation. Second,

$$\mathbb{O}_D \, ; \, (x_1, x_2 := 2, 3) = (false \vdash true) \, ; \, (true \vdash x_1' = 2 \wedge x_2' = 3)$$
$$= (false \vdash true) = \mathbb{O}_D \, ,$$

recalling that the design $\mathbb{O}_D$ represents non-termination. It is left absorbing, which is just what we expect from designs according to H1b. We now argue that the latter equation, although it is algebraically elegant, does not co-operate well with the first one, and hence cannot be upheld in a non-strict setting.

Consider the possible execution strategies for a program $R \, ; \, (x_1, x_2 := 2, 3)$, assuming we do not know whether $R = (x_1 := \tfrac{1}{0})$ or $R = \mathbb{O}_D$ holds, since this is undecidable in general. Conventionally, one would first execute R and then $(x_1, x_2 := 2, 3)$. This leads to non-termination if $R = \mathbb{O}_D$, but aborts if $R = (x_1 := 1/0)$, which is inconsistent with the first fact derived above. To avoid this error, one could alternatively start with $(x_1, x_2 := 2, 3)$, realising that the values of the variables prior to this assignment are not needed. The execution of R is thus omitted, which is inconsistent with the second fact if $R = \mathbb{O}_D$.

The conflict between both facts is summarised as follows: According to the first, it is possible to recover from undefinedness, but according to the second, it is impossible to recover from non-termination. To observe the latter, otherwise unnecessary calculations have to be performed. They possibly abort due to undefined expressions, contradicting the former.

Since it is our aim to model non-strict computations, we are forced to give up an equation like $\mathbb{O}_D \,;\, (x_1, x_2 := 2, 3) = \mathbb{O}_D$. This is an instance of the healthiness condition $\mathbb{O}_D \,;\, R = \mathbb{O}_D$ that every design R satisfies, called H1b above. 'However, a lazy functional language does not satisfy this law.'[14, page 24] Although we are not specifically concerned with functional programming languages, we therefore cannot use UTP's designs for our purpose.

3   Relational Preliminaries

In this section we set up the context of the investigation of non-strictness. We describe the relational model of imperative, non-deterministic programs in detail and introduce terminology, notation and conventions used in this paper.

Characteristic features of imperative programming are variables, states and statements. We assume an infinite supply $x_1, x_2, \ldots$ of variables. Associated with each variable x_i is its type or range D_i, a set comprising all values the variable can take. Each D_i shall contain two special elements $\bot$ and ∞ with the following intuitive meaning: If the variable x_i has the value $\bot$ *and* this value is needed, the execution of the program aborts. If the variable x_i has the value ∞ *and* this value is needed, the execution of the program does not terminate. Further structure is imposed on D_i in Sections 4.1 and 7.

A state is given by the values of a finite but unbounded number of variables $x_1, \ldots, x_m$ which we abbreviate as $\vec{x}$. Let $1..m$ denote the first m positive integers. Let $\vec{x}_I$ denote the subsequence of $\vec{x}$ comprising those x_i with $i \in I$ for a subset $I \subseteq 1..m$. By writing $\vec{x} = a$ where $a \in \{\infty, \bot\}$ we express that $x_i = a$ for all $i \in 1..m$. Let $D_I =_{\text{def}} \prod_{i \in I} D_i$ denote the Cartesian product of the ranges of the variables x_i with $i \in I$. A state is an element $\vec{x} \in D_{1..m}$.

The effect of statements is to transform states into new states. We therefore distinguish the values of a variable x_i before and after the execution of a statement. The input value is denoted just as the variable by x_i and the output value is denoted by x_i'. In particular, both $x_i \in D_i$ and $x_i' \in D_i$. Composed of the output values, the output state $(x_1', \ldots, x_n')$ is abbreviated as $\vec{x}'$. Statements may introduce new variables into the state and remove variables from the state; then $m \neq n$. Using UTP terminology, the input alphabet is $\{x_1, \ldots, x_m\}$ and the output alphabet is $\{x_1', \ldots, x_n'\}$ with possibly different m and n.

A computation is modelled as a relation $R = R(\vec{x}, \vec{x}') \subseteq D_{1..m} \times D_{1..n}$. An element $(\vec{x}, \vec{x}') \in R$ intuitively means that the execution of R with input values $\vec{x}$ *may* yield the output values $\vec{x}'$. The image of a state $\vec{x}$ is given by $R(\vec{x}) =_{\text{def}} \{\vec{x}' \mid (\vec{x}, \vec{x}') \in R\}$. Non-determinism is modelled by having $|R(\vec{x})| > 1$. Compared to designs, the new models get by with just one relation instead of two, and this is compensated by the additional special elements $\bot$ and ∞.

Another way to state the type of the relation is $R : D_{1..m} \leftrightarrow D_{1..n}$. The framework employed is that of heterogeneous relation algebra [31,32]; a homogeneous model would complicate the treatment of local variables in recursive calls (by stacks) and parallel composition (by merge). We omit any notational distinction of the types of relations and their operations and assume type-correctness in their use.

We denote the identity and universal relations by $\mathbb{I}$ and $\mathbb{T}$, respectively. Lattice join, meet and order of relations are denoted by $\cup$, $\cap$ and $\subseteq$, respectively. The Boolean complement of R is $\overline{R}$, and the converse (transposition) of R is $R^{\smile}$. Relational (sequential) composition of P and Q is denoted by $P \,;\, Q$ and PQ. Converse has highest precedence, followed by sequential composition, followed by meet and join with lowest precedence.

A relation R is a vector iff $R\mathbb{T} = R$, total iff $R\mathbb{T} = \mathbb{T}$ and univalent iff $R^{\smile}R \subseteq \mathbb{I}$. A relation is a mapping iff it is both total and univalent. Note that totality is exactly the healthiness condition H4.

Relational constants representing computations may be specified by set comprehension as, for example, in

$$R = \{(\vec{x}, \vec{x}') \mid x_1' = x_2 \wedge x_2' = 1\} = \{(\vec{x}, \vec{x}') \mid x_1' = x_2\} \cap \{(\vec{x}, \vec{x}') \mid x_2' = 1\} \,.$$

We abbreviate such a comprehension by its constituent predicate, that is, we write $R = (x_1' = x_2) \cap (x_2' = 1)$. In doing so, we use the identifier x in a generic way, possibly decorated with an index, a prime or an arrow. It follows, for example, that $\vec{x} = \vec{c}$ is a vector for every constant $\vec{c}$.

To form heterogeneous relations and, more generally, to change their dimensions, we use the following projection operation. Let I, J, K and L be index sets such that $I \cap K = \emptyset = J \cap L$. The dimensions of $R : D_{I \cup K} \leftrightarrow D_{J \cup L}$ are restricted by

$$(\exists \vec{x}_K, \vec{x}'_L : R) =_{\text{def}} \{(\vec{x}_I, \vec{x}'_J) \mid \exists \vec{x}_K, \vec{x}'_L : (\vec{x}_{I \cup K}, \vec{x}'_{J \cup L}) \in R\} : D_I \leftrightarrow D_J \,.$$

We abbreviate the case $L = \emptyset$ as $(\exists \vec{x}_K : R)$ and the case $K = \emptyset$ as $(\exists \vec{x}'_L : R)$. See Section 4.4 for the correspondence to variable (un)declaration.

Defined in terms of the projection, we furthermore use the following relational parallel composition operator, similar to that of [2,3,28]. The parallel composition of the relations $P : D_I \leftrightarrow D_J$ and $Q : D_K \leftrightarrow D_L$ is

$$P \| Q =_{\text{def}} (\exists \vec{x}'_K : \mathbb{I}) \,;\, P \,;\, (\exists \vec{x}_L : \mathbb{I}) \cap (\exists \vec{x}'_I : \mathbb{I}) \,;\, Q \,;\, (\exists \vec{x}_J : \mathbb{I}) : D_{I \cup K} \leftrightarrow D_{J \cup L} \,.$$

If necessary, we write $P_I \|_K Q$ to clarify the partition of $I \cup K$ (a more detailed notation would also clarify the partition of $J \cup L$). In our theory of non-strict computations the $\|$ operator corresponds to conjunction rather than the parallel composition of disjoint processes in [15, Section 7.1].

Recall that a non-empty subset S of a partially ordered set is directed iff each pair of elements of S has an upper bound in S. We apply the dual notion to the lattice of relations only: A set S of relations is *co-directed* iff it is directed with respect to $\supseteq$, that is, if $S \neq \emptyset$ and any two relations $P, Q \in S$ have a lower bound $R \in S$ with $R \subseteq P$ and $R \subseteq Q$.

4 Programming Constructs

We present a relational model of non-strict computations. Since we cannot use UTP's designs, we have to reformulate the respective theory. In particular, we give new definitions for most programming constructs and identify several health-iness conditions they satisfy. The latter starts with isotony and the unit laws in Section 4.5, followed by boundedness, continuity and totality in Section 5 and two dependence conditions in Section 7.

4.1 Values

The state of an imperative program is given by the values of its variables, taken from the ranges D_i introduced above. They contain the special elements $\bot$ and ∞ modelling undefinedness and non-termination. Instead of regarding D_i as an unstructured set, we augment the ranges to partially ordered structures. This is usual, for example, in the semantics of functional programming languages. Among the various suggested structures are directed or ω-complete (pointed) partial orders [1,30] or complete lattices [36]. We choose the *algebraic semilattices* of [6], which are complete semilattices having a basis of finite elements. They are closed under the constructions described below and adequate for our results.

In particular, each D_i is a partial order with a least element in which suprema of directed sets and infima of non-empty sets exist. We denote by $\preccurlyeq : D_i \leftrightarrow D_i$ the order on D_i, let ∞ be its least element, and write $\sup S$ for the supremum of the directed set S with respect to $\preccurlyeq$. The dual order of $\preccurlyeq$ is denoted by $\succcurlyeq =_{\mathrm{def}} \preccurlyeq^{\smile}$. An order similar to $\preccurlyeq$, in which $\bot$ is the least element, is introduced in Section 7.

Our data types are constructed as follows. Elementary types, such as the Boolean values $Bool =_{\mathrm{def}} \{\infty, \bot, true, false\}$ and the integer numbers $Int =_{\mathrm{def}} \mathbb{Z} \cup \{\infty, \bot\}$, are flat partial orders, that is, $x \preccurlyeq y \Leftrightarrow_{\mathrm{def}} x = \infty \lor x = y$. Thus $\bot$ is treated like any other value except ∞, with regard to $\preccurlyeq$. The union of a finite number of types D_i is given by their separated sum $\{\infty, \bot\} \cup \{(i, x) \mid x \in D_i\}$ ordered by $x \preccurlyeq y \Leftrightarrow_{\mathrm{def}} x = \infty \lor x = \bot = y \lor (x = (i, x_i) \land y = (i, y_i) \land x_i \preccurlyeq_{D_i} y_i)$. The product of a finite number of types D_i is $D_I = \prod_{i \in I} D_i$ ordered by the pointwise extension of $\preccurlyeq$, that is, $\vec{x}_I \preccurlyeq \vec{y}_I \Leftrightarrow_{\mathrm{def}} \forall i \in I : x_i \preccurlyeq_{D_i} y_i$. Values of function types are ordered pointwise and $\preccurlyeq$-continuous, that is, they distribute over suprema of directed sets. Recursive data types are built by the inverse limit construction, see [30].

Some results can be strengthened if we restrict our constructions to union and product. It is then easily proved by induction that every chain $C \subseteq D_i$ ordered by $\preccurlyeq$ is finite (a chain is a totally ordered subset). Even more, the lengths of the chains are bounded, so that the variable ranges are partial orders with finite height. Our previous work [11,12] restricts D_i to flat orders for reasons explained in Section 5. The new extension to more general orders is indispensable for infinite data structures, see Section 6.

The product construction plays a double role. It is not only used to build compound data types but also to represent the state of a computation with several variables. Hence the elements of the state $\vec{x} \in D_{1..m}$ are ordered by $\preccurlyeq$ and we may write $\vec{x} \preccurlyeq \vec{x}'$ to express that $x_i \preccurlyeq x_i'$ for each variable x_i.

4.2   Skip

In this and the following sections, we successively define our programming constructs using relations on the state and discuss essential algebraic properties. In particular, the order $\preccurlyeq$ is a relation on states which turns out to be fundamental. Indeed, we take it as the definition of the new relation modelling skip, denoted also by $\mathbb{1} =_{\mathrm{def}} \preccurlyeq$. While this action may appear strange, it can be compared to the redefinition of skip in [15, Section 9.1] to support procedure values. Although we do not treat such values in this paper, $\preccurlyeq$ can be interpreted as a kind of refinement [20,22]. Further explanation of $\mathbb{1}$ is provided by the following connection to designs.

Remark. The intention underlying the definition of $\mathbb{1}$ is to enforce an upper closure of the image of each state with respect to $\preccurlyeq$. Traces of such a procedure can be found in the healthiness conditions of designs: 'The healthiness condition H2 states formally that the predicate R is upward closed in the variable ok': as ok' changes from false to true, R cannot change from true to false.'[15, page 83] Since H3 implies H2, every H3-design is upper closed in this way. For H3-designs, [10] shows how to replace the auxiliary variables ok and ok' by a special element that corresponds to ∞ in our present discussion. In particular, [10, Lemma 9.2] formulates the upper closure as $\overline{R\top} \cap R \subseteq \overline{V^{\smile}}$, where V corresponds to the vector $\vec{x} = \infty$. By the Schröder law of relation algebra,

$$\overline{R\top} \cap R \subseteq \overline{V^{\smile}} \;\Leftrightarrow\; \overline{R\top} \cap V^{\smile} \subseteq \overline{R} \;\Leftrightarrow\; \overline{R}V^{\smile} \subseteq \overline{R}$$
$$\Leftrightarrow\; RV \subseteq R \;\Leftrightarrow\; RV \cup R = R \;\Leftrightarrow\; R(V \cup \mathbb{I}) = R \;.$$

If the state is a flat order, $V \cup \mathbb{I} = (x{=}\infty) \cup (x{=}x') = (x \preccurlyeq x')$, and we obtain the right unit law $R \;;\; \preccurlyeq \;=\; R$. Our definition of $\mathbb{1}$ refines this by distinguishing individual variables and non-flat orders. The refined right unit law corresponding to the healthiness condition H3 of designs is stated in the following definition.

As usual, skip should be a left and a right unit of sequential composition.

Definition 1. $\mathscr{H}_L(P) \Leftrightarrow_{\mathrm{def}} \mathbb{1} \;;\; P = P$ *and* $\mathscr{H}_R(P) \Leftrightarrow_{\mathrm{def}} P \;;\; \mathbb{1} = P$.

By reflexivity of $\mathbb{1}$ it suffices to demand $\subseteq$ instead of equality. We furthermore use $\mathscr{H}_E(P) \Leftrightarrow_{\text{def}} \mathscr{H}_L(P) \wedge \mathscr{H}_R(P)$. It follows that for $X \in \{E, L, R\}$ the relations satisfying $\mathscr{H}_X$ form a complete lattice. The next sections define programming constructs that satisfy or preserve these healthiness conditions.

4.3 Expressions

The assignment statement of UTP is the mapping $(\vec{x}:=\vec{e}) =_{\text{def}} (\vec{x}'=\vec{e})$, where each expression $e \in \vec{e}$ may depend on the input values $\vec{x}$ of the variables, and yields exactly one value $e(\vec{x})$ from the expression's type.

Our new relation modelling the assignment is $(\vec{x}\leftarrow\vec{e}) =_{\text{def}} \mathbb{1} \;;\; (\vec{x}:=\vec{e}) \;;\; \mathbb{1}$. We assume that each expression $e \in \vec{e}$ is $\preccurlyeq$-continuous, hence also $\preccurlyeq$-isotone. We write $(\vec{x}\leftarrow e)$ to assign the same expression e to all variables. The upper closure of the images perspicuously appears in the following lemma which intuitively states that $\mathbb{T}$ models the never terminating program.

Lemma 2. We have $(\vec{x}\leftarrow\infty) = \mathbb{T}$ and $(\vec{x}\leftarrow\vec{c}) = (\vec{x}'=\vec{c}) = (\vec{x}:=\vec{c})$ for every $\preccurlyeq$-maximal $\vec{c} \in D_{1..n}$. Moreover, $(\vec{x}\leftarrow\vec{e}) \;;\; (\vec{x}\leftarrow f(\vec{x})) = (\vec{x}\leftarrow f(\vec{e}))$ holds.

Resuming our introductory example we now obtain $(x_1, x_2\leftarrow\bot, 2) \;;\; (x_1\leftarrow x_2) = (x_1, x_2\leftarrow 2, 2)$ and furthermore $\mathbb{T} \;;\; (x_1, x_2\leftarrow 2, 2) = (x_1, x_2, \vec{x}_{3..n}\leftarrow 2, 2, \infty)$. If all expressions $\vec{e}$ are constant we have $\mathbb{T} \;;\; (\vec{x}\leftarrow\vec{e}) = (\vec{x}\leftarrow\vec{e})$. These properties hold instead of the healthiness condition H1b of designs, and demonstrate that computations in our setting are indeed non-strict.

Let us elaborate the assignment $(\vec{x}\leftarrow\vec{e})$ using $\preccurlyeq \;;\; (\vec{x}'=\vec{e}) \subseteq (\vec{x}'=\vec{e}) \;;\; \preccurlyeq$ which relationally states that the expressions $\vec{e}$ are $\preccurlyeq$-isotone [20]. The assignment then simplifies to $(\vec{x}\leftarrow\vec{e}) = (\vec{x}:=\vec{e}) \;;\; \mathbb{1}$ since

$$\mathbb{1} \;;\; (\vec{x}'=\vec{e}) \;;\; \mathbb{1} \subseteq (\vec{x}'=\vec{e}) \;;\; \mathbb{1} \;;\; \mathbb{1} = (\vec{x}'=\vec{e}) \;;\; \mathbb{1} \subseteq \mathbb{1} \;;\; (\vec{x}'=\vec{e}) \;;\; \mathbb{1} \;.$$

Hence $(\vec{x}\leftarrow\vec{e}) = (\vec{x}'=\vec{e}) \;;\; \mathbb{1} = \{(\vec{x}, \vec{x}') \mid \exists \vec{y} : \vec{y}=\vec{e}(\vec{x}) \wedge \vec{y}\preccurlyeq\vec{x}'\} = \{(\vec{x}, \vec{x}') \mid \vec{e}(\vec{x})\preccurlyeq\vec{x}'\}$. This means that the successor states of $\vec{x}$ under this assignment comprise the usual successor $\vec{e}(\vec{x})$ and its upper closure with respect to $\preccurlyeq$.

Consider the conditional statement $(P \triangleleft b \triangleright Q) = (b \cap P) \cup (\overline{b} \cap Q)$ of UTP, where the condition b is treated as a vector. In common terms this reads as 'if b then P else Q' but the definition does not take into account the possibility of b being undefined. Its extension to designs $(P \triangleleft b \triangleright Q) = (\mathcal{D}b \Rightarrow (b \cap P) \cup (\overline{b} \cap Q))$ does, but yields non-termination whenever the condition b is undefined. We therefore have to adapt the definition.

To this end, we no longer treat conditions as vectors but as $\preccurlyeq$-continuous expressions with values in $Bool$ that may depend on the input $\vec{x}$. Nevertheless, if b is a condition, the relation $b=c$ is a vector for each $c \in Bool$. Using $\vec{x}_{1..m}$ as input variables, we obtain that $(b=c) = \{(\vec{x}, \vec{x}') \mid b(\vec{x})=c\} : D_{1..m} \leftrightarrow D_{1..n}$ for arbitrary $D_{1..n}$ depending on the context. The new relation modelling the conditional 'if b then P else Q' is

$$(P \blacktriangleleft b \blacktriangleright Q) =_{\text{def}} b=\infty \cup (b=\bot \cap \vec{x}'=\bot) \cup (b=true \cap P) \cup (b=false \cap Q) \;.$$

The effect of an undefined condition in a conditional statement is to set all variables of the current state undefined. By Lemma 2 we can indeed replace $b=\infty \cup (b=\bot \cap \vec{x}'=\bot)$ with $(b=\infty \cap \vec{x}\leftarrow\infty) \cup (b=\bot \cap \vec{x}\leftarrow\bot)$. This models the fact that the evaluation of b is always necessary if the execution of the conditional is. Any non-termination or undefinedness is thus propagated.

As in UTP, the law $(P \blacktriangleleft b \blacktriangleright P) = P$ holds if b is defined, but not in general since an implementation cannot check if both branches of a conditional are equal. The conditional shall have lower precedence than sequential composition.

4.4   Variables

Variables are added to and removed from the current state by UTP's variable declaration **var** $x_i = (\exists x_i : \mathbb{I})$ and undeclaration **end** $x_i = (\exists x_i' : \mathbb{I})$. These relations are not homogeneous: The declaration includes x_i' in its range but not x_i in its domain, and the undeclaration the other way round.

Again we have to adapt the statements to respect the healthiness conditions $\mathscr{H}_L$ and $\mathscr{H}_R$. The new relations modelling the simultaneous (un)declaration of the variables $\vec{x}_K$ are **var** $\vec{x}_K =_{\text{def}} (\exists \vec{x}_K : \mathbb{1})$ and **end** $\vec{x}_K =_{\text{def}} (\exists \vec{x}_K' : \mathbb{1})$.

Since **var** $\vec{x}_K = \mathbb{1}$; $(\exists \vec{x}_K : \mathbb{I})$ can be shown, the declaration itself does not impose any restriction on the new variables. This means that accessing a declared but uninitialised variable results in non-termination. A more appropriate statement that yields undefinedness instead can be obtained by using **var** $\vec{x}_K$; $(\vec{x}_K \leftarrow \bot)$. Alternatively, the language designer may opt to allow only initialised variable declarations (**var** $\vec{x}_K \leftarrow \vec{e}_K$) $=_{\text{def}}$ **var** $\vec{x}_K$; $(\vec{x}_K \leftarrow \vec{e}_K)$. The expressions $\vec{e}_K$ must not refer to the new variables $\vec{x}_K$ in this case.

The alphabet extension is UTP's mechanism to hide local variables from recursive calls. It is given by $P_{+x_i} = (x_i'=x_i) \cap \textbf{end } x_i$; P ; **var** x_i, making explicit the change of P's type. The domain of P is extended by x_i and the range by x_i', and both are equated.

To adapt the alphabet extension to our setting, let $P : D_I \leftrightarrow D_J$ be a (possibly heterogeneous) relation and K such that $I \cap K = J \cap K = \emptyset$. The new alphabet extension of P by the variables $\vec{x}_K$ is $P^{+\vec{x}_K} : D_{I \cup K} \leftrightarrow D_{J \cup K}$ given by

$$P^{+\vec{x}_K} =_{\text{def}} \textbf{end } \vec{x}_I \ ; \ \textbf{var } \vec{x}_J \cap \textbf{end } \vec{x}_K \ ; \ P \ ; \ \textbf{var } \vec{x}_K \ .$$

Intuitively, the part **end** $\vec{x}_I$; **var** $\vec{x}_J$ preserves the values of $\vec{x}_K$ and the part **end** $\vec{x}_K$; P ; **var** $\vec{x}_K$ applies P to $\vec{x}_I$ to obtain $\vec{x}_J$. Just as the variable undeclaration may be seen as a projection, the alphabet extension is an instance of relational parallel composition. This follows since $P^{+\vec{x}_K} = (\mathbb{1}P\mathbb{1})_I\|_K \mathbb{1}$, which simplifies to $P_I\|_K \mathbb{1}$ if $\mathscr{H}_E(P)$ holds. While this resembles [15, Definition 9.1.3], the parallel composition of designs is different as regards termination. It is typically as complex to prove a result for the more general $P\|Q$ as it is for $P^{+\vec{x}_K}$.

4.5   Isotony and Neutrality

We have introduced a selection of programming constructs as summarised in the following definition. This selection subsumes the imperative, non-deterministic

core of UTP and hence is rich enough to yield a basic programming and specification language.

Definition 3. *We use the following relations and operations:*

skip	$\mathbb{1} =_{\text{def}} \preccurlyeq$
assignment	$(\vec{x} \leftarrow \vec{e}) =_{\text{def}} \mathbb{1} \; ; \; (\vec{x} := \vec{e}) \; ; \; \mathbb{1}$
variable declaration	$\boldsymbol{var} \; \vec{x}_K =_{\text{def}} (\exists \vec{x}_K : \mathbb{1})$
variable undeclaration	$\boldsymbol{end} \; \vec{x}_K =_{\text{def}} (\exists \vec{x}'_K : \mathbb{1})$
parallel composition	$P \| Q$
sequential composition	$P \; ; \; Q$
conditional	$(P \blacktriangleleft b \blacktriangleright Q) =_{\text{def}} b = \infty \cup (b = \bot \cap \vec{x}' = \bot) \cup$
	$\quad (b = \textit{true} \cap P) \cup (b = \textit{false} \cap Q)$
non-deterministic choice	$P \cup Q$
conjunction of co-directed set S	$\bigcap_{P \in S} P$
greatest fixpoint	$\nu f =_{\text{def}} \bigcup \{P \mid f(P) = P\}$

No new definitions are given for sequential composition, the non-deterministic
choice and the fixpoint operator. They are just the familiar operations of relation
algebra. This simplifies reasoning because it enables applying familiar laws, like
distribution of ; over $\cup$, also to programs. We use the *greatest* fixpoint to define the semantics of specifications given by recursive equations, and thus obtain
demonic non-determinism. This is consistent with UTP, which uses the term
'weakest fixed point' and the notation μ, but with the reverse order. The specification $P = f(P)$ is resolved as $\nu(\lambda P.f(P))$ which we abbreviate as $\nu P.f(P)$.
For example, the iteration *while b do P* is just $\nu X.(P \; ; \; X \blacktriangleleft b \blacktriangleright \mathbb{1})$.

We conclude our compendium of programming constructs by two useful results. The first states isotony of functions on programs with respect to refinement
$\sqsubseteq$, which is important for the existence of fixpoints needed to solve recursive
equations. Corresponding to the healthiness conditions H1a and H3 of designs,
the second result establishes $\mathbb{1}$ as a left and a right unit of sequential composition,
which is useful to terminate iterations and to obtain a one-sided conditional.

Theorem 4. *All functions composed of the constructs of Definition 3 are $\sqsubseteq$-
isotone. All relations composed of these constructs satisfy $\mathscr{H}_L$ and $\mathscr{H}_R$.*

Actually, these results hold for more constructs than those of Definition 3, for
example, also for the infinite choice $\bigcup$, least fixpoints, arbitrary conjunctions
and any constant relations satisfying $\mathscr{H}_L$ and $\mathscr{H}_R$, including assignments and
conditionals with isotone expressions. These additional constructs are further
investigated in [11] for flat D_i. The theory presented in this section is a proper
generalisation of the previous results to arbitrary partial orders containing $\bot$
and a least element ∞. Most results below also apply to further constructs.

5   Continuity

A function f on relations is called *co-continuous* iff it distributes over infima of
co-directed sets of relations, formally $f(\bigcap S) = \bigcap_{P \in S} f(P)$ for each co-directed

set S. The importance of continuity comes from the permission to represent the greatest fixpoint νf by the constructive $\bigcap_{n\in\mathbb{N}} f^n(\mathbb{T})$. This enables the approximation of νf by repeatedly unfolding f, which simulates recursive calls of the modelled computation. However, unbounded non-determinism breaks continuity as shown, for example, in [7, Chapter 9] and [4, Section 5.7]. Sources of unbounded non-determinism in our theory are the use of

- unrestricted non-deterministic choice $\bigsqcup$ and
- finite choice $\sqcup$ within (recursively constructed) infinite data structures.

Considering Definition 3, we have already banned $\bigsqcup$ and are about to replace its use by $\bigcap$ for the greatest fixpoint. The remaining source of unbounded non-determinism can be neutralised in either of two ways: by restriction to orders with finite height or to deterministic programs.

Our previous work [11] pursues the first approach by assuming D_i to be flat orders (actually, finite height suffices). Before presenting its main result, we characterise *boundedly non-deterministic* programs, see [7,13,35]. Traditionally, this requires that each state $\vec{x}$ has finitely many successor states $P(\vec{x})$, given by the image under the relation P. We adapt this to our context using the pointwise minima with respect to $\preccurlyeq$.

Definition 5. $\mathcal{H}_B(P) \Leftrightarrow_{\text{def}} \forall \vec{x} : |\min P(\vec{x})| \in \mathbb{N}$, *where the minimal elements of* $A \subseteq D_{1..n}$ *are* $\min A =_{\text{def}} \{x \mid x \in A \wedge \forall y : (y \in A \wedge y \preccurlyeq x) \Rightarrow y = x\}$.

This way the condition $\mathcal{H}_B$ accounts for the proper successor states, excluding those that have been added for technical reasons by forming the upper closure. Using $\mathcal{H}_B$ we can show the following statements.

Theorem 6. *Assume that the ranges* D_i *have finite height.*

1. *Relations composed of the constructs of Definition 3 satisfy* $\mathcal{H}_B$.
2. *Functions composed of the constructs of Definition 3 are co-continuous, that is, they distribute over infima of co-directed sets of relations satisfying* $\mathcal{H}_E$ *and* $\mathcal{H}_B$.
3. *Relations composed of the constructs of Definition 3 are total.*

The former approach suffices for basic data structures, but excludes functions as values and infinite data structures. However, the problem is not caused by the orders with infinite height, but by having non-determinism at the same time, since this introduces relations with infinitely many proper successor states. Our new proposal therefore is to restrict relations to represent deterministic programs. This is sufficient to show continuity even in the presence of infinite data structures. While the restriction to deterministic programs may seem harsh, it is characteristic of many programming languages and does not preclude the use of non-deterministic choice for specification purposes. Similarly to $\mathcal{H}_B$ above, we characterise deterministic computations in our context by the following $\mathcal{H}_D$.

Definition 7. $\mathcal{H}_D(P) \Leftrightarrow_{\text{def}} (\operatorname{lea} P)\mathbb{T} = \mathbb{T}$, *where* $\operatorname{lea} P =_{\text{def}} P \cap \overline{P; \succcurlyeq}$ *is the pointwise least elements of* P *with respect to* $\preccurlyeq$. *Moreover, let* $\mathcal{H}_C(P)$ *hold iff* $(\forall \vec{x} \in S : (\vec{x}, \vec{x}') \in P) \Rightarrow (\sup S, \vec{x}') \in P$ *for every directed set* S *ordered by* $\preccurlyeq$.

By taking the pointwise least elements, also $\mathscr{H}_D$ accounts for the proper successor states. The condition $\mathscr{H}_C$ is needed to prove part 2 of the following result and generalises $\preccurlyeq$-continuity to relations. If P satisfies $\mathscr{H}_R$ and $\mathscr{H}_D$, the relation lea P is a mapping that is $\preccurlyeq$-continuous iff P satisfies $\mathscr{H}_L$ and $\mathscr{H}_C$.

Theorem 8. *Consider Definition 3 without the choice operator.*

1. *Relations composed of these constructs satisfy $\mathscr{H}_D$ and $\mathscr{H}_C$. In particular, they are total.*
2. *Functions composed of these constructs are co-continuous, that is, they distribute over infima of co-directed sets of relations satisfying $\mathscr{H}_E$ and $\mathscr{H}_D$ and $\mathscr{H}_C$.*

We thus obtain a theory of non-strict computations over infinite data structures by restricting ourselves to deterministic programs. Future work shall investigate whether another trade-off is possible to reconcile non-determinism and infinite data structures. Theorems 4 and 8 are the main results to guarantee that the application of our theory in the next section is meaningful.

6   Infinite Data Structures

Supporting infinite data structures in a theory is nice, but one also needs means to construct and use them in programs. In this section we focus on lists, but our discussion also applies to more general structures such as infinite trees.

To see the difficulties involved, let us start with a simple example, the infinite list $ones = 1 : ones$. We assume that the type of lists of integers has been defined as $IntList = Nil + (Int : IntList)$ with non-strict constructors : and Nil. Our first attempt is a program P with one variable xs whose final value should be the required list:
$$P = (xs\leftarrow 1{:}xs) \; ; \; P \; .$$

However, its solution $\nu P.(xs\leftarrow 1{:}xs) \; ; \; P$ equals $\mathbb{T}$ by totality of the assignment. Obviously, non-strict computations do not prohibit programs from running into endless loops. But endless loops have no effect if their results are not needed, so we might instead try
$$P = P \; ; \; (xs\leftarrow 1{:}xs) \; .$$

And this works indeed, which we can confirm by calculating the greatest fixpoint of $f(P) = P \; ; \; (xs\leftarrow 1{:}xs)$. Using Theorem 8.2 we obtain $\nu f = \bigcap_{n\in\mathbb{N}} f^n(\mathbb{T})$ where

$$
\begin{aligned}
f^0(\mathbb{T}) &= \mathbb{T} \\
f^1(\mathbb{T}) &= \mathbb{T} \; ; \; (xs\leftarrow 1{:}xs) = (xs\leftarrow\infty) \; ; \; (xs\leftarrow 1{:}xs) = (xs\leftarrow 1{:}\infty) \\
f^2(\mathbb{T}) &= f(xs\leftarrow 1{:}\infty) = (xs\leftarrow 1{:}\infty) \; ; \; (xs\leftarrow 1{:}xs) = (xs\leftarrow 1{:}1{:}\infty) \\
f^3(\mathbb{T}) &= f(xs\leftarrow 1{:}1{:}\infty) = (xs\leftarrow 1{:}1{:}\infty) \; ; \; (xs\leftarrow 1{:}xs) = (xs\leftarrow 1{:}1{:}1{:}\infty)
\end{aligned}
$$

Lemma 2 is applied to calculate $f^1(\mathbb{T})$. Thus $f^n(\mathbb{T}) = (xs\leftarrow(1{:})^n\infty)$ and we have $\nu f = (xs\leftarrow ones)$.

Let us try to obtain the infinite list of natural numbers $nats = 0 : 1 : 2 : 3 : \ldots$ next. Our program should have two variables xs and c to hold the result and to count, respectively. Again the obvious first try $P = (xs\leftarrow c{:}xs)$; $(c\leftarrow c{+}1)$; P, assuming the initial value 0 for c, does not work. The above trick to reverse the construction is fruitless in this case, yielding

$$P = P \; ; \; (xs\leftarrow c{:}xs) \; ; \; (c\leftarrow c{+}1) \, .$$

In fact, this program assigns the infinite list $\infty : \infty : \infty : \ldots$ to xs. For example, if we try to access the first element of xs, the computation does not terminate, because to obtain the final value of c one has to unfold P infinitely. Even if the computation terminated, two further problems would arise: The constructed list would be decreasing (for example, the first element of xs is one larger than the second), and there is no initial value of c where this decreasing sequence could start. This could be avoided by using

$$P = P \; ; \; (c\leftarrow c{-}1) \; ; \; (xs\leftarrow c{:}xs) \, ,$$

and *somehow* ensuring that the final value of c is 0. Such a procedure we do not pursue, since not every computation can be inverted (like the increment of c by its decrement). The solution is to compute the value of c before the recursive call and to construct the sequence afterwards, as in

$$P = (c\leftarrow c{+}1) \; ; \; P \; ; \; (xs\leftarrow c{:}xs) \, .$$

We only have to make sure that the value of c is saved across the recursive call, so that it can be prepended to the list. The alphabet extension comes in handy:

$$P = (\textbf{var } t\leftarrow c) \; ; \; (c\leftarrow c{+}1) \; ; \; P^{+t} \; ; \; (xs\leftarrow t{:}xs) \; ; \; \textbf{end } t \, .$$

Using $f(P) = (\textbf{var } t\leftarrow c)$; $(c\leftarrow c{+}1)$; P^{+t} ; $(xs\leftarrow t{:}xs)$; $\textbf{end } t$, we obtain

$$
\begin{aligned}
f^0(\mathbb{T}) &= \mathbb{T} \\
f^1(\mathbb{T}) &= (\textbf{var } t\leftarrow c) \; ; \; (c\leftarrow c{+}1) \; ; \; \mathbb{T}^{+t} \; ; \; (xs\leftarrow t{:}xs) \; ; \; \textbf{end } t \\
&= (\textbf{var } t\leftarrow c) \; ; \; (c\leftarrow c{+}1) \; ; \; (\mathbb{T}_{xs,c}\|_t \mathbb{1}) \; ; \; (xs\leftarrow t{:}xs) \; ; \; \textbf{end } t \\
&= (\textbf{var } t\leftarrow c) \; ; \; (c\leftarrow c{+}1) \; ; \; (xs, c, t\leftarrow\infty, \infty, t) \; ; \; (xs\leftarrow t{:}xs) \; ; \; \textbf{end } t \\
&= (\textbf{var } t\leftarrow c) \; ; \; (c\leftarrow\infty) \; ; \; (xs\leftarrow t{:}\infty) \; ; \; \textbf{end } t \\
&= (xs, c\leftarrow c{:}\infty, \infty) \\
f^2(\mathbb{T}) &= (\textbf{var } t\leftarrow c) \; ; \; (c\leftarrow c{+}1) \; ; \; (xs, c\leftarrow c{:}\infty, \infty)^{+t} \; ; \; (xs\leftarrow t{:}xs) \; ; \; \textbf{end } t \\
&= (\textbf{var } t\leftarrow c) \; ; \; (xs, c, t\leftarrow c{+}1{:}\infty, \infty, t) \; ; \; (xs\leftarrow t{:}xs) \; ; \; \textbf{end } t \\
&= (xs, c\leftarrow c{:}c{+}1{:}\infty, \infty) \\
f^3(\mathbb{T}) &= (xs, c\leftarrow c{:}c{+}1{:}c{+}2{:}\infty, \infty)
\end{aligned}
$$

Thus $f^n(\mathbb{T}) = (xs, c\leftarrow c : c{+}1 : c{+}2 : \ldots : c{+}n{-}1 : \infty, \infty)$ and we obtain $(c\leftarrow 0)$; $\nu f = (xs, c\leftarrow nats, \infty)$.

The above program to construct $nats$ is motivated by the recursive definition $nats(c) = c : nats(c{+}1)$ of the natural numbers from c, also called *enumFrom* in Haskell. Its recursion pattern is the well-known symmetric linear recursion, which is sufficiently general to subsume cata-, ana-, hylo- and paramorphisms [19] or folds and unfolds [9] on lists. For example, in functional programming languages the latter are characterised by

$$unfold(p, f, g, x) = \textbf{if } p(x) \textbf{ then } Nil \textbf{ else } f(x) : unfold(p, f, g, g(x)) \ ,$$

where the parameter p represents the terminating condition, f constructs the values of the list and g modifies the seed x. Note that p, f and g are constant parameters. We may realise *unfold* by the program

$$P = (xs\leftarrow Nil \blacktriangleleft p(x) \blacktriangleright \textbf{var } t\leftarrow f(x) \ ; \ x\leftarrow g(x) \ ; \ P^{+t} \ ; \ xs\leftarrow t{:}xs \ ; \ \textbf{end } t) \ .$$

Instantiating $p(x) = false$, $f(x) = x$ and $g(x) = x{+}1$ we obtain the program for *nats*. Also *ones* may be recovered by $p(x) = false$ and $f(x) = g(x) = 1$. In such instances, where termination is not available or not guaranteed, our program P is more general than in strict UTP. Moreover, it is not necessary to compute the result entirely, but only to the required precision.

Let us now consider several further examples, starting with the list-consuming counterpart

$$foldr(f, z, xs) = \textbf{if } isNil(xs) \textbf{ then } z \textbf{ else } f(head(xs), foldr(f, z, tail(xs))) \ .$$

We may realise *foldr* by the program

$$P = (r\leftarrow z \blacktriangleleft isNil(xs) \blacktriangleright \textbf{var } t\leftarrow head(xs) \ ; \ xs\leftarrow tail(xs) \ ; \ P^{+t} \ ; \\ r\leftarrow f(t, r) \ ; \ \textbf{end } t)$$

that is able to process finite and infinite xs, provided f is non-strict. The dual *foldl* immediately returns from its recursive calls and therefore does not work on infinite lists in general, but *scanl* does. Instantiating *foldr* with $f(t, r) = g(t) : r$ and $z = Nil$ we obtain a program to compute $map(g, xs)$, leaving the result in r. Instantiating *foldr* with $f(t, r) = \textbf{if } p(t) \textbf{ then } t : r \textbf{ else } r$ and $z = Nil$ we obtain *filter*(p, xs). This shows that we can program using list comprehensions, even on infinite lists. For example, $[\ f(x) \mid x \leftarrow xs, \ p(x)\ ]$ is obtained by

$$P = (ys\leftarrow Nil \blacktriangleleft isNil(xs) \blacktriangleright \textbf{var } t\leftarrow head(xs) \ ; \ xs\leftarrow tail(xs) \ ; \ P^{+t} \ ; \\ (ys\leftarrow f(t){:}ys \blacktriangleleft p(t) \blacktriangleright \mathbb{1}) \ ; \ \textbf{end } t) \ .$$

It consumes the input list xs and produces the output list ys. We could also call the result xs, but generally its type differs from that of xs, hence P is a heterogeneous relation. Note that only the value of the variable xs is updated during the recursion, but there is no destructive update to the original list that is persistent and could be referenced by another variable.

As our final example, here is the 'unfaithful' prime number sieve [24], entirely in terms of the constructs of Section 4:

$$primes = from2 \ ; \ sieve$$
$$from2 = \textbf{var } c\leftarrow 2 \ ; \ (\nu R. \textbf{var } t\leftarrow c \ ; \ c\leftarrow c{+}1 \ ; \ R^{+t} \ ; \ xs\leftarrow t{:}xs \ ; \ \textbf{end } t) \ ; \ \textbf{end } c$$
$$sieve = \nu R. \textbf{var } p\leftarrow head(xs) \ ; \ xs\leftarrow tail(xs) \ ; \ remove \ ; \ R^{+p} \ ; \ xs\leftarrow p{:}xs \ ; \ \textbf{end } p$$
$$remove = \nu R. \textbf{var } q, t\leftarrow p, head(xs) \ ; \ xs\leftarrow tail(xs) \ ; \ R^{+q,t} \ ; \ p\leftarrow q \ ; \ div \ ; \ \textbf{end } q, t$$
$$div = (\mathbb{1} \blacktriangleleft p|t \blacktriangleright xs\leftarrow t{:}xs)$$

This may seem verbose compared to its Haskell equivalent, but it uses neither parameters and pattern matching, nor concise notations such as $[\,2..\,]$ for *from2* and $[\,t \mid t \leftarrow xs,\, p \nmid t\,]$ for *remove* available in Haskell. Such concepts shall be added to our language in the future. Our program can be executed in such a way that only so many prime numbers are computed as actually required. But also with finite data structures a lazy execution may be advantageous. For example, we have devised versions of mergesort and heapsort in our framework which, for lists of length n, perform at most $O(n \log n)$ comparisons, but fewer if only the initial elements of the sorted sequence are required.

7   Dependence

Undefined and defined variables may coexist according to our relational theory of computations. In this section we discuss two aspects of non-strictness that can be described in terms of dependence of variables. We first illustrate the issue for the case $m = n = 1$, that is, a single input and output variable, and then present the resulting, additional healthiness conditions.

Consider a relation R with an $x_1' \neq \bot$ such that $(\bot, x_1') \in R$, thus R produces a defined output for an undefined input. If x_1' is to be computed by a program, its value must not depend on the value of x_1 or else the input $x_1 = \bot$ would result in the output $x_1' = \bot$. In other words, there must be a constant assignment to x_1'. We therefore obtain the condition $(x_1, x_1') \in R$ for all x_1. Note that we do not conclude that R equals this constant assignment, since in general R may be composed by non-deterministic choice from the constant assignment and some non-constant computation.

Now consider a relation R with $(\bot, \bot) \notin R$, thus R does not produce an undefined output for an undefined input. Then indeed there cannot be non-constant computations and the value of x_1' must not depend on the value of the input x_1 at all. Hence we must ensure that *only* constant assignments occur. This is achieved by requiring $(x_1, x_1') \in R$ for all x_1, if $(x_1, x_1') \in R$ for some x_1. Note that choosing $x_1 = \bot$ yields a special case of the first condition, while $x_1' = \bot$ is prevented since it implies $(\bot, \bot) \in R$.

Both conditions can be generalised to arbitrary m and n, but the resulting formulae are very unwieldy. Fortunately, they have an elegant counterpart in order-theoretic terms, derived in [11] for flat orders, which we use directly. To this end, we introduce an order similar to $\preccurlyeq$, but now with respect to $\bot$. However, we have to restrict our data types by disallowing the use of functions as values.

The partial order $\sqsubseteq : D_i \leftrightarrow D_i$ with least element $\bot$ is constructed as follows. Elementary types are flat, that is, $x \sqsubseteq y \Leftrightarrow_{\mathrm{def}} x = \bot \vee x = y$. The finite union of D_i is ordered by $x \sqsubseteq y \Leftrightarrow_{\mathrm{def}} x = \bot \vee x = \infty = y \vee (x = (i, x_i) \wedge y = (i, y_i) \wedge x_i \sqsubseteq_{D_i} y_i)$. The finite product of types D_i is ordered by the pointwise extension of $\sqsubseteq$, that is, $\vec{x}_I \sqsubseteq \vec{y}_I \Leftrightarrow_{\mathrm{def}} \forall i \in I : x_i \sqsubseteq_{D_i} y_i$. The constituents of the inverse limit construction for recursive data types are ordered pointwise. Using the new order, we obtain an algebraic characterisation of the healthiness conditions, where $\sqsupseteq =_{\mathrm{def}} \sqsubseteq^{\smile}$ denotes the dual order of $\sqsubseteq$.

Definition 9. $\mathcal{H}_N(R) \Leftrightarrow_{\text{def}} \sqsupseteq\ ;\ R \subseteq R\ ;\ \sqsupseteq$ *and* $\mathcal{H}_A(R) \Leftrightarrow_{\text{def}} \sqsubseteq\ ;\ R \subseteq R\ ;\ \sqsubseteq$.

If R is a mapping, the condition $\mathcal{H}_N(R)$ is equivalent to $\mathcal{H}_A(R)$ and states that R is isotone with respect to $\sqsupseteq$. Actually, a relation R satisfying $ER \subseteq RE$ and $E^\smile R \subseteq RE^\smile$ for a partial order E is also called an 'isotone relation' [38] and an 'order preserving multifunction' [34]. These works investigate the 'relational fixed point property' [33], a property of the order E rather than of functions over relations.

Remark. The new healthiness conditions are related to the Egli-Milner order on powerdomains built from flat domains [27,30]. Indeed, one can interpret the conjunction of $\mathcal{H}_N$ and $\mathcal{H}_A$ as imposing the Egli-Milner order on the image sets of relations. This order is frequently used in semantics to define the least fixpoint of functions. Let us therefore emphasise that $\sqsubseteq$ serves to support our reasoning about undefinedness, that is, finite failure. It is not used to approximate fixpoints, which we do by the subset order $\subseteq$ that (with closure under $\preccurlyeq$) corresponds to an order based on wp. In [23] two orders based on wp and wlp are combined for approximation. In fact the Egli-Milner order models erratic non-determinism or general correctness, but UTP's and our definitions model demonic non-determinism or total correctness. The difference is expounded in [23,35] in more detail. A general correctness variant of UTP is explored in [8].

We can show that our programming constructs satisfy $\mathcal{H}_N$ and $\mathcal{H}_A$. To deal with the assignment and the conditional, we assume that the expressions are $\sqsubseteq$-isotone in addition to being $\preccurlyeq$-continuous.

Theorem 10. *Relations composed of the constructs of Definition 3 without the choice operator satisfy $\mathcal{H}_N$ and $\mathcal{H}_A$.*

The conditions $\mathcal{H}_N$ and $\mathcal{H}_A$ can also be seen as expressing an information preservation principle. In this interpretation $\sqsubseteq$ is the definedness information order and $\mathcal{H}_N$ and $\mathcal{H}_A$ convey definedness information. Corresponding healthiness conditions for the termination information order $\preccurlyeq$ are discussed in [11] and can also be generalised to the present setting of more general orders.

8   Conclusion

We have proposed a new relational approach to define the semantics of imperative programs. Let us summarise its key properties and its extensions to UTP.

- Undefinedness and non-termination are treated independently of each other. Finite and infinite failure can thus be distinguished, which is closer to practice and allows one to model recovery from errors. A fine distinction is offered by dealing with undefinedness separately for individual variables.
- The theory provides a relational model of dependence in computations. Additional healthiness conditions are stated in a compact algebraic form and can therefore be applied easily to new programs given as relations.

– The relations model non-strict computations in an imperative context. Efficiency can thus be improved by executing only those parts of programs necessary to obtain the final results. Programs can construct and process infinite data structures. The theory can serve as a basis to link to the semantics of functional programming languages.

The disadvantages of a possibly lazy evaluation are of course a potential overhead and reduced predictability of execution time, space and order.

We thus obtain a theory similar to that of designs but modelling non-strict computations. In particular, the left and right unit laws $\mathcal{H}_L$ and $\mathcal{H}_R$ and the totality property correspond to the healthiness conditions H1–H4 of designs without the left zero law $\mathbb{T} ; R = \mathbb{T}$. For elementary, sum and product types, all functions composed of programming constructs are continuous and all relations composed of programming constructs are boundedly non-deterministic. With infinite data types, continuity holds for the functions composed of deterministic programming constructs. Additionally, the relations satisfy the healthiness conditions $\mathcal{H}_N$ and $\mathcal{H}_A$ modelling the dependence of variables.

Our programming constructs introduced in Definition 3 are sufficiently similar to the original constructs of UTP to show that they yield the same results whenever the computations are defined and terminate. This correspondence is formally stated in [11] for elementary data types, but can be extended to the present, more general case. As another measure to ensure the adequacy of our framework, an operational semantics is outlined to describe the execution of programs. Future work shall extend the operational semantics to cover infinite data structures.

These observations also show the advantage of the UTP approach: We are able to compare different theories describing the semantics of programs within the same framework. Their similarities and differences are particularly apparent in the effective healthiness conditions. Such characterising properties are expressed concisely due to the fact that UTP is based on relations.

Connections to related work have been pointed out throughout this paper. In [12] we compare our work with further relational and functional approaches, including the Z notation [16,39], Haskell's I/O monad [17,25] and state transformers [18], and the multi-paradigm language Oz [29]. This is extended by the following notes.

Relations satisfying $\mathcal{H}_E$ are called 'ideal relations' by [20] and used to model higher order programming. The investigation aims at defining the semantics by predicate transformers rather than relations [21]. Accordingly, there is no special value to treat non-termination, which is not distinguished from undefinedness. Elementary data types have a discrete order. In [22], ideal relations are also used as 'couplings' to connect state spaces for data refinement.

Let us finally point out two topics that deserve further investigation. One of them is to explore our relational model as an intermediate for the translation of functional programming languages. The other is concerned with the connections to data flow networks [15, Section 8.3] and, in particular, to the algebra of stream processing functions [5].

Acknowledgement. I am grateful to the anonymous referees for their helpful remarks, fair criticism and interesting questions.

References

1. Abramsky, S., Jung, A.: Domain theory. In: Abramsky, S., Gabbay, D.M., Maibaum, T.S.E. (eds.) Handbook of Logic in Computer Science, Semantic Structures, vol. 3, ch. 1, pp. 1–168. Clarendon Press (1994)
2. Backhouse, R.C., de Bruin, P.J., Hoogendijk, P., Malcolm, G., Voermans, E., van der Woude, J.: Polynomial relators (extended abstract). In: Nivat, M., Rattray, C., Rus, T., Scollo, G. (eds.) Algebraic Methodology and Software Technology, pp. 303–326. Springer, Heidelberg (1992)
3. Berghammer, R., von Karger, B.: Relational semantics of functional programs. In: Brink, C., Kahl, W., Schmidt, G. (eds.) Relational Methods in Computer Science, ch. 8, pp. 115–130. Springer, Wien (1997)
4. Broy, M., Gnatz, R., Wirsing, M.: Semantics of nondeterministic and noncontinuous constructs. In: Bauer, F.L., Broy, M. (eds.) Program Construction. LNCS, vol. 69, pp. 553–592. Springer, Heidelberg (1979)
5. Broy, M., Ştefănescu, G.: The algebra of stream processing functions. Theoretical Computer Science 258(1–2), 99–129 (2001)
6. Davey, B.A., Priestley, H.A.: Introduction to Lattices and Order, 2nd edn. Cambridge University Press, Cambridge (2002)
7. Dijkstra, E.W.: A Discipline of Programming. Prentice Hall, Englewood Cliffs (1976)
8. Dunne, S.: Recasting Hoare and He's Unifying Theory of Programs in the context of general correctness. In: Butterfield, A., Strong, G., Pahl, C. (eds.) 5th Irish Workshop on Formal Methods. Electronic Workshops in Computing. The British Computer Society (July 2001)
9. Gibbons, J., Jones, G.: The under-appreciated unfold. In: Proceedings of the third ACM SIGPLAN International Conference on Functional Programming, pp. 273–279. ACM Press, New York (1998)
10. Guttmann, W.: Non-termination in Unifying Theories of Programming. In: MacCaull, W., Winter, M., Düntsch, I. (eds.) RelMiCS 2005. LNCS, vol. 3929, pp. 108–120. Springer, Heidelberg (2006)
11. Guttmann, W.: Algebraic Foundations of the Unifying Theories of Programming. PhD thesis, Universität Ulm (December 2007)
12. Guttmann, W.: Lazy relations. In: Berghammer, R., Möller, B., Struth, G. (eds.) RelMiCS/AKA 2008. LNCS, vol. 4988, pp. 138–154. Springer, Heidelberg (2008)
13. Hesselink, W.H.: Programs, Recursion and Unbounded Choice. Cambridge University Press, Cambridge (1992)
14. Hoare, C.A.R.: Theories of programming: Top-down and bottom-up and meeting in the middle. In: Wing, J.M., Woodcock, J., Davies, J. (eds.) FM 1999. LNCS, vol. 1708, pp. 1–27. Springer, Heidelberg (1999)
15. Hoare, C.A.R., He, J.: Unifying theories of programming. Prentice Hall Europe (1998)
16. ISO/IEC. Information technology: Z formal specification notation: Syntax, type system and semantics. ISO/IEC 13568:2002(E) (July 2002)
17. Launchbury, J.: Lazy imperative programming. In: Hudak, P. (ed.) Proceedings of the ACM SIGPLAN Workshop on State in Programming Languages. Yale University Research Report YALEU/DCS/RR-968, pp. 46–56 (June 1993)

18. Launchbury, J., Peyton Jones, S.: State in Haskell. Lisp and Symbolic Computation 8(4), 293–341 (1995)
19. Meijer, E., Fokkinga, M., Paterson, R.: Functional programming with bananas, lenses, envelopes and barbed wire. In: Hughes, J. (ed.) FPCA 1991. LNCS, vol. 523, pp. 124–144. Springer, Heidelberg (1991)
20. Naumann, D.A.: A categorical model for higher order imperative programming. Mathematical Structures in Computer Science 8(4), 351–399 (1998)
21. Naumann, D.A.: Predicate transformer semantics of a higher-order imperative language with record subtyping. Science of Computer Programming 41(1), 1–51 (2001)
22. Naumann, D.A.: Soundness of data refinement for a higher-order imperative language. Theoretical Computer Science 278(1–2), 271–301 (2002)
23. Nelson, G.: A generalization of Dijkstra's calculus. ACM Transactions on Programming Languages and Systems 11(4), 517–561 (1989)
24. O'Neill, M.E.: The genuine sieve of Eratosthenes. Journal of Functional Programming 19(1), 95–106 (2009)
25. Peyton Jones, S. (ed.): Haskell 98 Language and Libraries: The Revised Report. Cambridge University Press, Cambridge (2003)
26. Plasmeijer, R., van Eekelen, M.: Functional Programming and Parallel Graph Rewriting. Addison-Wesley, Reading (1993)
27. Plotkin, G.D.: A powerdomain construction. SIAM Journal on Computing 5(3), 452–487 (1976)
28. de Roever, W.-P.: Recursive program schemes: semantics and proof theory. Mathematical Centre Tracts, vol. 70. Mathematisch Centrum, Amsterdam (1976)
29. Van Roy, P., Haridi, S.: Concepts, Techniques, and Models of Computer Programming. MIT Press, Cambridge (2004)
30. Schmidt, D.A.: Denotational Semantics: A Methodology for Language Development. William C. Brown Publishers (1986)
31. Schmidt, G., Hattensperger, C., Winter, M.: Heterogeneous relation algebra. In: Brink, C., Kahl, W., Schmidt, G. (eds.) Relational Methods in Computer Science, ch. 3, pp. 39–53. Springer, Wien (1997)
32. Schmidt, G., Ströhlein, T.: Relationen und Graphen. Springer, Heidelberg (1989)
33. Schröder, B.S.W.: Ordered Sets: An Introduction. Birkhäuser, Basel (2003)
34. Smithson, R.E.: Fixed points of order preserving multifunctions. Proceedings of the American Mathematical Society 28(1), 304–310 (1971)
35. Søndergaard, H., Sestoft, P.: Non-determinism in functional languages. The Computer Journal 35(5), 514–523 (1992)
36. Stoy, J.E.: Denotational Semantics: The Scott-Strachey Approach to Programming Language Theory. MIT Press, Cambridge (1977)
37. Turner, D.A.: Miranda: A non-strict functional language with polymorphic types. In: Jouannaud, J.-P. (ed.) FPCA 1985. LNCS, vol. 201, pp. 1–16. Springer, Heidelberg (1985)
38. Walker, J.W.: Isotone relations and the fixed point property for posets. Discrete Mathematics 48(2–3), 275–288 (1984)
39. Woodcock, J., Davies, J.: Using Z. Prentice Hall, Englewood Cliffs (1996)

Monadic Maps and Folds for Multirelations in an Allegory

Clare E. Martin and Sharon A. Curtis

Oxford Brookes University, UK

Abstract. This paper contributes to the unification of semantic models and program development techniques by making a link from multirelations and predicate transformer semantics to algebraic semantics and the derivation of programs by calculation, as used in functional programming and relational program development. Two common ways to characterise iteration, namely the functional programming operators *map* and *fold*, are extended to multirelations, using concepts from category theory, power allegories and monads.

1 Introduction

Multirelations were introduced by Rewitzky [1] in the context of complete atomic boolean algebras, and they generalise relations in the same way that relations generalise functions: they are relations whose target type is a powerset type. Whilst ordinary relations model specifications by relating inputs to output values, multirelations relate inputs to guarantees (predicates) on the outputs, and are thus able to model two kinds of nondeterminism: angelic choices made in "our" interest, and demonic choices made by another party. The ability to express dual nondeterminism is extremely useful for modelling many different kinds of two-party transactions, and indeed multirelations have been used for a variety of such purposes. For example, Dunne [2] uses them to develop an extended substitution language, and in Martin and Curtis [3,4] they are used for specification of and calculation with resource-sharing and voting protocols.

In the Unifying Theories of Programming (UTP) [5], however, programs are modelled as alphabetised relations expressed as predicates, and only demonic nondeterminism is modelled in Hoare and He's work in [5]. Cavalcanti et al [6,7] extended the UTP model to include angelic nondeterminism, providing an explicit embedding of UTP predicates into the predicate transformer model, which is known to be isomorphic to the multirelational semantic model (see [8], or Section 3) and also to the choice semantics, as presented by Back and von Wright [9].

So why investigate properties of multirelations if they are isomorphic to other semantic models? And what contribution does this make to UTP?

The answer can be seen when considering the differences between different semantic models: the style of program development and proof in the UTP model or in that of predicate transformer semantics [10] is very different from that

A. Butterfield (Ed.): UTP 2008, LNCS 5713, pp. 102–121, 2010.

in algebraic semantics, where programs are directly manipulated within the semantic model. To achieve greater unification between different semantic models it would be greatly beneficial to be able to calculate with and reason about algebras that incorporate more kinds of nondeterminism than functional and relational algebras, for example the dual angelic and demonic nondeterminism seen in predicate transformers, choice semantics and multirelations.

It remains to be seen which semantic model of dual nondeterminism best suits the calculational style, but multirelations would seem to be a good candidate. As will be seen later in this paper, they have clean algebraic definitions, facilitating point-free calculation, and unlike weakest precondition semantics that transform postcondition predicates into precondition predicates, multirelations express programs in a forward manner, relating inputs to predicates on outputs, which is more convenient for humans to think about and manipulate.

Thus, this paper contributes to the unification of semantic models and program development techniques by expanding the multirelational calculus with operators and algebraic laws found within the algebraic style of calculation used for functional and relational program development by Bird and de Moor [11,12]. The resulting laws could then be mapped back into the UTP framework.

To that end, we (i) use point-free definitions of multirelations and their operators, engendering elegant and streamlined proofs, and (ii) extend common functional programming operators to the multirelational model, hopefully paving the way for similar treatment for more such operators. In particular, this paper addresses the *map* and *fold* operators, which have a more familiar form in multirelations than in predicate transformers.

Maps and folds are useful standard computations on datatypes: maps systematically alter data whilst leaving the overall data structure unchanged, and folds perform a computation over a whole data structure yielding a result value. This paper includes a monadic construction of multirelational maps and folds. Multirelational maps and folds are not new, in fact a different construction for them, using span categories, was presented in [4]. So why are we interested in a second construction? The answer is that ultimately, we hope that this monadic approach will help with the construction of a multirelational version of a further operator from functional programming: the *unfold* operator.

An unfold is a dual kind of computation to a fold [13]: in contrast to a fold, an unfold takes an input value and produces a data structure result. The unfold operator is particularly desirable for a calculus of multirelations because several application areas of angelic and demonic nondeterminism naturally involve an unfold type of computation. For example, many two-player games, with the angel and demon as the two players, are naturally expressed as an unfold: the input value is the starting position of the game, and as the game unfolds, the data structure that emerges is the history of the moves played in the game.

This is still work in progress; we do not currently have a multirelational unfold. The construction method used to define maps and folds in [4] does not obviously dualise, and so in this paper we consider a different technique that is sometimes known as the monadic extension [14], which is a method that has been successfully dualised in some different domains [15,16].

For this work we choose the setting of *power allegories*. Allegories [17] serve the algebra of sets and relations in the same way as categories serve the algebra of sets and total functions. Power allegories have some additional properties, including the existence of a power object, but excluding negation. The attraction of this setting (covered in more depth in [18]) is that it lends itself well to point-free reasoning, which engenders elegant and streamlined proofs.

Thus the contribution of this paper is two-fold: to give a clear and readable account of how to extend maps and folds to multirelations using a lax variant of the monadic method in the power allegory setting, and to also illustrate the elegance of point-free algebraic reasoning in the multirelational model. This paves the way for future work on the definition of unfolds.

For any readers not so familiar with the category theory that this work is based on, it is hoped that this paper will still provide a glimpse into the links between the algebraic semantics traditionally used in calculational program development and the semantic models of the UTP framework. In addition, such readers can feel reassured of the existence of solid mathematical foundations behind the development of the calculus of multirelations, including the familiar *map* and *fold* operators.

The paper is structured as follows. Some preliminary definitions are given in Section 2, and the definition of a multirelation in a power allegory is introduced in Section 3. This is followed in Section 4 by the introduction of an equivalent model in which multirelations are viewed as set-valued functions. The resulting Kleisli category is derived in Section 5, and maps and folds for this model are defined in Section 6. For all proofs of laws and lemmas contributed by this paper, please refer to the appendix.

2   Preliminaries

Binary multirelations have previously been defined in the context of sets and relations [1,3], but in this paper we choose the more general setting of power allegories, because it lends itself well to point-free reasoning in the style of Bird and de Moor [12]. Therefore we begin by covering the basic definition of an allegory as seen in [17], as well as looking at two particular varieties: division allegories and power allegories.

Familiarity with basic category theory is assumed; for more details see [19] for example. The notation $p\,;q$ will be used for the composition of each pair of arrows $p : A \to B$ and $q : B \to C$, and id_A is the identity arrow on object A. Function application will be denoted by juxtaposition.

2.1   Allegories

Recall that a category can be thought of as an abstraction of sets and functions, with objects of the category being analogous to sets, and arrows being analogous to functions. Similarly, an *allegory* is an abstraction of sets and relations:

Definition 2.1. *An allegory* A *is a category endowed with three additional operators* $\subseteq$, $\cap$ *and* $\circ$, *as follows:*

- *Any two arrows with the same source and target objects can be compared with a partial order $\subseteq$, with respect to which composition is monotonic.*
- *For every pair of arrows $r, s : X \rightarrow Y$ there is an arrow $r \cap s : X \rightarrow Y$, called the* meet *of r and s, and this is characterised by the following universal property, for all arrows $q : X \rightarrow Y$:*

$$q \subseteq r \cap s \;\; \equiv \;\; (q \subseteq r) \wedge (q \subseteq s)$$

- *For each arrow $r : X \rightarrow Y$ there is a* converse *arrow $r^\circ : Y \rightarrow X$ such that for all $s : X \rightarrow Y$, $t : Y \rightarrow Z$ and $u : X \rightarrow Z$*

$$
\begin{aligned}
(r^\circ)^\circ &= r \\
r \subseteq s &\equiv r^\circ \subseteq s^\circ \\
(r\,;t)^\circ &= t^\circ\,;r^\circ \\
(r;t) \cap u &\subseteq (r \cap (u;t^\circ));t \quad \text{(modular law)}
\end{aligned}
$$

The first of the above axioms, concerning the partial order $\subseteq$, says that A is an *order-enriched category.* Such an ordering can be useful for modelling program semantics: it is typically used to define a refinement ordering between arrows.

The category **Rel** of sets and relations is thus the archetypal example of an allegory: the ordering $\subseteq$ is the familiar subset inclusion, the meet of two relations is their intersection and the converse is the relational converse. One important subcategory of **Rel** is the category of sets and total functions (**Set**). The corresponding subcategory of an allegory is characterised via the following definitions:

Definition 2.2. *An arrow $m : X \rightarrow Y$ in an allegory* A *is a* function *arrow iff*

$$id_X \subseteq m\,;m^\circ \;\; and \;\; m^\circ\,;m \subseteq id_Y.$$

In particular, note that for any allegory A, its function arrows will include its identity arrows.

Definition 2.3. *Given an allegory* A, **Fun**(A) *is defined to be the subcategory of* A *consisting of the objects and function arrows of* A.

For example, the function arrows of the allegory **Rel** are simply those relations which are also total functions. Thus we have **Fun**(**Rel**) = **Set**.

2.2   Division Allegories

There are several varieties of allegory given in [17]. A *distributive allegory* has the property that the collection of all arrows with the same source and target type form a distributive lattice [20]:

Definition 2.4. *A* distributive allegory *is an allegory together with two opera-*
tors: a nullary operator $\emptyset$ *and a binary operator* $\cup$ *(called* join*). For every pair*
of objects, there is an arrow $\emptyset_{X,Y} : X \to Y$ *such that for every arrow* $r : X \to Y$,
$\emptyset_{X,Y} \subseteq r$ *and* $r; \emptyset_{Y,Z} = \emptyset_{X,Z}$. *Also, for every pair of arrows* $r, s : X \to Y$ *there*
is an arrow $r \cup s : X \to Y$, *which is characterised by the following universal*
property for all arrows $q : X \to Y$:

$$r \cup s \subseteq q \quad \equiv \quad (r \subseteq q) \wedge (s \subseteq q)$$

and which satisfies the following laws for all $p : W \to X$ *and* $q, r, s : X \to Y$:

$$p; (r \cup s) = p; r \cup p; s$$
$$q \cap (r \cup s) = (q \cap r) \cup (q \cap s)$$

In **Rel**, $\emptyset$ returns the empty relation, and join is relational union.

Definition 2.5. *A* division allegory *is a distributive allegory with an additional*
binary division operator \, *such that for each pair of arrows with common source*
$r : Z \to Y$ *and* $s : Z \to X$, $s \backslash r : X \to Y$ *is defined by the universal property*

$$t \subseteq s \backslash r \quad \equiv \quad s; t \subseteq r$$

The interpretation of $s \backslash r$ in **Rel** is $x \ (s \backslash r) \ y \ \equiv \ \forall z : z \, s \, x \Rightarrow z \, r \, y$.

  This division operator is especially useful for specifications that involve universal quantification. This operator is sometimes known as *left division* [12], or
weakest postspecification [5]. There is a dual right division operator; we use left
division because we will use it to define multirelations in Section 3.

2.3   Power Allegories

A power allegory [17] is a division allegory that contains an analogue of the
familiar notion of a powerset. Specifically,

Definition 2.6. *A division allegory* A *is a* power allegory *if there is*

 – *for each object* X, *an object* $\mathsf{P}X$ *called the* power-object *of* X
 – *a* power transpose Λ *that for each arrow* $r : X \to Y$ *returns a function arrow*
   $\Lambda r : X \to \mathsf{P}Y$
 – *a* membership *arrow* $\ni_X : \mathsf{P}X \to X$,

These three things are defined up to isomorphism by the universal property:

$$(f = \Lambda r) \quad \equiv \quad (f; \ni \ = r) \tag{2.1}$$

The converse of $\ni$ (the subscript X will usually be omitted for brevity) is denoted
by $\in$ and in **Rel** this represents the familiar set membership relation, with the
power-object being the powerset. The power transpose in **Rel** is the function
that defines the isomorphism between relations and set-valued functions via the
universal property (2.1). The following functor is also useful:

Definition 2.7. *The* existential image functor $\mathsf{E} : \mathsf{A} \to \mathbf{Fun}(\mathsf{A})$ *is defined as:*

$$\mathsf{E}r \ \hat{=} \ \Lambda(\ni; r)$$

3   Multirelations

Set Theoretic Definition
In **Rel**, a multirelation is a relation with a powerset target, and a multirelation
$r : X \to \mathbb{P}Y$ is said to be *up-closed* if for all $x \in X$ and $U, V \subseteq Y$

$$x \, r \, U \wedge U \subseteq V \;\Rightarrow\; x \, r \, V$$

Specifications can be modelled by up-closed multirelations [1], as follows.

Interpretation
A multirelation r relates a value x to a set U if and only if, given input x,
the angel can ensure that the program r will terminate with an output value
that satisfies postcondition U, where the set U is interpreted as a predicate. Of
course, if an output value satisfies U and $U \subseteq V$, then it must also satisfy V,
hence the up-closure property. This interpretation of multirelations thus relates
input values to guarantees (predicates) on the output, one of which is chosen by
the angel. The actual output value is chosen by the demon amongst values in
the angel's chosen guarantee set.

Predicate Transformer Correspondence
The weakest precondition predicate transformer $wp.r$ that corresponds to the
multirelation $r : X \to \mathbb{P}Y$ is given by

$$x \in wp.r.U \;\equiv\; (x, U) \in r$$

When multirelations are used to model programs and specifications, the up-
closure property corresponds to the monotonicity requirement of predicate transformer models.

3.1   Multirelations in an Allegory

The above set-theoretic definition of a multirelation is useful from an intuitive
point of view, but it is difficult to reason about equationally, as was seen in
[3], because the associated definition of multirelation composition is unwieldy to
calculate with. Therefore we now give a new alternative pointfree definition in
the setting of a power allegory, which is easier to reason about.

In allegories, multirelations are modelled as arrows whose targets are power
objects, and we have the corresponding definition:

Definition 3.1 (multirelation). *An* up-closed *multirelation* with source X
and target Y is an arrow $r : X \to \mathsf{P}Y$ in a power allegory such that

$$r \, ; \sqsubseteq_Y \;=\; r$$

where $\sqsubseteq_Y \mathrel{\widehat{=}} \in_Y \backslash \in_Y$; the subscript will usually be omitted.

Note that the family of arrows $\sqsubseteq$ coincides with the family of arrows $\subseteq$ in **Rel**.
We will abbreviate 'up-closed multirelation' by 'multirelation', and denote the

type of all multirelations with source X and target Y in a power allegory by $X \rightrightarrows Y$. Multirelations cannot be composed using ordinary composition for obvious type reasons. Instead, we have:

Definition 3.2 (multirelation composition). *The composition of two multirelations $r : X \rightrightarrows Y$, $s : Y \rightrightarrows Z$, denoted by $r \mathbin{\S} s : X \rightrightarrows Z$, is defined by*

$$r \mathbin{\S} s \;\hat{=}\; r ; (\in \backslash s)$$

Interpreting composition in set-theoretic terms, for all $x : X$ and $V : \mathbb{P}Z$, we have $x \ (r \mathbin{\S} s) \ V \iff (\exists U : x \ r \ U : (\forall y : y \in U : y \ s \ V))$. So, given input x, the angel can guarantee that $r \mathbin{\S} s$ will output a value satisfying V when he can ensure that r will establish an intermediate postcondition U such that, given any input value from U, he can guarantee that s will establish V. Whilst this pointwise definition provides useful intuition, laws like the following are more easily deduced from Definition 3.2 in the point-free style:

$$(r ; s) \mathbin{\S} t = r ; (s \mathbin{\S} t)$$

Definition 3.3 (multirelation identity). *The* identity *multirelation arrow is $\in_X$ for each object X.*

It is the case that multirelations form a category:

Lemma 3.4 (multirelations category). *The multirelations in a power allegory A form an order-enriched category with identity and composition as given in Definitions 3.2 and 3.3, and ordering $\subseteq$. This category will be referred to as* **Mul(A)**.

However, multirelations do not form a sub-category of the power allegory, because the category composition operator is different to that of the allegory.

4   Multifunctions in an Allegory

Relations can be interpreted as set-valued functions (multifunctions), and the arrows in a power allegory can be represented as function arrows in a similar way. So every multirelation can also be represented as a function, as shown below.

Definition 4.1 (up-closed multifunction). *An up-closed multifunction with source X and target Y is a function arrow $p : X \rightarrow \mathsf{P}^2 Y$ in a power allegory such that*

$$p ; \uparrow_Y = p$$

where the up-closure operator $\uparrow_Y \;\hat{=}\; \mathsf{E} \sqsubseteq_Y$; the subscript will usually be omitted.

Note that we may abbreviate 'up-closed multifunction' by 'multifunction'.

In **Rel**, $\uparrow$ is the standard up-closure function (e.g. see [20]). That is, for all $W \in \mathbb{P}^2 Y$, $\uparrow W = \{V \mid (\exists U : U \in W : U \subseteq V)\}$. So a function $p : X \to \mathbb{P}^2 Y$ is an up-closed multifunction if and only if for all $x \in X$ the set $p\,x$ is up-closed: if $U \in p\,x$ and $U \subseteq V$ then $V \in p\,x$. This is precisely the kind of function used in the *choice* semantics [9]; $p\,x$ produces a set of predicates (guarantees) that the angel can choose from.

Identity and composition for multifunctions are defined as follows:

Definition 4.2 (multifunction identity). *The* identity *multifunction arrow for each type* X *is denoted by* ι_X, *where* $\iota_X \,\hat{=}\, \Lambda \in_X$.

In set theory, the identity multifunction for all $x \in X$ is given by $\iota_X\, x = \uparrow \{\{x\}\}$.

Definition 4.3 (multifunction composition). *The* composition *of each pair of up-closed multifunctions* $p : X \to \mathsf{P}^2 Y$ *and* $q : Y \to \mathsf{P}^2 Z$ *is defined by*

$$p \star q \;\hat{=}\; p\,;\mathsf{E}^2 q\,;\mathsf{E}\cap\,;\cup$$

where $\cap \,\hat{=}\, \Lambda(\in\backslash\ni)$ *and* $\cup \,\hat{=}\, \Lambda(\ni\,;\ni)$.

In set theory the arrows $\cap$ and $\cup$ represent generalised intersection and union, so for all $x : X$, the value of $(p \star q)x$ is $\bigcup\{\bigcap\{q\,w \mid w \in W\} \mid W \in p\,x\}$. Hence given input x, the angel can only ensure that $p \star q$ will establish a postcondition U if he can choose a postcondition W for p (given input x) such that he can ensure that q establishes U for every input value in W. The following two laws would be fiddly to prove using set-theoretic notation, but in this allegorical setting, are immediate from Definition 4.3:

$$(p\,;q) \star r = p\,;(q \star r) \tag{4.1}$$
$$(p\,;\mathsf{E}^2 q) \star r = p \star (q\,;r) \tag{4.2}$$

Multifunctions also form a category within a power allegory:

Lemma 4.4 (multifunctions category). *The up-closed multifunctions in a power allegory* A *form an order-enriched category* **MFun**(A), *with identity and composition as in Definitions 4.2 & 4.3, where the ordering* $\leq$ *on the arrows* $p, r : X \to \mathsf{P}^2 Y$ *is defined by*

$$p \leq r \;\hat{=}\; p\,;\ni \,\subseteq\, r\,;\ni$$

The isomorphism between multirelations and multifunctions is stated below:

Lemma 4.5. *There is an order-isomorphism of categories* **MFun**(A) $\cong$ **Mul**(A) *as given by the universal property (2.1) for* Λ *and* $\ni$.

There are a number of useful operators for converting between functions, relations, multirelations and multifunctions, but the only one we require here is a lifting operator to convert a function to its multifunction equivalent:

Definition 4.6 (lifting). *Let* $f : X \to Y$ *in* **Fun**(A), *for power allegory* A. *Then the* lifting $\widehat{f} : X \to \mathsf{P}^2Y$ *in* **MFun**(A) *is defined by*

$$\widehat{f} \,\widehat{=}\, f\,;\iota$$

The lifting operator is a functor and satisfies many elegant algebraic properties, some of which are listed below for subsequent use:

$$\widehat{f} \star m = f\,;m \tag{4.3}$$

$$\widehat{f} \star \widehat{g} = \widehat{f\,;g} \tag{4.4}$$

$$m \star \widehat{f} = m\,;\mathsf{E}^2 f\,;\uparrow \tag{4.5}$$

$$\widehat{f}\,;\ni = f\,;\in \tag{4.6}$$

To recap, we have now arrived at the point where, given any power allegory A, we can characterise its multirelation arrows by **Mul**(A), and its multifunction arrows by **MFun**(A). Futhermore, these two categories arising within A are order-isomorphic to each other. The semantic models of multirelations and multifunctions are not new, but their presentation in the context of allegories is new. We have defined **MFun**(A) because it provides a useful stepping stone to cast **Mul**(A) as a Kleisli category of multirelations, in order to construct the monadic maps and folds, as will be seen in the following section.

5   Kleisli Categories

This section constructs a Kleisli category order-isomorphic to that of multifunctions, and thus also to that of multirelations. In order to describe what Kleisli categories are, we will need the concept of a monad (e.g. see [19]):

Definition 5.1 (monad). *A* monad $\langle \mathsf{M}, \eta, \mu \rangle$ *in a category* C *consists of a functor* $\mathsf{M} : \mathsf{C} \to \mathsf{C}$ *and two natural transformations, the* unit $\eta : I_\mathsf{C} \to \mathsf{M}$ *and* multiplication $\mu : \mathsf{M}^2 \to \mathsf{M}$ *such that*

$$\mathsf{M}\eta\,;\mu = id = \eta\mathsf{M}\,;\mu \quad and \quad \mu\mathsf{M}\,;\mu = \mathsf{M}\mu\,;\mu$$

Every monad can be used to form a Kleisli category in the following way:

Definition 5.2 (Kleisli category). *Given a monad* $\langle \mathsf{M}, \eta, \mu \rangle$ *in a category* C, *the* Kleisli category C^M *has the same objects as* C *and the arrows from* X *to* Y *in* C^M *are the arrows of type* $X \to \mathsf{M}Y$ *in* C. *Each object* X *has identity arrow* η_X, *and for each* $f : X \to \mathsf{M}Y$ *and* $g : Y \to \mathsf{M}Z$, *their* Kleisli composition $f\,;_\mathsf{M} g : X \to \mathsf{M}Z$ *is defined by*

$$f\,;_\mathsf{M} g \,\widehat{=}\, f\,;\mathsf{M}g\,;\mu$$

Some laws derivable from the definition of $;_\mathsf{M}$ can be found in [21].

Example 5.3. If A is a power allegory then the triple $\langle \mathsf{P}, \eta, \cup \rangle$ is a monad in **Fun(A)**, where $\eta = \Lambda id$, $\cup = \Lambda(\ni\,;\ni)$ and $\mathsf{P} = \mathsf{J}\,;\mathsf{E}$, where J is the embedding functor $\mathsf{J} : \mathbf{Fun(A)} \to \mathsf{A}$.

Translating this to set theory, taking A to be **Rel**, η is the function that maps each element to its singleton set, $\cup$ returns the generalised union of a set of sets, and P is the functor that maps each object to its powerset and applies each function to all the elements of a set: $\mathsf{P}\,f\,X = \{f\,x \mid x \in X\}$. Thus $\mathbf{Fun(Rel)}^{\mathsf{P}}$, also known as $\mathbf{Set}^{\mathsf{P}}$, is the category of sets and set-valued functions.

Note that the universal property (2.1) defines an isomorphism between the Kleisli category of this monad and the original allegory A.   □

The example above was a relatively simple illustration of a monad and its corresponding Kleisli category. The monad required to build the Kleisli category corresponding to multifunctions (and hence multirelations) is not so simple.

5.1 Multifunctions as a Kleisli Category

We will approach the construction of multifunctions as a Kleisli category in small steps. Firstly, in **Fun(A)** we will need the existence of equalisers:

Definition 5.4 (equaliser). *The* equaliser *of a pair of arrows* $f, g : Y \to Z$ *in a category is an arrow* $eq : X \to Y$ *such that for all* $h : W \to Y$ *with* $h\,;f = h\,;g$ *there is a unique* $k : W \to X$ *with* $k\,;eq = h$. *The source object of eq, namely* X, *is called the* object *of the equaliser.*

Rel is an allegory such that **Fun(Rel)** has equalisers; there are others, for example every tabular allegory A has equalisers in **Fun(A)** (see [17] for details).

We will need a suitable monad $\langle \mathsf{N}, \eta, \mu \rangle$ to form the Kleisli category for multifunctions in **Fun(A)**. The definition below of $\mathsf{N} : \mathbf{Fun(A)} \to \mathbf{Fun(A)}$ is presented separately on objects and arrows:

Definition 5.5 (action of N on objects). *Let A be a power allegory such that* **Fun(A)** *has equalisers. For each object* Y *in A,* $\mathsf{N}\,Y$ *is defined to be the object of the equaliser of* $id_{\mathsf{P}^2 Y}$ *and* $\uparrow_Y$ *in* **Fun(A)**.

Interpreting the above with $\mathsf{A} = \mathbf{Rel}$, $\mathsf{N}\,Y = \{Z \in \mathbb{P}^2 Y \mid Z \text{ is up-closed}\}$.

From Definition 4.1 and the definitions above we can now define the following:

Definition 5.6 (embedding *e*, projection '). *Let A be a power allegory such that* **Fun(A)** *has equalisers. Then there is an arrow* $e_Y : \mathsf{N}\,Y \to \mathsf{P}^2 Y$ *for each object* Y *in A, such that* e_Y *is an up-closed multifunction. Furthermore, for all* $p : W \to \mathsf{P}^2 Y$ *in* **MFun(A)** *there is a unique* $p' : W \to \mathsf{N}\,Y$ *characterised by the universal property*

$$ u = p' \quad \equiv \quad u\,;e_Y = p $$

We are now ready to complete the definition of N:

Definition 5.7 (action of N on arrows). *Let* A *be a power allegory such that* **Fun(A)** *has equalisers. For each arrow* $f : Y \to Z$ *in* **Fun(A)**,

$$N f \;\widehat{=}\; (e_Y \star \widehat{f})'$$

Interpreting the above definition with $A = \mathbf{Rel}$ using property (4.5), applying Nf to an up-closed set of sets Z results in $N f\, Z =\uparrow \{\{E f z\} \mid z \in Z\}$. This applies f to all the values in the sets belonging to Z and then takes their upclosure.

Lemma 5.8. $N : \mathbf{Fun(A)} \to \mathbf{Fun(A)}$ *as defined above is a functor.*

The functor N can now be used to form a monad:

Lemma 5.9. *Let* A *be a power allegory such that* **Fun(A)** *has equalisers, and let* N *be defined as above. For each object* Y *in* A*, let* $\eta : I_{\mathbf{Fun(A)}} \,\dot{\to}\, N$ *and* $\mu : N^2 \,\dot{\to}\, N$ *be defined by*

$$\eta_Y \;\widehat{=}\; \iota'_Y,$$
$$\mu_Y \;\widehat{=}\; (e_{NY} \star e_Y)'.$$

Then $\langle N, \eta, \mu \rangle$ *is a monad.*

The set-theoretic interpretations of η and μ are as follows: $\eta\, y =\uparrow \{\{y\}\}$ and $\mu Y = \bigcup \{\bigcap X \mid X \in Y\}$.

The universal property from Definition 5.6 shows that for each object X, there is a one-to-one correspondence between the up-closed multifunctions with target X and the functions with target $N\,X$. This can be extended to an order-isomorphism of categories:

Theorem 5.10. *Suppose the monad* $\langle N, \eta, \mu \rangle$ *is defined as in Lemma 5.9 and let the ordering on arrows in* $\mathbf{Fun(A)}^N$ *be defined for all* $u, v : W \to N Y$ *by*

$$u \preceq_N v \;\;\equiv\;\; u\,;e_Y\,;\ni \;\subseteq\; v\,;e_Y\,;\ni$$

Then there is an order-isomorphism of categories $\mathbf{Fun(A)}^N \cong \mathbf{MFun(A)}$ *given by the universal property from Definition 5.6.*

Corollary 5.11. *There is an order-isomorphism of categories* $\mathbf{Fun(A)}^N \cong \mathbf{Mul(A)}$.

6   Monadic Extensions

It is known [14,15] that if $\langle M, \eta, \mu \rangle$ is a monad in some category C, then every functor $F : C \to C$ can be extended to $F^M : C^M \to C^M$, which is a functor under certain conditions. In this section we examine the properties of the extension F^M for the monad of Lemma 5.9 for a restricted class of functors. We start by recalling some standard definitions concerning functors and datatypes.

6.1   Functors and Initial Algebras

Definition 6.1 (polynomial functor). *A polynomial functor* in a category *with products and coproducts is one of the following:*

- *The identity functor* Id,
- *A constant functor* K_X *for some object* X,
- *The composition* FG, *pointwise sum* F + G *or pointwise product* F × G *of two polynomial functors* F *and* G.

Here the juxtaposition FG denotes F after G, so $(FG)f = F(Gf)$.

Definition 6.2 (initial algebra). *Let* F : C → C *be a functor. By definition, an* F-algebra *is an arrow of type* $FX \rightarrow X$. *An* F-algebra $\alpha : FT \rightarrow T$ *is* initial *if, for each* F-algebra $p : FX \rightarrow X$, *there exists a (unique) arrow* $([p]) : T \rightarrow X$ *that satisfies the equivalence*

$$\alpha ; q = Fq ; p \quad \equiv \quad q = ([p])$$

That is, α *is an initial object in the category of* F-*algebras.*

Arrows of the form $([p])$ are called *catamorphisms*, and are also known as *folds*.

Example 6.3. Consider the recursively defined datatype of cons-lists over an arbitrary type X:

$$list\ X ::= nil \mid cons(X, list\ X)$$

From this description, we can construct a functor L_X, where $L_X(Y) = 1 + (X \times Y)$ and $L_X(f) = id + (id \times f)$. If we are working within a category that supports the existence of initial algebras, such as **Set**, then the above definition of *list X* describes the datatype of cons-lists as an initial L_X-algebra that is the coproduct $[nil, cons]_X : L_X(list\ X) \rightarrow list\ X$. □

Initial algebras are used to characterise datatypes, but they can also be used to construct functors. Suppose the datatype's functor is written as a bifunctor; for example, writing $L_X(Y)$ above as $L(X, Y)$. In general, if F is a bifunctor with initial algebra $\alpha_X : F(X, TX) \rightarrow TX$, then a *type functor* T can be defined, such that TY is the target object of α_Y, and for all $f : X \rightarrow Y$

$$Tf \ \hat{=} \ ([F(f, id_{TY}) ; \alpha_Y]) \tag{6.1}$$

Example 6.4. Given the datatype definition of *list X* above in the category **Set**, equation (6.1) translates to:

$$list\ f\ [\ ] = [\ ]$$
$$list\ f\ (x : xs) = f\ a\ :\ list\ f\ xs,$$

where $[\ ]$ is the empty list constructed by *nil*, and $x : xs$ is an abbreviation for *cons* (x, xs). Thus the type functor *list* is the well-known *map* operator of functional programming, where *list f* applies f to every element of the list. □

The class of functors we will consider in the remainder of this section are polynomial functors, type functors, or those obtained via the closure of such operations.

6.2   The Monadic Extension of a Functor

The monadic extension of a functor is defined [14,15] as follows:

Definition 6.5 (monadic extension). *Let* $\mathsf{F} : \mathsf{C} \to \mathsf{C}$ *be a functor, let* $\langle \mathsf{M}, \eta, \mu \rangle$ *be a monad in* C, *and let* $\delta^\mathsf{F} : \mathsf{FM} \overset{\cdot}{\to} \mathsf{MF}$. *The extension* $\mathsf{F}^\mathsf{M} : \mathsf{C}^\mathsf{M} \to \mathsf{C}^\mathsf{M}$ *is defined for any object* X *and arrow* $f : Y \to Z$ *as*

$$\mathsf{F}^\mathsf{M} X \;\hat{=}\; \mathsf{F} X$$
$$\mathsf{F}^\mathsf{M} f \;\hat{=}\; \mathsf{F} f \,;\, \delta^\mathsf{F}_Z$$

To explain, note that the arrow $f : Y \to Z$ in C^M is an arrow $f : Y \to \mathsf{M} Z$ in the category C. Applying F to f results in an arrow $\mathsf{F} f : \mathsf{F} Y \to \mathsf{FM} Z$, but the extension $\mathsf{F}^\mathsf{M} : \mathsf{C}^\mathsf{M} \to \mathsf{C}^\mathsf{M}$ requires the type of $\mathsf{F}^\mathsf{M} f$ to be $\mathsf{F} Y \to \mathsf{MF} Z$. Thus $\mathsf{F} f$ is composed with a suitable $\delta^\mathsf{F}_Z : \mathsf{FM} Z \to \mathsf{MF} Z$, which obtains an arrow of the correct type.

Naturally, we would like F^M to be a functor, and this requires conditions on δ^F:

Definition 6.6 (lifting). F^M *as defined above is called a* lifting *when it is a functor in* C^M, *which is the case if and only if it satisfies the following conditions:*

$$\mathsf{F} \eta_X \,;\, \delta^\mathsf{F}_X = \eta_{\mathsf{F} X} \tag{6.2}$$
$$\mathsf{F} \mu_X \,;\, \delta^\mathsf{F}_X = \delta^\mathsf{F}_{\mathsf{M} X} \,;_\mathsf{M} \delta^\mathsf{F}_X \tag{6.3}$$

Note that the above definitions generalise to functors of types $\mathsf{F} : \mathsf{C}^n \to \mathsf{C}$ in an obvious way, where $\mathsf{C}^n = \mathsf{C} \times \ldots \times \mathsf{C}$ (n times), and $\delta^\mathsf{F} : \mathsf{FM}^n \overset{\cdot}{\to} \mathsf{MF}$.

The following definition [14,15] gives an inductive way to define the natural transformation δ^F associated with the lifting of any functor defined using the polynomial and/or type functor constructors. The definition is valid for any monad; the only value that depends on the chosen monad is the choice of ϕ^M in the definition of $\delta^{\mathsf{F} \times \mathsf{G}}$:

Definition 6.7. *Let* $\langle \mathsf{M}, \eta, \mu \rangle$ *be a monad, then* δ *is given by*

$$\delta^{\mathsf{K}_X}_X \;\hat{=}\; \eta_X \qquad\qquad \delta^{\mathsf{F}+\mathsf{G}}_{(X,Y)} \;\hat{=}\; [\delta^\mathsf{F}_X \,;\, \mathsf{M}\, inl \;,\;\; \delta^\mathsf{G}_Y \,;\, \mathsf{M}\, inr]$$

$$\delta^{\mathsf{Id}}_X \;\hat{=}\; id_{\mathsf{M} X} \qquad\qquad \delta^{\mathsf{F} \times \mathsf{G}}_{(X,Y)} \;\hat{=}\; (\delta^\mathsf{F}_X \times \delta^\mathsf{G}_Y) \,;\, \phi^\mathsf{M}$$

$$\delta^{\mathsf{FG}}_X \;\hat{=}\; \mathsf{F}\delta^\mathsf{G}_X \,;\, \delta^\mathsf{F}_{\mathsf{G} X} \qquad\qquad \delta^\mathsf{T}_X \;\hat{=}\; (\!(\delta^{\mathsf{H}_X}_{\mathsf{T} X} \,;\, \mathsf{M}\alpha_X)\!)$$

Above, inl *and* inr *are the injection arrows of the coproduct. The natural transformation* $\phi^\mathsf{M} : \mathsf{M} X \times \mathsf{M} Y \overset{\cdot}{\to} \mathsf{M}(X \times Y)$ *is associated with monad* M. T *is the type functor for a bifunctor* H, *with initial algebra* $\alpha_X : \mathsf{H}(X, \mathsf{T} X) \to \mathsf{T} X$ *and associated functor* $\mathsf{H}_X(Y) = \mathsf{H}(X, Y)$.

It is known [14,15] that all of the components of the above definition, apart from ϕ^M, are natural transformations that satisfy appropriately typed forms of conditions (6.2) and (6.3). Moreover, if F is defined using any of the constructors used in the above definition, then δ^F is a natural transformation if ϕ^M is one, and properties (6.2) and (6.3) hold for δ^F if they are true for ϕ^M.

6.3   Lax Liftings of Functors on Multirelations

The monadic extension of functors described in the previous section cannot be applied directly to the monad associated with multirelations of Lemma 5.9. Instead, we introduce a weaker definition which we will call a *lax lifting*.

Definition 6.8 (lax lifting). *Let* $\langle M, \eta, \mu \rangle$ *be a monad in a category* C *and suppose that* C^M *is enriched with an ordering* $\preceq$. *Let* $F : C \to C$ *be a functor and let* δ^F *be a family of arrows such that for every object* X *there is an arrow* $\delta^F_X : FMX \to MFX$, *and for all* $p : X \to Y$ *in* C,

$$FMp \, ; \delta^F_Y \preceq \delta^F_X \, ; MFp \tag{6.4}$$

Suppose further that

$$F\eta_X \, ; \delta^F_X = \eta_{FX} \tag{6.5}$$

$$F\mu_X \, ; \delta^F_X \preceq \delta^F_{MX} \, ;_M \delta^F_X \tag{6.6}$$

Then we define the lax lifting $F^M : C^M \to C^M$ *on objects as* $F^M X = FX$ *and on arrows* $f : Y \to Z$ *in* C^M *as* $F^M f = Ff \, ; \delta^F_Z$.

Lemma 6.9. *If* F^M *is a lax lifting then it preserves identities, and for all* p, q *it is the case that* $F^M(p \,;_M q) \preceq F^M p \,;_M F^M q$.

If F is defined using constructors from polynomial and/or type functors, then properties (6.4), (6.5) and (6.6) will hold for F provided that they hold for $\times$, since it is known that all the other constructors are natural transformations that satisfy the stronger analogues (6.2) and (6.3).

It remains to define the transformation ϕ in the Kleisli category associated with multirelations and examine its properties. The definition of ϕ given below requires the existence of *relational products* in the allegory A, which are constructed using the left and right projections *outl* and *outr* of the product in **Fun**(A), provided that it has finite products. These exist if A is a unitary tabular allegory, for example **Rel** (see [12] for details).

$$r \times s \; \hat{=} \; (outl \, ; r \, ; outl^\circ) \cap (outr \, ; s \, ; outr^\circ)$$

The relational product is a monotonic bifunctor, but it is not a categorical product. We can now define ϕ^N for multirelations:

Definition 6.10. *Suppose that* $\langle N, \eta, \mu \rangle$ *is the monad of Lemma 5.9. Using the notation of (5.6),* ϕ^N *is defined by*

$$\phi^N_{(X,Y)} \; \hat{=} \; ((e_X \times e_Y) \, ; \Lambda((\ni \times \ni) \, ; ((\in \times \in) \backslash \in)))'$$

To understand ϕ^N, it may help to consider the relation $(\ni \times \ni) \, ; ((\in \times \in) \backslash \in))$, in a set-theoretic setting:

$$(A, B) \, ((\ni \times \ni) \, ; ((\in \times \in) \backslash \in))) \, Z \; \equiv$$
$$\exists p_A, p_B : p_A \in A \wedge p_B \in B \wedge (\forall a, b : a \in p_A \wedge b \in p_B : (a, b) \in Z)$$

Thus for two sets A, B of postconditions, Z contains (but is not limited to) all pairs of outcomes (a, b) where a satisfies p_A and b satisfies p_B. The rest of the definition of ϕ^N involves Λ, which returns all possible such Zs, and the embeddings and projection, which convert between the appropriate types of arrows and ensure upclosure of the output of ϕ^N.

Lemma 6.11. ϕ^N *satisfies conditions (6.4), (6.5) and (6.6).*

It follows that if A is a power allegory then any functor extension defined in $\mathbf{Fun}(A)^N$ using any of the constructors of Definition 6.7 is a lax lifting.

6.4   Monadic Multirelational Maps

It is now possible for us to construct multirelational map operators for datatypes. We shall illustrate how to do this for lists, by constructing a lax lifting of the *list* functor, otherwise known as *map*.

Taking L_X as the base functor for lists as defined in Example 6.3, we have

$$\delta_{list\,X}^{\mathsf{L}_X} = [\ \eta\,;\mathsf{N}\,inl\ ,\ \ (\eta \times id)\,;\phi^N\,;\mathsf{N}\,inr\ ]$$

Then from the definition of δ (Definition 6.7), we obtain

$$\delta_X^{list} = (\!|\ \delta_{list\,X}^{\mathsf{L}_X}\,;\mathsf{N}[nil, cons]_X\,|\!)$$

In $\mathbf{Set}^N$ this definition can be expanded as follows:

$$\delta_X^{list} = (list\ e_X\,;\Lambda((listr\ \ni)\,;((listr\ \in)\backslash \in)))'$$

where $list$ was defined in Example 6.4, and $listr$ is defined for relations as follows:

$$
\begin{array}{rcl}
[\,]\ (listr\ r)\ [\,] & \equiv & true \\
(x : xs)\ (listr\ r)\ (y : ys) & \equiv & x\ r\ y\ \wedge\ xs\ (listr\ r)\ ys
\end{array}
$$

Having defined δ^{list}, Definition 6.8 can be used to calculate the monadic extension of the *list* functor in $\mathbf{Set}^N$. Suppose $p : X \to NY$, then we have

$$
\begin{array}{ll}
list^N\ p\ [\,] & = \uparrow \{\{[\,]\}\} \\
list^N\ p\ (x : xs) = \{U \mid \exists Z, V : Z \in p\,x \wedge V \in list^N\ p\ xs \\
\qquad\qquad\qquad \wedge\ (\forall w, ws : w \in Z \wedge ws \in V : (w : ws) \in U)\}
\end{array}
$$

This completes the derivation of the *list* (or *map*) functor for $\mathbf{Set}^N$ where N was defined in Lemma 5.9.

The corresponding definition for $list^N$ applied to an up-closed multifunction $p : X \to \mathbb{P}^2 Y$ is textually the same as the above, it is only the types that change, and when translated back to multirelations this gives the same definition as in [4]. There may be other choices for ϕ^N that generate alternative definitions for $list^N$ but it is beyond the scope of this paper to examine these.

The above illustrated a multirelational map operator for lists; it is of course possible to obtain multirelational map operators for other datatypes in a similar way, by using the construction functors for those datatypes in place of the *list* functor.

6.5   Monadic Multirelational Folds

Folds in the Kleisli category can be derived from folds in the base category. This definition is the same as that in [14], except that the functor extension is replaced by a lax lifting:

Lemma 6.12. *Let* $\langle M, \eta, \mu \rangle$ *be a monad in category* C. *Then if* $F : C \to C$ *has initial algebra* α *then the lax lifting* $F^M : C^M \to C^M$ *has initial algebra* $\alpha \,;\, \eta$. *If* $\psi : FX \to X$ *in* C^M, *then the fold in* C^M *is given by* $(\!|\psi|\!)_M = (\!|\delta_X^F \,;_M\, \psi|\!)$.

Now the above lemma can be used to find the *foldr* operator on lists in a Kleisli category, since *foldr* is defined as the fold associated with the base functor for lists L_X of Example 6.3. Let $\langle N, \eta, \mu \rangle$ be the monad of Lemma 5.9 and let $f : L_X(Y) \to Y$ in $\mathbf{Set}^N$. If we let $g \mathrel{\hat{=}} \delta_Y^{L_X} \,;_N\, f$, then by Lemma 6.12, $(\!|f|\!)_N = (\!|g|\!)$ and by Definition 6.2

$$[nil, cons]_X \,;\, (\!|g|\!) = (1 + id \times (\!|g|\!)) \,;\, g$$

In a set-theoretic setting, this definition can be expanded to the point level using the definition from Section 6.4 and Kleisli composition to give the following (where the arrow $f : L_X(Y) \to Y$ in $\mathbf{Set}^N$ has been replaced by two components p and a): Let $p : X \times Y \to NY$ and $a : NY$ then

$$foldr \; p \; a \; [\,] = a$$
$$foldr \; p \; a \; (x : xs) = \bigcup \{ \bigcap \{p \; x \; y \mid y \in Y\} \mid Y \in foldr \; p \; a \; xs\}$$

Intuitively, Y is a postcondition established from the fold so far on xs, y is an outcome satisfying Y, and $p \, x \, y$ is the (upclosed) set of possible postconditions after performing this step p of the fold on intermediate result y with the list element x. Thus the set $\bigcap \{p \, x \, y \mid y \in Y\}$ contains postconditions that can be guaranteed whatever the choice of y satisfying Y, and the $\bigcup$ ensures the inclusion of all possible such guaranteed postconditions, for all choices of Y.

It follows from the isomorphism between the category of multifunctions and the Kleisli category that the definition of *foldr* for multifunctions is textually the same as the above, if $p : X \to \mathbb{P}^2 Y$ is a multifunction and $a : \mathbb{P}^2 Y$ is an up-closed set. This multirelational definition of *foldr* is identical to that constructed by the alternative method of [4].

The above illustrated a multirelational fold operator for lists; similarly, the use of other functors to construct datatypes results in multirelational folds over more general datatypes.

It is interesting to analyse the relationship between maps and folds since in functional and relational programming algebras, it is the case that the map functor is an instance of a fold. The following lemma gives a lax analogue of some results of [14] and shows that for type functors, map is an instance of a fold in the base category but is only related to the monadic fold by an inequation:

Lemma 6.13. *Let* T *be the type functor associated with base bifunctor* F *with initial algebra* $\alpha_X : \mathsf{F}(X, \mathsf{T}X) \to \mathsf{T}X$ *and let* F^M *be a lax lifting in the category* C^M *which is order-enriched with* $\preceq$, *then if* $f : X \to Y$ *in* C^M

$$\mathsf{T}^\mathsf{M} f \;=\; (\!|\mathsf{F}(f, id_{\mathsf{MT}Y}) ; \delta^\mathsf{F}_{(Y,\mathsf{T}Y)} ; \mathsf{M}\alpha_Y|\!)$$

$$\mathsf{T}^\mathsf{M} f \;\preceq\; (\!|\mathsf{F}^\mathsf{M}(f, \eta_{\mathsf{T}Y}) ;_\mathsf{M} (\alpha_Y ; \eta_{\mathsf{T}Y})|\!)_\mathsf{M}$$

6.6   Unfolds

The technique of extending folds as described in the previous section has been dualised to unfolds in [15] and [16], but unfortunately the methods used there do not apply here. The problem with [15] is that it only applies to a strong monad, and the monad described in Section 5 is not strong. The more recent method of [16] fails on two counts. First, it requires a strictness property that does not generally hold for multifunctions: it is not generally the case that $p ;_\mathsf{M} abort = abort$ where $abort = (\varLambda\emptyset)'$ and as a result the category of multifunctions does not have a terminal object. The other problem is that the extension of the *list* functor is not itself a functor, it is only a lax functor. So the search for the definition of unfold continues. It is hoped that one of these existing methods could be generalised to produce a lax unfold of some kind, but it is beyond the scope of this paper to construct such a definition.

7   Conclusions

Much of the material presented above is standard theory, included in order to provide sufficient background information to make it possible to present this paper's contribution of monadic multirelational maps and folds. To be precise, the definitions of allegories in Section 2 are standard [17], as are the definitions of Kleisli categories in Section 5 [19] and monadic extensions in Section 6.1 [14]. Moreover, the multifunctional model of Section 4 was previously discovered by Back and von Wright [9], the associated monad has been described by Dawson [22] and even the multirelational definitions of map and fold have been documented elsewhere [4].

However, the particular contributions of this paper are several. Firstly, looking from an overall perspective, this paper draws together these varied strands of work from within different semantic models into the setting of power allegories, thus contributing to unification work between different models of program semantics. In particular, through the isomorphism between up-closed multirelations and monotonic predicate transformers [8], multirelations have strong links to UTP [5] and predicate transformer semantics. Thus being able to provide algebraic semantics for multirelations, including all the algebraic definitions and datatypes and operators and laws that make it possible to reason about multirelations to use them for calculational program development, is a very important link.

Secondly, looking at the details of the work in this paper, this construction of maps and folds for multirelations using a monadic extension is also new. Whilst it may seem futile to construct new definitions of map and fold for multirelations when such operators already exist, this work should not be seen as an end in itself, but rather as a firm foundation from which to explore the existence of other operators and algebraic laws, in particular concerning the potentially useful unfold. This paper has given a rigorous treatment of monadic extensions for multirelations, which has resulted in a weakened version of the standard theory. The definition given here was chosen to be compatible with previous work [4], but the monadic extension is not unique, and preliminary investigations suggest that there are other definitions that may also yield useful operators. Through this work, it has been possible to see precisely why previous methods for dualising monadic catamorphisms fail here, but it remains to be seen whether these methods might also be weakened in some way that could be applied to multirelations.

Finally, this paper illustrates the use of point-free definitions and calculation for multirelations. This results in elegant definitions and a style of reasoning more transparent than that used in traditional set-theoretic proofs. In particular, the set-theoretic definition of composition is so cumbersome that it renders calculations at best error-prone and at worst virtually impossible. The point-free alternative is much more concise and manageable, and any doubts of its value can easily be dispelled by attempting any of the proofs using the set-theoretic definitions instead.

To summarise, this paper contains a contribution to the development of the algebra of multirelations, presenting a different view of maps and folds from that described in [4], and this has resulted in a weakening of the standard monadic extension. Future work includes establishing whether an unfold operator can be defined, and this would further contribute to unification of the functional, relational and multirelational calculi.

Acknowledgements

We would like to thank the anonymous referees for their helpful comments.

References

1. Rewitzky, I.: Binary multirelations. In: de Swart, H., Orłowska, E., Schmidt, G., Roubens, M. (eds.) Theory and Applications of Relational Structures as Knowledge Instruments. LNCS, vol. 2929, pp. 259–274. Springer, Heidelberg (2003)
2. Dunne, S.: Chorus angelorum. In: Julliand, J., Kouchnarenko, O. (eds.) B 2007. LNCS, vol. 4355, pp. 19–33. Springer, Heidelberg (2006)
3. Martin, C.E., Curtis, S.A., Rewitzky, I.: Modelling angelic and demonic nondeterminism with multirelations. Science of Computer Programming 65(2), 140–158 (2007)
4. Martin, C.E., Curtis, S.A.: Nondeterministic folds. In: Uustalu, T. (ed.) MPC 2006. LNCS, vol. 4014, pp. 274–298. Springer, Heidelberg (2006)
5. Hoare, C.A.R., Jifeng, H.: Unifying Theories of Programming. Prentice-Hall, Englewood Cliffs (1998)

6. Cavalcanti, A., Woodcock, J.C.P., Dunne, S.E.: Angelic nondeterminism in the unifying theories of programming. Formal Aspects of Computing 18(3), 288–307 (2006)
7. Cavalcanti, A., Woodcock, J.C.P.: Angelic nondeterminism and unifying theories of programming. In: Derrick, J., Boiten, E. (eds.) REFINE 2005, vol. 137. Elsevier, Amsterdam (2005)
8. Hesselink, W.: Multirelations are predicate transformers. Technical Report, Dept. of Computing Science, Groningen, The Netherlands (2004)
9. Back, R., Wright, J.: Refinement Calculus: A Systematic Introduction. Springer, New York (1998)
10. Morgan, C.C.: Programming from Specifications, 2nd edn. Prentice-Hall, Englewood Cliffs (1994)
11. Bird, R.: An Introduction to Functional Programming using Haskell. Prentice-Hall, Englewood Cliffs (1998)
12. Bird, R., Moor, O.: The Algebra of Programming. Prentice-Hall, Englewood Cliffs (1997)
13. Gibbons, J., Jones, G.: The under-appreciated unfold. In: Proceedings 3rd ACM SIGPLAN Int. Conf. on Functional Programming, ICFP'98, Baltimore, MD, USA, September 26–29, vol. 34(1), pp. 273–279. ACM Press, New York (1998)
14. Fokkinga, M.M.: Monadic maps and folds for arbitrary datatypes. Memoranda Informatica 94-28 (1994)
15. Pardo, A.: Monadic corecursion - definition, fusion laws, and applications. Electronic Notes in Theoretical Computer Science 11, 105–139 (1998)
16. Hasuo, I., Jacobs, B., Sokolova, A.: Generic trace theory. Electronic Notes in Theoretical Computer Science 164(1), 47–65 (2006)
17. Freyd, P., Ščedrov, A.: Categories, Allegories. Springer, Heidelberg (1993)
18. Martin, C.E., Curtis, S.A.: The algebra of multirelations (2009) (in preparation)
19. MacLane, S.: Categories for the Working Mathematician, 2nd edn. Springer, Heidelberg (1998)
20. Davey, B.A., Priestley, H.A.: Introduction to Lattices and Order, 2nd edn. Cambridge University Press, Cambridge (2002)
21. Martin, C.E., Curtis, S.A.: Supplement to this paper (2009), http://cms.brookes.ac.uk/staff/SharonCurtis/publications/mf-supp.pdf
22. Dawson, J.E.: Compound monads in specification languages. In: Proceedings of Programming Languages meets Program Verification, PLPV 2007, pp. 3–10. ACM Press, New York (2007)

Appendix

To keep within space constraints, and also because pages of calculational proofs can be tedious, we include one sample proof to illustrate the point-free calculational style. The full proofs for all results contributed by this paper can be found online in a supplement for this paper [21].

Proof. of Lemma 5.8 To show that N is a functor, we need to demonstrate that it preserves identities and distributes through composition. For identity preservation, we have:

$\mathsf{N}\,id$

$=$ {Action of N on arrows (Definition 5.7)}

$(e_Y \star \widehat{id})'$

$=$ {Definition (4.6)}

$(e_Y \star \iota)'$

$=$ {Identity of $\star$}

e'_Y

$=$ {(5.6)}

id

As for composition, first note that by Definition 5.6, every up-closed multifunction $p : X \to \mathsf{P}^2 Y$ has the property that $p' ; e = p$, and so using equation (4.1) we can see that for all $q : Y \to \mathsf{P}^2 Z$,

$$p' ; (e_Y \star q)' ; e_Z = p \star q \qquad (A.1)$$

Definition 5.6 also implies that for any $p, q : X \to \mathsf{N}Y$,

$$(p = q) \quad \equiv \quad (p ; e_Y = q ; e_Y) \qquad (A.2)$$

So now we can calculate

$\mathsf{N}\,f ; \mathsf{N}\,g ; e_Z$

$=$ {Action of N on arrows (Definition 5.7)}

$(e_X \star \widehat{f})' ; (e_Y \star \widehat{g})' ; e_Z$

$=$ {Equation (A.1)}

$e_X \star \widehat{f} \star \widehat{g}$

$=$ {Equation (4.4)}

$e_X \star \widehat{(f ; g)}$

$=$ {Actions of N (Definitions 5.5 and 5.7)}

$\mathsf{N}(f ; g) ; e_Z$

which establishes the result by equation (A.2).   □

Unifying Theories of Interrupts

Alistair A. McEwan[1] and Jim Woodcock[2]

[1] Department of Engineering, University of Leicester, UK
[2] Department of Computing, University of York, UK

Abstract. The concept of an interrupt is one that appears across many paradigms, and used in many different areas. It may be used as a device to assist specifications to model failure, or to describe complex interactions between non co-operating components. It is frequently used in hardware to allow complex scheduling patterns. Although interrupts are ubiquitous in usage, the precise behaviour of a system incorporating interrupts can be difficult to reason about and predict. In this paper, a complete theory of the interrupt operator presented by Hoare in his original treatment of CSP is proposed. The semantics are given in the CSP model in Unifying Theories of Programming. New and existing algebraic laws are proposed and justified. The contribution of the paper is therefore a denotational semantics of an interrupt operator, and a collection of algebraic laws that assist in reasoning about systems incorporating interrupts.

1   Introduction

The concept of an interrupt is useful in modelling reactive systems. For instance, an operating system may be interrupted by a user pressing a key, or by a high priority job becoming ready for processing. Alternatively, a piece of hardware may have an interrupt line built in to require it to process inputs immediately they become available. Interrupts may also be used to model component failure in specifications—where a system is suddenly, and unexpectedly, required to evolve into one with very different behaviour. For instance, a piece of equipment failing may cause it to refuse to offer the service for which it was intended: here, the interrupt is used to describe the occurrence of the failure. Furthermore, interrupts can be used to model more abstract situations in software. In object-oriented programming, it is common to build exception handlers that may, or may not, choose to respond to the act of another component indicating an erroneous situation. If the event handler is the process which can be interrupted, then the willingness, or otherwise, to respond immediately to an exception can be modelled by enabling, or disabling, interrupt events.

The theory of Communicating Sequential Processes (CSP) is presented by Hoare in [4], although it was originally presented in earlier works [3]. It is further built on by Roscoe in [8]. It is a mathematical formalism for reasoning about concurrent, communicating entities in a system. Each entity in the system is represented by a *process*, which engages in atomic actions, called *events*. An event is an observable action in the life of a process, and acts as a communication, or

A. Butterfield (Ed.): UTP 2008, LNCS 5713, pp. 122–141, 2010.

synchronisation between co-operating processes. An *alphabet* is a set of events. The role of alphabets in the semantic domain differs between [4] and [8]. In the former, processes have alphabets, while in the latter, it is the process combinators that are alphabetised.

Complex descriptions of behaviour are built up as networks of processes, using CSP operators. CSP is a process algebra: descriptions of processes can be re-written and manipulated in accordance with algebraic laws; the correctness of these laws being justified within the semantic models associated with CSP.

The interrupt operator $\widehat{}$ is introduced into CSP in [4]. It is described as being an unusual form of sequential composition, where the termination of a process is not required for the initiation of a latter process: the latter process can be thought of as forcing the termination of the former. In a sequential composition such as P; Q, the successful termination of P is required before execution of Q may begin. However, in the expression $P \widehat{} Q$, the initials of Q (i.e, the set of events in which Q is initially willing to engage) can interrupt P at any time. Hoare presents a *traces* model of this operator, defining it in terms of the observable interactions recorded with the environment, along with several algebraic laws. The most significant of these laws is a *step law*. This step law uniquely defines the operator.

This is followed by a variation of the operator, called the *catastrophic inter-rupt*: $P\widehat{\iota}Q$. In this version, the interrupt event ι is unique, and its appearance in a trace of $P\widehat{\iota}Q$ signals the termination of P and the initiation of Q. The step law for this version of the operator uniquely characterizes it for deterministic processes, although it may be extended to non-deterministic processes where it is shown to be strict, and to distribute over non-determinism in both arguments.

The catastrophic operator is the one used in [8], where a failures semantics for the operator is given. This version takes the form $P \triangle_i Q$, and describes the situation where the process P can be interrupted by the event i, and subsequent behaviour is that of Q. It can be seen that $\widehat{\iota}$ and $\triangle_i$ are the same (given that ι describes a unique event, which equates to i) as they both adhere to the same step law. In this paper, the syntax of [8] ($\triangle_i$) is adopted for the interrupt operator. In doing so, we adhere to the operator precedences of [5], which follow from [8].

The main contribution of this paper is to define a semantics for the interrupt operator $\triangle_i$ in the Unifying Theories of Programming model of CSP. This is achieved firstly by adopting the step law as the definitive characterization, and showing that some obvious and desirable laws fall trivially out of this character-ization. Following this, a new denotational semantics is given which is correct with respect to the step law. The semantics is also shown to be sufficient and complete in theoretical terms as it is shown to be strict and to distribute over disjunction in both arguments. A definition of a conditional version of this oper-ator is given where the interruptible process can enable or disable the possibility of an interrupt, and the justification is extended to this version of the operator. For clarity and ease of reading, proofs are omitted from this paper.

The paper is structured as follows: Section 2 presents an overview of reactive processes in the Unifying Theory, and the CSP model is given in Section 3. Section 4 presents the step law for the unconditional and conditional versions of the interrupt operator and some relevant laws. Denotational semantics for the unconditional version of the operator, along with the justification that the semantics is correct with respect to the step law are given in Section 5, and this is followed by the same for the conditional version in Section 6. Conclusions are drawn, and areas in need of further consideration are highlighted in Section 7.

1.1   Examples

Example 1. Interruptible and interrupting processes: $P \triangle_i Q$

We use the name *interrupting process* to refer to the behaviour of the process resulting after the interrupt event has occurred. This is the process Q of Example 1, and the event i is the *interrupt event*. The name *interruptible process* refers to the normal behaviour that may be interrupted: this is the process P of Example 1. Therefore in this example, the event i can occur during execution of P, and subsequent behaviour will then be Q, with no further observations of P being possible.

Example 2. A simple process and an interrupt: $a \rightarrow b \rightarrow STOP \triangle_i STOP$

In Example 2 the *interruptible* process is $a \rightarrow b \rightarrow STOP$. The possible traces which may be observed of this process are $\{\langle\rangle, \langle a \rangle, \langle a, b \rangle\}$. However, this process may be interrupted by the process $i \rightarrow STOP$. Therefore the possible traces of the composition are those of the interruptible process, and those which may be observed if the interrupt occurs. These are: $\{\langle\rangle, \langle a \rangle, \langle a, b \rangle, \langle i \rangle, \langle a, i \rangle, \langle a, b, i \rangle\}$. These traces show that the occurrence of the interrupt event passes control to the process on the right hand side of the operator.

Example 3. Restartable processes: $P^R(i) \cong \mu X \bullet (P \triangle_i X)$

One possible requirement of a process is to be able to restart it: for instance, a user of a computer may wish to reboot it after an error. Example 3 shows that interrupt extends easily to this notion, as in [4]. Here, P is the process to be made restartable. The recursively defined process X behaves as P until an interrupt occurs, after which its behaviour is that of X again. The notation P^R denotes a restartable version of P, parameterised by the interrupt i.

2   Reactive Processes

The fundamental property of a sequential process is that behaviour may be adequately described by observations made only at initialization and at termination. A *reactive process* however is characterized by the fact that it also admits intermediate observations between initialization and termination. These intermediate observations are typically interactions with the environment. A reactive program may not be characterized by its final state alone: information about interactions with the environment *must* also be recorded as many reactive programs never terminate, and therefore have no final state.

A sequence of interactions with the environment is called a *trace*, and is recorded by the variable tr. The variable tr contains the sequence of interactions before the process started, and the variable tr' contains the sequence of interactions recorded so far. The expression $tr' - tr$ therefore gives the sequence of interactions performed by the current process up to the current point in time.

The boolean variable *wait* describes the quiescence of a process, indicating whether or not the observations made are intermediate or final. If *wait* is true, the preceding process is in an intermediate state and no observations of this process can be made. If it is false, the predecessor terminated and the process may begin. Similarly, if $wait'$ is true, all observations of the current process are intermediate, and when it is false, observations are of the process in its terminating state. For instance, all the intermediate states of a given process P (when $P.wait = true$) are also intermediate states of the process P; Q, for any given Q. For control to pass from P to Q, P must be in a terminating state: i.e. $P.wait' = false$.

In any non-terminated state, a process may refuse to engage in a specific event, or set of events. The variable ref (an abbreviation of *refusals*) records the set of events in which a process may refuse to engage. The value of ref' indicates the events in which a process is refusing to engage in any of its intermediate states, or its final terminating state. The behaviour of a process, is not dependent upon the initial value of ref, as it is not dependent upon the refusals of the predecessor.

The final observational variable of reactive processes is one which describes program stability—the variable *okay*. If, for a given process P, $P.okay = true$, then the process P has started, and the predecessor terminated in a stable state; if $P.okay = false$, then P has not started and even the initial values of the process variables are unobservable. In the case where $P.okay' = true$ and $P.wait' = true$, the process is in a stable state and is awaiting interaction with the environment. In the case where $P.okay' = true$ and $P.wait' = false$, the process has terminated in a stable state. In the case where $P.okay' = false$, the process is in a non-stable state and the value of the other observational variables are meaningless—commonly known as *divergence*.

Not every relation including these observational variables in its alphabet describes a reactive process. In order to be considered a reactive process, a predicate must satisfy a number of conditions—referred to as *healthiness conditions*. A healthiness condition restricts the lattice of relations that can be described in the theory. Processes that do not satisfy these conditions are not in the lattice of reactive processes. The healthiness conditions presented in this section are taken from [5].

Definition 1. R1: $P = P \wedge tr \leq tr'$

The first healthiness condition for a reactive process **R1** ensures that processes only ever extend the trace—they can not change the record of events that have already happened. The simplicity of **R1** leads to many obvious algebraic laws: for instance, it distributes through conjunction and disjunction; and its scope may be extended over other conjunctions. The result of applying any of the reactive program combinators to an **R1** healthy process is another **R1** healthy process. That is, **R1** is closed under conjunction, disjunction, conditional and sequence.

Definition 2. R2$_1$: $\mathbf{R2}_1(P, (tr, tr')) = \sqcap_s \bullet P(s, s \frown (tr' - tr))$

Definition 3. R2$_2$: $\mathbf{R2}_2(P(tr, tr')) = P(\langle\rangle, tr' - tr)$

Whilst a reactive process is sensitive to the value of *okay*—it cannot be started until *okay* is true—there is no reason why it needs to be sensitive to the value of tr. The healthiness condition **R2** therefore requires a reactive process is not sensitive to the value of tr. In fact, there are two definitions for **R2** given in [5]. The first of these states that behaviour should not change if tr is replaced by an arbitrary value, and the same change is made to tr'. The second requires that behaviour is not changed if tr is replaced with the empty sequence.

A relation that is **R2$_1$** healthy is also **R2$_2$** healthy—for every relation P, **R2$_2$**(P) is a fixed point of **R2$_1$**. In this paper we assume Definition 3 for **R2**. Not all properties that hold for **R2$_2$** hold for **R2$_1$**—this point is discussed further in [2], but is not directly relevant to the remainder of this paper. The programming operators are closed with respect to **R2**.

Definition 4. J: $J \mathrel{\widehat{=}} (okay \Rightarrow okay') \wedge II$

The predicate J of Definition 4 is a special case of a reactive process. The role played by J is that it permits a change in the value of *okay* whilst keeping the other variables constant. If *okay* is changed, it may be weakened, but not strengthened. One might capture this point by stating that a process may not be made to recover from instability; and becoming unstable does not change history. J is **R2** healthy. Furthermore, it is a left unit of sequential composition. This predicate is later used to build a healthiness condition for CSP processes. II is the identity: it ensures that all other observational variables remain unchanged.

Definition 5. R3: $\mathbf{R3}(P) = (II \lhd wait \rhd P)$

The third and final healthiness condition for a reactive process is one that makes sequential composition well-defined, given in Definition 5. If the process on the left of the sequential composition is in a wait state, then the program on the right is also. This is intuitively what one might expect from a reactive process: if this were not true, then the right hand side would be able to engage in some activity before its predecessor had successfully and stably terminated.

The healthiness condition **R3** is of vital importance to this paper: the interrupt operator both *requires*, and *violates*, some conditions of **R3**. Like all healthiness conditions, **R3** is idempotent. **R3** distributes through disjunction.

3   A Unified Model of CSP

The model of reactive processes in the previous section has been used in [5] to describe a number of paradigms, including the *Algebra of Communicating Processes* [1], and the well known *Calculus of Communicating Systems*[6,7]. The Unifying Theories model of CSP follows directly from that of reactive processes. In fact, a CSP process is a reactive process that observes some additional healthiness conditions—the healthiness conditions for reactive processes coupled with those for CSP processes define what it means for an alphabetised relation to be a CSP process. In this section, these conditions are presented and explained.

3.1   Healthiness Conditions

Definition 6. CSP1: $P = (\neg\ okay \wedge tr \leq tr') \vee P$

R1 insisted that a process will only ever extend the trace. However, CSP processes also model divergence, and in the presence of divergence the final values of variables cannot be meaningfully observed. The first healthiness condition, **CSP1**, ensures (like **R1**) that a process can only ever extend the trace. However it also states that if the process is in a divergent state ($\neg\ okay$) then there are no other guarantees. **CSP1** distributes over disjunction and conjunction.

Definition 7. CSP2:
$P = P;\ okay \Rightarrow okay' \wedge tr' = tr \wedge ref' = ref \wedge wait' = wait$

Definition 8. *Alternative* **CSP2**: $\mathbf{CSP2}(P) = P;\ J$

The second condition necessary for a CSP process is given in Definition 7. A CSP process cannot explicitly be required to diverge: processes must be monotonic in $okay'$. **CSP2** enforces this condition. Where the predecessor diverged ($okay = false$) nothing may be assumed about $okay'$, but in the case where it did not, $okay'$ cannot be required to be false. **CSP2** may also equivalently be defined in terms of Definition 4, J, given in Definition 8. **CSP2** is closed over disjunction, sequential composition and conditional.

3.2   Stop, Skip, and Chaos

In this section, some well known CSP processes are presented in terms of their semantics in the Unifying Theories model.

Definition 9. *The identity process* II_{CSP}:

$$II_{CSP} \,\widehat{=}\,$$
$$(okay' = okay \wedge tr' = tr \wedge ref' = ref \wedge wait' = wait) \lhd okay \rhd tr \leq tr'$$

Definition 9 is the identity process for CSP. In the event that the predecessor did not diverge, then nothing changes. In the event that it did, then the only guarantee is that the trace may be extended. The heathiness condition Definition 5 must be reformulated for CSP processes to take into account this identity.

Definition 10. *The process SKIP:* $SKIP \mathrel{\widehat{=}} \exists\, ref \bullet II_{CSP}$

The process commonly known as *SKIP* is a special example of the identity, where the refusals of the previous process are ignored—the existential quantifier has the effect of making the final refusals of the previous process—therefore the initial refusals of this process—irrelevant to its behaviour. The unit law for left composition of the identify follows from this; as does the well known left unit law for *SKIP*. Another interesting law concerns external choice and *SKIP*: if one component may terminate immediately, then a refinement is the program that may terminate immediately.

Definition 11. *The process STOP:* $STOP \mathrel{\widehat{=}} \mathbf{R1} \circ \mathbf{R2} \circ \mathbf{R3}(wait := true)$

The deadlock process *STOP* is one which is always in a wait state. No observation can be made of this process which extends the trace so that tr' is longer than tr. The expected left zero law for *STOP* exists.

Definition 12. *The process CHAOS:* $CHAOS \mathrel{\widehat{=}} \mathbf{R1} \circ \mathbf{R2} \circ \mathbf{R3}(true)$

The worst CSP process imaginable can perform any action in its alphabet at will. It may non-deterministically choose to perform any action, or to perform no action and deadlock, or even to perform infinite internal actions. This is the process *CHAOS* of Definition 12. Surprisingly, this definition is strictly stronger than the predicate *true*: even a process as non-deterministic as this is still required to preserve the healthiness conditions for CSP processes. For instance, it may not begin until the previous process has terminated and it may not change history even though its future is unpredictable.

3.3   Choice

Definition 13. *Internal choice:* $P \sqcap Q \mathrel{\widehat{=}} P \vee Q$

An internal (non-deterministic) choice between two CSP processes is the disjunction of the two processes.

Definition 14. *External choice:* $P \,\square\, Q \mathrel{\widehat{=}} \mathbf{CSP2}((P \wedge Q) \lhd STOP \rhd (P \vee Q))$

An external choice between two CSP processes P and Q is given in Definition 14. This definition states that the external choice has both possible behaviours of P and Q if no choice has been made—that is, if no observation has been made and termination has not occurred. This is characterized by the condition where $STOP = true$—recalling that *STOP* is merely a predicate in this semantic model, then its use in a conditional statement such as this one is simply a short-hand notation. Alternatively, if an observation had been made—characterized by the observational variables not representing $STOP$ then behaviour will be either that of P or that of Q depending upon which choice was made. The purpose of **CSP2** in this definition is one of *closure*: the negation of $STOP$ is not a **CSP2** healthy process. By applying **CSP2**, then only those points in the resultant lattice that are healthy are permitted.

3.4   Communication, Events, and Prefixing

Event prefixing is a powerful tool in building the description of a CSP process. The prefix operator is a *binary infix* operator: it takes an event as the left hand argument and a process as the right. The result is a process that will engage in the left hand operand, and afterwards its behaviour is described by the right hand process.

The definition of prefixing in the Unifying Theory relies on several related definitions: in this section these are presented and explained.

Definition 15. *B:* $B \cong ((tr' = tr) \wedge wait') \vee (tr < tr')$

Definition 16. *Φ:* $\Phi \cong (\mathbf{R1} \circ \mathbf{R2} \circ \mathbf{R3}) \wedge B$

Definition 15 insists that while a process is waiting, the trace remains unchanged. After it has terminated it will have extended the trace. Φ insists that in addition to this, the whole process observes the healthiness conditions for reactive processes. The two important conditions are that the construction does not tamper with the other observational variables while it is in a waiting state, and particularly that it is not dependent upon the initial value of tr. The application of **R2** and **R3** ensures that this is the case.

Definition 17. *do:* $do_{\mathcal{A}}(a) \cong \Phi(a \notin ref' \lhd wait' \rhd tr' = tr \cap \langle a \rangle)$

Definition 17, $do_{\mathcal{A}}$, describes the effect of observing the occurrence of the event a: there are exactly two stable states. Either $wait' = true$ and the process has not terminated and was not refusing an a, or it has terminated and a has been appended to the trace.

Definition 18. *Simple prefix:* $a \rightarrow SKIP \cong \mathbf{CSP1}(okay' \wedge do_{\mathcal{A}}(a))$

The construction $a \rightarrow SKIP$ is referred to as *simple prefix*, and its behaviour is described in terms of the observational variables, given in Definition 18. On termination, the simple prefix has not diverged ($okay'$), and the changes to the other observational variables are described by the function $do_{\mathcal{A}}$.

Definition 19. *Prefix:* $a \rightarrow P \cong a \rightarrow SKIP; P$

Definition 19 gives the real meaning of prefix operator. It is actually a shorthand way of writing a sequential composition, and comprises the process $a \rightarrow SKIP$

and P. The process $a \rightarrow SKIP$ waits to perform an a, after which it terminates successfully and passes control to P using sequential composition.

CSP processes are closed under sequential composition. A consequence of this is that CSP processes are also closed under prefixing as this has been defined in terms of sequential composition.

3.5   Additional Healthiness Conditions

The healthiness conditions **CSP1** and **CSP2** are not alone strong enough to characterize a model containing *only* relations corresponding to processes that can be written using CSP operators. Three further conditions are needed—these are given below.

Definition 20. CSP3: $\text{CSP3}(P) \mathrel{\widehat{=}} SKIP;\ P$

The condition **CSP3** states that the behaviour of a process does not depend on the initial value of the refusals; i.e. it should be the case that when a process P starts, whatever the previous process could, or did refuse should be irrelevant. This follows intuitively from the definition of $SKIP$, which throws away the value of the refusals on termination. Expanding this condition gives $\neg\ wait \Rightarrow (P = \exists ref \bullet P)$. If the previous process diverged ($\neg\ okay$) then **CSP1** guarantees the behaviour of P is already independent of ref. So **CSP3** is relevant to the situation $okay \wedge \neg\ wait$—when the process has started and is in a stable state.

Several laws are relevant to **CSP3**. Firstly, as expected it is idempotent. The others concern closure properties: as CSP processes are not closed with respect to conjunction (hence the **CSP2** clause in Definition 14), closure is concerned with disjunction, conditional, and sequential composition. The laws for closure all carry the proviso that $P = \text{CSP3}(P)$ and $Q = \text{CSP3}(Q)$.

Definition 21. CSP4: $\text{CSP4}(P) \mathrel{\widehat{=}} P;\ SKIP$

CSP4 requires that on termination or divergence, the value of ref' is irrelevant. If P terminates without diverging then the value of ref' is irrelevant; whereas if P has not terminated then the value of ref' is that of P. If P diverges the only guarantee is that the trace is extended: all other observational variables are irrelevant.

$SKIP$, $STOP$, and $CHAOS$ are all **CSP4** healthy. Additionally, the usual closure properties also hold, with the usual proviso that $P = \text{CSP4}(P)$ and $Q = \text{CSP4}(Q)$.

Definition 22. *Interleaving* ($\interleave$):

$$P \interleave Q \mathrel{\widehat{=}}$$
$$(\ wait' = (P.wait \vee Q.wait)\ \wedge$$
$$ref' = (P.ref \cap Q.ref)\ \wedge$$
$$tr' - tr \in (P.tr' - tr \interleave Q.tr' - tr)\ \wedge$$
$$ok' \wedge (P.ok \wedge Q.ok)\ );\ SKIP$$

Definition 22 presents the interleaving operator. In this definition. Each of the actions of the interleaving of P and Q is an action of either P or of Q. If one of either P or Q can not have engaged in an action, then it must have been performed by the other; if both could have engaged in the action then the choice between them is non-deterministic. An action can only be refused when it is refused by P and Q, and terminates only when both P and Q terminate.

Definition 23. CSP5: $\mathbf{CSP5}(P) \mathrel{\widehat{=}} P \;\|\!|\!|\; SKIP$

Finally, **CSP5** has the effect of insisting that refusals of a process are subset closed. That is to say, at an arbitrary subsequent observation—which may be an intermediate state or a terminating one—a process may have been refusing any of the events in ref'; it must also therefore have been able to refuse all the events in any subset of ref'—including the empty set. The interleaving operator used in Definition 23 is given in Definition 22.

4   Unconditional and Conditional Interrupts

In this section, the existing step law of [4,8] for the interrupt operator is presented. This is extended to a conditional version of the operator. Several obvious and practically useful laws are shown to follow.

4.1   Characterizing Unconditional Interrupt

Law 1. $\triangle_i$-*step:* $(a \rightarrow P) \triangle_i Q = (a \rightarrow (P \triangle_i Q)) \mathbin{\square} (i \rightarrow Q)$

Law 1 presents the step law given in [4,8]. This recursive law states that the interrupt event i is available as an external choice in all states in the interruptible process.

[4] states that this law is sufficient to uniquely characterize the operator for deterministic processes. This may be seen to follow intuitively: if a process is interruptible, it should be interruptible in all states—and this is achieved by the recursion in the law. Moreover, the interruptible process should not itself be able to control when it is interrupted—the external choice with the interrupt event i ensures that it is the environment that chooses when the interrupt event happens, if it happens at all. Furthermore, both [4] and [8] argue that if the operator is shown to distribute through non-determinism, and is shown to be strict, then the law is also a unique characterization of the operator for non-deterministic processes.

It follows that where this is shown to be the case, the step law is sufficient to establish a notion of theoretical completeness for the operator—it may be used in any situation to eliminate the operator from any specification. This is demonstrated by the normal form for CSP processes—in which the operator may be eliminated—presented in [8].

4.2   Laws of Unconditional Interrupt

A couple of laws follow from this definition.

Law 2. *STOP-$\triangle_i$:*   *STOP* $\triangle_i Q = i \to Q$

Firstly, the deadlock process *STOP* may be interrupted: if a process is interruptible and it is not engaging in any activity and waiting indefinitely, then only the interrupt event may occur.

Definition 24. *Refinement ($\sqsubseteq$):* $P \sqsubseteq Q \mathrel{\widehat{=}} [Q \Rightarrow P]$

Law 3. *SKIP-$\triangle_i$:*   *SKIP* $\triangle_i Q \sqsubseteq SKIP$

An attempt to interrupt *SKIP* may not succeed: it may terminate before the interrupt occurs. The only useful information that may be determined is that *SKIP* is itself a possible implementation of the scenario. The proofs of these laws are trivial, and rely on the step law and laws of external choice.

4.3   Characterizing Conditional Interrupt

Another useful operator is one where the interruptible process may choose whether to enable or disable the interrupt. Such a situation may be, for instance, a high priority process running on a processor disabling the outside world from de-scheduling it, and this is a common occurrence in modern, pre-emptive schedulers. In this section, a characterization of this version of the operator is given, along with the related versions of the laws in the previous section.

Definition 25. *Guard & :* $x \& Y \mathrel{\widehat{=}} (Y \lhd x \rhd STOP)$

Law 4. $\triangle_{c\&i}$-*step:* $(a \to P) \triangle_{c\&i} Q = (a \to (P \triangle_{c\&i} Q)) \mathbin{\square} (c \mathbin{\&} i \to Q)$

A conditional interrupt is one where the interrupting process can assign to a boolean control variable c, and the value of c indicates whether or not it is willing to engage in an interrupt.

This characterization, not presented in either [4] or [8], draws from the step law for unconditional interrupt, and therefore follows that it too is sufficient to uniquely characterize this operator. The environment is responsible for choosing when an interrupt event happens, if at all. However, importantly, the interruptible process has the ability to enable or disable this choice, depending on the value of the guard c. This value need not be fixed: for instance it may be true initially, and later false in $P(x)$. In this way, it is possible for the interruptible process to enable and disable its potential to be interrupted.

4.4   Laws of Conditional Interrupt

As with unconditional interrupt, the same couple of laws fall out of this definition.

Law 5. *STOP-$\triangle_{c\&i}$:* $STOP \triangle_{c\&i} Q = c \& i \rightarrow Q$

Firstly, the deadlock process *STOP* may or may not be be interrupted: if a process is interruptible and it is not engaging in any activity and waiting indefinitely, then only the interrupt event may occur. However, if the guard c is *false*, then the interrupt event may be refused and the deadlocked process cannot progress.

Law 6. *SKIP-$\triangle_{c\&i}$:* $SKIP \triangle_{c\&i} Q \sqsubseteq SKIP$

The condition with *SKIP* is more complicated: if the guard were enabled, then the attempt to interrupt it may or may not succeed; if the guard were disabled then it will certainly fail. As before, the proofs of these laws rely on the step law, and those for external choice.

5   A Denotational Semantics for Interrupt

In the previous sections, definitions of interrupt were given that relied on the step law in [4,8]. In this section, a denotational semantics for unconditional interrupt is given. This denotational semantics is correct as it respects the step law. Furthermore, by showing that the definition meets those requirements to allow it to uniquely characterize non-deterministic systems, it is shown to be theoretically complete. Whilst [4] argues that the step law is sufficient, it may also be the case that other laws are found to be useful for pragmatic reasons— and the denotational semantics allows for the proving of these laws. The section opens by presenting a new healthiness condition that allows a process to interfere with behaviours of the processes preceding it. This is followed by an operator that allows alphabets of a process to be added to, and finally a new operator called *interrupt prefix* that allows events to be forced into choice with preceding events is given. Together these are used to give the semantics of the interrupt operator in a style similar to that of sequential composition, choice and prefixing for regular CSP processes.

5.1   A Healthiness Condition Allowing Interference

Definition 26 presents a new healthiness condition **I3**. An **I3** healthy process may interfere with the behaviours of its predecessor, and may only execute while the predecessor is in a wait state—i.e. has not terminated. If the predecessor has terminated—i.e. *P.wait = false* it behaves as the identity. We name this condition **I3** to reflect its relation to **R3**.

Definition 26. I3: $\mathbf{I3}(P) = P \triangleleft wait \triangleright II_{CSP}$

Example 4. **I3** processes left-commuting through history: $P; \mathbf{R3}(Q; \mathbf{I3}(R))$

In Example 4, for all processes P, Q, and R, the process $(P; \mathbf{R3}(Q; \mathbf{I3}(R)))$ is **R3** healthy along with any additional assumptions about P, Q, and R. The process R is made **I3** healthy by an application of **I3**. The behaviours of R can therefore left-commute through history, and an observation of Q may contain some observation of R. This is not what would have been expected had R been a process that was **R3** healthy: normally no observations of R would be expected until Q had terminated. The composition of Q and R is made **R3** healthy to stop the behaviours of R left-commuting further—into the observations of P.

Law 7. R3(I3(P)) = II_{CSP}

Although a process X of the form **I3**(X) is not a CSP (or even reactive) process as it contradicts **R3**, it can form part of a process that is, as in Law 7, which states that an **I3** process that is required to be **R3** healthy will in fact behave as the identity. The proof follows from the definitions of **R3** and **I3**.

Law 8. I3-$\vee$-*dist*: I3($P \vee Q$) = I3(P) $\vee$ I3(Q)

Moreover, **I3** distributes over disjunction—given as Law 8. The proof follows from the disjunctive properties of the conditional operator.

5.2   Extending Alphabets

The alphabet of a process P is the observational variables and $\mathcal{A}P$, the set of events in which P can potentially engage.

Definition 27. *Alphabet extension* $^+$: $P^{+i} \mathrel{\widehat{=}} P \wedge (i \notin ref' \lhd wait' \rhd P)$

Definition 27 presents a new operator, *alphabet extension*, $^+$. This operator takes a given process and adds an event i into its alphabet. In ensuring that the expression is well defined, several considerations must be made. During execution of P, the event i was not in the alphabet of P; therefore the event is added to $\mathcal{A}P$ on termination. It is certainly the case that P was not willing to engage in i during execution—therefore the event may be added to the final refusals of P.

Law 9. $^+$-$\vee$-*dist*: $(P \vee Q)^{+i} = P^{+i} \vee Q^{+i}$

Law 10. $^+$-;-*dist*: $(P;\ Q)^{+i} = P;\ Q^{+i}$

Alphabet extension distributes through disjunction. In the case of sequential composition however, it does not distribute leftwards: this is because it affects the final refusals of a process, and these are always the final refusals of the rightmost process in the sequential composition. Of course, by **CSP3** these are in general not relevant to the behaviour of the process—but are in fact crucial to the behaviour of an interruptible process.

5.3   Communication, Events, and Prefixing

The prefix operator $\rightarrow$ given in Definition 18 describes standard CSP prefixing of events. However this definition is not sufficient for describing the case where an event is forced to occur despite apparent opposition—precisely the situation when a process is being interrupted. In this section, we develop the definition of a new operator, *interrupt prefix* ($\triangle$) to describe this.

Definition 28. $try(a, P) \cong ((a \notin ref' \land II_{CSP}) \lhd wait' \rhd tr' = tr \frown \langle a \rangle); \ P$

Definition 29. $try(a) \cong (a \notin ref' \land II_{CSP}) \lhd wait' \rhd tr' = tr \frown \langle a \rangle$

The process $try(a, P)$ of Definition 28 does not refuse to communicate a before termination; and when it has terminated, an a has been appended to the trace. Following this will be the process P. This is similar to the use of do_A in simple prefixing (Definition 17), except that the reactive healthiness conditions are not imposed. Definition 29 presents the special case where P is *SKIP*.

Definition 30. $force(a, P) \cong \mathbf{I3}(try(a, P))$

Definition 31. $force(a) \cong \mathbf{I3}(try(a))$

The definition of *force* in Definition 30 is a process that can interact with its environment only in the event that its predecessor has not terminated—by requiring it to be **I3** healthy. In this scenario it behaves as $try(a, P)$; when the predecessor terminates it behaves as the identity, meaning that the whole construct terminates. Definition 29 presents the special case where P is *SKIP*.

Definition 32. *Interrupt prefix:* $i \, \triangle \, Q \cong \mathbf{CSP1}(ok' \land force(i, Q))$

Definition 33. *Simple interrupt prefix:* $i \, \triangle \, SKIP \cong \mathbf{CSP1}(ok' \land force(i))$

Definition 32 presents the Interrupt prefix operator. This is similar in style to Definition 18: when the process is not diverging, behaviour is well defined—given by the function *force* of Definition 30. By ensuring that it is **CSP1** healthy, behaviour in the event of divergence is also well defined. Definition 33 presents the equivalent definition for the simple interrupt prefix.

Example 5. Care with interrupt prefix

$$(P; \ (i \to Q)) \ = \ (P; \ (i \to SKIP); \ Q)$$
$$(P; \ (i \, \triangle \, Q)) \ \neq \ (P; \ (i \, \triangle \, SKIP); \ Q)$$

Example 5 shows that care needs to be taken with the interrupt prefix operator—in particular with associative properties of sequential composition that do not hold. Prefixing for normal events ($\to$) is defined in terms of a simple prefix sequentially composed with subsequent behaviours. In the case where $Q \neq SKIP$, this is not true of the interrupt prefix ($\triangle$). The definition of **I3** states that a process which is **I3** healthy may be active before its predecessor terminated. In the case where the predecessor P successfully terminates, the **I3** healthy process is never observed. Therefore, in the case $P; \ i \, \triangle \, Q$, if P successfully terminates then no behaviours of $i \, \triangle \, Q$ will ever be observed. This is not true of $P; \ i \, \triangle \, SKIP; \ Q$. In this case, if P terminates successfully, no behaviours of $i \, \triangle \, SKIP$ may be observed, and control is immediately passed to Q.

5.4   Definition of Unconditional Interrupt

Definition 34. *Unconditional interrupt* $\triangle_i$:

$$P \triangle_i Q \;\hat{=}\; \mathbf{R3} \circ \mathbf{CSP2}(P^{+i}; \; i \triangle Q)$$

In this definition an unconditional interrupt is the interruptible process P with the interrupt event i added to its alphabet, sequentially composed with the **I3** healthy interfering process $i \triangle Q$.

If the interrupting process $(i \triangle Q)$ has not done anything, it terminates when the interruptible process (P^{+1}) terminates. Therefore the whole construct terminates. This is a consequence of $i \triangle Q$ being **I3** healthy. Should an i have been observed however, subsequent behaviour is only that of Q, so the construct terminates when Q terminates. It is necessary to require the whole construct to be **R3** healthy. In doing so, as in Example 4, it ensures $P \triangle_i Q$ is a valid CSP process. If the whole construct were not required to be **R3** healthy then the interrupt prefix could left commute through the predecessors of P—in Example 4 it would allow the interrupting process R to not only interrupt the process Q—which was the intention—but also to interrupt the process P, which was not. The purpose of the **CSP2** is is to preserve properties of divergence that would normally be imposed on an external choice.

5.5   Proving the Correctness of the Denotational Semantics

In order to prove that this denotational semantic model of the interrupt operator is correct, it is necessary to prove that it respects the step law, Law 1. As the step law is accepted to uniquely characterize the operator, we assert that if the denotational semantics respects this step law, then it is correct. The full proof is very long and is omitted from this paper; however in this section we present some new laws and corollaries that support the proof, and we conclude this section by briefly discussing the structure of the proof.

Law 11. $\triangle_i$-;-*dist*:

$$(P; \; Q) \triangle_i R = ((P \wedge wait') \triangle_i R) \vee (P \wedge \neg \; wait'; \; (Q \triangle_i R))$$

The expression $(P; \; Q) \triangle_i R$ describes the situation where the sequential composition of P and Q may be interrupted by $i \triangle R$. Three possibilities exist: either P is interrupted before it has terminated normally, or P terminated normally and Q is interrupted, or both processes terminated normally. In the case where P is interrupted, subsequent behaviour is $i \triangle R$, and no observations are made of Q. However, if P terminated normally, Q may be interrupted, and subsequent behaviour is $i \triangle R$. In the third case, where Q terminates normally, the whole construct terminates and no observations of $i \triangle R$ are ever made.

Law 12. $\triangle_i$-*elim*: $a \rightarrow SKIP \triangle_i Q = a \rightarrow SKIP \;\square\; i \rightarrow Q$

If the intention is to interrupt the simple prefix $a \rightarrow SKIP$, then the choice of both $a \rightarrow SKIP$ and $i \rightarrow Q$ is available. This allows for the elimination of the interrupt operator in specific situations.

Corollary 1. $\triangle_i$-elim1:

$$(a \rightarrow SKIP \wedge wait') \triangle_i Q = (a \rightarrow SKIP \wedge wait') \square i \rightarrow Q$$

Corollary 2. $\triangle_i$-elim2:

$$(a \rightarrow SKIP \wedge \neg wait') \triangle_i Q = (a \rightarrow SKIP \wedge \neg wait') \square i \rightarrow Q$$

Two corollaries follow from this and the law of the excluded middle. In Corollary 1, the interruptible process has not terminated and the external choice is still possible. In Corollary 2 the interruptible process has terminated successfully, but the external choice was still a possibility.

Law 13. $\triangle_i$-step:

$$(a \rightarrow P) \triangle_i Q = (a \rightarrow (P \triangle_i Q)) \square (i \rightarrow Q)$$

The proof of the correctness of the denotational semantics relies on these corollaries. Firstly, it observes that the process $a \rightarrow P$ can be rewritten as a simple prefix—meaning that the laws for distribution of interrupt through sequential composition apply. The most useful and applicable law therefore is the elimination of the interrupt operator, resulting in the introduction of an external choice with the waiting simple prefix. Once the external choice has been factored out of the internal choice, the final two steps of the proof reconstruct the definition of interrupt.

5.6 Proving Properties of Distribution and Strictness

In Section 4, conditions were stated which must be met in order to prove that an operator is applicable to both non-deterministic and deterministic systems. These conditions are that non-determinism must distribute through the operator, and that the operator must be strict. In this section, laws are presented that justify these claims about the denotational semantics for the interrupt operator. The conclusion is that the denotational semantics are sufficient for non-deterministic systems, and therefore Law 1 ($\triangle_i$-step) is shown to be theoretically sufficient: i.e, it is applicable to the interrupt operator in all circumstances.

Law 14. $\sqcap - \triangle_i$-dist: $(P \sqcap Q) \triangle_i R = (P \triangle_i R) \sqcap (Q \triangle_i R)$

Example 6. Multiple interrupts: $(P \triangle_i Q \triangle_j R) = ((P \triangle_i Q) \triangle_j R)$

Law 14 considers the distribution of disjunction through the left hand operand of the interrupt operator. The syntax of the interrupt operator requires that the choice of interrupt event i is unique. If a model requires multiple interrupt events, then multiple interrupts need to be specified (and the interrupt operator binds as tightly as the prefix operator), and this is demonstrated in Example 6. Given then, that $i \rightarrow P \sqcap i \rightarrow Q = i \rightarrow (P \sqcap Q)$, the right hand will always be deterministic with regards to the interrupt event. Therefore Law 14 is the only one necessary to satisfy the requirements for distribution through disjunction.

Law 15. *CHAOS-$\triangle_i$:*   *CHAOS* $\triangle_i$ Q = *CHAOS*

The second requirement for applicability to non-deterministic systems is that the operator is strict: that $f(\perp) = \perp$. Law 15 describes this for the left operand (the interruptible process).

In a similar manner to that for non-determinism in the left argument, it is not necessary to consider strictness in the right argument as the interrupting process may not be chaotic. This follows from the fact that the interrupt event i must be unique, and $i \to CHAOS \neq CHAOS$—the syntax of the operator therefore does not permit interrupting behaviour to be urgently chaotic—the first event observed is deterministic.

5.7   Distribution of Interrupt Through Variable Scope

The Unifying Theories model of CSP allows for the declaration of variables, and the ending of variable scope. This introduces a piece of syntax not considered in the applicability of the step law of [4,8]. However, the denotational semantics allow for a law that demonstrates that this additional piece of syntax does not affect the applicability of the step law.

Law 16.   **var** -$\triangle_i$-*dist*

$$(\textbf{ var } x; \; P; \; \textbf{ end } x) \triangle_i \; Q = \textbf{ var } x; \; P \triangle_i \; Q; \; \textbf{ end } x$$
$$[\textit{ provided } x \notin \alpha Q \;]$$

If P contains some state that is in scope until P terminates, then that scope also extends to the interrupting process. In other words, the local state will remain in scope until Q terminates.

Therefore, the step law may now be applied to the interrupt operator inside the variable declaration. In fact, although this law is necessary to show that the new syntax does not affect the applicability of the law, its use extends further than this: to the preservation of user state through the modelling of failure.

6   Conditional Interrupt, Denotationally

In the conditional version of the operator, c is the condition that enables or disables the interrupt, and i is the interrupting event. When c is true, the interrupt prefix $i \triangle Q$ is enabled, and when c is false, it behaves as the identity.

Definition 35. *Conditional interrupt* $\triangle_{c\&i}$:

$$P \triangle_{c\&i} \; Q \; \widehat{=} \; \textbf{R3} \circ \textbf{CSP2}(P^{+i}; \; (i \triangle Q) \triangleleft c \triangleright II_{CSP})$$

Similar laws apply to the conditional version of the operator as to the unconditional version. It left-distributes through sequential composition. It may be eliminated when interrupting a simple prefix—the difference is that the interrupt event i is guarded by the condition c. In the case where c is always true, these laws reduce to the laws given in the previous section for the unconditional version of the operator. Therefore the unconditional version of the operator can be regarded as a special case of the conditional version, with the added condition that $c = true$ is invariant.

Law 17. $\triangle_{c\&i}$-;-*dist:*

$$(P; \; Q) \triangle_{c\&i} R = ((P \wedge wait') \triangle_{c\&i} R) \vee (P \wedge \neg \; wait'; \; (Q \triangle_{c\&i} R))$$

Law 18. $\triangle_{c\&i}$-*elim:* $a \rightarrow SKIP \triangle_{c\&i} Q = a \rightarrow SKIP \; \square \; c \& i \rightarrow Q$

Corollary 3. $\triangle_{c\&i}$-*elim1:*

$$(a \rightarrow SKIP \wedge wait') \triangle_{c\&i} Q = (a \rightarrow SKIP \wedge wait') \; \square \; c \& i \rightarrow Q$$

Corollary 4. $\triangle_{c\&i}$-*elim2:*

$$(a \rightarrow SKIP \wedge \neg \; wait') \triangle_{c\&i} Q = (a \rightarrow SKIP \wedge \neg \; wait') \; \square \; c \& i \rightarrow Q$$

Law 19. $\triangle_{c\&i}$-*step denotationally:*

$$(a \rightarrow P) \triangle_{c\&i} Q = (a \rightarrow (P \triangle_{c\&i} Q)) \; \square \; (c \& i \rightarrow Q)$$

6.1   Proving Properties of Distribution and Strictness

Law 20. $\sqcap - \triangle_{c\&i}$-*dist:* $(P \sqcap Q) \triangle_{c\&i} R = (P \triangle_{c\&i} R) \sqcap (Q \triangle_{c\&i} R)$

Law 21. $CHAOS$-$\triangle_{c\&i}$: $CHAOS \triangle_{c\&i} Q = CHAOS$

Properties of distribution and strictness also hold for the conditional version. That is, non-determinism distributes through the left hand operand; and it is strict. The syntax does not allow for non-determinism or urgently chaotic behaviour in the right hand operand due to the uniqueness of the interrupting event.

6.2   Distribution of Conditional Interrupt through Variable Scope

As expected, the fact that the interrupt is conditional does not affect the preservation of local state; as shown by the following law.

Law 22.   var -$\triangle_{c\&i}$-*dist*

$$(\; \textbf{var } x; \; P; \; \textbf{end } x) \triangle_{c\&i} Q = \; \textbf{var } x; \; P \triangle_{c\&i} Q_{+x}; \; \textbf{end } x$$
$$[\; provided \; x \notin \alpha Q \;]$$

7   Summary

In this paper, a semantics for the interrupt operator of CSP was given in the Unifying Theory. A traces semantics was given in [4], and failures semantics in [8]; the definition in this paper is equivalent to a failures-divergences semantics and is the most complete treatment of the operator recorded. Existing algebraic laws hold, in particular the step law—concluding that the definition presented in this paper respects all the properties of that in [4,8].

An interesting aspect of the semantics is that a new construct (healthiness condition $I3$) was required for the definition. This healthiness condition is not suitable for a CSP process—in fact it contravenes some conditions necessary for a process to be considered a CSP process. However, the aggregate construct of an interruptible and interrupting process *is* still a CSP process. The ability to construct this definition, in particular the ability to include a non-CSP process in this manner, is itself evidence that the Unifying Theories semantic model of CSP is more expressive than the well accepted failures-divergences model of [8].

Other works such as [11] have shown the usefulness of the interrupt operator in modelling systems failures and faults. Therefore including a definition of this operator in the Unifying Theories semantic model of CSP allows its application in these areas. Moreover, as the semantic model of *Circus*[9,10] is based on this model, we postulate that this definition will be applicable to *Circus* processes.

[2] demonstrates how the failures-divergences of a Unifying Theories CSP process can be calculated from its semantics. We have not attempted to calculate the failures-divergences of our operator in this paper, but to do so, and compare the failures-divergences semantics with the failures semantics of [8] would be an interesting future exercise. Another exercise that we leave for future work is to compare the behaviours of our operator with other notions of interrupts—both in formal notations, and in programming languages and hardware systems, and to investigate how our notion of interrupt generalizes across different languages and paradigms.

References

1. Bergstra, J.A., Klop, J.W.: Algebra of communicating processes with abstraction. Theoretical Computer Science 37(1), 77–121 (1985)
2. Cavalcanti, A., Woodcock, J.: A tutorial introduction to CSP in Unifying Theories of Programming. In: Pernambuco Summer School on Software Engineering 2004: Refinement. Springer, Heidelberg (2005)
3. Hoare, C.A.R.: Communicating sequential processes. Comm. ACM 21(8), 666–677 (1978)
4. Hoare, C.A.R.: Communicating Sequential Processes. Prentice-Hall International Series in Computer Science. Prentice-Hall, Englewood Cliffs (1985)
5. Hoare, C.A.R., Jifeng, H.: Unifying Theories of Programming. Prentice-Hall Series in Computer Science. Prentice-Hall, Englewood Cliffs (1998)
6. Milner, R.: A Calculus of Communication Systems. LNCS, vol. 92. Springer, Heidelberg (1980)

7. Milner, R.: Communication and Concurrency. International Series in Computer Science. Prentice-Hall, Englewood Cliffs (1989)
8. Roscoe, A.W.: Theory and Practice of Concurrency. Prentice Hall Series in Computer Science. Prentice Hall, Englewood Cliffs (1998)
9. Woodcock, J.C.P., Cavalcanti, A.L.C.: A concurrent language for refinement. In: 5th Irish Workshop on Formal Methods (2001)
10. Woodcock, J.C.P., Cavalcanti, A.L.C.: The semantics of Circus. In: Bert, D., Bowen, J.P., Henson, M.C., Robinson, K. (eds.) Formal Specification and Development in Z and B. ZB 2002, pp. 184–203. Springer, Heidelberg (2002)
11. Woodcock, J.C.P., McEwan, A.A.: Verifying the safety of a railway signalling device. In: Ehrig, H., Kramer, B.J., Ertas, A. (eds.) Proceedings of IDPT 2002, The 6th Biennial World Conference on Integrated Design and Process Technology, Society for Design and Process Science, vol. 1 (2002)

UTP Semantics for Handel-C

Juan Ignacio Perna and Jim Woodcock

Computer Science Department
The University of York
York - United Kingdom
{jiperna,jim}@cs.york.ac.uk

Abstract. Only limited progress has been made so far towards an axiomatic semantics or discovering the algebraic rules that characterise Handel-C programs. In this paper we present a UTP semantics together with extensions we needed to include in order to express Handel-C properties that were not addressable with standard UTP. We also show how our extensions can be abstracted to a more general context and prove a set of algebraic rules that hold for them. Finally, we use the semantics to prove some properties about Handel-C constructs.

1 Introduction

Handel-C [10] is a Hardware Description Language (HDL) based on the syntax of the C language extended with constructs to deal with parallel behaviour and process communications based on CSP [11]. The language is designed to target synchronous hardware components with multiple clock domains, usually implemented in Field Programmable Gate Arrays (FPGAs).

In this paper we present a denotational semantics for a subset of Handel-C. Our semantics is based on the theory of designs as presented in the Unifying Theories of Programming (UTP) [12]. Special attention is paid to the way in which parallelism is captured, as the UTP model for parallel composition is more restrictive than the one used in Handel-C. The major difference between the two parallel models lies in the fact that the shared-variable parallel model presented in UTP is based on the parallel processes terminating at the same time. As this restriction does not hold for Handel-C programs, we propose an extension of this UTP theory that is capable of handling the kind of parallelism we required. We also used the semantics to prove a set of algebraic rules about Handel-C programs.

We also generalise the notions in our parallel operator for Handel-C and provide a more general parallel operator that is able to handle processes that may take a different amount of clock cycles to finish. We also address the algebraic laws of our operator together with the healthiness conditions that it preserves.

The rest of this paper is organised as follows: section 2 presents the syntax of the subset of Handel-C we address in this work together with an informal account of its semantics. Section 3 presents our parallel-by-merge operator for Handel-C that handles parallel composition of processes of different length. This section

A. Butterfield (Ed.): UTP 2008, LNCS 5713, pp. 142–160, 2010.

also covers the algebraic laws we have proved about the operator together with the healthiness conditions the operator preserves. Section 4 presents the UTP semantics for Handel-C and motivates the changes we introduced in UTP in order to be able to capture Handel-C's timing model and restrictions. This section also includes a set of algebraic laws we have proved from the semantics together with examples of the semantics in action. In section 5 we propose an abstraction of our parallel-by-merge operator suitable for more general synchronous environments. Finally, section 6 presents the related research and section 7 the conclusions and future extensions of this work.

2   Handel-C in More Detail

In order to provide semantics for the language, a simplified subset that captures the major constructs in the Handel-C language is being used. Most constructs in the language can be built by combining constructs in this subset, with exception of the prioritised choice construct and function calls. Our subset of Handel-C constructs is presented in figure 1.

$\langle program \rangle ::= \textbf{main} \{ \langle statements \rangle \}$

$\langle statements \rangle ::= \langle statement \rangle \, \mathbin{;} \langle statements \rangle \mid \langle statements \rangle \mathbin{\overset{\parallel}{_{HC}}} \langle statements \rangle \mid \langle statement \rangle$

$\langle statement \rangle ::= \textbf{if} \langle boolean\ expression \rangle \textbf{ then } \langle statements \rangle \textbf{ else } \langle statements \rangle$

$\qquad \mid \textbf{while} \langle boolean\ expression \rangle \textbf{ do } \langle statements \rangle$

$\qquad \mid \langle variable\ list \rangle \overset{:=}{_{HC}} \langle expression\ list \rangle \mid \delta^{HC} \mid \Pi_{HC}$

$\qquad \mid \langle channel\ name \rangle ? \langle variable\ name \rangle \mid \langle channel\ name \rangle ! \langle expression \rangle$

Fig. 1. Restricted syntax for Handel-C programs

As described in the language documentation [10], programs are comprised of at least one **main** function and, possibly, some additional functions. Multiple main functions (within the same file) produces the parallel execution of their bodies under the same clock domain. It is possible to produce the same effect in our reduced subset by means of the parallel operator.

All C-based constructs in Handel-C behave as defined in ANSI-C [14] but with some additional restrictions regarding the clock-based, synchronous nature of the language. In this sense, the evaluation of expressions is performed by means of combinatorial circuitry and it is completed within the clock cycle in which it is initiated (expressions are considered to be evaluated "for free" [10] due to this semantic interpretation).

This way of evaluating conditions affects the timing of all the constructs in the language. In the case of selection, the branch selected for execution (depending on the condition) will start execution within the same clock cycle in which the whole construct is initiated. The **while** construct behaves in a similar way when its condition is true (i.e., it starts its body in the same clock cycle in which its condition is evaluated) and, because of the same reason, terminates within the same clock cycle in which its condition becomes false. Assignment, on the other hand, happens at the end of the clock cycle. This definition of the assignment construct allows swapping of variables without the need of temporary variables.

From the remaining non-C constructs, parallel composition of statements executes in a *real* parallel fashion as it refers to independent pieces of hardware running in the same clock domain. Delay leaves the state unchanged but takes a whole clock cycle to finish and $\mathit{II}_{\mathsf{HC}}$ leaves the state unchanged and finishes immediately (in fact, no hardware is generated for it).

Finally, input and output have the standard blocking semantics: if the two parts are ready to communicate, the value outputted at one end is assigned to the variable associated with the input side. Both sides of the communication take one full clock cycle to successfully communicate. A process trying to communicate over a channel without the other side being ready will block (delay) for a single clock cycle and try again.

3   Extended Parallel by Merge

As mentioned before, we intend to define the semantics of Handel-C constructs in terms of synchronous UTP designs. The first problem we faced in this context is the fact that the parallel-by-merge approach used in UTP (see [12] chapter 7), is only applicable to parallel processes that take the same amount of time to terminate. This is a very strong restriction, especially in the context of Handel-C where parallel composition is unrestricted in this sense.

The rest of this section outlines the definitions and algebraic laws that hold for a new parallel-by-merge operator that can handle processes that do not necessarily take the same amount of time to finish.

3.1   The Merge Predicate

The first step towards the definition of our operator is to instantiate the merge predicate M that will join the results of two *single-step* parallel process. By *single-step* we mean a process that performs all its actions in a single time unit (e.g., a single clock cycle in the context of synchronous hardware). The intuition behind our definition is that M will update the shared variables to the value of the process that has modified it or will leave it unchanged if none of the parallel processes modified it. More precisely, we define M as follows:

$$M(ok, m, 0.m, 1.m, m', ok') =$$
$$ok \Rightarrow ok' \wedge$$
$$\qquad ((m' = m) \lhd m = 1.m \rhd (m' = 1.m))$$
$$\qquad \lhd m = 0.m \rhd$$
$$\qquad ((m' = 0.m) \lhd m = 1.m \rhd (m' = 1.m \sqcap m' = 0.m))$$

Handel-C semantics allows at most one write to any shared variable per clock cycle. In this context, our definition for M behaves as expected as it will be applied at the end of each clock cycle where we know that, at most, one of the processes has changed the value in its local copy of m.

We "totalised" the definition of M in order to cover the (impossible) case where the two parallel processes modify m, as we needed M to be symmetric in order to prove our operators associative later in this section. In this context, the result of multiple assignment to the same variable during the same clock cycle is the internal choice of updating the store with either of the values being assigned. This unexpected non-determinism can be explained at the hardware level by the unpredictable value that will be stored in a register when it is fed with more than one value at the same time.

Following Hoare and He [12], we define the single-step parallel composition operator $\|_M$ as $P \|_M Q =_{df} ((P; U0) \| (Q; U1)); M$. Here $U0$ and $U1$ are separating simulations that will generate the local copies of the shared state.

We are interested in proving some standard algebraic laws about our merge predicate:

L1 $P \|_M Q = Q \|_M P$ $\qquad\qquad\qquad\qquad\qquad\qquad$ $\|_M$-comm

L2 $P \|_M (Q \|_M R) = (P \|_M Q) \|_M R$ $\qquad\qquad\qquad$ $\|_M$-assoc

L3 $(\mathit{II}_X \|_M \mathit{II}_Y) = \mathit{II}_{X \cup Y}$ $\qquad\qquad\qquad\qquad\qquad$ $\|_M$-II

L4 **true** $\|_M P = $ **true** $\qquad\qquad\qquad\qquad\qquad\qquad$ $\|_M$-**true**

L5 $(P \lhd b \rhd Q) \|_M R = ((P \|_M R) \lhd b \rhd (Q \|_M R))$ $\qquad$ $\|_M$-$\lhd\rhd$

L6 $(P \sqcap Q) \|_M R = (P \|_M R) \sqcap (Q \|_M R)$ $\qquad\qquad$ $\|_M$-$\sqcap$

L7 $(\bigsqcup S) \|_M R = \bigsqcup_n (S_n \|_M R)$ $\qquad\qquad\qquad\qquad$ $\|_M$-$\bigsqcup$

$\qquad$ for any descending chain $S = \{S_n \mid n \in \mathcal{N}\}$

L8 $(x := e; P) \|_M Q = (x := e); (P \|_M Q)$

$\qquad$ provided that $x := e$ does not mention m

Instead of proving all these laws for our operator, we can take advantage of an already proved result from UTP that guarantees properties **L1** - **L7** above to hold iff M is a *valid merge*. We proved M to be valid by showing it satisfies:

V1 $(0.m, 1.m := 1.m, 0.m); M = M$ $\qquad\qquad\qquad$ M is symmetric

V2 $(0.m, 1.m, 2.m := 1.m, 2.m, 0.m); M3 = M3$ $\qquad$ M is associative

$\qquad$ where $M3 = \exists x, t \bullet M(ok, m, 0.m, 1.m, x, t) \wedge M(t, m, x, 2.m, m', ok')$

V3 $(\mathbf{var}\ 0.m, 1.m := m, m; M) = \mathit{II}$

We were also able to prove two expected properties from our definition of M: if one of the branches remains idle (i.e., does not modify the shared variable), then the shared variable will be updated according to the other branch (M-unit); and if the two processes modify the variable in the same way then the shared variable will be updated to that value (M-idemp). More formally stated:

$$(0.m = v); M(v, 0.m, 1.m, m') = (m' = 1.m) \qquad \textit{M-unit}$$
$$(0.m, 1.m := v, v); M(m, 0.m, 1.m, m') = m' = v \qquad \textit{M-idemp}$$

We also proved that M preserves healthiness conditions **H1** to **H4**, by proving (again, by a result from UTP) that $\|_M$ is **H1** to **H4**.

3.2   The Final Merge Predicate

In the context of UTP synchronous parallel process, time is captured by a global counter c and each parallel process has its own copy of the store. Each process has access to the global state by means of a pair of vectors indexed by time: in and out that can be interpreted as the values of the global variables at the beginning and end of the clock cycle respectively. Processes behave independently from each other, signalling the end of their actions at each clock cycle by performing a **sync** action. The merge predicate is then used to calculate the global value of the store for that clock cycle and to propagate the value to the processes through the in observation.

So far we have defined how to merge the result of a single step in the computations of parallel processes. The next step is to define a final merge predicate $\hat{M}$ (i.e., a predicate that will take the result of two arbitrary processes and will compute the final outcome of their parallel execution) that is capable to handle different-length parallel processes. The main issue when trying to define such an operator is how to state that if one of the processes takes less clock cycles to finish than the other one, then it should do nothing but wait. More important, how to produce this "missing behaviour" while preserving properties **L1** to **L8** from the previous section.

The above idea could be expressed in the UTP by forcing the shorter process to perform the missing **sync** actions it is not doing (i.e., advancing the local counter c and updating out_c and the shared resource m appropriately). There are several alternative ways to achieve this effect but, even though all of them are operationally correct, they fail when trying to prove some of the desired properties for the parallel merge operator. The main reason for this being the *behavioural padding* we are using to generate the missing behaviour for the shorter process not being associative and not distributing over $\hat{M}$.

The evidence above suggests that we need a way of denoting the padding in a less explicit way. In fact, we need to find a way to establish the right values in the variables used to control the parallel execution for the shorter processes and to denote the fact that the local copy of the shared resource m is keeping its previous value while the clock counter is advancing.

To achieve this effect we first introduce a new variable f recording the clock cycle count in which the whole program finishes. In this way, we keep the local copies of the counter c to the actual termination times for each branch while we are able to express actions for the whole duration of the program. We also introduce the $0.m.in$ inspired after the in vector in the UTP formulation. We initialise $0.m.in$ to behave like the standard feedback loop in a flip-flop (at each clock cycle, it holds the same value it had during the previous clock cycle). In this way, we are avoiding an explicit mention of how the variable is preserving its previous value during the cycles in which the process is inactive.

We also need to account for the communication primitives and how our parallel operator handles them. We define the input and output commands to rely upon a set of special variables that are not included in the list of program variables. The special set of variables associated to a given channel ch include $ch?, ch!$ and ch standing, respectively, for the requests for inputting, outputting and the value to be transmitted over ch. We also assume that $ch?, ch!$ (the requests for communication) will remain in the logical value $false$ unless they are used. This assumption is consistent with the hardware implementation of communications, where the requests are wires that remain in a "low state" unless they are explicitly fed with current when the request is done.

Finally, we introduce the fixed, but arbitrary value ARB. As with the $false$ logical value for the communication requests, this value will be the default value for all channels when they are not being used. This is a refinement of what happens at the hardware level where the value of this kind of buses is left unconstraint when they are not being used.

We now extend the standard definition of the separating simulation $U0$ (and similarly $U1$) to include $m.in$ together with the channel request wires:

$$U0 =_{df} \mathbf{var}\ 0.m.in, 0.c, 0.ch?, 0.ch!, 0.ch := m.in, c, ch?, ch!, ch;$$
$$\mathbf{end}\ m.in, c, ch?, ch!, ch$$

With these definitions in place we now define the final merge predicate:

$$\hat{M} =_{df} (c := max(0.c, 1.c)\ \|$$
$$\{M(m_{i-1}, 0.m.in_i, 1.m.in_i, m.in_i')|c \le i \le f\}\ \|$$
$$\{M(false, 0.ch_i, 1.ch_i, ch_i')|c \le i \le f\}\ \|$$
$$\{M(false, 0.ch?_i, 1.ch?_i, ch?_i')|c \le i \le f\}\ \|$$
$$\{M(\text{ARB}, 0.ch!_i, 1.ch!_i, ch!_i')|c \le i \le f\});$$
$$\mathbf{end}\ 0.c, 1.c, 0.ch?, 1.ch?, 0.ch!, 1.ch!, 0.ch?, 1.ch?, 0.ch, 1.ch;$$
$$\{\mathit{II}_{m.in_i, m_i, \text{com}(ch)_i}|i < c\}$$

There are several aspects of this definition that are worth noticing:

- Even though the introduction of f in our model allows the local counters ($0.c$ and $1.c$) to be different, we know one of them (the bigger one) matches the actual cycle count for the parallel execution of both processes. We choose the longest execution time to update the global cycle counter.
- All our updates to the shared store (generically referred to as m) are based on the value of the resource being updated at the previous clock cycle. Updates to the communication requests and bus values, on the other hand, are based on their respective default values.

The rationale behind the behaviour for the store is that we are modelling sequential hardware, where the next value of registers (variables) will depend on the state of the machine in the previous clock cycle. A similar explanation holds for communication requests and buses, where the default values are used to detect if any of the processes has changed them. In both cases, M acts as a multiplexer that selects between preserving the old/default value or routing the updated value.

- Regarding Hoare and He's initial formulation, we removed the presence of the *out* sequence in our model. In UTP, the *out* vector is used to record the intermediate results produced by the process over the shared variables and avoid variable capture. The fact that our variables are themselves sequences allows us to remove *out* and reuse the local copy of m for this purpose.

Finally, we define the parallel-by-merge operator as:

$$P \parallel_{\hat{M}} Q =_{df} ((P;U0) \parallel (Q;U1)); \hat{M}$$

3.3 Algebraic Laws and Healthiness Conditions

In this section we provide the set of laws we proved about our parallel-by-merge operator. Most of the laws are similar to the ones presented earlier in the paper for the $\parallel_M$ operator, but we recast them here for clarity.

L1 $P \parallel_{\hat{M}} Q = Q \parallel_{\hat{M}} P$ $\hfill \parallel_{\hat{M}}\text{-comm}$

L2 $P \parallel_{\hat{M}} (Q \parallel_{\hat{M}} R) = (P \parallel_{\hat{M}} Q) \parallel_{\hat{M}} R$ $\hfill \parallel_{\hat{M}}\text{-assoc}$
   provided that P, Q and R are **H4**

L3 $(II \parallel_{\hat{M}} P) = P$ $\hfill \parallel_{\hat{M}}\text{-}II$

L4 $\textbf{true} \parallel_{\hat{M}} P = \textbf{true}$ $\hfill \parallel_{\hat{M}}\textbf{-true}$

L5 $(P \triangleleft b \triangleright Q) \parallel_{\hat{M}} R = ((P \parallel_{\hat{M}} R) \triangleleft b \triangleright (Q \parallel_{\hat{M}} R))$ $\hfill \parallel_{\hat{M}}\text{-}\triangleleft\triangleright$

L6 $(P \sqcap Q) \parallel_{\hat{M}} R = (P \parallel_{\hat{M}} R) \sqcap (Q \parallel_{\hat{M}} R)$ $\hfill \parallel_{\hat{M}}\text{-}\sqcap$

L7 $(\bigsqcup S) \parallel_{\hat{M}} R = \bigsqcup_{n} (S_n \parallel_{\hat{M}} R)$ $\hfill \parallel_{\hat{M}}\text{-}\bigsqcup$
   for any descending chain $S = \{S_n \mid n \in \mathcal{N}\}$

L8 $x := e; (P \parallel_{\hat{M}} Q) = (x := e; P) \parallel_{\hat{M}} Q$ $\hfill :=\text{-}\parallel_{\hat{M}}$

L9 $(P \parallel_{M_{\{m,ch\}}} Q); \textbf{tick}; (R \parallel_{\hat{M}} S) = (P; \textbf{tick}; R) \parallel_{\hat{M}} (Q; \textbf{tick}; S)$ $\hfill \parallel_M\text{-}\parallel_{\hat{M}}$
   provided that P and Q do not perform any **tick** event
   where $\parallel_{M_{\{m,ch\}}} =_{df} M(m, 0.m.in, 1.m.in, m.in') \parallel$
$$M(\text{com}(ch), 0.\text{com}(ch), 1.\text{com}(ch), \text{com}(ch)')$$

We start by proving two of the three validity properties of the $\|_{\hat{M}}$ operator by showing:

$$(0.st, 1.st := 1.st, 0.st); \hat{M} = \hat{M} \qquad\qquad \hat{M}\text{-symmetric}$$

$$\text{where } st =_{df} m_{0..f}, c, ch?, ch!, ch$$

$$(0.st, 1.st, 2.st := 1.st, 2.st, 0.st); \hat{M}3 = \hat{M}3 \qquad\qquad \hat{M}\text{-associative}$$

$$\text{where } \hat{M}3 =_{df} \exists x.st \bullet \hat{M}(st, 0.st, 1.st, x.st) \wedge \hat{M}(st, x.st, 2.st, st')$$

With these results, we easily proved ($\|_{\hat{M}}$-comm) and ($\|_{\hat{M}}$-assoc).

The key result regarding our parallel-by-merge operator's capability to handle processes of different length lies in property 3.3**L3**, as the spreadsheet principle (3.3**L9**) will eventually reduce the shorter process to $\mathit{II}_{\mathsf{HC}}$.

Proof of 3.3**L3**: For the proof, consider:

$$P =_{df} c, m.in, ch, ch?, ch! :=$$
$$c + t, P.m.in \frown \langle m.in_{c+t+1}, ..., m.in_f \rangle, P.ch_{c..c+t} \frown \langle \mathsf{ARB}, ..., \mathsf{ARB} \rangle,$$
$$P.ch?_{c..c+t} \frown \langle false, ..., false \rangle, P.ch!_{c..c+t} \frown \langle false, ..., false \rangle))$$

Then we have:

$$\mathit{II}_{\{m.in, \mathrm{com}(ch), c\}} \|_{\hat{M}} P$$

$= [\|_{\hat{M}}$'s definition, $U0$ and $U1$ definition and predicate calculus]

$$((0.c, 0.m.in_{c..f}, 0.ch_{c..f}, 0.ch?_{c..f}, 0.ch!_{c..f} :=$$
$$c, \langle m.in_{c-1}, ..., m.in_{f-1} \rangle, \langle \mathsf{ARB}, ..., \mathsf{ARB} \rangle, \langle false, ..., false \rangle, \langle false, ..., false \rangle) \|$$
$$(1.c, 1.m.in_{c..f}, 1.ch_{c..f}, 1.ch?_{c..f}, 1.ch!_{c..f} :=$$
$$c + t, P.m.in \frown \langle m.in_{c+t+1}, ..., m.in_f \rangle, P.ch_{c..c+t} \frown \langle \mathsf{ARB}, ..., \mathsf{ARB} \rangle,$$
$$P.ch?_{c..c+t} \frown \langle false, ..., false \rangle, P.ch!_{c..c+t} \frown \langle false, ..., false \rangle)); \hat{M}$$

$= [\hat{M}$-unit]

$$(c, m.in_{c..f}, ch_{c..f}, ch?_{c..f}, ch!_{c..f} :=$$
$$c + t, P.m.in \frown \langle m.in_{c+t+1}, ..., m.in_f \rangle, P.ch_{c..c+t} \frown \langle \mathsf{ARB}, ..., \mathsf{ARB} \rangle,$$
$$P.ch?_{c..c+t} \frown \langle false, ..., false \rangle, P.ch!_{c..c+t} \frown \langle false, ..., false \rangle)$$

$= [$Definition of $P]$

$$P$$

Laws **L4-L8** can be easily proved from the fact that $\hat{M}$ is defined in terms of $\|$ and these properties hold for the disjoint-alphabet parallel operator. **L9** can be proved following the proof sketched in [12].

Regarding the healthiness conditions and their preservation through the $\|_{\hat{M}}$ operator, we begin by observing that even though we have not explicitly stated that $\hat{M}$ is a design, this can be easily shown if we first note that all the parallel elements in its definition are designs:

$$\hat{M}$$
$$= [\hat{M}\text{'s definition}]$$
$$(\textbf{true} \vdash c := max(0.c, 1.c)) \parallel$$
$$\{(\textbf{true} \vdash M(m_{i-1}, 0.m_i, 1.m_i, m.in_i'))|c \le i \le f\} \parallel$$
$$\{(\textbf{true} \vdash M(ch_{i-1}, 0.ch_i, 1.ch_i, ch_i))|0 < i < f\} \parallel$$
$$\{(\textbf{true} \vdash M(ch?_{i-1}, 0.ch?_i, 1.ch?_i, ch?_i))|0 < i < f\} \parallel$$
$$\{(\textbf{true} \vdash M(ch!_{i-1}, 0.ch!_i, 1.ch!_i, ch!_i))|0 < i < f\} \parallel$$
$$\textbf{end } 0.c, 1.c, 0.ch?, 1.ch?, 0.ch!, 1.ch!, 0.ch?, 1.ch?, 0.ch, 1.ch$$
$$= [\parallel \text{ composition of designs, } \mathbb{M} \text{ for } \hat{M}\text{'s body}]$$
$$(\textbf{true} \vdash \mathbb{M})$$

By being a design, $\hat{M}$ satisfies **H1** and **H2**. $\hat{M}$'s simple assumption (**true**) makes it trivial to prove that it also satisfies **H3**. Finally, **H4** follows naturally from M being **H4**. We use these results together with the fact that our definition of $\parallel_{\hat{M}}$ follows the UTP parallel-by-merge template to ensure that $\parallel_{\hat{M}}$ is implementable and preserves the four healthiness conditions.

4   Handel-C Semantics

In this section we present the semantic expressions that give meaning to Handel-C constructs. The first problem we face when trying to produce a UTP-based semantics is the property of the assignment design that allows us to flatten a sequence of assignments to a single (possibly multiple) assignment (law 3.1.**L2** in UTP). For example, UTP algebraic laws for assignment and sequential composition allow us to reduce $(x := 1; x := x + 1)$ to $x := 2$. Even though the equivalent Handel-C program also finishes by storing the value 2 in x, it does so after two clock cycles and we are interested in preserving the information about $x = 1$ for a whole clock cycle before changing into its final value (this is fundamental when parallel composition is taken into account).

We address this problem by turning the variables in the program into sequences of values indexed by clock cycle. In this way, it does not hold that $(x \mathbin{\underset{\mathsf{HC}}{:=}} 1 \mathbin{\mathring{,}} x \mathbin{\underset{\mathsf{HC}}{:=}} x + 1) = x \mathbin{\underset{\mathsf{HC}}{:=}} 2$. For this idea to work we need to introduce a way to keep track of the current clock cycle and how each construct behaves with respect to it. With this in mind, we extend the scope of the observational variable c from just parallel regions to the full scope of the program. We also add a single action capturing the notion of the clock *ticking*:

$$\textbf{tick} =_{df} c := c + 1$$

We also take advantage of the *in* vector as defined in section 3.2. In the context of the semantics, it plays a key role because it allows us to unify the sequential and parallel worlds and preserve the compositionality of the approach (we will address this issue in more detail at the end of this section).

To keep the presentation compact, we introduce the notation com(ch) to stand for all the variables associated to channel ch ($ch?$,$ch!$,ch) and com$_{idle}$ to the set of values associated to a channel when it is idle (i.e., it's default values).

In these terms, the semantics of assignment, the one-clock-cycle delay and II_{HC} can be stated as follows:

$$[\![x \mathbin{\overset{:=}{_{HC}}} e]\!] =_{df} (x.in_c, v.in_c, \text{com}(c) := [\![e]\!], v_{c-1}, \text{com}_{idle}); \textbf{tick}$$
$$[\![\delta^{HC}]\!] =_{df} (v.in_c, \text{com}(c) := v_{c-1}, \text{com}_{idle}); \textbf{tick}$$
$$[\![II_{HC}]\!] =_{df} II_D$$

Here v stands for the remaining variables in the state space of the program. Thus, v_c refers to the values of the variables mentioned in v at clock cycle c and $v.in_{c+1}$ to the value for the *in* vectors associated to each of them at clock cycle $c + 1$. On the other hand, the semantics of an expression e are defined in the usual way with the exception that variable accesses (i.e., reads) are indexed by the clock cycle in which they happen.

The basic sequential constructs of the language can be given semantics by their UTP counterparts:

$$[\![P \mathbin{;} Q]\!] =_{df} [\![P]\!]; [\![Q]\!]$$
$$[\![\textbf{if } c \textbf{ then } P \textbf{ else } Q]\!] =_{df} [\![P]\!] \lhd [\![c]\!] \rhd [\![Q]\!]$$
$$[\![\textbf{while } c \textbf{ do } P]\!] =_{df} \mu X \bullet ([\![P]\!]; X) \lhd [\![c]\!] \rhd II$$

We use the communication requests introduced in section 3.2 and include three new signals $\overleftarrow{ch}, \overrightarrow{ch}$ and $\overleftrightarrow{ch}$ standing for the granted request for input and output over ch together with the actual value transmitted over the bus ch. In this context, the semantics of the input/output primitives can be stated as follows:

$$[\![ch?m]\!] =_{df}$$
$$\mu X \bullet ch?_c := true;$$
$$((m.in_c, v.in_c, ch!_c, ch_c := \overleftrightarrow{ch}'_c, v_{c-1}, false, \text{ARB}; \textbf{tick})$$
$$\lhd \overrightarrow{ch}'_c = true \rhd$$
$$(v.in_c, ch!_c, ch_c := v_{c-1}, false, \text{ARB}; \textbf{tick}; X))$$
$$[\![ch!x]\!] =_{df}$$
$$\mu X \bullet ch!_c, ch_c := true, [\![x]\!];$$
$$((v.in_c, ch?_c := v_{c-1}, false; \textbf{tick})$$
$$\lhd \overleftarrow{ch}'_c = true \rhd$$
$$(v.in_c, ch?_c := v_{c-1}, false; \textbf{tick}; X))$$

It is worth noticing that none of the *granted-request* variables are modified by the communicating processes (i.e., they do not appear in the output alphabet of the processes). In this way, the same variable can be mentioned in multiple parallel without risking to interfere with each other.

The semantics for parallel composition is defined in terms of the $\|_{\hat{M}}$ operator:

$$[\![P \,_{\mathrm{HC}}\|\, Q]\!] =_{df} [\![P]\!] \,\|_{\hat{M}}\, [\![Q]\!]$$

We have addressed $\|_{\hat{M}}$ in full detail in section 3.2. For the present discussion it is relevant to highlight that it produces local copies of the state and the channels (thanks to the separating simulations) that each process will access and modify. The merge predicate $\hat{M}$ is then be used to merge these copies back into the original shared variables.

Finally, we use the top-level **main** function to introduce the clock cycle count c together with the traces for the store, their associated in variables and the channel request/granted signals. We also initialise the shared variables (with their corresponding in vectors) to behave like a flip-flop. We apply a similar technique to establish the default value for channel requests and to set the default value transmitted over the channels to ARB. In this way, we satisfy the assumptions about default values we made when defining $\|_{\hat{M}}$ in section 3.2.

$[\![\textbf{main } \{P\}]\!] =_{df}$

 var $c, m, m.in, f, ch?, ch!, ch, \overleftarrow{ch}, \overrightarrow{ch}, \overleftrightarrow{ch}; ch?, ch!, ch;$

  $c, m_{0..f}, m.in_{0..f} := 1, \lambda c \bullet \mathrm{ARB} \lhd c = 0 \rhd m_{c-1}, \lambda c \bullet \mathrm{ARB} \lhd c = 0 \rhd m_{c-1};$

  $ch?_{0..f}, ch!_{0..f}, ch_{0..f} := \lambda c \bullet false; \lambda c \bullet false; \lambda c \bullet \mathrm{ARB};$

  $[\![P]\!] \wedge (m = m.in') \wedge (f = c') \wedge (\overrightarrow{ch}' = ch!') \wedge (\overleftarrow{ch}' = ch?') \wedge (\overleftrightarrow{ch}' = ch');$

 end $m.in, f, ch?, ch!, ch, \overleftarrow{ch}, \overrightarrow{ch}, \overleftrightarrow{ch}$

It is worth noting the mapping we are producing between m and $m.in'$. In this way, the register storing m is copying what is fed to it through the in channel at every clock cycle. The simple relation this equation establishes is the key for the compositionality of the approach. In the context of sequential fragments, each sub-process will modify in according to its needs and this will be reflected in m. In the context of parallel processes, the in variable will be replicated (i.e., locally copied), generating multiple inputs to the same register. The $\hat{M}$ operator will appropriately merge (select) the right one and transfer the final value to the global in, ensuring homogeneous operation and compositionality.

We also constrain the value of f to the final value of the clock counter, making it consistent with our requirements in section 3. Regarding granted/request signals, they are used to avoid variable-capture when producing the local copies of the state within the parallel operator. The restrictions imposed here to keep them equal to the communication requests at all times, allows the feedback of the merged result (captured in the primed version of the requests) to the recursive equations used in the communication.

4.1 Properties about the Semantics

So far we have introduced a way to express the semantics for Handel-C in the theory of designs in UTP. At this point we are interested in using the semantics to find out which properties hold true for Handel-C syntactic constructs. We devote the rest of this section to describe the results we have proved so far towards this goal.

L1 $\quad P \,\semi\, (Q \,\semi\, S) = (P \,\semi\, Q) \,\semi\, S$ $\hfill \semi\text{-assoc}$

L2 $\quad P \parallel_{HC} Q = Q \parallel_{HC} P$ $\hfill \parallel_{HC}\text{-comm}$

L3 $\quad (P \parallel_{HC} Q) \parallel_{HC} R = P \parallel_{HC} (Q \parallel_{HC} R)$ $\hfill \parallel_{HC}\text{-assoc}$

L4 $\quad P \,\semi\, \Pi_{HC} = P = \Pi_{HC} \parallel_{HC} P$ $\hfill \semi\text{-skip}$

L5 $\quad \Pi_{HC} \parallel_{HC} P = P$ $\hfill \parallel_{HC}\text{-}\Pi_{HC}$

L6 $\quad x :=_{HC} e \,\semi\, (P \parallel_{HC} Q) = (x :=_{HC} e \,\semi\, P) \parallel_{HC} (x :=_{HC} e \,\semi\, Q)$ $\hfill \parallel_{HC}\text{-}:=_{HC}$

L7 $\quad x :=_{HC} e \,\semi\, (P \parallel_{HC} Q) = (x :=_{HC} e \,\semi\, P) \parallel_{HC} (\delta^{HC} \,\semi\, Q)$ $\hfill \parallel_{HC}\text{-}:=_{HC}\text{-}\delta^{HC}$

L8 $\quad x, y :=_{HC} e_1, e_2 \,\semi\, (P \parallel_{HC} Q) = (x :=_{HC} e_1 \,\semi\, P) \parallel_{HC} (y :=_{HC} e_2 \,\semi\, Q)$ $\hfill \parallel_{HC}\text{-multiple-}:=_{HC}$

L9 $\quad (ch?x \,\semi\, P) \parallel_{HC} (ch!e \,\semi\, Q) =$

$\qquad (x, ch?, ch!, ch :=_{HC} e, true, true, e) \,\semi\, (P \parallel_{HC} Q)$ $\hfill ?!\text{-}_{HC}$

$\quad$ Provided that $(ch?', ch!', ch' = \overleftarrow{ch'}, \overrightarrow{ch'}, \overleftrightarrow{ch'})$

L10 $\quad (ch?x \,\semi\, P) \parallel_{HC} (ch!e \,\semi\, Q) \parallel_{HC} (ch?y \,\semi\, R) =$

$\qquad (x, y, ch?, ch!, ch :=_{HC} e, e, true, true, e) \,\semi\, (P \parallel_{HC} Q \parallel_{HC} R)$ $\quad ?!\text{-multiple-readers}$

$\quad$ Provided that $(ch?', ch!', ch' = \overleftarrow{ch'}, \overrightarrow{ch'}, \overleftrightarrow{ch'})$

L11 $\quad (ch?x \,\semi\, P) \parallel_{HC} Q =$

$\qquad ((ch?, ch!, ch :=_{HC} true, false, \mathsf{ARB}) \,\semi\, ch?x \,\semi\, P) \parallel_{HC} Q$ $\hfill ?\text{-copy-rule}$

$\quad$ Provided that there is no process writing into ch during the first clock cycle in the execution of the parallel region

L12 $\quad (ch!e \,\semi\, P) \parallel_{HC} Q =$

$\qquad ((ch?, ch!, ch :=_{HC} false, true, e) \,\semi\, ch?x \,\semi\, P) \parallel_{HC} Q$ $\hfill !\text{-copy-rule}$

$\quad$ Provided that there is no process reading from ch during the first clock cycle in the execution of the parallel region

The proofs for **L1** to **L5** are straightforward from our definition of the semantics and the properties of the underlying sequential and parallel composition operators. In particular, **L4** holds because the semantics of all our constructs in the language can be expressed as designs (Π is a left unit) that are also **H3** healthy (Π_D is a right unit).

Proof of **L6** (the proofs of **L7** and **L8** follow the same proof outline).

$$(x \mathrel{\overset{:=}{_{HC}}} e \mathbin{\overset{\circ}{_9}} P) \mathbin{\overset{\|}{_{HC}}} (x \mathrel{\overset{:=}{_{HC}}} e \mathbin{\overset{\circ}{_9}} Q)$$

$$= [\text{Semantics of } \mathrel{\overset{:=}{_{HC}}}, \mathbin{\overset{\circ}{_9}} \text{ and } \mathbin{\overset{\|}{_{HC}}}]$$

$$(x_c, v_c, \mathsf{com}(c) := e, v_{c-1}, \mathsf{com_{idle}}; \mathbf{tick}; P) \mathbin{\|_{\hat{M}}}$$
$$(x_c, v_c, \mathsf{com}(c) := e, v_{c-1}, \mathsf{com_{idle}}; \mathbf{tick}; Q)$$

$$= [\|_M\text{-}\|_{\hat{M}}]$$

$$((x_c, v_c, \mathsf{com}(c) := e, y_{c-1}, \mathsf{com_{idle}}) \mathbin{\|_{M_{\{x,v,\mathsf{com}(ch)\}}}}$$
$$(x_c, v_c, \mathsf{com}(c) := e, v_{c-1}, \mathsf{com_{idle}})); \mathbf{tick}; (P \mathbin{\|_{\hat{M}}} Q)$$

$$= [M\text{-idemp}]$$

$$(x_c, v_c, \mathsf{com}(c) := e, v_{c-1}, \mathsf{com_{idle}}); \mathbf{tick}; (P \mathbin{\|_{\hat{M}}} Q)$$

$$= [\text{Semantics of } \mathrel{\overset{:=}{_{HC}}}, \mathbin{\overset{\circ}{_9}} \text{ and } \mathbin{\overset{\|}{_{HC}}}]$$

$$x \mathrel{\overset{:=}{_{HC}}} e \mathbin{\overset{\circ}{_9}} (P \mathbin{\overset{\|}{_{HC}}} Q)$$

4.2   The Semantics in Action

In this section we present two simple cases to illustrate the way the semantics work on an environment of shared variables. The first example shows a program that first initialises one of the shared variables to them modify them in an uneven-length parallel subprocess:

$$\mathbf{main} \ \{x \mathrel{\overset{:=}{_{HC}}} 8 \mathbin{\overset{\circ}{_9}} ((x \mathrel{\overset{:=}{_{HC}}} x + 1) \mathbin{\overset{\|}{_{HC}}} (y \mathrel{\overset{:=}{_{HC}}} 1 \mathbin{\overset{\circ}{_9}} x \mathrel{\overset{:=}{_{HC}}} x + y + 1))\}$$

$$= [\mathbin{\overset{\|}{_{HC}}}\text{-multiple-}\mathrel{\overset{:=}{_{HC}}}]$$

$$\mathbf{main} \ \{x \mathrel{\overset{:=}{_{HC}}} 8 \mathbin{\overset{\circ}{_9}} (x, y \mathrel{\overset{:=}{_{HC}}} x + 1, 1) \mathbin{\overset{\circ}{_9}} (\varPi_{HC} \mathbin{\overset{\|}{_{HC}}} x \mathrel{\overset{:=}{_{HC}}} x + y + 1)\}$$

$$= [\mathbin{\overset{\|}{_{HC}}}\text{-}\varPi_{HC}]$$

$$\mathbf{main} \ \{x \mathrel{\overset{:=}{_{HC}}} 8 \mathbin{\overset{\circ}{_9}} (x, y \mathrel{\overset{:=}{_{HC}}} x + 1, 1) \mathbin{\overset{\circ}{_9}} x \mathrel{\overset{:=}{_{HC}}} x + y + 1\}$$

As expected, the program can be flattened into a sequence of parallel assignments. We can apply the semantic expressions for the constructs in Handel-C to obtain the trace:

$$\mathbf{var} \ c, x, y := 3, \langle \mathsf{ARB}, 8, 9, 11 \rangle, \langle \mathsf{ARB}, \mathsf{ARB}, 1, 1 \rangle$$

Our next example addresses the case where one process is trying to communicate with another one that is not ready:

$$\mathbf{main} \ \{(ch?x) \mathbin{\overset{\|}{_{HC}}} (y := 10 \mathbin{\overset{\circ}{_9}} ch!y)\}$$

$$= [?\text{-copy-rule}]$$

$$\mathbf{main} \ \{(ch?, ch!, ch \mathrel{\overset{:=}{_{HC}}} true, false, \mathsf{ARB} \mathbin{\overset{\circ}{_9}} (ch?x)) \mathbin{\overset{\|}{_{HC}}} (y := 10 \mathbin{\overset{\circ}{_9}} ch!y)\}$$

$$= [\mathbin{\overset{\|}{_{HC}}}\text{-multiple-}\mathrel{\overset{:=}{_{HC}}}]$$

$$\mathbf{main} \ \{(y, ch?, ch!, ch \mathrel{\overset{:=}{_{HC}}} 10, true, false, \mathsf{ARB}) \mathbin{\overset{\circ}{_9}} (ch?x \mathbin{\overset{\|}{_{HC}}} ch!y)\}$$

$= [?!\text{-} \underset{\mathsf{HC}}{:=}]$

main $\{(y, ch?, ch!, ch \underset{\mathsf{HC}}{:=} 10, true, false, \mathsf{ARB})\ \S$

$(x, ch?, ch!, ch \underset{\mathsf{HC}}{:=} y, true, true, y)\ \S\ (\mathit{\Pi}_{\mathsf{HC}} \underset{\mathsf{HC}}{\|} \mathit{\Pi}_{\mathsf{HC}})\}$

$= [\underset{\mathsf{HC}}{\|}\text{-}\mathit{\Pi}_{\mathsf{HC}},\ \S\text{-skip}]$

main $\{(y, ch?, ch!, ch \underset{\mathsf{HC}}{:=} 10, true, false, \mathsf{ARB})\S(x, ch?, ch!, ch \underset{\mathsf{HC}}{:=} y,$

$true, true, y)\}$

From the final equation above, it is easy to see that there was a failed attempt of communication during the first clock cycle, and that the communication was carried out during the following clock cycle. Expanding the semantics of the **main** function and assignment we can get the actual trace of the program:

var $c, x, y, ch?, ch!, ch := 2, \langle \mathsf{ARB}, \mathsf{ARB}, 10 \rangle, \langle \mathsf{ARB}, 10, 10 \rangle,$

$\langle false, true, true \rangle, \langle false, false, true \rangle, \langle \mathsf{ARB}, \mathsf{ARB}, 10 \rangle$

5   Generalising the Parallel by Merge Operator

Up to this point we have presented an extension of the parallel-by-merge theory presented in [12] that is able to handle different-length parallel processes in the context of the semantic expressions we are generating for Handel-C.

In this section we explore the possibilities of extending this notion to a more general case in order to make our results available to a broader application domain.

For the remainder of this section, we return to the framework in which this theory was initially developed by assuming a context in which inter-process communication, as described in earlier sections of this paper, is not required[1]. We are also going to remove the need to use sequences to represent the store, as it was introduced because of a particular need of the semantics for Handel-C.

Recasting from the previous section, we need to establish the properties that the merge predicate M must satisfy. Apart from being a valid merge (to guarantee properties 3.1.L1, 3.1.L2 and 3.1.L4 to 3.1.L7) we also require M to satisfy M-unit and M-idemp. We need the former to ensure that $\mathit{\Pi}$ is the unit for parallel composition inside shared regions and the later to prove that equality distributes over parallel composition with final merge.

We can interpret $(M\text{-unit})$ as defining the behaviour of the merge predicate when one of the parallel processes is idle. As the $\hat{M}$ operator is based on M, we can easily lift the property to $\hat{M}$ and prove:

$$(0.st = st); \hat{M}(st, 0.st, 1.st, st') = (st' = 1.st) \qquad \hat{M}\text{-unit}$$
$$\text{provided that } 1.c = j,\ f > c \text{ and } j > 0$$

Based on M satisfying the properties above, we intend to produce a final-merge operator that satisfies the laws 3.3.L1 to 3.3.L8 in this paper. In this

---

[1] We also assume the reader is familiar with the contents in chapter 7: *Concurrency* of UTP.

sense, we still need to provide a *valid* $\hat{M}$ predicate and, hence, we still have
the problem of handling the behavioural padding of the shorter processes in the
parallel composition. We take advantage of the f variable introduced earlier to
deal with this problem and define our more general formulation as:

$$U0(m) =_{df} \mathbf{var}\ 0.out, 0.c, 0.m;$$
$$0.c := c;$$
$$\{0.out_i := in_{i-1}|0 < i \leq f\};$$
$$0.out = 0.out \oplus out; 0.out_{0.c} = m; \tag{1}$$
$$0.m = 0.out_f; \tag{2}$$
$$\mathbf{end}\ out, c, m$$

Not surprisingly, we needed to re-introduce the *out* variable and we use the
same trace-like approach we defined before to perform the behavioural padding.
We also keep the same overriding behaviour we used before (line (1)) but we
also include the final value of the local copy of m at the end of *out* (note that
process 0 modifies the *out* sequence only within the index range $[0..(0.c-1)]$).
The reason for transferring the value of m to the *out* sequence is to cover the case
where $0.c < f$ (the process finishes earlier than other processes in the parallel
composition). In this context, the value of the local copy of m should be merged
with the corresponding outcome of the other processes at clock cycle $0.c$, and
these values are stored in the corresponding copies of *out* at this particular index
(clock cycle).

Finally, line (2) sets the value of the local copy of m to the outcome of the
current process at clock cycle f. In this way, we make $0.m$'s value independent
of the actual execution time for process 0 (we will take advantage of this fact to
define an associative $\hat{M}$ operator).

We are now ready to define the final-merge operator $\hat{M}$ as:

$$\hat{M} =_{df}\ c' = max(0.c, 1.c)\ \|$$
$$M(m \lhd f = c \rhd in_{f-1}, 0.m, 1.m, m')\ \| \tag{3}$$
$$\{M(m \lhd i = c \rhd in_{i-1}), 0.out_i, 1.out_i, out'_i|c \leq i < f\}\ \| \tag{4}$$
$$\{\mathbb{I}_{\{out_i\}}|i < c\};$$
$$\mathbf{end}\ 0.c, 1.c, 0.out, 1.out$$

Apart from the change in the way the clock is handled (already introduced in
the previous section), the main point to be noted here is that we changed Hoare
and He's initial formulation by replacing m with $m \lhd f = c \rhd in_{f-1}$ as the
first argument for M. The reason for this change is the fact that the initial
formulation by Hoare and He will ignore the intermediate changes to the shared
store and will calculate m's final value based on its value before the parallel
branches started executing (i.e., the value in m).

As mentioned earlier, we are interested in a clock-wise update of the shared
variable. To achieve this goal, assignments consume a clock cycle (i.e., they

produce a **sync** event) so synchronisation (and, hence, *merging*) happens on every clock cycle.

Moreover, our definition of M calculates the next value of m based on the local copy of the store that changed during the previous clock cycle. Thus, the final value for m should be calculated from the last update (stored in the *in* sequence at the current clock cycle minus one $0.c - 1$) rather than based on the value of m before the execution of the parallel processes (as several changes from that value may have happened to m since the parallel composition started and it would be impossible to find out which process made a modification during the last clock).

Finally, we need to define the way in which f is introduced (and calculated). As it only makes sense to mention f in the context of parallel processes sharing variables, we add it to the set of variables introduced in the **shared** declaration. In turn, we use the same "loop-back" approach used by Hoare and He to feed-back the *out* values produced by the parallel composition into the *in* vector to update f and define:

$$(\textbf{shared } m \mathbin{\fatsemi} P \mathbin{\fatsemi} \textbf{end } m) =_{df} \textbf{var } c, in, out, f \mathbin{\fatsemi}$$
$$(c := 0) \mathbin{\fatsemi} (P \wedge (in = out') \wedge (f = c')) \mathbin{\fatsemi}$$
$$\textbf{end } c, in, out, f$$

5.1 Validity, Algebraic Laws and Healthiness Conditions

Based on the properties we assumed for the merge predicate together with the associativity and commutativity of the max function, it is easy to show that our definition of $\hat{M}$ satisfies the symmetric and associative properties from the valid merge definition. Regarding the last valid property, the presence of f in the definition makes it impossible to be proved unless M satisfies (M-idemp).

Even though we can prove the third property in the *valid merge* definition, this result is not useful in the proof we intend to conduct. Instead, the proof relies on M satisfying (M-unit) as defined at the beginning of this section.

With the results above together with the laws for $\parallel$ we can prove that our general $\parallel_{\hat{M}}$ satisfies 3.3.L1 to 3.3.L7.

The proof of 3.3.**L8** relies in the following additional results we have proved about the UTP:

$$(v, m := x, v') = (v := x; m := v) \qquad \text{Primed assignment unfold}$$
$$\textbf{var } v; v_{0..j} := \langle v_0, v_1, ..., v_{j-1}, v_j \rangle; P(v_{j-1}); \textbf{end } v = \qquad \text{Partial end of scope}$$
$$\textbf{var } v; v_{0..j-1} := \langle v_0, v_1, .., v_{j-1} \rangle \wedge P(v_{j-1}); \textbf{end } v$$

Regarding the healthiness of our operator, we follow the same approach we used for the parallel-by-merge operator we defined for Handel-C. By a similar argument, our general final merge predicate can also be expressed as a design with trivial precondition **true**. In this way, we are sure it is **H1** to **H3** healthy. The proof of **H4** is based on the fact that $\hat{M}$ is a design and that M is also **H4**.

6   Related Work

Operational [7] and denotational [6,4,5] semantics have been proposed for Handel-C, providing interpretations for most constructs, ranging from simple assignments to prioritised choices (priAlts). Denotational semantics have also been proposed for the compilation into hardware [15] and used to formally verify some correctness properties of the generated hardware [16]. All these papers describe works based either in a branching-sequences semantic domain or a flattened version of the branching structure based on merge functions. In general, all these works were based on the notion of state-transformers, were each step in the semantics was expressing the effect of the construct over the state space of the program. The time model of Handel-C also directed all these works towards adopting a clock cycle as a unit and to split it into two disjoint sets of actions (i.e., combinatorial and sequential actions). The complexity of this kind of semantic domains made it quite difficult to use the semantics to validate/discover algebraic laws about Handel-C programs. In fact, only [8] used the semantics to prove some standard algebraic properties that also hold for Handel-C (e.g., $[\varPi\text{-}; \text{unit}]$, $[\|\text{-assoc}]$, etc).

In [9], initial steps towards the unification of most of these works in semantics are presented. The goal of this work is to provide a framework where a timed version of *Circus* [18] can be used as the specification language and several lower level languages (Handel-C among them) can be used to implement such a specification. The work is based on the reactive processes model provided in UTP. The rationale behind the selection of a reactive processes formalism lies in the need to cope with nondeterminism and refusals (present in the Circus language). The expressiveness of the acceptance-refusals model underlying the reactive theory in UTP is also likely to allow this framework to cover the recent trend in hardware design of interconnecting hardware working at different clock speeds (multiple clock domains). The price to be paid for this richness in expressivity is a more complicated theory, where it is necessary to deal with several intermediate observation points during each process' execution.

Our work is similar to [9] in the sense that it tends towards unifying the existing semantics for Handel-C and is oriented towards the algebraic rules satisfied by Handel-C programs. On the other hand, we have based our work on the theory UTP designs, preempting us from covering multiple clock domains but allowing a more compact and elegant representation of Handel-C programs aiming at single-clocked domains. We believe we will be able to profit from the elegance of our model when trying to prove algebraic laws about Handel-C operators/constructs.

UTP denotational semantics has also been been proposed for a subset of Verilog [13] that is similar to ours but includes guarded events (a non existing feature in Handel-C) and excludes recursion. The semantics are derived from an operational semantics model and they also include some algebraic reduction rules for parallel composition. The work is based in the reactive-processes theory of UTP (a subset of it, as they avoid healthiness condition **R2**). Our work is based on the simpler theory of designs and our focus is not in the derivation of the semantics from existing operational ones but in finding a comprehensive set of deduction rules for Handel-C.

Regarding other HDL languages (such as VHDL or SystemC), their semantics are informally provided in terms of a simulator [1,2]. Most works on the semantics of these languages follow these simulation models [3,17], making them quite different in purpose in comparison to our work.

7   Conclusions and Future Work

We have presented semantics for a subset of Handel-C including parallelism and communication. We have done so by using UTP's theory of designs as the semantic domain. The main contribution of this work is a denotational semantics for Handel-C that is well suited for reasoning and finding properties about the constructs of the language. Our usage of the theory of designs to describe the semantics for a HDL is also novel, as all existing works in the field address the semantics from the more powerful, yet more complex, theory of reactive processes (or a subset of it).

In the process of capturing the semantics of Handel-C in UTP we found several points in which we needed to extend or modify some aspects of UTP. The most interesting of these extensions is a parallel-by-merge operator that can handle parallel processes of uneven length. We have provided such an operator for the context of the semantics and proved a significant set of algebraic laws and healthiness conditions about it.

We also abstracted the key features of our parallel-by-merge operator and provided a more general formulation that we expect to be useful in a larger application domain. We also summarised the additional constraints that has to be satisfied by the single-step merge predicate in order for the general parallel merge to satisfy additional rules.

Finally, we have been able to take advantage of existing algebraic laws from UTP together with the rules provided in this work to easily prove an interesting set of algebraic laws about Handel-C programs. Some of these laws have been used to derive the semantics of example programs involving fixed-points in a few steps.

As future work we intend to keep on exploring the set of algebraic laws we can prove about the semantics. We are also interested in completing our work on semantics for Handel-C by covering priorities and procedure calls.

References

1. Multivalue Logic System for VHDL Model Interoperability (Std_logic_1164). IEEE Standard 1164-1993 (1993)
2. Standard SystemC Language Reference Manual (LRM). IEEE Standard 1666-2005 (2005)
3. Breuer, P.T., Fernández, L.S., Kloos, C.D.: Proof theory and a validation condition generator for VHDL. In: Euro-VHDL '94, pp. 512–517 (1994)

4. Butterfield, A.: Denotational semantics for prialt-free Handel-C. Technical report, The University of Dublin, Trinity College (December 2001)
5. Butterfield, A., Woodcock, J.: Semantic domains for Handel-C. Electronic Notes in Theoretical Computer Science, vol. 74 (2002)
6. Butterfield, A., Woodcock, J.: Semantics of prialt in Handel-C. In: Concurrent Systems Engineering. IOS Press, Amsterdam (2002)
7. Butterfield, A., Woodcock, J.: Prialt in handel-c: an operational semantics. International Journal on Software Tools Technology Transfer 7(3), 248–267 (2005)
8. Butterfield, A., Woodcock, J.: A Hardware Compiler Semantics for Handel-C. In: MFCSIT 2004, Dublin, Ireland, August 2006. ENTCS, vol. 161, pp. 73–90 (2006)
9. Butterfield, A., Sherif, A., Woodcock, J.: Slotted-circus. In: IFM, pp. 75–97 (2007)
10. Celoxica Ltd. DK3: Handel-C Language Reference Manual (2002)
11. Hoare, C.A.R.: Communicating sequential processes. Commun. ACM 26(1), 100–106 (1983)
12. Hoare, C.A.R., Jifeng, H.: Unifying Theories of Programming. Prentice-Hall, Englewood Cliffs (1998)
13. Huibiao, Z., Bowen, J.P., Jifeng, H.: From operational semantics to denotational semantics for verilog. In: Margaria, T., Melham, T.F. (eds.) CHARME 2001. LNCS, vol. 2144, pp. 449–471. Springer, Heidelberg (2001)
14. Kernighan, B.W.: The C Programming Language. Prentice Hall Professional Technical Reference (1988)
15. Perna, J.I., Woodcock, J.: A denotational semantics for Handel-C hardware compilation. In: ICFEM, pp. 266–285 (2007)
16. Perna, J.I., Woodcock, J.: Wire-Wise Correctness for Handel-C Synthesis in HOL. In: ETAPS'08 - Seventh International Workshop on Designing Correct Circuits (DCC), March 2008, pp. 86–100 (2008)
17. Salem, A.: Formal semantics of synchronous systemc. In: DATE '03: Proceedings of the conference on Design, Automation and Test in Europe, Washington, DC, USA, p. 10376. IEEE Computer Society, Los Alamitos (2003)
18. Woodcock, J., Cavalcanti, A.: A concurrent language for refinement. In: Butterfield, A., Strong, G., Pahl, C. (eds.) IWFM, Workshops in Computing. BCS (2001)

Unifying Theories of Locations

Michael Anthony Smith[1,2] and Jeremy Gibbons[1]

[1] Oxford University, UK
[2] Systems Assurance Group, QinetiQ, UK
anthony.smith@kellogg.oxon.org,
Jeremy.Gibbons@comlab.ox.ac.uk

Abstract. We present a Unifying Theories of Programming (UTP) model of locations, where a location is either *shareable* or *containable* depending on whether its value can be dereferenced by a pointer. Our model of locations is similar to previous work on pointers within the UTP; the main difference is that the previous work on pointers only modelled shareable locations. We explain why containable locations (whose values must be copied rather than aliased) are useful, present an outline of our UTP model, and compare it to existing work on UTP. We hope to convince the reader that a general model of pointers within the UTP ought to be able to represent both shareable and containable locations.

1 Introduction

Hoare and He's Unifying Theories of Programming (UTP) [3] uses the notion of a relational predicate to model various programming paradigms and features, such as imperative, functional, and parallel programming. Here, a relational predicate is a predicate that defines a relationship between observable input and output variables (i.e. the variables in the predicate's alphabet). For example, the UTP model in [1] supports the notion of a compound data structure via the introduction of a record datatype, which essentially maps distinct labels to values. These labels are also used when unambiguously specifying the location of a value and determining whether it is shared.

An object can be modelled in a similar manner to that of the record. For example, in C++ and C# the object and record types are defined by the class and struct datatype constructors respectively. Here, a variable of an object type contains a pointer to an object, whereas a variable of a record type contains the record itself. It is this distinction between variables of object and record types that we believe is important to explicitly model in a general theory of UTP pointers. Specifically, the contents of a record are duplicated, whereas the contents of an object are aliased (shared).

The UML class diagram in Figure 1 provides a high level overview of our model, which ensures that: each location has precisely one value; only shareable locations can be directly accessed via a reference value; and field names (labels) of a compound value represent containable locations. Such a model of locations can be used to support our earlier UTP model of objects [9].

A. Butterfield (Ed.): UTP 2008, LNCS 5713, pp. 161–180, 2010.
© Springer-Verlag Berlin Heidelberg 2010

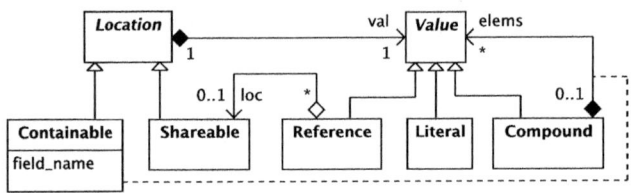

Fig. 1. Location Model – Class Diagram

1.1 Scope

The model of locations we present in this paper is not intended to support the concepts of object ownership or reference containment, such as discussed in ownership models [2,5] and separation logics [7]. Nor is this model of locations intended to support low-level pointer operations, such as those operations that create a new pointer by adding an arbitrary offset to an existing pointer (e.g. $p = p+2$) or get the address of a record's element (e.g. $p = \&(r.x)$). Having said this, it is straightforward to write C^{++} and C$^{\#}$ programs that do not directly use such low-level pointer operations and this ought to be syntactically checkable. For example, in C$^{\#}$ this could be achieved by banning the use of the unsafe keyword.

1.2 Family Tree

Within this paper we use instances of the family tree class diagram in Figure 2 to provide data structures for us to model. Here, shareable (hollow diamond) and composite (solid diamond) aggregations are used to distinguish between shareable and containable locations, respectively; aggregations that have any number of instances are represented by lists.

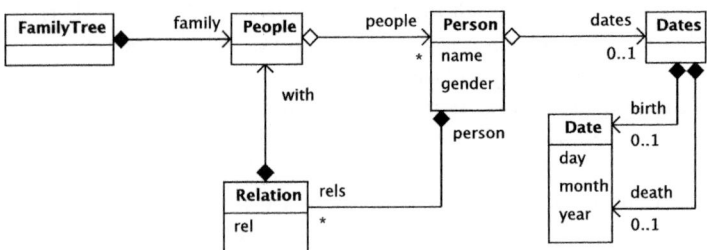

Fig. 2. Family Tree Example – Class Diagram

1.3 Structure

This paper continues by presenting a concrete model of locations (Section 2), which is abstracted (Section 3) and then integrated into the UTP (Section 4).

Having done this, the work is related to other UTP work on pointers (Section 5) and summarised (Section 6).

2   Concrete Representation

2.1   Concrete Value Notation

The two types of *literal value* used within this paper are the integers (e.g. -32) and the strings (e.g. "Some text"). There is also a special *unset* literal constant, denoted by ¿; this is used to represent the contents of a freshly created location, and the value of a missing element.

The two remaining types of concrete value are the *compound* and *reference* values. A compound value is represented by a partial map from field names (which we identify with containable locations) to concrete values. It is denoted by $\{_{i=1}^{k} nm_i = v_i\}$, where the name nm_i indexes the concrete value v_i. A name is denoted by an alpha-numeric word starting with a letter or the dollar symbol. The name represented purely by a single dollar symbol, which we refer to as the 'dollar name', is reserved for denoting a shareable location, and thus cannot be used as a compound value's field name.

A reference value is either null or an index to a shareable location. Such values are denoted by $\ominus$ and ℓ_i respectively, where two non-null reference values ℓ_i and ℓ_j index distinct shareable locations whenever $i \neq j$.

Figure 3 provides both an instance of the family tree's Dates class and a concrete value representation of this instance (object). Here, the Dates object explicitly sets only one of its two optional Date fields, birth, to 12 Aug 1980. The other optional field, death, is left unset. This data structure can be drawn as a graph, as illustrated in Figure 4, where: a literal value is denoted by a boxed node containing the literal; and a compound value is denoted by a circular node, whose outgoing edges are labelled with its distinct field names. Reference values are denoted by a diamond node that contains the reference (Figures 6 & 8).

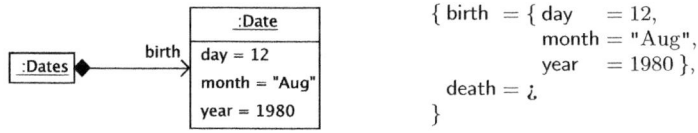

Fig. 3. Dates – object diagram and concrete representation

In addition to defining the concrete representations of the values used within this paper, it is useful to provide some meta-variables for representing each of the different types of value. Here we use i, j and k to represent integers; s to represent strings; lv to represent literal values; cv to represent compound values; rv to represent reference values; and v to represent a concrete value.

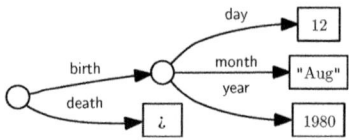

Fig. 4. Dates – concrete graph representation

We also use meta-variable t for representing a concrete term, where a concrete term includes the concrete values, field names, and the yet-to-be terms such as location graphs. These meta-variables are typically used to define functions, as illustrated by the following example, which extracts the shareable locations contained within a term. This example also uses the generalised term notation, $t\{^k_{i=1} t_i\}$, which denotes a term t with k sub-terms, $t_1, \ldots, t_k$, where a term that has no subterms is denoted by either $t\{\}$ or $t\{^0_{i=1} t_i\}$.

$$
\begin{aligned}
sLocs\; \ell_i &\;\widehat{=}\; \{\ell_i\} \\
sLocs\; t\{^k_{i=1} t_i\} &\;\widehat{=}\; \bigcup\{^k_{i=1} sLocs\; t_i\}
\end{aligned}
$$

We read such definitions by pattern-matching from top to bottom, accepting the first equation that matches an actual argument. Thus, the order in which the lines of a function are presented may affect its meaning. In this case, swapping the order would produce a function that returns the empty set.

The $sLocs$ function is applied to terms that are yet to be defined, such as the heap value term in Section 2.2. Note that this does not require an update to the $sLocs$ function as these terms are already handled by the second definitional line, which can be applied to any term (i.e. a general term).

2.2   Concrete Location Heap

A *location heap* is a partial map from shareable locations to values; it is denoted by $\{_{i:N}\; \ell_i \mapsto v_i\}$, where N is some finite subset of the natural numbers. For example, the object diagram in Figure 5 illustrates that Jane Doe is married to John Doe, where only the instances of the Person class are considered to be shareable. It can be represented by the following concrete location heap, where the contents of shared locations ℓ_3 and ℓ_5 contain the John Doe and Jane Doe Person objects respectively.

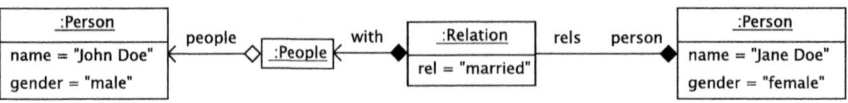

Fig. 5. Marriage example – object diagram

$\{ \ell_3 \mapsto \{$ name $=$ "John Doe", gender $=$ "male", dates $= \ominus$, rels $= \, \rlap{\llap{\textrm{\textlnot}}} \,\}$,
   $\ell_5 \mapsto \{$ name $=$ "Jane Doe", gender $=$ "female", dates $= \ominus$,
          rels $= \{ \$1 = \{$ rel $=$ "married", person $= \ell_5$, with $= \{$ people $= \{ \$1 = \ell_3 \} \} \} \}$
       $\}$
$\}$

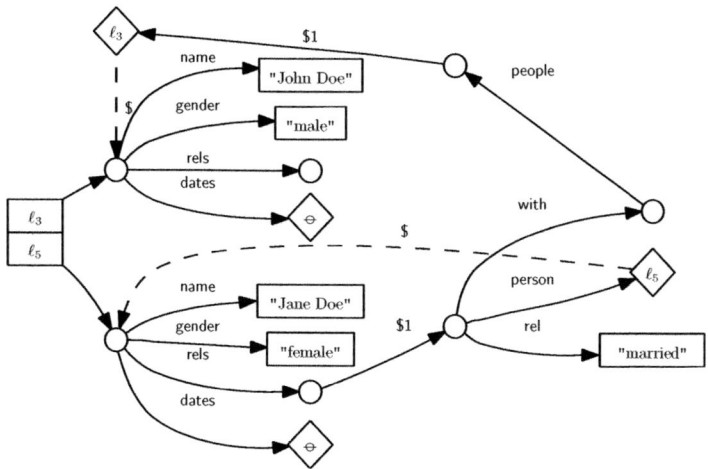

Fig. 6. Marriage example – concrete heap graph

Figure 6 provides the alternative graph representation of the example, where the dashed edges are used to link a reference value to its contents. Note that these edges are labelled with the dollar name ($) as discussed in Section 2.1.

Before moving on to present the concrete location model, we observe that a concrete heap can reference a shareable location that it does not define; i.e. a concrete heap can contain reference values that are not in the domain of the heap's partial map. In order to classify location heaps that do not have this undesirable property, we introduce a healthiness condition, which considers a heap to be healthy whenever all references to shared locations within the graph's values are defined by the graph itself.

$$\mathrm{HC_H} \ H \quad \widehat{=} \quad sLocs \ H \subseteq \mathrm{dom} \ H$$

where:

H	is the meta variable representing a concrete location heap
$\mathrm{dom}\,\_$	returns the domain of a relation or function

Further, any heap can be made healthy by adding an entry for each missing shared location and setting that location's value to the unset value ($\rlap{\llap{\textrm{\textlnot}}}$), as follows:

$$\mathrm{MH_H} \ H \quad \widehat{=} \quad H \cup \{ r \mapsto \rlap{\llap{\textrm{\textlnot}}} \mid r \in (sLocs \ H) \setminus (\mathrm{dom} \ H) \}$$

Note that a healthy heap is unaffected by the application of $\mathrm{MH_H}$ (and vice-versa), because all the shareable locations in the heap are contained within its domain; i.e. $(\mathrm{MH_H} \ H = H) \Leftrightarrow \mathrm{HC_H} \ H$.

The notion of equivalence ($\_ \equiv \_$) between location heaps is more complex than that for concrete values, which is mathematical equality (where the ordering of elements within a set or map is not significant). Here, the equivalence relationship between heaps allows for the renaming of shareable locations. Specifically, two heaps are considered to be equivalent if there exists a bijective map (f) that can be applied to one heap to produce the other.

$$H_1 \equiv H_2 \quad \Leftrightarrow \quad \exists f \bullet H_1 = rename(H_2, f)$$

where

$$rename(\ell_i, f) \quad \widehat{=} \quad \ell_{f(i)}$$
$$rename(t\{^k_{i=1} t_i\}, f) \quad \widehat{=} \quad t\{^k_{i=1} rename(t_i, f)\}$$

2.3   Concrete Location Model

Location models extend this notion of the heap by adding a starting point, which is represented by a concrete value. Therefore, a location model is denoted by a value-heap pair (v, H). Here, the idea is that the value v represents the root of a computational unit, such as a program, whose elements can share data via the shareable locations in the heap H.

Like the location heap that preceded it, location models have a healthiness condition which ensures that the heap is valid; that is, all the shareable locations referenced within a model are defined by the heap.

$$HC1_L(v, H) \quad \widehat{=} \quad sLocs(v, H) = \operatorname{dom} H$$

A location model can be made $HC1_L$-valid in a similar manner to a heap.

$$MH1_L(v, H) \quad \widehat{=} \quad (v, H \cup \{r \mapsto \text{¿} \mid r \in sLocs(v, H) \setminus (\operatorname{dom} H)\})$$

Locations in the model are considered to be *reachable* if they are either contained within the starting value v or indirectly contained within the contents of v's reference values. For $HC1_L$-healthy models, this can be formalised by the following functions, where R and R' represent the shareable locations that have already been taken into account and are contained within a value respectively.

$$reachable(v, H) \quad \widehat{=} \quad reachValue(v, H, \emptyset)$$
$$reachValue(v, H, R) \quad \widehat{=} \quad sLocs\ v \cup reachDeref(sLocs\ v, H, R)$$
$$reachDeref(R', H, R) \quad \widehat{=} \quad \bigcup\{reachValue(H\ r, H, R' \cup R) \mid r \in R' \setminus R\}$$

The following normal-form healthiness condition ensures that there is no unreachable information within the model; i.e. every shareable location that is defined by a model's heap is reachable.

$$\mathrm{HC2_L}(v, H) \ \widehat{=} \ \operatorname{dom} H = reachable(\mathrm{MH1_L}(v, H))$$

Note that we apply the $\mathrm{MH1_L}$ healthiness constructor prior to performing the reachability calculation, in order to ensure that $\mathrm{HC2_L}$ calculation is defined. If a location model is not in normal form (i.e. $\mathrm{HC2_L}$-healthy), it can be made so by ensuring that it is $\mathrm{HC1_L}$-healthy and then removing all the unreachable locations.

$$\mathrm{MH2_L}(v, H) \ \widehat{=} \ \text{let } (v_1, H_1) \ \widehat{=} \ \mathrm{MH1_L}(v, H) \text{ in}$$
$$(v_1, \{rv \mid rv \in H_1 \land (\textit{first } rv) \in reachable(v_1, H_1)\})$$

where $first(x, y) \widehat{=} x$.

We are now in a position to define an equivalence relation over location models. It is similar to that of heaps, except that we first ensure that models are made healthy before performing the check, as we only want to consider reachable elements in a model's heap. In other words, two location models are equivalent iff there exists some bijective shareable-location-renaming function f that enables two normalised heaps to be made equal.

$$(v_1, H_1) \equiv (v_2, H_2)$$
$$\Leftrightarrow$$
$$\exists f \bullet \mathrm{MH2_L}(v_1, H_1) = rename(\mathrm{MH2_L}(v_2, H_2), f)$$

It is this notion of equivalence up to which our UTP model of locations is fully abstract, as described in Section 4.3.

The family tree example can now be extended to illustrate a concrete location model, by adding an object to represent the family tree, as illustrated in Figure 7. The concrete graph representation of this example is provided by Figure 8, where the explicit visualisation of the heap has been removed, as it is no longer required for representing the shareable locations. Such locations are now represented by the dashed edges within the graph, which are now guaranteed to exist due to the reachability healthiness condition.

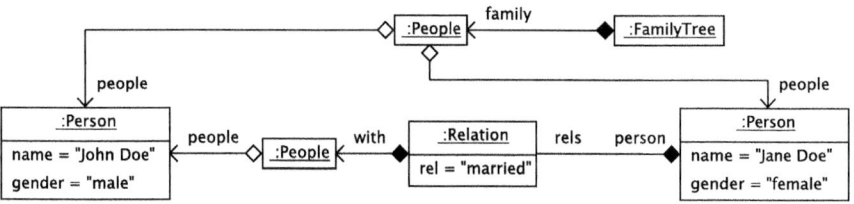

Fig. 7. Family tree example – object diagram

2.4 Paths and Their Operations

A *compound value path* describes a route from a compound value to one of its elements, via a non-empty dot-separated sequence of field names. Compound

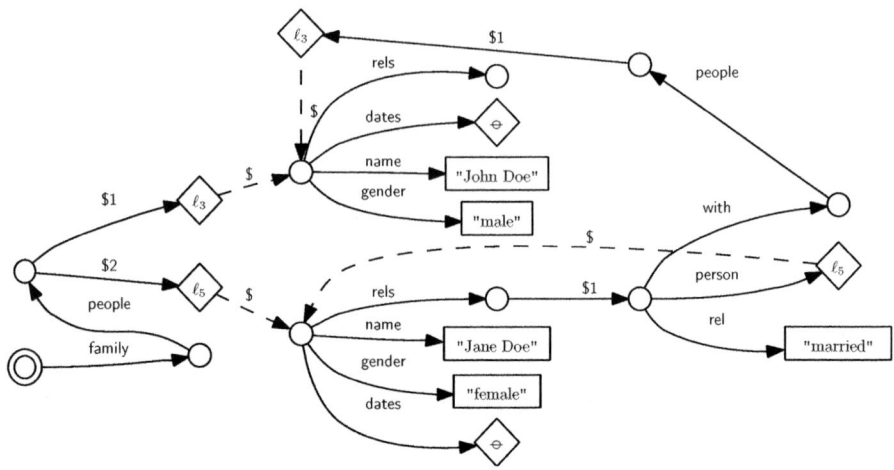

Fig. 8. Family tree example – concrete model graph

value paths are essentially used to describe routes to contained locations, which we can access and update by using the following functions:

$$*cv.nm \quad \widehat{=} \quad cv \; nm$$
$$cv.nm := v \quad \widehat{=} \quad cv \oplus \{nm \mapsto v\}$$
$$cv.nm.p := v \quad \widehat{=} \quad cv \oplus \{nm \mapsto (*cv.nm).p := v\}$$

where p is the meta-variable for paths, $(\_\ \_)$ is the function or map application operation, and $(\_ \oplus \_)$ is the function override operation. This notion of a path is extended to define location model update and access functions as follows:

$$*(v, L) \quad \widehat{=} \quad v$$
$$*(v, L).p \quad \widehat{=} \quad *v.p$$
$$*(v, L).\ell_i \quad \widehat{=} \quad L \; \ell_i$$
$$*(v, L).\ell_i.p \quad \widehat{=} \quad (L \; \ell_i).p$$
$$(v, L) := v' \quad \widehat{=} \quad (v', L)$$
$$(v, L).p := v' \quad \widehat{=} \quad (v.p := v', L)$$
$$(v, L).\ell_i := v' \quad \widehat{=} \quad (v, L \oplus \{\ell_i \mapsto v'\})$$
$$(v, L).\ell_i.p := v' \quad \widehat{=} \quad (v, L \oplus \{\ell_i \mapsto (L \; \ell_i).p := v'\})$$

Further, it is possible to extend this notion to copy a value from one location to another, as follows:

$$(v, L).lp := (v, L).lp' \quad \widehat{=} \quad (v, L).lp := *(v, L).lp'$$

where: $\varnothing$ denotes the empty path and lp denotes either a path (p), a shareable location index (ℓ_i), or a shareable location index followed by a path $(\ell_i.p)$; and $(v, L).\varnothing$ denotes (v, L).

It is also straightforward to define other operations, such as for deleting elements from compound values and the heap; we omit these constructions for reasons of space.

3   Abstract Model

In Section 2.3, graphs represented healthy concrete location models, where:

- the solid and dashed edges denote distinct compound and potentially shared shareable locations, respectively;
- the rectangular, circular, and diamond nodes denote literal, compound, and reference values, respectively.

This section presents: a brief overview of the trace-based graph abstraction; some utility operations for manipulating traces; a model of nodes as a set of traces; and an overview of the trace-based location graph model.

3.1   Graph Abstraction

We can determine the value of dereferencing a reference node of a concrete location graph by following that node's outbound edge (as shown in Figure 8). That is, the shareable location index contained within a reference node is not required. Thus, this unused data can, and will, be ignored in our abstraction.

We observe that the outbound edges of each node within a healthy concrete location graph have distinct labels. Therefore, we can use a finite non-empty sequence of names to unambiguously define a path from a graph's root node to any other node. Such a path is from now on referred to as an *absolute path*.

The location of a node within a concrete location graph can be modelled by the set of all absolute paths to that node, which we from now on refer to as an *absolute path-set*. Hence, one way of providing a UTP model of locations would be as a partial map from such an absolute path-set to an appropriate abstraction of the data directly associated with its corresponding node. For example, the data associated with:

- a literal or null-reference node could be modelled by its concrete value;
- a compound node could be modelled by its set of outbound edge labels;
- a non-null reference node could be modelled by its outbound edge label.

Such a model of locations is similar to that presented in [1], which uses the idea of an entity group to model shared locations. Here each group contains the set (equivalence class) of fully qualified variables that share the same location.

Another approach is to change the notion of an absolute path-set, from representing the location of a node to representing both the location and contents of a node. To avoid confusion, we refer to such paths as *traces*. Here, the idea is that the last value in a trace represents its content, and the front of the trace its location. In other words, a trace is a path p followed by a trace label l, where l represents either a name, a literal value, or the null-reference value; it is denoted by $p.l$. This is the basis of the UTP model of locations we present in this paper (Section 4). Such a model of locations is similar to that presented in [4], which uses trace-sets to model both locations and values. Here, the main difference is in our introduction of a containable location and its effect on assignment (which [4] refers to as 'pointer swing'). Specifically, within our model the contents of contained locations need to be duplicated, whereas the contents of shared locations are referenced.

3.2   Traces

As previously stated, a trace is denoted by $p.l$, where p is a path and l is a trace label (i.e. a name, a literal, a null-reference). One consequence of this is that it is only possible to concatenate two traces (denoted by $tr_1.tr_2$) when the last label in the first trace tr_1 is a name, as only names are allowed within a path.

The remainder of this section defines some utility operations on traces and trace-sets, that are used in the construction of our abstract model of locations. First we introduce two operations front and last for extracting the location and content components of a non-empty trace.

$$\text{front } p.l \;\; \widehat{=} \;\; p \qquad\qquad \text{last } p.l \;\; \widehat{=} \;\; l$$

The front operation can be used to generate the set of locations visited by a trace, as characterised by their paths, where each path within this set is considered to be a *prefix* of the original trace. Such a set of paths is referred to as the *proper prefixes* of the given trace. The function prefixes_T defines the non-proper version of the prefix set.

$$\begin{aligned}
\text{prefixes}_\text{T}\, \varnothing &\;\; \widehat{=} \;\; \{\varnothing\} \\
\text{prefixes}_\text{T}\, tr &\;\; \widehat{=} \;\; \{tr\} \cup \text{prefixes}_\text{T}(\text{front } tr)
\end{aligned}$$

The prefixes also provide a natural ordering over traces.

$$\begin{aligned}
tr_1 <_\text{T} tr_2 &\;\; \widehat{=} \;\; \text{prefixes}_\text{T}(tr_1) \subset \text{prefixes}_\text{T}(tr_2) \\
tr_1 \leq_\text{T} tr_2 &\;\; \widehat{=} \;\; \text{prefixes}_\text{T}(tr_1) \subseteq \text{prefixes}_\text{T}(tr_2)
\end{aligned}$$

Having defined an ordering over traces, it is now possible to use that ordering to define a subtraction operation. This is eventually used to define the relative paths between nodes in a set.

$$(\_ -_\text{T} \_) \;\; \widehat{=} \;\; \lambda\, tr_1, tr_2 \mid tr_2 \leq_\text{T} tr_1 \bullet \text{pick}\{tr \mid tr_1 = tr_2.tr\}$$

where the pick function picks the singleton element from a set (i.e. $\text{pick}\{x\} \widehat{=} x$).

Before leaving the trace utilities, we lift the definitions of the front, last, and prefixes_T operations to trace-sets. The first two are lifted by applying their definitions to each non-empty trace with the set. The latter one is lifted to a trace-set (denoted by TR) by applying the prefixes operation to each trace within the set and merging the results.

$$\text{frontTraces } TR \quad \widehat{=} \quad \{\text{front } tr \mid tr \in (TR \setminus \{\varnothing\})\}$$

$$\text{lastLabels } TR \quad \widehat{=} \quad \{\text{last } tr \mid tr \in (TR \setminus \{\varnothing\})\}$$

$$\text{prefixes}_{\text{N}} \ TR \quad \widehat{=} \quad \bigcup\{\text{prefixes}_{\text{T}} \ tr \mid tr \in TR\}$$

3.3   Trace-Based Node

A trace-based graph node is modelled by a set of traces that satisfies two healthiness conditions. Both of these conditions follow from the observation that the only way a concrete location graph node may have more than one incoming edge, is if all these edges are labelled with the dollar name. Consequently, every trace to a node is guaranteed to end with the same label, except for the root node which has no label. This is modelled by the first healthiness condition, which states that all incoming edges to a node have the same label.

$$\text{HC1}_{\text{N}}(n) \quad \widehat{=} \quad \#\,\text{lastLabels}(n) \leq 1$$

Another consequence of the observation is that a node may only have multiple parents if it is stored in a shareable location. This is modelled by the second healthiness condition, which states that the trace to any node that has more than one parent must end with the special shareable location label.

$$\text{HC2}_{\text{N}}(n) \quad \widehat{=} \quad \#\,\text{lastLabels}(\text{frontTraces}(n)) > 1 \Rightarrow \text{lastLabels}(n) = \{\$\}$$

Any healthy node can be denoted by $P.l$, where each path in the path-set P is extended by the trace-label l to form the trace-set $\{p.l \mid p \in P\}$. The remainder of this section now presents some useful utility relations and operations on nodes.

Node relations: The *child-of* and *descendant-of* relations test whether one node is an immediate child of or a descendant of another node. These tests assume that the nodes come from a healthy graph, where all the routes to the parent are contained within the child.

$$n_1 \ \text{childOf} \ n_2 \qquad \widehat{=} \qquad n_2 \in \text{frontTraces}(n_1)$$

$$n_1 \ \text{descendantOf} \ n_2 \quad \widehat{=} \quad n_2 \in \text{prefixes}_{\text{N}}(\text{frontTraces}(n_1))$$

In addition to knowing whether two nodes are related, it is sometimes useful to identify the relative traces from a parent to child node.

$$\text{traces}_{\text{N}}(n_1, n_2) \quad \widehat{=} \quad \{tr_2 -_{\text{T}} tr_1 \mid tr_1 \in n_1 \land tr_2 \in n_2 \land tr_1 \leq_{\text{T}} tr_2\}$$

Such trace-sets are used to determine whether two nodes are related via shareable or via containable locations. Here, two nodes are related by a shareable location if one of the traces within the trace-set includes the dollar label. Similarly they are related by a containable location if one of the traces within the trace-set does not contain the dollar label.

$$n_1 \ \text{shareDescOf} \ n_2 \qquad \widehat{=} \qquad n_1 \ \text{descendantOf} \ n_2 \land \$ \in_{\text{T}} \text{traces}_{\text{N}}(n_2, n_1)$$

$$n_1 \ \text{containDescOf} \ n_2 \quad \widehat{=} \quad n_1 \ \text{descendantOf} \ n_2 \land \$ \notin_{\text{T}} \text{traces}_{\text{N}}(n_2, n_1)$$

where $l \in_{\text{T}} tr \ \widehat{=} \ \exists p \bullet p.l \in \text{prefixes}_{\text{T}} \ tr$.

Note that the only way a node can be both a shareable and a containable descendant of another node, is if the nodes are both contained in the same cycle. In this case, all the containable descendants are also shareable descendants.

Node unlinking (deletion): Part of the assignment process involves the removal of previously held data. This is the purpose of the following unlinking operations, which remove all traces of either a node (n_1) or its children from the specified target node (n_2).

$$\text{unlink}_N \ n_1 \text{ from } n_2 \quad \widehat{=} \quad n_2 \setminus \{ tr_2 \mid tr_1 \in n_1 \wedge tr_2 \in n_2 \wedge tr_1 \leq_T tr_2 \}$$
$$\text{unlinkChildren}_N \ n_1 \text{ from } n_2 \quad \widehat{=} \quad n_2 \setminus \{ tr_2 \mid tr_1 \in n_1 \wedge tr_2 \in n_2 \wedge tr_1 <_T tr_2 \}$$

These operations can be lifted to the graph context by unlinking a given node from a node-set.

$$\text{unlink}_G(N, n) \quad \widehat{=} \quad \{ (\text{unlink}_N \ n \text{ from } n') \mid n' \in N \}$$
$$\text{unlinkChildren}_G(N, n) \quad \widehat{=} \quad \{ (\text{unlinkChildren}_N \ n \text{ from } n') \mid n' \in N \}$$

Node duplication (replacement): It is sometimes useful to construct a new node from a pair of existing nodes, a source node (n_2) and one of its descendants (n_3). Here the idea is to extract the traces between the source and descendant nodes, and then append them to a new source node (n_1), which is the target of the duplication.

$$\text{replace}_N \ n_1 \text{ for } n_2 \text{ in } n_3 \quad \widehat{=} \quad \{ tr_1.tr \mid tr_1 \in n_1 \wedge tr \in \text{traces}_N(n_2, n_3) \}$$

Instead of replacing one parent for another, we may want to add a parent; for example, when copying a reference to a shareable location. This is essentially achieved by performing the replacement operation and merging in the original data.

$$\text{add}_N \ n_1 \text{ to } n_2 \text{ in } n_3 \quad \widehat{=} \quad (\text{replace}_N \ n_1 \text{ for } n_2 \text{ in } n_3) \cup n_3$$

These operations can then lifted so that they operate on node-sets, by reparenting each node in the set.

$$\text{replace}_G \ n_1 \text{ for } n_2 \text{ in } N \quad \widehat{=} \quad \{ (\text{replace}_N \ n_1 \text{ for } n_2 \text{ in } n) \mid n \in N \}$$
$$\text{add}_G \ n_1 \text{ to } n_2 \text{ in } N \quad \widehat{=} \quad \{ (\text{add}_N \ n_1 \text{ to } n_2 \text{ in } n) \mid n \in N \}$$

We use these operations to prepare a subgraph for being moved or copied to a new location.

3.4   Trace-Based Graph

A *trace-based graph* is a set of trace-based nodes that satisfies four healthiness conditions. The first healthiness condition states that each of the graph's nodes is healthy.

$$\text{HC1}_G(G) \quad \widehat{=} \quad \forall n \mid n \in G \bullet \text{HC1}_N(n) \wedge \text{HC2}_N(n)$$

The second healthiness condition states that the nodes of a graph are disjoint. This ensures that an absolute trace can be used to identify a single node.

$$\text{HC2}_\text{G}(G) \;\; \hat{=} \;\; \forall\, n_1, n_2 \mid \{n_1, n_2\} \subseteq G \wedge n_1 \neq n_2 \bullet n_1 \cap n_2 = \emptyset$$

For a graph (G) that satisfies condition HC2$_\text{G}$, it is possible to define an operation for extracting the node (n) that has an absolute trace (p), so long as the trace is within the graph.

$$\text{node}_\text{G}(G, tr) \;\; \hat{=} \;\; \lambda\, G, tr \mid \text{HC2}_\text{G}(G) \wedge tr \in_\text{G} G \bullet \text{pick}(\{n \mid tr \in n \in G\})$$

where the ($\_ \in_\text{G} \_$) relation determines whether a trace is in the graph:

$$p \in_\text{G} G \,\hat{=}\, p \in (\textstyle\bigcup G)$$

The third healthiness condition states that each of a node's traces is consistently extended; i.e. if it is possible to take an edge with label l from node n_1 to node n_2, then the trace-set formed by appending the label l to each of n_1's traces is a subset of n_2's trace-set.

$$\begin{aligned}
\text{HC3}_\text{G}(G) \;\; \hat{=} \;\; & \forall\, n_1, n_2, tr_1, tr_2, l \mid \\
& \{n_1, n_2\} \subseteq G \wedge \{tr_1, tr_2\} \in n_1 \bullet \\
& \quad tr_1.l \in n_2 \Rightarrow tr_2.l \in n_2
\end{aligned}$$

The fourth healthiness condition states that the parents of a node are contained within the graph; in other words, the traces within a graph are prefix closed.

$$\text{HC4}_\text{G}(G) \;\; \hat{=} \;\; \forall\, tr, l \mid tr.l \in_\text{G} G \bullet tr \in_\text{G} G$$

The combination of the first three graph healthiness conditions defines what it means for the trace model to have a consistent, but not necessarily complete, set of nodes. Thus, these conditions should be satisfied by any healthy subgraph.

The remainder of this section provides operations for manipulating the contents of a location graph model, such as operations for: extracting a subgraph; extracting the value at a location; and assigning a value to a location.

Children and descendants subgraphs: Subgraphs can be formed by selecting only some of a graph's nodes. The childOf and descendantOf relations can be used to filter a graph to form children and descendants subgraphs respectively.

$$\begin{aligned}
\text{children} \;\; &\hat{=} \;\; \lambda\, G, n \mid n \in G \bullet \{n' \mid n' \in G \wedge n' \text{ childOf } n\} \\
\text{descendants} \;\; &\hat{=} \;\; \lambda\, G, n \mid n \in G \bullet \{n' \mid n' \in G \wedge n' \text{ descendantOf } n\}
\end{aligned}$$

Note that a node can be a descendant of itself if, and only if, there is a non-empty sequence of edges back to itself.

Dereferencing a location's value: A location is represented by a healthy node whose last label is either a field name or the dollar name. Such a node can be represented by a path-set, as each trace within this node may only contain names. The value of a location node is determined by recursively examining its children, or more specifically its child labels. There are three cases to consider.

1. There is a single null-reference or literal value (nlv) child label. In this case, the label value is returned as the location's value.
2. There is a single child label that contains the dollar name. In this case the path-set (reference value) that models the child node is returned.
3. There is a set of child-labels that contain field names. In this case a compound value is recursively constructed from its children.

$$
\begin{aligned}
*_G(G, p) &\;\widehat{=}\; *_G(G, \mathsf{node}_G(G, p)) \\
*_G(G, P) &\;\widehat{=}\; *_G(G, \mathsf{children}(G, P)) \\
*_G(G, \{P.nlv\}) &\;\widehat{=}\; nlv \\
*_G(G, \{P.\$\}) &\;\widehat{=}\; P.\$ \\
*_G(G, \{_{i=1}^{k} P.nm_i\}) &\;\widehat{=}\; \{_{i=1}^{k} nm_i = *_G(G, P.nm_i)\}
\end{aligned}
$$

Recall that we introduced $P.l$ as an alternative notation for denoting a healthy node, in Section 3.3, where $P.l \;\widehat{=}\; \{p.l \mid p \in P\}$.

Preparing a location for assignment: The preparation required for assigning a value to a location depends on a number of factors, such as whether the location already exists. We could limit assignments to existing locations, but then this would not mirror our concrete model, which defined assignment in terms of the map overriding operation ($\_ \oplus \_$). Instead we categorise a potential location as either existing (E_{pm}), freshly containable (C_{pm}), freshly shareable (S_{pm}), or invalid (U_{pm}), as follows:

$$
prepMode(G, P.nm) \;\widehat{=}\;
\begin{cases}
E_{pm}, & \text{if } P.nm \in G \\
S_{pm}, & \text{if } P.nm \notin G \wedge nm = \$ \\
C_{pm}, & \text{if } P.nm \notin G \wedge nm \neq \$ \wedge *_G(G, P) \in CV \\
U_{pm}, & \text{otherwise}
\end{cases}
$$

where CV denotes the set compound values (i.e. the compound value type). Note that the above definition of freshly created locations ensures that a compound value may only contain containable locations (and vice versa). In general, a path-set P is considered to represent an assignable location within a graph G whenever it has a valid assignable location mode.

$$
P \; \mathsf{assignableIn}_G \; G \;\widehat{=}\; prepMode(G, P) \neq U_{pm}
$$

It is now possible to define the preparation for an assignable location by ensuring that it exists and contains no contents. This can involve the clearing (unlinking) of an existing node's contents and the creation of a new location node.

$$prep_G(G, P) \quad \widehat{=} \quad prep(G, P, prepMode(G, P))$$
$$prep(G, P, E_{pm}) \quad \widehat{=} \quad \text{unlinkChildren}_G(G, P)$$
$$prep(G, P.l, S_{pm}) \quad \widehat{=} \quad \text{unlinkChildren}_G(G, P) \cup \{P.\$\}$$
$$prep(G, P.l, C_{pm}) \quad \widehat{=} \quad G \cup \{P.l\}$$

Assigning a null-reference or literal value: A null-reference or literal value (*nlv*) can be assigned to a graph location by preparing the location and setting its contents to the given value.

$$(G, p) :=_G nlv \quad \widehat{=} \quad (G, \text{node}_G(G, p)) :=_G nlv$$
$$(G, P) :=_G nlv \quad \widehat{=} \quad \text{prep}_G(G, P) \cup \{P.nlv\}$$

Assigning an encapsulated compound value: An encapsulated compound value is a concrete compound value that contains no shareable locations (i.e. a compound value in the set $\{cv \mid sLocs\ cv = \emptyset\}$). Such values are represented by the meta-variable *ecv*. It can be assigned to a location by preparing the location and setting its contents to the subtree that represents the compound value.

$$(G, p) :=_G ecv \quad \widehat{=} \quad (G, \text{node}_G(G, p)) :=_G ecv$$
$$(G, P) :=_G ecv \quad \widehat{=} \quad \text{prep}_G(G, P) \cup \bigcup\{P.tr \mid tr \in (cvTrs\ ecv)\}$$

where the *cvTrs* function converts an encapsulated compound value into a prefix closed set of traces, representing each trace through the compound value's structure.

Assigning the contents of an existing location: In the concrete model, we referred to this as the copying of a location's value. This is more tricky than the previous cases for a number of reasons. One significant reason is that the location we are copying may be contained within the target location that we are assigning to. In such a case, the location preparation process could remove (clear) the location we want to copy. This limitation can be overcome by a three-step process. First, copy the value to a fresh temporary location, which is not contained within the contents of the target location. Second, prepare the target location and copy the value of the temporary location to it. Last, remove the temporary location.

What would make a good temporary location is dependant on what the location graph is being used to model, so in general we cannot specify this. Having said that, what we can do is specify how to assign the contents of a location to a prepared location node.

Assigning to a cleared location node: When assigning the contents of a cleared location, care has to be taken to ensure that the contents of reference values are pointed to rather than duplicated. In order to facilitate this, two utility operations are defined: one for identifying the referenced nodes (copyRefSG); and the other to add the copied pointer (path) to these identified nodes (copyRefNodes).

$$\text{copyRefSG}(G, n) \quad \widehat{=} \quad \{n' \mid n' \in G \wedge n' \text{ shareDescOf } n\}$$
$$\text{copyRefNodes } n_1 \text{ to } n_2 \text{ in } G \quad \widehat{=} \quad \text{add}_G \ n_2 \text{ for } n_1 \text{ in copyRefSG}(G, n_1)$$

Care also has to be taken to ensure that a duplicate of the value nodes are added to the copy node. This is facilitated by two utility operations: one for identifying the nodes to be duplicated (copyValSG); and the other to perform the duplication (copyValNodes) using the node replacement operation.

$$\text{copyValSG}(G, n) \quad \widehat{=} \quad \{n' \mid n' \in G \wedge n' \text{ containDescOf } n\}$$
$$\text{copyValNodes } n_1 \text{ to } n_2 \text{ in } G \quad \widehat{=} \quad \text{replace}_G \ n_2 \text{ for } n_1 \text{ in copyValSG}(G, n_1)$$

It is now possible to define the graph transformation operation of copying the contents of a source node to the empty location as the union of: the appropriately updated reference nodes; the descendant nodes that were not updated; the non-descendant nodes; and the duplicated value nodes.

$$\begin{aligned}
\text{copy}_G \ n_1 \text{ to } n_2 \text{ in } G \quad \widehat{=} \quad & (\text{copyRefNodes } n_1 \text{ to } n_2 \text{ in } G) \\
\cup \quad & \text{descendants}(G, n_1) \setminus \text{copyRefSG}(G, n_1) \\
\cup \quad & G \setminus \text{descendants}(G, n_1) \\
\cup \quad & (\text{copyValNodes } n_1 \text{ to } n_2 \text{ in } G)
\end{aligned}$$

Now given that the location with path \$copy is an assignable location that does not exist within the graph, the copy assignment can be defined as follows:

$$\begin{aligned}
(G, p) :=_G p' \quad \widehat{=} \quad & (G, p) :=_G \text{node}_G(G, p') \\
(G, p) :=_G P' \quad \widehat{=} \quad & (G, \text{node}_G(G, p)) :=_G P' \\
(G, P) :=_G P' \quad \widehat{=} \quad & \text{let } G_1 \widehat{=} (\text{copy}_G \ P' \text{ to } \{\$copy\} \text{ in } (G \cup \{\$copy\})) \\
& \qquad G_2 \widehat{=} (\text{copy}_G \{\$copy\} \text{ to } P \text{ in } \text{prep}_G(G_1, P)) \\
& \text{in } \text{unlink}_G(G_2, \{\$copy\})
\end{aligned}$$

4   UTP Model

Our UTP model of locations uses the Abstract Location Trace Graph (ALTG) of Section 3.4 to provide a semantics of locations, where the special logical variables $altg$ and $altg'$ to represent the before and after states of the graph. The contents of this ALTG are then linked to the normal UTP program variables, using a technique inspired by [1]. In our case, the values of normal program variables are mirrored by correspondingly named first-level nodes in the graph. For example, the logical input and output variables for a UTP program variable x are represented by the node $\{x\}$ in the $altg$ and $altg'$ graphs respectively. Note that whenever there could be confusion between whether a variable is being used to denote its name rather than its value, we prefix the variable with a dash to get its name. For example, the predicate $x = *_G(altg, 'x)$ holds whenever the value of variable x equals the value of extracting its corresponding element from the graph $altg$ (i.e. the one with the path name $'x$).

The remainder of this section introduces the healthiness conditions on the UTP model of locations, provides the definitions for a few operations, such as assignment, and relates the abstract and concrete models. Here the meta variable Q denotes a relational predicate that defines a UTP location model program.

4.1   Healthiness Conditions

Before we formalise the relationship between a program's variables and the ALTG, it is worth introducing a healthiness condition to ensure that both the *altg* and *altg'* graphs are healthy (as defined in Section 3.4).

$$\text{HC1}_\text{U}(Q) \;\;\widehat{=}\;\; Q = (\,Q \wedge \text{HC}_\text{U}(altg) \wedge \text{HC}_\text{U}(altg')\,)$$
$$\text{HC}_\text{U}(G) \;\;\widehat{=}\;\; \text{HC1}_\text{G}(G) \wedge \text{HC2}_\text{G}(G) \wedge \text{HC3}_\text{G}(G) \wedge \text{HC4}_\text{G}(G)$$

The first step in formalising the link between the graph and program variables is by insisting that the first-level nodes within the graph correspond precisely to the UTP program variables other than the model variables (i.e. *altg* and *altg'*).

$$\text{HC2a}_\text{U}(Q) \;\;\widehat{=}\;\; Q = (\,Q \wedge \{\,'x \mid x \in inv\alpha Q\} = \text{labels}_\text{G}(altg, \varnothing)\,)$$
$$\text{HC2b}_\text{U}(Q) \;\;\widehat{=}\;\; Q = (\,Q \wedge \{\,'x \mid x' \in outv\alpha Q\} = \text{labels}_\text{G}(altg', \varnothing)\,)$$
$$\text{HC2}_\text{U}(Q) \;\;\widehat{=}\;\; \text{HC2a}_\text{U}(Q) \wedge \text{HC2b}_\text{U}(Q)$$

where: $inv\alpha Q$ and $outv\alpha Q$ represent the input and output alphabets of program Q except for the model variables *altg* and *altg'* respectively; and the child labels of graph path are defined by $\text{labels}_\text{G}(G, p) \widehat{=} \{l \mid P.l \in \text{children}(G, \text{node}_\text{G}(G, p))\}$.

The second, and last, step in formalising the link between the graph and program variables is to ensure that the value of a variable is the same as the value stored within the ALTG.

$$\text{HC3a}_\text{U}(Q) \;\;\widehat{=}\;\; Q = (\,Q \wedge (\textstyle\bigwedge_{x \in inv\alpha Q} x = *_\text{G}(altg, 'x))\,)$$
$$\text{HC3b}_\text{U}(Q) \;\;\widehat{=}\;\; Q = (\,Q \wedge (\textstyle\bigwedge_{x' \in outv\alpha Q} x' = *_\text{G}(altg', 'x))\,)$$
$$\text{HC3}_\text{U}(Q) \;\;\widehat{=}\;\; \text{HC3a}_\text{U}(Q) \wedge \text{HC3b}_\text{U}(Q)$$

4.2   Operations

Due to space limitations, we only present those operations that significantly differ from those of the standard UTP relational model, as presented in Chapter 2 of [3]: specifically, the assignment and program variable management operations.

The assignment operation is broken down into three cases, depending on the type of the r-value (i.e. the value to be assigned). These mirror the three cases presented in the trace-based graph model, except that the location is always defined in terms of a possibly empty path from a UTP program variable. It is defined as follows:

$$x.p := nlv \;\;\widehat{=}\;\; \text{HCs}_\text{U}(altg' = ((altg, 'x.p) :=_\text{G} nlv))$$
$$x.p := ecv \;\;\widehat{=}\;\; \text{HCs}_\text{U}(altg' = ((altg, 'x.p) :=_\text{G} ecv))$$
$$x.p := y.p_1 \;\;\widehat{=}\;\; \text{HCs}_\text{U}(altg' = ((altg, 'x.p) :=_\text{G} 'y.p_1))$$

where $x.\varnothing = x$ and $\mathrm{HCs}_\mathrm{U}(Q) \mathrel{\widehat{=}} \mathrm{HC3}_\mathrm{U}(\mathrm{HC2}_\mathrm{U}(\mathrm{HC1}_\mathrm{U}(Q)))$. Note that the combined healthiness condition ensures that the consequences of updating shared values can be seen by all participating UTP program variables.

The variable introduction and elimination operations are also defined in terms of their effects on the ALTG. Here the variable introduction operation provides a default unset value to the introduced variable; and the variable elimination operation removes all references to the value from the graph.

$$\mathsf{var}\, x \quad \mathrel{\widehat{=}} \quad \exists\, x \bullet \mathrm{HCs}_\mathrm{U}(altg' = ((altg, 'x) :=_\mathrm{G} \dot{\iota}))$$
$$\mathsf{end}\, x \quad \mathrel{\widehat{=}} \quad \exists\, x' \bullet \mathrm{HCs}_\mathrm{U}(altg' = \mathsf{unlink}_\mathrm{G}(altg, 'x))$$

4.3 Full Abstraction

The ALTG-based UTP model of locations, outlined here, is fully abstract in the sense described earlier: two concrete location graphs are equivalent, as defined in Section 2.3, iff their corresponding ALTGs are equal. This is essentially because the underpinning ALTG model is fully abstract by design; it removes the need for explicitly indexed shareable locations. Here, each location has precisely one path-set that represents it.

5 Related Work

Our model of locations was inspired by Hoare and He's trace-based model of pointers [4]. It introduces the notion of a containable location. This significantly complicates the — already non-trivial — notion of assignment, which in [4] is defined in terms of *swinging* the pointer of the assigned location to its new contents. In our model, several contained pointers can be swung at once by an assignment operation, as the contents of:

- a containable location are duplicated on assignment;
- a shareable location are referenced (shared) on assignment;
- a location can include many shareable and containable locations.

The benefit of this extra complexity is that our location model enables the atomicity of assignment to be directly specified (or supported). For example, the copying of a `struct` in C^{++} or a `record` in Pascal can be captured.

Schieder has also adapted Hoare and He's work on trace-based pointers to provide a weakest precondition semantics for pointers [8]. Here, the object maps have been totalised in order to avoid undefinedness; this leads to the null pointer being modelled by a node that has outbound edges (all of which point to itself). However, like [4] it does not support the notion of a containable location.

Cavalcanti, Harwood, and Woodcock have an *entity group* [6] inspired model of pointers and records [1]. Here, an entity group contains the set of path names that can be used to access the same value, where a path name is either:

1. a *simple name* of a UTP user variable; or
2. a *rooted field name*, which is a simple name extended by a dot-separated sequence of record field labels.

This notion of a path is similar to the one we use, in the sense that both use dot-separated labels to define a route from a given starting point to a location. The main difference is that every location in [1] is potentially shareable, whereas only some of the locations within our model are shareable. Specifically, [1] does not support the notion of a containable location.

A further difference between our model and those of [4], [8] and [1] is that we have an explicit notion of a pointer value (i.e. sharable location), as represented by a path-set of the form '$P.\$$'. One consequence of this is that our model directly supports the notion of a *handle*, which is a pointer to a pointer. Here the second pointer value (path-set) includes a path of the form '$p.\$.\$$'.

6   Conclusions

6.1   Summary

This paper augments the general relational model of the UTP with an Abstract Location Trace Graph (ALTG), which enables complex relationships between locations and their data to be represented. Here, both shareable and containable locations are modelled by a path-set. They differ in that only shareable locations can be dereferenced by a pointer, whose value is the shareable location's path-set itself. The key point is that containable locations actually contain rather than reference their contents, thus when they are copied their contents are duplicated rather than referenced. This mirrors situations where the whole of a compound value, such as a Pascal `record` or a C^{++} `struct`, is duplicated on assignment. In general, being able to control the amount of data that gets duplicated on assignment provides a means for directly supporting different levels of containment within a data structure.

One consequence of modelling a pointer's value as the path-set that defines its location is that it is possible to directly represent the concept of a handle (i.e. a pointer to a pointer). The combination of having direct support for contained locations and pointer values mirrors the features of our UTP model of objects [9]; it is what led to the development of this model from [4] and [1].

Overall, we argue that a general UTP model of pointers ought to consider both shareable and containable locations. Such models will provide support for languages like C$^{\#}$ (and our UTP object model), which have language constructs for building containable locations and handles.

6.2   Future Work

In this paper we have presented both concrete and abstract models of locations. What we have not done is prove that the two models are consistent. We have also not shown how this model of locations can be applied to either UTP designs or objects [3,9]. Finally, we have not considered the issues of:

- location ownership and encapsulation (e.g. as presented in [2,5,7]);
- location typing (e.g. augment a location with the type of its contents);
- location visibility (e.g. augment a location with read-only or scope modifiers).

Augmenting the UTP model of locations to handle any of these issues is left as future work.

References

1. Cavalcanti, A., Harwood, W., Woodcock, J.: Pointers and records in the unifying theories of programming. In: Dunne, S., Stoddart, B. (eds.) UTP 2006. LNCS, vol. 4010, pp. 200–216. Springer, Heidelberg (2006)
2. Clarke, D.: Object Ownership and Containment. PhD thesis, University of New South Wales (October 2002)
3. Hoare, C.A.R., He, J.: Unifying Theories of Programming. Computer Science. Prentice-Hall, Englewood Cliffs (1998)
4. Hoare, C.A.R., He, J.: A trace model for pointers and objects. In: 13th European Conference on Object-Oriented Programming, pp. 1–17 (1999)
5. Noble, J., Clarke, D., Potter, J.: Object ownership for dynamic alias protection. In: Technology of Object-Oriented Languages and Systems, TOOLS (1999)
6. Paige, R.F., Ostroff, J.S.: Erc: an object-oriented refinement calculus for Eiffel. Formal Aspects of Computing 16(1), 51–79 (2004)
7. Reynolds, J.C.: Separation logic: A logic for shared mutable data structures. In: 17th Annual IEEE Symposium on Logic in Computer Science (2002)
8. Schieder, B.: Pointer theory and weakest preconditions without addresses and heap. In: Kozen, D., Shankland, C. (eds.) MPC 2004. LNCS, vol. 3125, pp. 357–380. Springer, Heidelberg (2004)
9. Smith, M.A., Gibbons, J.: Unifying Theories of Objects. In: Davies, J., Gibbons, J. (eds.) IFM 2007. LNCS, vol. 4591, pp. 599–618. Springer, Heidelberg (2007)

Unifying Input Output Conformance

Martin Weiglhofer[1,2] and Bernhard K. Aichernig[1,*]

[1] Institute for Software Technology, Graz University of Technology, Austria
[2] Competence Network Softnet Austria

Abstract. Model-based conformance testing aims to assess the correctness of an implementation with respect to a specification. This raises the question of a proper conformance relation that should be established between implementations and specifications. One commonly used conformance relation is the so-called input output conformance (**ioco**), which is defined over labeled transition systems. In this paper we investigate a denotational semantics of the input output conformance relation over reactive processes. We formalize the underlying assumptions of the **ioco** relation in terms of formal healthiness conditions and by adopted choice operators. Finally, we show that our denotational version of **ioco** can be generalized in the same way as the original relation. Our work aims to provide a unification of input output conformance by lifting the definition from labeled transition systems to reactive processes.

Keywords: Input output conformance, ioco, unifying theories of programming, reactive processes, quiescence, fairness, model-based testing.

1 Introduction

Software development is a complex and error-prone task. Failures in safety-critical applications may be life-threatening. At least software failures cause high costs during and after the software development process. Therefore, software engineers need the support of tools, techniques, and theories in order to reduce the number of software failures.

Model-based black-box testing techniques aim to assess the correctness of a reactive system, i.e., the implementation under test (IUT), with respect to a given specification. The IUT is viewed as a black-box with an interface that accepts inputs and produces outputs. The goal of model-based black-box testing is to check if the observable behavior of the IUT conforms to a specification with respect to a particular conformance relation.

Industrial specifications are mostly incomplete and due to abstraction non-deterministic. Hence, a conformance relation being useful in industry needs to cope with incompleteness and non-determinism. One of the most popular of such conformance relations is the input output conformance (**ioco**) relation [1].

Mature research prototypes (e.g. [2,3]) and successful industrial case studies (e.g. [4,5]) have shown the usability of this conformance relation in practice.

---

* Authors are listed in reverse alphabetical order.

A. Butterfield (Ed.): UTP 2008, LNCS 5713, pp. 181–201, 2010.

However, the used theory is given in an operational semantics and some of the underlying assumptions have been stated informally only. It is the contribution of this paper to redefine **ioco** in the denotational predicative semantics of UTP. The benefits of this new theory can be summarized as follows: (1) Instead of describing the assumptions of **ioco** informally, the UTP formalization presents the underlying assumptions as unambiguous healthiness conditions and by adopted choice operators over reactive processes; (2) A UTP formalization naturally relates **ioco** and refinement in one theory; (3) The denotational version of **ioco** enables formal, machine checkable, proofs. (4) Due to the predicative semantics of UTP, test case generation based on the presented theory can be seen as a satisfiability problem. This facilitates the use of modern sat modulo theory techniques (e.g. [6]) for test case generation. (5) Finally, the UTP version of **ioco** broadens the scope of **ioco** to specification languages with similar UTP semantics, e.g. to generate test cases from Circus [7] specifications. Hence our work enriches UTP's reactive processes with a practical testing theory.

The rest of this paper is structured as follows. Section 2 reviews the input output conformance relation. Section 3 comprises the formalization of **ioco** in the UTP-framework. Finally, we discuss our results and further research in Section 4.

2   Conformance of Labeled Transition Systems

This section reviews the **ioco** relation [1] which is defined over labeled transition system (LTS). When testing reactive systems one distinguishes between inputs and outputs. Thus, the alphabet of an LTS is partitioned into inputs and outputs.

Definition 1 (Labeled transition system with inputs and outputs). *A labeled transition system is a tuple $M = (Q, A \cup \{\tau\}, \rightarrow, q_0)$, where Q is a finite set of states, $A = A_I \cup A_O$ a finite alphabet partitioned into an input alphabet A_I and an output alphabet A_O where $A_I \cap A_O = \emptyset$. $\tau \notin A$ an unobservable action, $\rightarrow \subseteq Q \times (A \cup \{\tau\}) \times Q$ is the transition relation, and $q_0 \in Q$ is the initial state.*

The class of labeled transition systems with inputs A_I and outputs in A_O is denoted by $\mathcal{LTS}(A_I, A_O)$ [1]. We use the following common notations for LTSs:

Definition 2. *Given a labeled transition system $M = (Q, A_I \cup A_O \cup \{\tau\}, \rightarrow, q_0)$ and let $q, q', q_i \in Q, a_{(i)} \in A_I \cup A_O$ and $\sigma \in (A_I \cup A_O)^*$.*

$$q \xrightarrow{a} q' =_{df} (q, a, q') \in \rightarrow$$

$$q \xrightarrow{a} =_{df} \exists q' \bullet (q, a, q') \in \rightarrow$$

$$q \xnrightarrow{a} =_{df} \nexists q' \bullet (q, a, q') \in \rightarrow$$

$$q \xRightarrow{\epsilon} q' =_{df} (q = q') \vee \exists q_0, \dots, q_n \bullet (q = q_0 \xrightarrow{\tau} q_1 \wedge \cdots \wedge q_{n-1} \xrightarrow{\tau} q_n = q')$$

$$q \xRightarrow{a} q' =_{df} \exists q_1, q_2 \bullet q \xRightarrow{\epsilon} q_1 \xrightarrow{a} q_2 \xRightarrow{\epsilon} q'$$

$$q \xRightarrow{a_1 \dots a_n} q' =_{df} \exists q_0, \dots, q_n \bullet q = q_0 \xRightarrow{a_1} q_1 \dots q_{n-1} \xRightarrow{a_n} q_n = q'$$

$$q \xRightarrow{\sigma} =_{df} \exists q' \bullet q \xRightarrow{\sigma} q'$$

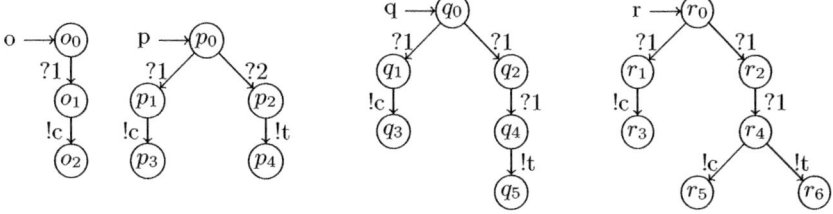

Fig. 1. Examples of input output labeled transition systems

According to [1], we use $init(q)$ to denote the actions enabled in state q and $traces(q)$ to denote the traces enabled in state q. Furthermore, we denote the states reachable by a particular trace σ by q **after** σ. More precisely,

Definition 3. *Given a labeled transition system* $M = (Q, A_I \cup A_O \cup \{\tau\}, \rightarrow, q_0)$ *and let* $q \in Q, C \subseteq Q$ *and* $\sigma \in (A_I \cup A_O)^*$.

$$init(q) =_{df} \{a \in A_I \cup A_O \cup \{\tau\} | q \xrightarrow{a} \} \qquad traces(q) =_{df} \{\sigma | q \xRightarrow{\sigma} \}$$

$$q \textbf{ after } \sigma =_{df} \{q' | q \xRightarrow{\sigma} q'\} \qquad C \textbf{ after } \sigma =_{df} \bigcup_{q \in C} (q \textbf{ after } \sigma)$$

Note that we will not always distinguish between an LTS and its initial state and write $M \Rightarrow$ instead of $q_0 \Rightarrow$.

Example 1. Figure 1 shows four labeled transition systems o, p, q, and r. The input alphabet is given by $A_I = \{1, 2\}$ and the output alphabet is $A_O = \{c, t\}$. We denote input actions by the prefix "?", while output actions have the prefix "!". For example, p_0 **after** $?1 = \{p_1\}$ while q_0 **after** $?1 = \{q_1, q_2\}$.   □

The **ioco** conformance relation employs the idea of observable quiescence. That is, it is assumed that a special action, i.e. θ, is enabled in the case where the labeled transition system does not provide any output action. This θ-labeled transitions allow to detect implementations that do not provide outputs while the specification requires some output (see Example 4: $\neg(y \textbf{ ioco } s)$). The input output conformance relation identifies quiescent states as follows: A state q of a labeled transition system is quiescent if neither an output action nor an internal action (τ) is enabled in q.

Definition 4. *Let* M *be a labeled transition system* $M = (Q, A_O \cup A_I \cup \{\tau\}, \rightarrow, q_0)$, *then a state* $q \in Q$ *is quiescent, denoted by* $\theta(q)$, *if* $\forall a \in A_O \cup \{\tau\} \bullet q \not\xrightarrow{a}$.

Usually, δ is used as special action denoting quiescence. Because of a name clash with UTP's deadlock symbol δ [8] we use θ for representing quiescence. By adding θ-labeled transitions to LTSs the quiescence symbol can be used as any other action. By the use of suspension automata θ becomes observable.

Definition 5 (Suspension automata). *Let* M *be a labeled transition system* $M = (Q, A_I \cup A_O \cup \{\tau\}, \rightarrow, q_0)$ *then the suspension automaton* M_θ *is given by*

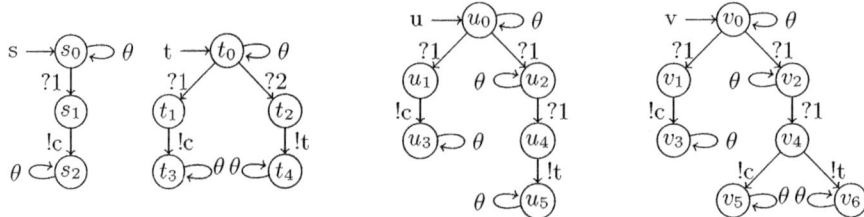

Fig. 2. Examples of suspension automata

$(Q, A_I \cup A_O \cup \{\tau, \theta\}, \rightarrow \cup \rightarrow_\theta, q_0)$ *where* $\rightarrow_\theta =_{df} \{q \xrightarrow{\theta} q | q \in Q \wedge \theta(q)\}$. *The suspension traces of* M_θ *are* $Straces(M_\theta) =_{df} \{\sigma \in (A_I \cup A_O \cup \{\theta\})^* | M_\theta \xRightarrow{\sigma}\}$.

Unless otherwise indicated, we use from now on M_θ instead of M, i.e. we usually include θ in the transition relations.

Example 2. Fig. 2 shows the suspension automata for the LTSs illustrated in Fig. 1. For example, the states u_0, u_2, u_3, and u_5 are quiescent states since they do not have outgoing edges labeled with an output nor with a τ action. Among others, u comprises the suspension traces $\langle ?1, !c, \theta \rangle$ and $\langle \theta, ?1, \theta, ?1, !t, \theta \rangle$.   □

A major hypothesis of the input output conformance relation is that the implementation can be represented as a labeled transition system. It is not assumed that this LTS is known in advance, but only its existence is required. This is known as a testing hypothesis [9,10].

The models used for representing implementations are input output transition systems. Since implementations are not allowed to refuse inputs, their models obey to the same restriction. This means that implementations are assumed to be input-enabled and so are their models.

Definition 6 (Input output transition system). *An input output transition system is an LTS* $M = (Q, A_I \cup A_O \cup \{\tau\}, \rightarrow, q_0)$ *where all input actions are enabled (possibly preceded by* τ-*transitions) in all states:* $\forall a \in A_I, \forall q \in Q \bullet q \xRightarrow{a}$

The class of input output transition systems with inputs A_I and outputs in A_O is given by $\mathcal{IOTS}(A_I, A_O) \subseteq \mathcal{LTS}(A_I, A_O)$ [1].

Example 3. The IOTSs for the suspension automata of Fig. 2 are depicted in Fig. 3. Note that the reason for the τ transitions in state z_4 is not input-enabledness but the restrictions on choices (see Section 3.3).   □

Before giving the definition of the **ioco** relation we need to define what are the outputs of a particular state and what are the outputs of a set of states.

Definition 7. *Given an LTS* $M = (Q, A_I \cup A_O \cup \{\tau\}, \rightarrow, q_0)$ *and let* $q \in Q$ *and* $C \subseteq Q$, *then* $out(q) =_{df} \{a \in A_O | q \xrightarrow{a}\} \cup \{\theta | \theta(q)\}$ *and* $out(C) =_{df} \bigcup_{q \in C}(out(q))$.

Now we are ready to give the definition of the **ioco** relation. Informally, the input output conformance relation states, that an implementation under test (IUT)

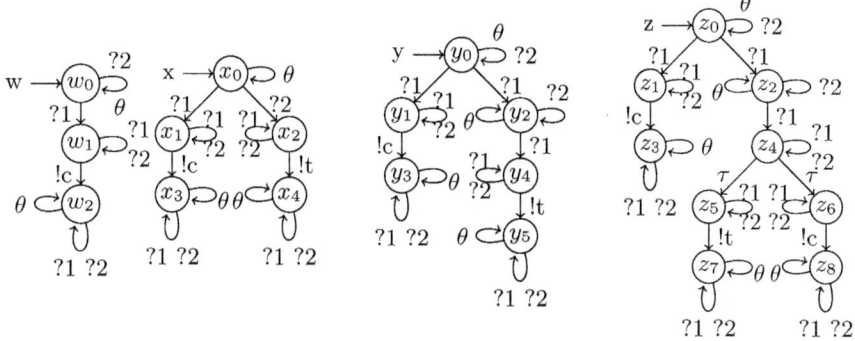

Fig. 3. Examples of input output transition systems (input-enabled by definition)

conforms to a specification S, iff the outputs of the IUT are outputs of S after an arbitrary suspension trace of S. More formally,

Definition 8 (Input output conformance). *Given a set of inputs A_I and a set of outputs A_O then* **ioco** $\subseteq \mathcal{IOTS}(A_I, A_O) \times \mathcal{LTS}(A_I, A_O)$ *is defined as:*

$$IUT \textbf{ ioco } S =_{df} \forall \sigma \in Straces(S) \bullet out(IUT \textbf{ after } \sigma) \subseteq out(S \textbf{ after } \sigma)$$

Example 4. Consider the LTSs of Figure 2 to be specifications and let the IOTSs of Figure 3 be implementations. Then we have w **ioco** s and x **ioco** t. We also have x **ioco** s because ?2 is not a trace of s. Thus, this branch is not relevant with respect to **ioco**. y does not conform to s, i.e. $\neg(y \textbf{ ioco } s)$, because $out(y_0 \textbf{ after}_y\ ?1) = \{!c, \theta\} \not\subseteq \{!c\} = out(s_0 \textbf{ after}_s\ ?1)$. Furthermore $\neg(z \textbf{ ioco } s)$ because $out(z_0 \textbf{ after}_z\ ?1) = \{!c, \theta\} \not\subseteq \{!c\} = out(s_0 \textbf{ after}_s\ ?1)$. Due to the use of suspension traces we also have $\neg(z \textbf{ ioco } u)$ because $out(z_0 \textbf{ after}_z\ ?1\ \hat{\theta}\ ?1) = \{!c, !t\} \not\subseteq \{!t\} = out(u_0 \textbf{ after}_u\ ?1\ \hat{\theta}\ ?1)$. □

The **ioco** definition from above can be lifted to a more general definition where different instantiations correspond to different conformance relations:

Definition 9 (Generic input output conformance). *Given a set of inputs A_I and a set of outputs A_O then* **ioco**$_\mathcal{F} \subseteq \mathcal{IOTS}(A_I, A_O) \times \mathcal{LTS}(A_I, A_O)$ *is defined as:* $IUT \textbf{ ioco}_\mathcal{F}\ S =_{df} \forall \sigma \in \mathcal{F} \bullet out(IUT \textbf{ after } \sigma) \subseteq out(S \textbf{ after } \sigma)$

Using **ioco**$_\mathcal{F}$ we can now express different relations by selecting a proper set of sequences for $\mathcal{F}$. The input output testing relation ($\leq_{iot}$) is given by **ioco**$_{A^*}$, while the input output refusal relation ($\leq_{ior}$) can be defined as **ioco**$_{(A \cup \{\theta\})^*}$. **ioconf** is given by **ioco**$_{traces(S)}$.

Example 5. The IOTS y and the IOTS z of Fig. 3 serve to illustrate the differences between these conformance relations: $z \leq_{iot} y$, $\neg(z \leq_{ior} y)$, z **ioconf** y, $\neg(z \textbf{ ioco } y)$, x **ioconf** w, x **ioco** w, $\neg(x \leq_{iot} w)$ and $\neg(x \leq_{ior} w)$. □

By the use of a particular set of test cases one wants to test if a given implementation conforms to its specification. In the **ioco** framework a test case is again a labeled transition system [1]:

Definition 10 (Test case). *A test case t is an LTS $t = (Q, A_I \cup A_O \cup \{\theta\}, \rightarrow$, q_0) such that (1) t is deterministic and has finite behavior; (2) Q contains terminal states pass and fail; and (3) for any state $q \in Q$ where $q \neq pass$ and $q \neq fail$, either $init(q) = \{a\}$ for some $a \in A_I$, or $init(q) = A_O \cup \{\theta\}$*

Test cases are extracted from specifications by some algorithm (e.g. [1,3]). Basically, test cases consist of some trace of the specification where at each state allowed outputs lead to pass verdict states, while forbidden outputs lead to fail verdict states. Testing is then conducted by running a test case t in parallel with the implementation i. A test run is a trace of the synchronous parallel composition $t\|i$ leading to a terminal state of t.

3   Input Output Conformance of Processes

This section presents our denotational version of the **ioco** conformance relation. We formulate **ioco** over UTP's reactive processes. As **ioco**, the denotational version is applicable to incomplete specifications. That is, implementations may behave arbitrarily after unspecified inputs.

3.1   Reactive Processes

Basically, the process of testing is modelled as an interaction between two reactive processes, the implementation under test (IUT) and the test case. A reactive process with respect to the unified theories of programming is defined as follows:

Definition 11 (Reactive process). *A reactive process P is one which satisfies the healthiness conditions **R1**, **R2**, **R3** where $R1(X) =_{df} X \wedge (tr \leq tr')$, $R2(X(tr, tr')) =_{df} \bigsqcap_s X(s, s\hat{\ }(tr' - tr))$, and $R3(X) =_{df} \mathbb{I} \lhd wait \rhd X$. The alphabet of P consists of the following:*

- *A, the set of events in which it can potentially engage.*
- *tr : A^*, the sequence of events which have happened up to the time of observation.*
- *ref : $\mathcal{P}A$, the set of events refused by the process during its wait.*
- *wait : Bool, which distinguishes its waiting states from its terminated states.*
- *ok, ok' : Bool, indicating start and termination of a process*

The skip predicate ($\mathbb{I}$) is defined as in [8]: $\mathbb{I} =_{df} \neg ok \wedge (tr \leq tr') \vee ok' \wedge (tr' = tr) \wedge \cdots \wedge (wait' = wait)$.

   The input output conformance relation distinguishes between inputs and outputs. Outputs are actions that are initiated by and under control of an implementation under test, while input actions are initiated by and under control of the system's environment [1]. Hence, the alphabet A of a process consists of two disjoint sets $A = A_{in} \cup A_{out}$. In addition, we will also differentiate between refused inputs $ref_{in} =_{df} ref \cap A_{in}$ and refused outputs $ref_{out} =_{df} ref \cap A_{out}$. Thus, also refusals form a partition: $ref_{in} \cap ref_{out} = \emptyset$ and $ref = ref_{in} \cup ref_{out}$. Note that we use ? and ! to indicate inputs and outputs for processes. For example, a process having as input alphabet $\mathcal{A}_{in} = \{1\}$ and as output alphabet $\mathcal{A}_{out} = \{c\}$ is written as $do_\mathcal{A}(?1); do_\mathcal{A}(!c)$.

A process offering a single event $a \in \mathcal{A}$ for communication is expressed in terms of $do_\mathcal{A}(a)$, where

$$do_\mathcal{A}(a) =_{df} \Phi(a \notin ref' \lhd wait' \rhd tr' = tr \,\widehat{}\, \langle a \rangle)$$
$$\Phi =_{df} \mathbf{R} \circ and_B = and_B \circ \mathbf{R}, \quad B =_{df} ((tr' = tr) \wedge wait' \vee (tr < tr'))$$
$$\mathbf{R} =_{df} \mathbf{R1} \circ \mathbf{R2} \circ \mathbf{R3}$$

For sequential composition we rely on UTP's standard sequential composition operator: $P(v, v'); Q(v, v') =_{df} \exists v_0 \bullet (P(v, v_0) \wedge Q(v_0, v'))$.

3.2   IOCO Specifications

For technical reasons, that is the computability of particular sets during the test case generation, the reactive processes used in the **ioco** framework need to satisfy an additional healthiness condition. The processes need to be strongly responsive, i.e. processes do not comprise livelocks. If there is a livelock a process may execute while it never offers communication. Hence, the healthiness condition for specifications excludes livelocks:

IOCO1 $P = P \wedge (ok \Rightarrow (wait' \vee ok'))$

Within Tretmans theory [1] quiescence denotes the absence of outputs and the absence of internal actions. Quiescence is encoded by the presence of a particular action θ. Although, quiescence can be classified by $wait'$ and ref' it is necessary to include θ into the traces of processes (see Example 4 $\neg z$ **ioco** u).

Since **ioco** uses traces containing quiescence we need to include θ in the traces of our processes. Thus, we extend set of events for reactive processes $\mathcal{A}$ by θ. In the sequel we use the following abbreviation $\mathcal{A}_\theta =_{df} \mathcal{A} \cup \{\theta\}$. A UTP process is quiescent after a particular trace iff either it has finished its execution or it refuses to do any output action

$$quiesence =_{df} \neg wait' \vee \forall o \in \mathcal{A}_{out} \bullet o \in ref'$$

Quiescent communication is expressed in terms of $do_\mathcal{A}^\theta$, which adds quiescence (θ) to the traces and to the refusal set of a process.

Definition 12 (Quiescent communication). *Let $a \in \mathcal{A}$ be an action of a process' alphabet, then*

$$do_\mathcal{A}^\theta(a) =_{df} \begin{cases} \Phi^i(do_\mathcal{A}(a)) & \text{if } a \in \mathcal{A}_{out} \\ \Phi^i(\{\theta, a\} \nsubseteq ref' \wedge tr' - tr \in \theta^* \lhd wait' \rhd \\ \qquad\qquad tr' - tr \in \theta^* \,\widehat{}\, \langle a \rangle) & \text{if } a \in \mathcal{A}_{in} \end{cases}$$

where $\Phi^i =_{df}$ ***IOCO1*** $\circ \mathbf{R} \circ and_B$

Consider the case where a is an input action, i.e., $a \in A_{in}$: In the case of $wait'$ the process $do_A^\theta(a)$ allows an arbitrary number of θ events (see the θ-loops in Fig. 2). After termination the event a has happened preceded by an arbitrary - possible empty sequence - of quiescence events, i.e. $tr' - tr \in \theta^* \widehat{\ } \langle a \rangle$. For the sake of simplicity we sometimes write θ^* instead of $\{\theta\}^*$. Note that $\theta^* \widehat{\ } \langle a \rangle$ denotes the set of events where every element of θ^* is concatenated with $\langle a \rangle$.

The possible occurrence of θ events is formalized as follows:

IOCO2 $P = P \wedge (\neg wait \Rightarrow (wait' \Rightarrow (\theta \notin ref' \Rightarrow quiescence)))$

IOCO3 $P = P \wedge (\neg wait \Rightarrow (wait' \Rightarrow (\theta \notin ref' \Rightarrow \exists s \bullet tr' - tr = s \widehat{\ } \theta^*)))$

The antecedence $\neg wait$ is necessary due to the same reasons as in **R3**.

By introducing the observability of quiescence we need to change the definition of the skip ($\mathbb{I}$) element: Processes always need to respect the properties of quiescence. Even in the case of divergence θ can be observed if and only if there is no output. This leads to $\mathbb{I}^\theta$, which is defined as follows.

$$\mathbb{I}^\theta =_{df} \left(\begin{array}{c} \neg ok \wedge (tr \leq tr') \wedge (wait' \Rightarrow (\theta \notin ref' \Rightarrow \\ (quiescence \wedge (\exists s \bullet tr' - tr = s \widehat{\ } \theta^*)))) \end{array} \right) \vee \left(\begin{array}{c} ok' \wedge \\ (v' = v) \end{array} \right)$$

In the above definition the variables v and v' denote the observation vectors, i.e., $v = \{ok, wait, tr, ref\}$ and $v' = \{ok', wait', tr', ref'\}$, respectively.

By introducing a new skip element we also need to change the definition of the healthiness condition **R3**. We will denote this modified healthiness condition as $\mathbf{R3}^\theta(P) =_{df} \mathbb{I}^\theta \lhd wait \rhd P$.

Since the quiescence event θ encodes the absence of output events it may occur at any time. This is even true for the deadlock process.

Definition 13 (Quiescent deadlock)

$$\delta^\theta =_{df} \mathbf{R3}^\theta (tr' - tr \in \theta^* \wedge wait')$$

Consequently, the classical deadlock process indicating absolute inactivity does not exist within the **ioco** theory.

Although quiescence is preserved by sequential composition, we need to redefine internal and external choices in order to preserve the properties of quiescence. Basically, the composition of processes that start with input actions (i.e. the processes are quiescent initially) is quiescent. If one of the two composed processes is not quiescent initially, the composition is not quiescent either.

For our quiescence preserving composition operators ($\sqcap^\theta$, $+^\theta$) we use an approach similar to parallel by merge [8]. The idea of parallel by merge is to run two processes independently and merge their results afterwards. In order to express independent execution we need a relabeling function. Given an output alphabet $\{v_1', v_2', \ldots, v_n'\}$, U_l is defined as follows

Definition 14 (Relabelling)

$$\alpha U_l(\{v_1', v_2', \ldots, v_n'\}) =_{df} \{v_1, v_2, \ldots, v_n, l.v_1', l.v_2', \ldots, l.v_n'\}$$

$$U_l(\{v_1', v_2', \ldots, v_n'\}) =_{df} (l.v_1' = v_1) \wedge (l.v_2' = v_2) \wedge \cdots \wedge (l.v_n' = v_n)$$

Independent execution of P and Q is now expressed by relabeling:

Definition 15 (Independent execution)

$$P \, \big\lambda \, Q =_{df} P; U_0(out\alpha P) \wedge Q; U_1(out\alpha Q)$$

An internal choice, which takes care of θ within the resulting process, can be defined as follows:

Definition 16 (Quiescence preserving internal choice)

$$P \ \sqcap^\theta \ Q =_{df} (P \, \big\lambda \, Q); M_\sqcap \quad with \quad M_\sqcap =_{df} M_\sqcap^{\delta^\theta} \lhd \delta^\theta \rhd M^{\neg\delta^\theta}$$

As this definition illustrates we need two merge relations for the quiescence preserving internal choice: $M_\sqcap^{\delta^\theta}$ and $M^{\neg\delta^\theta}$. $M_\sqcap^{\delta^\theta}$ merges the very beginning of the two processes P and Q. After that, $M^{\neg\delta^\theta}$ takes care that $P \ \sqcap^\theta \ Q$ behaves like P or Q. As proven in [11], this operator is idempotent and commutative.

$M_\sqcap^{\delta^\theta}$ and $M^{\neg\delta^\theta}$ share some common properties, formalized by M^θ: (1) Parts of P and Q are only merged if their *wait'* values are equal, and (2) potentially the initial θ has to be removed from all traces.

Definition 17 (Internal choice - Common merge)

$$M^\theta =_{df} (0.wait \Leftrightarrow 1.wait) \wedge wait' = 0.wait \wedge (ok' = (0.ok \wedge 1.ok)) \wedge$$
$$((\neg initQuiet(0.tr - tr) \vee \neg initQuiet(1.tr - tr)) \Rightarrow \neg initQuiet(tr' - tr))$$
$$where \ initQuiet(t) =_{df} t \notin (\{s \hat{\ } u | s \in \mathcal{A} \wedge u \in \mathcal{A}_\theta^*\} \cup \{\langle\rangle\})$$

$M_\sqcap^{\delta^\theta}$ is defined by the use of M^θ. In addition to M^θ, $M_\sqcap^{init}$ merges traces and refusal sets of P and Q into new traces and new refusal sets.

Definition 18 (Internal choice - Initial merge)

$$M_\sqcap^{\delta^\theta} =_{df} M^\theta \wedge M_\sqcap^{init}$$
$$M_\sqcap^{init} =_{df} ((tr' = 0.tr \wedge ref' = (0.ref \setminus \{\theta\}) \cup (\{\theta\} \cap (0.ref \cup 1.ref))) \vee$$
$$(tr' = 1.tr \wedge ref' = (1.ref \setminus \{\theta\}) \cup (\{\theta\} \cap (0.ref \cup 1.ref))))$$

By adding $\{\theta\} \cap (0.ref \cup 1.ref)$ to the set of refused actions the new process refuses θ only if one of the two processes refuse to exhibit a θ event. In other words, only if both processes do not refuse θ, i.e., $\theta \notin 0.ref \wedge \theta \notin 1.ref$, the resulting process does not refuse θ as well, i.e., $\theta \notin ref'$.

$M^{\neg\delta^\theta}$ takes care that finally $P \ \sqcap^\theta \ Q$ behaves like P or Q. Additionally, M^θ is applied in order to potentially remove θ from the traces.

Definition 19 (Internal choice - Terminal merge)

$$M^{\neg\delta^\theta} =_{df} M^\theta \wedge M^{term}$$
$$M^{term} =_{df} ((tr' = 0.tr \wedge ref' = 0.ref) \vee (tr' = 1.tr \wedge ref' = 1.ref))$$

A quiescence preserving external choice operator is given by

Definition 20 (Quiescence preserving external choice)

$$P +^\theta Q =_{df} (P \wedge Q); M_+ \quad with \quad M_+ =_{df} M_+^{\delta^\theta} \vartriangleleft \delta^\theta \vartriangleright M^{\neg\delta^\theta}$$

Except the merge relation $M_+^{\delta^\theta}$ the external choice is equivalent $\sqcap^\theta$. The difference is how the very beginning of P and Q is combined to form $P +^\theta Q$. The external choice operator is idempotent and commutative [11].

Definition 21 (External choice merge relation)

$$M_+^{\delta^\theta} =_{df} M^\theta \wedge M_+^{init}$$
$$M_+^{init} =_{df} (ref' = ((0.ref \cap 1.ref) \setminus \{\theta\}) \cup (\{\theta\} \cap (0.ref \cup 1.ref))) \wedge$$
$$(tr' = 0.tr \vee tr' = 1.tr)$$

Specification processes for the **ioco** framework are defined as follows:

Definition 22 (ioco specification). *An **ioco** specification is a reactive process satisfying the healthiness conditions **IOCO1**, **IOCO2** and **IOCO3**. In addition its set of possible events is partitioned into the quiescent event, input events, and output events:* $\mathcal{A} = \mathcal{A}_{out} \cup \mathcal{A}_{in} \cup \{\theta\}$ *where* $\mathcal{A}_{out} \cap \mathcal{A}_{in} = \emptyset$ *and* $\theta \notin \mathcal{A}_{out} \cup \mathcal{A}_{in}$

Processes expressed in terms of $do_\mathcal{A}^\theta$, ;, $+^\theta$ and $\sqcap^\theta$ are **ioco** specifications. **ioco** specifications are closed under these operators. For proofs we refer to [11].

Remark 1. The class of labeled transition systems (LTS) used for the **ioco** relation is restricted to image finite LTSs [12]. Image finite LTSs are limited in their possible non-deterministic choices, i.e. image finite LTSs are bounded in terms of non-determinism. This requirement is only due to the properties of Tretmans' test case generation algorithm. Since we are interessted in a predicative semantics we do not face the problem of image-finiteness.   □

Remark 2. The TGV tool [3], which claims to generate test cases with respect to **ioco**, uses a different notion of quiesence: $quiesence_{TGV} =_{df} quiesence \vee (\neg ok' \wedge \neg wait')$. Note that we rely on *quiescence* rather than on $quiescence_{TGV}$.   □

3.3 IOCO Implementations

The input output conformance relation uses labeled transition systems to represent implementations. As mentioned in Section 2, it is not assumed that this LTS is known in advance, but only its existence is required. Our formalization requires something similar: implementations can be expressed as processes.

Processes for representing implementations in terms of the **ioco** relation need to satisfy the properties of specifications plus three additional properties: some restrictions on allowed choices, input-enabledness, and fairness.

Restrictions on choices. An implementation is not allowed to freely choose between the actions enabled in a particular state. The **ioco** relation distinguishes between inputs and outputs not only by partitioning a process' alphabet, but also by assigning responsibilities to these two alphabets (see Section 3.1.

In terms of choices this means that for implementations choices between outputs are internal choices. Internal choices are represented by a disjunctions over the refused actions, thus we restrict the choices between outputs:

IOCO4 $P = P \wedge (\neg wait \Rightarrow (wait' \Rightarrow (|\mathcal{A}_{out}| - 1) \leq |ref'_{out}|))$

Example 6. Because of this healthiness condition the τ transitions in state z_4 of Figure 3 are required, i.e. the choice between $!t$ and $!c$ is an internal choice. Thus, as required by **IOCO4**, after the trace $\langle ?1, \theta, ?1 \rangle$ z does not offer $!t$ and $!c$ for communication, i.e. $!t \notin ref' \wedge !c \notin ref'$. Instead, it non-deterministically offers only one of the two actions for communication, i.e. $!t \notin ref' \vee !c \notin ref'$. □

Contrary, input actions are under control of the system's environment. That is, choices between inputs are external choices. This restriction is enforced by requiring input-enabledness (see **IOCO5**).

In addition, if there are inputs and outputs enabled in a particular state of an implementation the choice between input and output is up to the environment. That is, choices between inputs and outputs are external choices. Again, this restriction is covered by having input-enabled implementations (see **IOCO5**).

Remark 3. Note that, as identified in [13], external choices between inputs and outputs allows the environment to prevent the system from providing an output. Therefore, the constraints on the semantics of choices within implementations have been relaxed [12]. By changing the properties of test cases (see Remark 4 in Section 3.5), choices between inputs and outputs are now choices of the implementation. Our work focuses on the original definition of **ioco**.   □

Input-enabledness. Input-enabledness requires that an implementation accepts every input in every (waiting) state. More precisely, an implementation cannot prevent the environment from providing an input, while running.

IOCO5 $P = P \wedge (\neg wait \Rightarrow (wait' \Rightarrow (ref'_{in} = \emptyset)))$

As for specifications we need to redefine $\mathbb{I}$ such that even in the case of divergence the additional properties of implementations are satisfied.

$$\mathbb{I}^\theta_\iota =_{df} \begin{pmatrix} \neg ok \wedge (tr \leq tr') \wedge \\ (wait' \Rightarrow (((|\mathcal{A}_{out}| - 1) \leq |ref'_{out}|) \wedge (ref'_{in} = \emptyset)) \wedge \\ (\theta \notin ref' \Rightarrow (quiescence \wedge (\exists s \bullet tr' - tr = s \hat{\ } \theta^*)))) \end{pmatrix} \vee \begin{pmatrix} ok' \wedge \\ (v' = v) \end{pmatrix}$$

Using this new version of the $\mathbb{I}$-relation within the healthiness condition **R3** leads to **R3**$^\theta_\iota$ which is used for implementations

$$\mathbf{R3}^\theta_\iota(P) =_{df} \mathbb{I}^\theta_\iota \lhd wait \rhd P$$

While specifications are expressed in terms of $do_{\mathcal{A}}^{\theta}$, implementations use $\iota_{\mathcal{A}}$. More precisely, we express implementations by the use of $\iota_{\mathcal{A}}^{\theta}$. But let us start with $\iota_{\mathcal{A}}$ first. $\iota_{\mathcal{A}}$ takes care of the input-enabledness of processes.

For the sake of simplicity we use the following abbreviation to denote a sequence of inputs without a particular action: $\mathcal{A}_{in\setminus a}^{*} =_{df} (\mathcal{A}_{in} \setminus \{a\})^{*}$.

Definition 23 (Input-enabled communication). *Let $a \in \mathcal{A}$ be an action of a process' alphabet, then*

$$\iota_{\mathcal{A}}(a) =_{df} \Phi^{i}(ref'_{in} = \emptyset \wedge a \notin ref' \wedge tr' - tr \in \mathcal{A}_{in\setminus a}^{*} \lhd wait' \rhd tr' - tr \in \mathcal{A}_{in\setminus a}^{*} \widehat{\;} \langle a \rangle)$$

$\iota_{\mathcal{A}}(a)$ is similar to $do_{\mathcal{A}}(a)$. It denotes that the process $\iota_{\mathcal{A}}(a)$ cannot refuse to perform an a-action. Furthermore, $\iota_{\mathcal{A}}(a)$ cannot refuse to perform any input action. After executing any input action sequence ended by an a action the process $\iota_{\mathcal{A}}(a)$ terminates successfully.

Input enabledness also affects the representation of a deadlock. An input-enabled process needs to accept an input action at any time. That is an input-enabled process can only deadlock on outputs. Therefore, the deadlock process δ_{ι}, which substitutes δ in the case of input-enabled processes, is given by:

Definition 24 (Output deadlock)

$$\delta_{\iota} =_{df} \mathbf{R}\mathcal{S}_{\iota}^{\theta}(tr' - tr \in \mathcal{A}_{in}^{*} \wedge wait')$$

Again, as for the non-input-enabled case, we need a quiescent version of $\iota_{\mathcal{A}}$. $\iota_{\mathcal{A}}^{\theta}(a)$ has θ events within its traces if a is an input event.

Definition 25 (Input-enabled quiescent communication). *Let $a \in \mathcal{A}$ be an action of a process' alphabet, then*

$$\iota_{\mathcal{A}}^{\theta}(a) =_{df} \begin{cases} \iota_{\mathcal{A}}(a) & \text{if } a \in \mathcal{A}_{out} \\ \Phi^{i}(ref'_{in} = \emptyset \wedge \theta \notin ref' \wedge tr' - tr \in (\mathcal{A}_{in\setminus a} \cup \theta)^{*} \\ \qquad \lhd wait' \rhd tr' - tr \in (\mathcal{A}_{in\setminus a} \cup \theta)^{*} \widehat{\;} \langle a \rangle) & \text{if } a \in \mathcal{A}_{in} \end{cases}$$

Combining input-enabledness with quiescence again requires a slight modification of the deadlock process. This leads to the output quiescent deadlock:

Definition 26 (Quiescent output deadlock)

$$\delta_{\iota}^{\theta} =_{df} \mathbf{R}\mathcal{S}_{\iota}^{\theta}(tr' - tr \in (\mathcal{A}_{in} \cup \theta)^{*} \wedge wait')$$

Fairness. Fairness is especially important for allowing theoretical exhaustive test case generation algorithms. The fairness assumption for the **ioco** relation requires that an implementation eventually shows all its possible non-deterministic behaviors when it is re-executed with a particular set of inputs. Without assuming fairness of implementations there is not even a theoretical possibility of generating a failing test case for any non-conforming implementation. An unfair implementation may always lead a test case away from its errors. To express this fairness on an implementation we use a probabilistic choice operator similar to He and Sanders [14]. According to [14] a probabilistic choice between two processes A and B is expressed with $A \ _p\oplus B$ where $0 \leq p \leq 1$. This expression equals A with probability p and B with probability $1-p$. For example, $A \ _{0.9}\oplus B$ denotes that during execution A is chosen in 90% of the cases.

The probabilistic version of our quiescence preserving internal choice, i.e. $\sqcap^\theta$, is given by $_p\odot^\theta$. The laws for $_p\odot^\theta$ are similar to the laws for $_p\oplus$, i.e.,

$$P \ _1\odot^\theta \ Q = P$$
$$P \ _p\odot^\theta \ Q = Q \ _{1-p}\odot^\theta \ P$$
$$P \ _p\odot^\theta \ P = P$$
$$(P \ _p\odot^\theta \ Q) \ _q\odot^\theta \ R = P \ _{pq}\odot^\theta \ (Q \ _r\odot^\theta \ R), \qquad r = ((1-p)q)/(1-(pq))$$
$$(P \ _p\odot^\theta \ Q); R = (P; R) \ _p\odot^\theta \ (Q; R))$$

A quiescence preserving internal choice is given by the non-deterministic choice of all possible probabilistic choices, i.e.

$$P \ \sqcap^\theta \ Q = \sqcap\{P \ _p\odot^\theta \ Q | 0 \leq p \leq 1\} \sqsubseteq P \ _p\odot^\theta \ Q$$

Relying on probabilistic choices means that when one implements a choice the specification is refined by choosing a particular probability for this choice. Fairness is expressed by restricting the probabilities p to $0 < p < 1$:

Definition 27 (Internal fair (quiescence preserving) choice)

$$P \ \sqcap_f^\theta \ Q =_{df} \sqcap\{P \ _p\odot^\theta \ Q | 0 < p < 1\}$$

Thus, when executing a test case on the implementation the implementation will eventually exhibit all its possible behavior. As stated by the following lemma fair internal quiescence preserving choices are valid implementations of internal quiescence preserving choices. This guarantees that our internal quiescence preserving choice can be safely implemented by its fair version.

Lemma 1. $P \ \sqcap^\theta \ Q \sqsubseteq P \ \sqcap_f^\theta \ Q$

Proof

$$
\begin{aligned}
P \ \sqcap_f^\theta \ Q = & \qquad\qquad\qquad\qquad \{\text{definition of } \sqcap_f^\theta\} \\
= \sqcap\{P \ _p\odot^\theta \ Q | 0 < p < 1\} & \qquad\qquad\qquad\qquad \{\text{definition of } \sqcap\} \\
\sqsupseteq \sqcap\{P \ _p\odot^\theta \ Q | 0 < p < 1\} \sqcap P \sqcap Q & \qquad\qquad\qquad\qquad \{\text{laws for } _p\odot^\theta\} \\
= \sqcap\{P \ _p\odot^\theta \ Q | 0 < p < 1\} \sqcap P \ _1\odot^\theta \ Q \sqcap P \ _0\odot^\theta \ Q & \qquad\qquad \{\text{definition of } \sqcap\} \\
= \sqcap\{P \ _p\odot^\theta \ Q | 0 \leq p \leq 1\} & \qquad\qquad\qquad\qquad \{\text{laws for } _p\odot^\theta\} \\
= P \ \sqcap^\theta \ Q &
\end{aligned}
$$

Given the notion of input-enabledness and fairness we can now define which processes serve to represent **ioco** testable implementations:

Definition 28 (ioco testable implementation). *An* **ioco** *testable implementation is a reactive process satisfying the healthiness conditions* **IOCO1-IOCO5.** *In addition, an* **ioco** *testable implementation must be fair.*

Processes expressed in terms of $\iota_{\mathcal{A}}^{\theta}$, $;$, $+^{\theta}$, and $\sqcap_{f}^{\theta}$ are **ioco** testable implementations if their choices obey to the following rules: (1) Choices between outputs are fair internal choices ($\sqcap_{f}^{\theta}$); (2) Choices between inputs and choices between inputs and outputs are external choices ($+^{\theta}$). Implementation processes are closed under these operators. For proofs please refer to [11].

3.4   Predicative Input Output Conformance Relation

Recall that informally an IUT conforms to a specification S, iff the outputs of the IUT are outputs of S after an arbitrary suspension trace of S.

Thus, we need the (suspension) traces of a process, which are obtained by hiding all observations except the traces

Definition 29 (Traces of a process)

$$Trace(P) =_{df} \exists ref, ref', wait, wait', ok, ok' \bullet P$$

In addition to all traces of a particular process we need the traces after which a process is quiescent. Due to the chosen representation of quiescence (see Section 3.2) we use the following predicate in order to obtain the traces after which a process is quiescent

Definition 30 (Quiet traces of a process)

$$Quiet(P) =_{df} \exists ref'_{in} \bullet (P[false/wait'] \vee P[A_{out}/ref'_{out}])$$

Using these two predicates the input output conformance relation between implementation processes (see Definition 28) and specification processes (see Definition 22) can be defined as follows:

Definition 31 ($\sqsubseteq_{ioco}$). *Given an implementation process I and a specification process S, then*

$$S \sqsubseteq_{ioco} I =_{df} [\forall t \in \mathcal{A}_{\theta}^{*}, \forall o \in \mathcal{A}_{out} \bullet$$
$$((Trace(S)[t/tr'] \wedge Trace(I)[\hat{t}\,o/tr']) \Rightarrow Trace(S)[\hat{t}\,o/tr']) \wedge$$
$$((Trace(S)[t/tr'] \wedge Quiet(I)[t/tr']) \Rightarrow Quiet(S)[t/tr'])]$$

In order to distinguish the input output conformance given in denotational semantics from its operational semantics version we use different symbols. Note that because $\sqsubseteq_{ioco}$ is related to refinement I **ioco** S is given by $S \sqsubseteq_{ioco} I$.

ioco relates the outputs (including quiescence) of I and S for all suspension traces of S. Contrary, our $\sqsubseteq_{ioco}$ definition comprises two different parts. The first part considers only outputs while the second part deals with quiescence.

Using the predicative definition $\sqsubseteq_{ioco}$ we can now show the relation between the input output conformance relation and refinement.

Theorem 1. $\sqsubseteq \subseteq \sqsubseteq_{ioco}$

Proof. In order to prove $\sqsubseteq \subseteq \sqsubseteq_{ioco}$, we have to show that $S \sqsubseteq I \Rightarrow S \sqsubseteq_{ioco} I$

$S \sqsubseteq I$ {definition of $\sqsubseteq$ and propositional calculus}
$= [I \Rightarrow S] \wedge ([I \Rightarrow S] \vee [I \Rightarrow S])$ {substitution}
$= [I \Rightarrow S] \wedge [(I[false/wait'] \Rightarrow S[false/wait'])] \vee$
$\quad [(I[A_{out}/ref'_{out}] \Rightarrow S[A_{out}/ref'_{out}])]$ {def. of [] and prop. calculus}
$= [I \Rightarrow S] \wedge [(I[false/wait'] \wedge I[A_{out}/ref'_{out}]) \Rightarrow$
$\quad (S[false/wait'] \vee S[A_{out}/ref'_{out}])]$ {propositional calculus}
$\Rightarrow [(I \Rightarrow S) \wedge ((\exists ref'_{in} \bullet (I[false/wait'] \vee I[A_{out}/ref'_{out}])) \Rightarrow$
$\quad (\exists ref'_{in} \bullet (S[false/wait'] \vee S[A_{out}/ref'_{out}])))]$
$\qquad\qquad\qquad$ {propositional calculus and definition of $Quiet$}
$\Rightarrow [((\exists ref, ref', wait, wait', ok, ok' \bullet I) \Rightarrow (\exists ref, ref', wait, wait', ok, ok' \bullet S)) \wedge$
$\quad (Quiet(I) \Rightarrow Quiet(S))]$ {prop. calculus and def. of $Trace$}
$\Rightarrow [\forall t \in \mathcal{A}^*_\theta \bullet (Trace(I)[t/tr'] \Rightarrow Trace(S)[t/tr']) \wedge$
$\quad \forall t \in \mathcal{A}^*_\theta \bullet (Quiet(I)[t/tr'] \Rightarrow Quiet(S)[t/tr'])]$ {propositional calculus}
$\Rightarrow [\forall t \in \mathcal{A}^*_\theta, \forall o \in \mathcal{A}_{out} \bullet (Trace(I)[\hat{t}\,o/tr'] \Rightarrow Trace(S)[\hat{t}\,o/tr']) \wedge$
$\quad \forall t \in \mathcal{A}^*_\theta \bullet (Quiet(I)[t/tr'] \Rightarrow Quiet(S)[t/tr'])]$
$\qquad\qquad\qquad$ {propositional calculus and definition of $Trace$}
$\Rightarrow [\forall t \in \mathcal{A}^*_\theta, \forall o \in \mathcal{A}_{out} \bullet$
$\quad ((Trace(S)[t/tr'] \wedge Trace(I)[\hat{t}\,o/tr']) \Rightarrow Trace(S)[\hat{t}\,o/tr']) \wedge$
$\quad \forall t \in \mathcal{A}^*_\theta \bullet ((Trace(S)[t/tr'] \wedge Quiet(I)[t/tr']) \Rightarrow Quiet(S)[t/tr'])]$
$\qquad\qquad\qquad$ {distributivity of $\forall$}
$= [\forall t \in \mathcal{A}^*_\theta, \forall o \in \mathcal{A}_{out} \bullet$
$\quad (((Trace(S)[t/tr'] \wedge Trace(I)[\hat{t}\,o/tr']) \Rightarrow Trace(S)[\hat{t}\,o/tr']) \wedge$
$\quad ((Trace(S)[t/tr'] \wedge Quiet(I)[t/tr']) \Rightarrow Quiet(S)[t/tr']))]$ {def. of $\sqsubseteq_{ioco}$}
$= S \sqsubseteq_{ioco} I$ $\square$

Although, $\sqsubseteq_{ioco}$ and **ioco** are not transitive in general, an interesting property is that refining a conforming implementation does not break conformance.

Theorem 2. $((S \sqsubseteq_{ioco} I_2) \wedge (I_2 \sqsubseteq I_1)) \Rightarrow S \sqsubseteq_{ioco} I_1$

Proof. $S \sqsubseteq_{ioco} I_2 \wedge I_2 \sqsubseteq I_1$ {definition of $\sqsubseteq$ and propositional calculus}
$= (S \sqsubseteq_{ioco} I_2) \wedge [I_1 \Rightarrow I_2] \wedge [I_1 \Rightarrow I_2]$ {def. of $\exists$, $Trace$, and $Quiet$}
$\Rightarrow (S \sqsubseteq_{ioco} I_2) \wedge [Trace(I_1) \Rightarrow Trace(I_2)] \wedge [Quiet(I_1) \Rightarrow Quiet(I_2)]$
$\qquad\qquad\qquad$ {propositional calculus}
$\Rightarrow [\forall t \in \mathcal{A}^*_\theta, \forall o \in \mathcal{A}_{out} \bullet$
$\quad (((Trace(S)[t/tr'] \wedge Trace(I_2)[\hat{t}\,o/tr']) \Rightarrow Trace(S)[\hat{t}\,o/tr']) \wedge$
$\quad (Trace(I_1)[\hat{t}\,o/tr'] \Rightarrow Trace(I_2)[\hat{t}\,o/tr'])) \wedge$
$\quad \forall t \in \mathcal{A}^*_\theta \bullet (((Trace(S)[t/tr'] \wedge Quiet(I_2)[t/tr']) \Rightarrow Quiet(S)[t/tr']) \wedge$
$\quad (Quiet(I_1)[t/tr'] \Rightarrow Quiet(I_2)[t/tr']))]$ {prop. calculus}
$\Rightarrow [\forall t \in \mathcal{A}^*_\theta, \forall o \in \mathcal{A}_{out} \bullet$
$\quad (((Trace(S)[t/tr'] \wedge Trace(I_1)[\hat{t}\,o/tr']) \Rightarrow Trace(S)[\hat{t}\,o/tr']) \wedge$
$\quad ((Trace(S)[t/tr'] \wedge Quiet(I_1)[t/tr']) \Rightarrow Quiet(S)[t/tr']))]$ {def. of $\sqsubseteq_{ioco}$ }
$= S \sqsubseteq_{ioco} I_1$ $\square$

Although, the definition of $\sqsubseteq_{ioco}$ corresponds to the definition of **ioco** we can reformulate our definition to a more generic version $\sqsubseteq_{ioco}^{P}$ which corresponds to **ioco**$_{\mathcal{F}}$. Like $\mathcal{F}$ in **ioco**$_{\mathcal{F}}$, P is used to select the proper set of traces.

Definition 32 ($\sqsubseteq_{ioco}^{P}$). *Given an implementation process I and a specification process S, then*

$$S \sqsubseteq_{ioco}^{P} I =_{df} [\ \forall t \in \mathcal{A}_\theta^*, \forall o \in \mathcal{A}_{out} \bullet$$
$$((P(S,I,t) \wedge Trace(I)[t\widehat{\ }o/tr']) \Rightarrow Trace(S)[t\widehat{\ }o/tr']) \wedge$$
$$((P(S,I,t) \wedge Quiet(I)[t/tr']) \Rightarrow Quiet(S)[t/tr']) \ ]$$

The conformance relations listed in Section 2 can now be defined as follows:

Definition 33 (Conformance relations)

$$S \sqsubseteq_{iot} I =_{df} S \sqsubseteq_{ioco}^{P_{iot}} I, \text{ where } P_{iot}(S,I,t) = t \in \mathcal{A}_\theta^*$$
$$S \sqsubseteq_{ior} I =_{df} S \sqsubseteq_{ioco}^{P_{ior}} I, \text{ where } P_{ior}(S,I,t) = t \in \mathcal{A}^*$$
$$S \sqsubseteq_{ioconf} I =_{df} S \sqsubseteq_{ioco}^{P_{ioconf}} I, \text{ where } P_{ioconf}(S,I,t) = Trace(S)[t/tr'] \wedge t \in \mathcal{A}^*$$
$$S \sqsubseteq_{ioco} I =_{df} S \sqsubseteq_{ioco}^{P_{ioco}} I, \text{ where } P_{ioco}(S,I,t) = Trace(S)[t/tr'] \wedge t \in \mathcal{A}_\theta^*$$

3.5   Test Cases, Test Processes, and Test Suites

Testing for conformance is done by applying a set of test cases to an implementation. Test cases are processes satisfying additional properties.

A test process has finite behavior such that testing can be eventually stopped. In the case of divergence one needs to interrupt testing externally.

TC1 $P(tr,tr') = P \wedge (\exists n \in \mathbb{N} \bullet length(tr' - tr) \leq n)$

Furthermore, a test case either accepts all responses from an implementation, i.e., inputs from the view of the test case, or it accepts no inputs at all:

TC2 $P = P \wedge (\neg wait \Rightarrow (wait' \Rightarrow (ref'_{in} = \mathcal{A}_{in} \vee ref'_{in} = \emptyset)))$

If the test case has to provide a particular stimuli to the IUT it is always clear which output (from the view of the test case) should be send:

TC3 $P = P \wedge (\neg wait \Rightarrow (wait' \Rightarrow (|ref'_{out}| \geq |\mathcal{A}_{out}| - 1)))$

Furthermore, testing should be a deterministic activity, i.e. test cases should be deterministic. Determinism includes that a tester can always deterministically decide what to do: send a particular stimuli to the IUT or wait for a possible response. This is ensured by the following two healthiness conditions.

TC4 $P = P \wedge (\neg wait \Rightarrow (wait' \Rightarrow ((|ref'_{out}| = |\mathcal{A}_{out}| - 1) \Leftrightarrow ref'_{in} = \mathcal{A}_{in})))$
TC5 $P = P \wedge (\neg wait \Rightarrow (wait' \Rightarrow ((ref'_{in} = \emptyset) \Leftrightarrow (ref'_{out} = \mathcal{A}_{out}))))$

After termination a test case should give a verdict about the test execution

TC6 $P = P \wedge (\neg wait' \Rightarrow (pass' \Rightarrow \neg fail'))$

Note that we use separate variables because some test case selection strategies (e.g. [3]) make use of inconclusive verdicts, i.e., $\neg pass' \wedge \neg fail'$.

As for specifications and implementations we make $\mathbb{I}$ suitable for test cases:

$$\mathbb{I}^{TC} =_{df} \left(\begin{array}{l} \neg ok \wedge (tr \leq tr') \wedge (\exists n \in \mathbb{N} \bullet length(tr' - tr) \leq n) \wedge \\ wait' \Rightarrow ((ref'_{in} = \mathcal{A}_{in} \vee ref'_{in} = \emptyset) \wedge \\ (|ref'_{out}| \geq |\mathcal{A}_{out}| - 1) \wedge \\ ((|ref'_{out}| = |\mathcal{A}_{out}| - 1) \Leftrightarrow ref'_{in} = \mathcal{A}_{in}) \wedge \\ ((ref'_{in} = \emptyset) \Leftrightarrow (ref'_{out} = \mathcal{A}_{out}))) \wedge \\ (\neg wait' \Rightarrow (pass' \Rightarrow \neg fail')) \end{array}\right) \vee \left(\begin{array}{l} ok' \wedge \\ (v' = v) \end{array}\right)$$

$\mathbb{I}^{TC}$ ensures that even in the case of divergence we respect the properties of test cases. For test cases **R3** becomes $\mathbf{R3}^{TC} =_{df} \mathbb{I}^{TC} \lhd wait \rhd P$.

Definition 34 (Test process). *A test process P is a reactive process, which satisfies the healthiness conditions $\mathbf{TC1} \ldots \mathbf{TC6}$ and $\mathbf{IOCO1}$. The set of events in which a test case can potentially engage is given by $\mathcal{A}$, where $\mathcal{A} = \mathcal{A}_{out} \cup \mathcal{A}_{in}$, $\mathcal{A}_{out} \cap \mathcal{A}_{in} = \emptyset$ and $\theta \in \mathcal{A}_{in}$. The observations are extended by: $pass, fail : Bool$, which denote the pass and fail verdicts, respectively.*

Remark 4. Due to the results of Petrenko et al. [13], the properties of test cases have been changed recently [12]. Test cases are now input-enabled, i.e. they are not able to block any input (i.e. outputs of the IUT) anymore. Hence, test cases accept every output of the IUT in every state. Note that this conflicts with healthiness condition **TC5** and **TC6**. During the test execution one has now to decide non-deterministically whether to send an input or to wait for an output. However, we use the original version of **ioco** in this paper.   □

Test cases are reactive processes expressed in terms of $do_{\mathcal{A}}(a)$. We use the following abbreviations for indicating pass (✓) and fail (✗) verdicts.

$$✓ =_{df} (\neg wait' \Rightarrow pass') \qquad ✗ =_{df} (\neg wait' \Rightarrow fail')$$

Due to the properties of test cases the only choices of a test case are choices between inputs. Since the chosen input to a test case, i.e. output of the IUT, are up to the IUT this choice is given in terms of an external choice:

$$P + Q =_{df} P \wedge Q \lhd \delta \rhd P \vee Q \quad \text{with} \quad \delta =_{df} \mathbf{R3}(tr' = tr \wedge wait')$$

Test cases are closed under $\{+, ;\}$. For proofs please refer to [11].

Example 7. A test case T with $A_{in} = \{c, t, \theta\}$ and $A_{out} = \{1\}$ that sends a stimulus and subsequently accepts a c but neither accepts t nor θ is given by

$$T =!1; ((?c \wedge ✓) + (?t \wedge ✗) + (\theta \wedge ✗)) = \{\text{def. of } do_{\mathcal{A}}, ✓, ✗, \text{ and } +\}$$

$$= \left(\begin{array}{l} !1 \notin ref' \wedge tr' = tr \vee \\ \{?c, ?t, \theta\} \nsubseteq ref' \wedge tr' = tr^\frown \langle !1 \rangle \end{array}\right) \lhd wait' \rhd \left(\begin{array}{l} tr' = tr^\frown \langle !1, ?c \rangle \wedge pass' \vee \\ tr' = tr^\frown \langle !1, ?t \rangle \wedge fail' \vee \\ tr' = tr^\frown \langle !1, \theta \rangle \wedge fail' \end{array}\right)_{\Box}$$

A test suite is a set of test cases. Because of the use of global verdicts (see Definition 38), a test suite is given by the nondeterministic choice of a set of test cases.

Definition 35 (Test suite). *Given a set of N test processes $T_1, \ldots, T_N$, then a test suite TS is defined as: $TS =_{df} \bigcap_{i=1,\ldots,N} T_i$*

3.6   Testing Implementations

Test case execution in the input output conformance testing framework is modeled by executing the test case in parallel to the system under test. We model this parallel execution again as parallel merge (see Section 3.2).

The execution of a test case t on an implementation i is denoted by $t\rceil\rceil i$. This new process $t\rceil\rceil i$ consists of all traces present in both, the test case and the implementation. Furthermore, $t\rceil\rceil i$ gives $fail'$ and $pass'$ verdicts after termination.

Such an execution operator is inspired by CSPs parallel composition [15], i.e, the parallel composition of a test case and an implementation can only engage in a particular action if both processes participate in the communication.

Since a test case swaps inputs and outputs of the IUT we need to rename alphabets. Therefore, we define an alphabet renaming operator for a process P denoted by $\overline{P}$ as follows: $A\overline{P} =_{df} AP$; $A_{out}\overline{P} =_{df} A_{in}P$; $A_{in}\overline{P} =_{df} A_{out}P$.

Definition 36 (Test case execution). *Let TC be a test case process and IUT be an implementation process, then $A(TC\rceil\rceil IUT) =_{df} A\overline{TC} \cup AIUT$ and $TC\rceil\rceil IUT =_{df} (\overline{TC} \;\lambda\; IUT); M_{ti}$.*

The relation M_{ti} merges the traces of the test case and the implementation. The result comprises the pass and fail verdicts of the test case as well as traces that are allowed in both, the test case and the implementation. Because of our representation of quiescence, there is no θ that indicates termination of the IUT, i.e., $\neg 1.wait$. M_{ti} takes care of that when merging the traces.

Definition 37 (Test case/impl. merge)

$$M_{ti} =_{df} pass' = 0.pass \wedge fail' = 0.fail \wedge wait' = (0.wait \wedge 1.wait) \wedge$$
$$ref' = (0.ref \cup 1.ref) \wedge ok' = (0.ok \wedge 1.ok) \wedge$$
$$(\exists u \bullet ((u = (0.tr - tr) \wedge u = (1.tr - tr) \wedge tr' = tr\,\widehat{}\,u) \vee$$
$$(u\,\widehat{}\,A_{in}^* \,\widehat{}\, \langle\theta\rangle = (0.tr - tr) \wedge u = (1.tr - tr) \wedge tr' = tr\,\widehat{}\,\langle u, \theta\rangle) \wedge \neg 1.wait))$$

Due to the lack of symmetry of our merge operator the test case execution operator $\rceil\rceil$ is not symmetric. However, it still distributes over $\sqcap$, i.e., let T_1, T_2 be test cases and let P be an implementation, then $(T_1 \sqcap T_2)\rceil\rceil P = (T_1\rceil\rceil P) \sqcap (T_2\rceil\rceil P)$.

This law allows one to run a set of N test cases $T_1, \ldots, T_N$, i.e. a test suite $TS =_{df} \sqcap_{i=1,\ldots,N} T_i$, against an implementation process P:

$$TS\rceil\rceil P = \bigsqcap_{i=1,\ldots,N} T_i\rceil\rceil P = (T_1 \sqcap \ldots \sqcap T_N)\rceil\rceil P$$

Since our test cases do not consist of a single trace but of several traces there may be different verdicts given at the end of different traces. An implementation passes a test case if all possible test runs lead to the verdict pass:

Definition 38 (Global verdict). *Given a test process (or a test suite) T and an implementation process IUT, then*

$$IUT \text{ passes } T =_{df} \forall r \in A_\theta^* \bullet (((T\rceil\rceil IUT)[r/tr'] \wedge \neg wait') \Rightarrow pass')$$
$$IUT \text{ fails } T =_{df} \exists r \in A_\theta^* \bullet (((T\rceil\rceil IUT)[r/tr'] \wedge \neg wait') \Rightarrow fail')$$

Example 8. Now we can calculate verdicts by executing test cases on implementations. For example, consider the test case of Example 7, i.e. $T = !1; ((?c \land \checkmark) + (?t \land \boldsymbol{X}) + (\theta \land \boldsymbol{X}))$, and the IUT $\mathcal{P}_w = \iota_\mathcal{A}^\theta(?1); \iota_\mathcal{A}^\theta(!c)$ (representing the IUT w of Figure 3). Executing T on the IUT $\mathcal{P}_w$, i.e. $T \| \mathcal{P}_w$, is conducted as follows:

$$T \| \mathcal{P}_w = \qquad\qquad\qquad\qquad\qquad \{\text{def. of } \| \text{ and renaming}\}$$

$$= (?1; ((!c \land \checkmark) + (!t \land \boldsymbol{X}) + (\theta \land \boldsymbol{X})) \, \mathbb{\lambda} \, \iota_\mathcal{A}^\theta(?1); \iota_\mathcal{A}^\theta(!c)); M_{ti} \quad \{\text{def. of } \mathbb{\lambda} \text{ and } M_{ti}\}$$

$$= \begin{pmatrix} ?1 \notin ref' \land tr' = tr \lor \\ !c \notin ref' \land tr' = tr \hat{\ } \langle ?1 \rangle \end{pmatrix} \triangleleft wait' \triangleright (tr' = tr \hat{\ } \langle ?1, ?c \rangle \land pass')$$

Thus, we have $\mathcal{P}_w$ passes T because

$$\mathcal{P}_w \text{ passes } T \qquad\qquad\qquad\qquad\qquad \{\text{def. of passes}\}$$

$$= \forall r \in \mathcal{A}_\theta^* \bullet (((T \| \mathcal{P}_w)[r/tr'] \land \neg wait') \Rightarrow pass') \qquad \{t \| \mathcal{P}_w\}$$

$$= \forall r \in \mathcal{A}_\theta^* \bullet ((\neg wait' \land r = tr \hat{\ } \langle ?1 \rangle \hat{\ } \langle ?c \rangle \land pass') \Rightarrow pass') \qquad \{\text{prop. calc.}\}$$

$$= \forall r \in \mathcal{A}_\theta^* \bullet TRUE = TRUE \qquad\qquad\qquad\qquad \square$$

4   Conclusion and Future Work

This paper lifts the input output conformance (**ioco**) theory of Tretmans [1] for functional black-box testing of reactive systems to UTP's reactive processes [8].

The presented operators make the absence of output events, i.e. quiescence, observable for reactive processes. Furthermore, we show how to express input enabled processes and introduce a formal notion of fairness. By the use of specification processes and implementation processes we define $\sqsubseteq_{ioco}$. This conformance relation gives a notion of correctness of an implementation with respect to a specification in terms of UTP's reactive processes.

Although, the presented theory is more complex than Tretmans' original formulation there are many benefits in embedding **ioco** in UTP. First, the presented healthiness conditions are mostly simple and formalize the assumptions behind **ioco**. To the best of our knowledge, this is the first time that these assumptions have been presented in a formal way. Second, we can formally prove properties of $\sqsubseteq_{ioco}$, and check proofs automatically. For example, particular steps of some proofs of [11] have been checked using satisfiability solvers (e.g. [6]). Thanks to the predicative style of $\sqsubseteq_{ioco}$ such decision procedures cannot only be used for proof checking, but also for test case generation by expressing test case generation as a satisfiability problem. Finally, formulating **ioco** in terms of UTP make specifications with a UTP semantics useable for **ioco** testing.

Although, this paper gives the basic notion of specifications, implementations, test cases and conformance there is plenty of work left. While we related refinement and $\sqsubseteq_{ioco}$, there are many other laws that should be investigated. Another open task is to instantiate this framework for a particular process algebra, e.g., CSP. Furthermore, there are many extensions to the ioco theory. For example,

Lestiennes and Gaudel [16] presented *rioco*, which relaxes the property of input-enabledness. Another variation of **ioco** considers the presence of time, i.e. **tioco** [17]. It would be interesting to study these conformance relations in terms of UTP and compare arising healthiness conditions to the presented healthiness conditions.

Acknowledgments. The research herein is conducted within the competence network Softnet Austria and funded by the Austrian Federal Ministry of Economics (bm:wa), the province of Styria, the Steirische Wirtschaftsförderungsgesellschaft mbH. (SFG), and the city of Vienna in terms of the center for innovation and technology (ZIT). This research is also funded by the EU FP7 project MO-GENTES ICT-216679.

References

1. Tretmans, J.: Test generation with inputs, outputs and repetitive quiescence. Software - Concepts and Tools 17(3), 103–120 (1996)
2. Tretmans, J., Brinksma, E.: TorX: Automated model based testing. In: 1st European Conference on Model-Driven Software Engineering, pp. 13–25 (2003)
3. Jard, C., Jéron, T.: TGV: theory, principles and algorithms. International Journal on Software Tools for Technology Transfer 7(4), 297–315 (2005)
4. de Vries, R.G., Belinfante, A., Feenstra, J.: Automated testing in practice: The highway tolling system. In: 14th International Conference on Testing Communicating Systems. IFIP Proceedings, vol. 210, pp. 219–234 (2002)
5. Aichernig, B.K., Peischl, B., Weiglhofer, M., Wotawa, F.: Protocol conformance testing a SIP registrar: An industrial application of formal methods. In: 5th Int'l. Conference on Software Engineering and Formal Methods, pp. 215–224. IEEE, Los Alamitos (2007)
6. Dutertre, B., de Moura, L.: The yices smt solver (2008), http://yices.csl.sri.com/tool-paper.pdf
7. Oliveira, M.V.M., Cavalcanti, A.L.C., Woodcock, J.C.P.: A UTP Semantics for *Circus*. Formal Aspects of Computing 21(1), 3–32 (2007)
8. Hoare, C., He, J.: Unifying Theories of Programming. Prentice-Hall, Englewood Cliffs (1998)
9. Bernot, G.: Testing against formal specifications: A theoretical view. In: Abramsky, S. (ed.) TAPSOFT 1991, CCPSD 1991, and ADC-Talks 1991. LNCS, vol. 494, pp. 99–119. Springer, Heidelberg (1991)
10. Tretmans, J.: A Formal Approach to Conformance Testing. PhD thesis, University of Twente, Enschede (December 1992)
11. Weiglhofer, M., Aichernig, B.K.: Input output conformance testing in the unifying theories of programming. Technical Report SNA-TR-2008-1P6, Softnet Austria (2008), http://www.ist.tugraz.at/staff/weiglhofer/publications
12. Tretmans, J.: Model based testing with labelled transition systems. In: Hierons, R.M., Bowen, J.P., Harman, M. (eds.) FORTEST. LNCS, vol. 4949, pp. 1–38. Springer, Heidelberg (2008)
13. Petrenko, A., Yevtushenko, N., Huo, J.L.: Testing transition systems with input and output testers. In: Hogrefe, D., Wiles, A. (eds.) TestCom 2003. LNCS, vol. 2644, pp. 129–145. Springer, Heidelberg (2003)

14. He, J., Sanders, J.W.: Unifying probability. In: Dunne, S., Stoddart, B. (eds.) UTP 2006. LNCS, vol. 4010, pp. 173–199. Springer, Heidelberg (2006)

15. Hoare, C.: Communicating Sequential Processes. Prentice-Hall, Englewood Cliffs (1985)

16. Lestiennes, G., Gaudel, M.C.: Test de systèmes réactifs non réceptifs. Journal Européen des Systèmes Automatisés, Modélisation des Systèmes Réactifs 39(1-3), 255–270 (2005) (Technical Report in English available)

17. Krichen, M., Tripakis, S.: Black-box conformance testing for real-time systems. In: Graf, S., Mounier, L. (eds.) SPIN 2004. LNCS, vol. 2989, pp. 109–126. Springer, Heidelberg (2004)

The Miracle of Reactive Programming

Jim Woodcock

Department of Computer Science
University of York
jim@cs.york.ac.uk

Abstract. Reactive miracles are rather unexplored in Unifying Theories of Programming. We present two simple properties: prefixing a miracle with an event, and offering an external choice between a process and a miracle. Both are strange processes, each violating an important axiom of the standard failures-divergences model for CSP.

1 Introduction

Communicating Sequential Processes (CSP) is a formal language for describing patterns of interaction in concurrent systems. It was first introduced by Tony Hoare in 1978 [Hoa78], although that view of CSP has changed much in 30 years. The most useful textbooks are by Hoare [Hoa85], Roscoe [Ros97], and Schneider [Sch00]. As well as an axiomatic and operational semantics (see, *e.g.*, [Sch00]), the language has a variety of different denotational semantic models reflecting, for instance, untimed [BHR84], timed [RoR88], probabilistic [Low93], and synchronous behaviour [Bar93]. The three major denotational models of untimed CSP are the traces, stable failures, and failures-divergences models (see both [Ros97] and [Sch00] for accounts of each of these models).

The *traces model* defines the meaning of a process as the set of traces of events that the process can be observed to perform. The *stable failures model* extends the traces model with refusal sets, which are sets of events that a process can refuse to perform. A failure is a pair consisting of a trace and a set of events that the process may refuse after the trace. The *failures-divergences model* extends the failures model with another set of traces, each of which leads to a divergence of the process.

More recently, Hoare & He have given a new semantics to CSP in *Unifying Theories of Programming (UTP)* [HoH98] in the style of Hehner's *Predicative Programming* [Heh84a, Heh84b]. The semantic setting provided by the UTP is the theory of alphabetised relations, and interesting sub-theories are built by defining mappings corresponding to healthiness conditions capturing different aspects of the sub-theory. Hoare and He first build a sub-theory of precondition-postcondition pairs within the relational calculus; this is the theory of designs (see [WoC04] for a tutorial introduction to designs). Next, they build a theory of reactive processes, which is disjoint from the theory of designs. Finally, they use the reactive healthiness conditions to embed designs within the theory of

A. Butterfield (Ed.): UTP 2008, LNCS 5713, pp. 202–217, 2010.

reactive processes. The result is the theory of CSP processes (see [CaW04] for a tutorial account of this embedding).

All three theories are complete lattices, rather than the complete partial orders of the standard models for CSP. As complete lattices, they each have a top element. The top of the design lattice is the familiar miracle from the refinement calculus: $w : [\, true, false\,]$ [Mor88]. This design is always guaranteed to terminate if it is started, and when it does terminate, it achieves the impossible. As well as representing intermediate results in refinement, it gives a semantics to naked guarded commands, allowing them to wait [Mor90].

The tops of the reactive and the CSP lattices are, to the best of our knowledge, completely unexplored. In this paper, we give an insight into the nature of the reactive miracle and give just a glimpse into how it might be useful in developing reactive systems.

The paper is structured as follows. We begin by introducing the theory of designs in UTP in Sect. 2, followed by the theory of reactive processes in Sect. 3. In Sect. 4, we describe the semantics of CSP in terms of reactive designs. In Sect. 5 and Sect. 6 we give our two small properties of reactive miracles. In Sect. 7, we discuss some novel applications of these properties, and in Sect. 8, we conclude the paper.

2   Designs in Unifying Theories of Programming

Relations in the sub-theory of designs can be split into *assumption-commitment* pairs, which are called *designs*. These are very similar to the specification statements of the refinement calculus (see, *e.g.*, [Mor90]). The theory of designs in UTP unifies various theories of programming, such as the assertional technique [Gri81], B [Abr96], the refinement calculus [Mor90], VDM [Jon90], and Z [Spi88, Spi92, WoD96].

Designs have two observations: ok and ok' record the observations that the program has started and has terminated, respectively. For predicates P and Q not containing ok or ok', the design with precondition P and postcondition Q is defined as:

$$(P \vdash Q) \;\hat{=}\; (ok \wedge P \Rightarrow ok' \wedge Q)$$

This definition may be read as "if the program starts in a state satisfying P, then it will terminate, and on termination Q will be true".

Refinement in UTP is universal inverse-implication. That is, one relation P is refined by another Q, denoted $P \sqsubseteq Q$, providing $[\, Q \Rightarrow P\,]$, where the brackets indicate universal quantification over all variables in the alphabet. Refinement of designs is just the same, giving rise to the familiar laws for refinement of specification statements.

$$P_1 \vdash Q_1 \;\sqsubseteq\; P_2 \vdash Q_2$$
$$= \{\, \text{definition of } \sqsubseteq \,\}$$

$$[\,(\,P_2 \vdash Q_2\,) \Rightarrow (\,P_1 \vdash Q_1\,)\,]$$
$= \{\,\text{design, twice}\,\}$
$$[\,(\,ok \wedge P_2 \Rightarrow ok' \wedge Q_2\,) \Rightarrow (\,ok \wedge P_1 \Rightarrow ok' \wedge Q_1\,)\,]$$
$= \{\,\text{case split } ok\,\}$
$$[\,(\,P_2 \Rightarrow ok' \wedge Q_2\,) \Rightarrow (\,P_1 \Rightarrow ok' \wedge Q_1\,)\,]$$
$= \{\,\text{case split } ok'\,\}$
$$[\,(\neg P_2 \Rightarrow \neg P_1\,) \wedge (\,(\,P_2 \Rightarrow Q_2\,) \Rightarrow (\,P_1 \Rightarrow Q_1\,))\,]$$
$= \{\,\text{propositional calculus}\,\}$
$$[\,(\,P_1 \Rightarrow P_2\,) \wedge (\,(\,P_2 \Rightarrow Q_2\,) \Rightarrow (\,P_1 \Rightarrow Q_1\,))\,]$$
$= \{\,\text{predicate calculus}\,\}$
$$[\,P_1 \Rightarrow P_2\,] \wedge [\,P_1 \wedge Q_2 \Rightarrow Q_1\,]$$

The final conjuncts can be read as the familiar slogan "weaken preconditions, strengthen postconditions".

Designs are closed under the program operators of sequential composition, nondeterministic choice, conditional, and (least-fixed point) recursion. We give the two of these properties:

$$(P \vdash Q)\,;(S \vdash T) \;=\; (P \wedge (Q \; \mathbf{wp} \; S)) \vdash (Q \,;\, T)$$

$$(P_1 \vdash P_2) \lhd b \rhd (Q_1 \vdash Q_2) \;=\; (P_1 \lhd b \rhd Q_1) \vdash (P_2 \lhd b \rhd Q_2)$$

We assume that neither P nor S contain dashed variables. This is actually the subject of another (optional) healthiness condition [HoH98]. Hoare & He use the convention that P is a relation (predicate on dashed and undashed variables, and p a condition (predicate on undashed variables only0.

The bottom of the design lattice is the extreme point, **true**, which arises from the design (**false** $\vdash P$), a design with precondition false and postcondition P, which may be arbitrary.

$\quad$**false** $\vdash$ **false**
$= \{\,\text{definition of design}\,\}$
$\quad ok \wedge \mathbf{false} \Rightarrow ok' \wedge \mathbf{false}$
$= \{\,\mathbf{false} \text{ zero for conjunction}\,\}$
$\quad \mathbf{false} \Rightarrow ok' \wedge \mathbf{false}$
$= \{\,\text{vacuous implication}\,\}$
$\quad \mathbf{true}$

This is the imperative program *abort*, and as it is the bottom of the lattice, we denote it by $\perp_D$. The other extreme point is $\neg\, ok$, which arises from the design (**true** $\vdash$ **false**), as we now show:

$$\textbf{true} \vdash \textbf{false}$$
$$= \{ \text{definition of design} \}$$
$$ok \wedge \textbf{true} \Rightarrow ok' \wedge \textbf{false}$$
$$= \{ \textbf{true} \text{ unit for conjunction} \}$$
$$ok \Rightarrow ok' \wedge \textbf{false}$$
$$= \{ \textbf{false} \text{ zero for conjunction} \}$$
$$ok \Rightarrow \textbf{false}$$
$$= \{ \text{contradiction} \}$$
$$\neg ok$$

This is the imperative program *miracle*, and as it is the lattice top, we denote it by $\top_D$. The design miracle is an interesting program. Originally, Dijkstra proposed a healthiness condition for his predicate transformers, *The Law of the Excluded Miracle*, to outlaw such a program [Dij76] (he wasn't considering specifications). This healthiness condition also exists in UTP, where it is known as **H4** (feasibility):

$$P \; ; \textbf{true} = \textbf{true}$$

This states (perhaps a little cryptically) that for *every* initial value there is a final value satisfying the postcondition, as we can see from the following derivation characterising the **H4** healthiness condition:

$$P \; ; \textbf{true} = \textbf{true}$$
$$= \{ \text{universal truth} \}$$
$$[P \; ; \textbf{true}]$$
$$= \{ \text{relational calculus} \}$$
$$[\exists \, ok', v' \bullet P]$$

where v' is the list of program variables. So **H4** excludes miracles. Designs may or may not satisfy **H4**; those that do are implementable; those that don't aren't.

Dijkstra expressed his healthiness condition using his *weakest precondition predicate transformer*, which may be defined in terms of designs as

$$(P_1 \vdash P_2 \; \textbf{wp} \; r) = (P_1 \wedge \neg (P_2 \; ; \neg r))$$

His healthiness condition can then be stated as:

$$Q \; \textbf{wp} \; \textbf{false} = \textbf{false}$$

We can see that this follows from our formulation. Consider the design $(Q_1 \vdash Q_2)$, and assume that it is **H4**, and that Q_1 has no dashed variables. This has the following consequence:

$$(Q_1 \vdash Q_2) \; ; \textbf{true} = \textbf{true}$$

$= \{\,\text{design bottom, twice}\,\}$

$(Q_1 \vdash Q_2)\,;(\mathbf{false} \vdash \mathbf{true}) \;=\; (\mathbf{false} \vdash \mathbf{true})$

$= \{\,\text{design sequence}\,\}$

$((Q_1 \wedge \neg (Q_2\,;\mathbf{true})) \vdash (Q_2\,;\mathbf{true})) \;=\; (\mathbf{false} \vdash \mathbf{true})$

$= \{\,\text{design bottom}\,\}$

$\neg\,(Q_1 \wedge \neg (Q_2\,;\mathbf{true}))$

$= \{\,\text{weakest precondition}\,\}$

$\neg\,((Q_1 \vdash Q_2)\;\mathbf{wp}\;\mathbf{false})$

Miracles are used to give semantics to *naked guarded commands*, which are defined as [Mor90]:

$$b \to P \;\widehat{=}\; b \wedge P$$

Notice that this really is a design:

$b \wedge (P_1 \vdash P_2)$

$= \{\,\text{conditional}\,\}$

$(P_1 \vdash P_2) \vartriangleleft b \vartriangleright \mathbf{false}$

$= \{\,\text{design bottom}\,\}$

$(P_1 \vdash P_2) \vartriangleleft b \vartriangleright (\mathbf{true} \vdash \mathbf{false})$

$= \{\,\text{design closure}\,\}$

$(P_1 \vartriangleleft b \vartriangleright \mathbf{true}) \vdash (P_2 \vartriangleleft b \vartriangleright \mathbf{false})$

$= \{\,\text{conditional}\,\}$

$b \Rightarrow P_1 \vdash b \wedge P_2$

The naked guarded command P is enabled in states where it behaves non-miraculously. To see this, first consider the $\mathbf{wp}$-semantics for the naked guarded command:

$(b \to (P_1 \vdash P_2))\;\mathbf{wp}\;q$

$= \{\,\text{weakest precondition}\,\}$

$(b \Rightarrow P_1) \wedge \neg\,((b \wedge P_2)\,;\neg\,q)$

$= \{\,\text{relational calculus}\,\}$

$(b \Rightarrow P_1) \wedge \neg\,(b \wedge (P_2\,;\neg\,q))$

$= \{\,\text{propositional calculus}\,\}$

$(b \Rightarrow P_1) \wedge (b \Rightarrow \neg\,(P_2\,;\neg\,q))$

$= \{\,\text{propositional calculus}\,\}$

$b \Rightarrow P_1 \wedge \neg\,(P_2\,;\neg\,q)$

$= \{\,\text{weakest precondition}\,\}$

$b \Rightarrow ((P_1 \vdash P_2)\;\mathbf{wp}\;q)$

Now think about the case where the guard is false:

$$(\textbf{false} \rightarrow P) \ \textbf{wp false}$$
$$= \ \textbf{false} \Rightarrow (P \ \textbf{wp false})$$
$$= \ \textbf{true}$$

One of the characteristic properties of the theory of designs is that $\textbf{true}$ is a left unit for sequential composition. So, once a guard is false, control flow is stuck. As Morgan puts it, miracles can wait [Mor90].

3   Reactive Processes

Reactive process have four pairs of observational variables; tr, ref, ok, $wait$, and their dashed counterparts. The tr and ref observations constitute a failure in the sense explained in Sect. 1. The ok and $wait$ observations (and their dashed cousins) describe whether a process is started (or finishes) in a stable, waiting, or unstable state. Reactive processes have three healthiness conditions:

R1 $P \ = \ P \wedge tr \leq tr'$
R2 $P(tr, tr') \ = \ \sqcap_s \bullet P(s, s \ ^\frown (tr' - tr))$
R3 $P \ = \ (\mathbb{I} \lhd wait \rhd P)$

(Here, $\mathbb{I}_R$ is the identity relation.) The first healthiness condition ensures that once an event is observed in a trace it can't be forgotten: the trace only gets longer. The second says that, while history is important, a process can't depend on the previous value of the trace taking a particular form. The final healthiness condition says that, if a process is initiated in the waiting state of a predecessor, then it too will have to wait.

CSP processes are a special kind of reactive process that satisfy two additional healthiness conditions:

CSP1 $P \ = \ (\neg \ ok \wedge tr \leq tr') \vee P$
CSP2 $P \ = \ P \ ; J$
where $J \ \widehat{=} \ (ok \Rightarrow ok') \wedge \mathbb{I}(tr, ref, wait, v)$

which are analogues of the design healthiness conditions:

H1 $P \ = \ \neg \ ok \vee P$
H2 $P \ = \ P \ ; J_D$
where $J_D \ \widehat{=} \ (ok \Rightarrow ok') \wedge \mathbb{I}(v)$

Every design satisfies these two conditions. A predicate has the healthiness condition **H1** if it is a fixed point of the equation; in this case, if the program hasn't started ($\neg \ ok$), then no further observation can be made. If the predicate is **H2**, then it is monotonic in the value of ok'. This rules out predicates such as $\neg \ ok'$, which, although it appears to insist on nontermination, isn't a design at all: it cannot be expressed in the form $P \vdash Q$. The nonterminating program is described by the lattice bottom, $\textbf{true}$, which doesn't constrain ok' at all. The intuition for this comes from refinement, which says when one design Q is better than another P: it terminates more often, and with more strongly defined results. Every other design is better than $true$, and this must include all those designs that require termination.

Reactive programs are not designs: the two theories are disjoint. This follows from the antagonistic nature of $H1$ and $R1$. In general, a theory of CH-healthy predicates must be disjoint from the theory of designs, since on abortion a design provides no guarantees, but a CH-healthy predicate still requires ψ to hold, although there is an approximate relationship between the two theories [HCW08]. It can be shown that the image of designs through the reactive healthiness conditions gives the lattice of CSP processes (those reactive predicates that also satisfy $CSP1$ and $CSP2$ [HoH98, CaW04].

We can make the difference between designs and reactive processes smaller by reformulating $R3$ to restrict designs to those predicates sensitive to the $wait$ observation. This leaves $R1$ as the only impediment to design-hood. Recall the definition of the design identity from [HoH98]:

$$\mathbb{I}_D \mathrel{\widehat{=}} H1(\mathbb{I})$$

and that of the reactive identity:

$$\mathbb{I}_{rea} \mathrel{\widehat{=}} R1(\mathbb{I}_D)$$

The reactive identity is clearly not a design: it always guarantees $tr \le tr'$, even when $\neg\, ok$. So, in the $R3$ healthiness condition:

$$R3(P) \mathrel{\widehat{=}} (\mathbb{I}_{rea} \vartriangleleft wait \vartriangleright P)$$

even if P is a design, $R3(P)$ isn't. We therefore introduce a new healthiness condition to make a design behave like the design identity when waiting:

$$R3j(P) \mathrel{\widehat{=}} (\mathbb{I}_D \vartriangleleft wait \vartriangleright P)$$

Clearly, $R3j(P)$ is a design if P is. Two simple properties follow from this:

$$R1 \circ R3j \;=\; R3 \circ R1$$

$$R1 \circ R3j \;=\; R1 \circ R3$$

The second result is a consequence of the first, and the fact that $R1$ and $R3$ commute. The first result follows from the fact that $R1$ is conjunctive, and therefore distributes through the conditional.

Proof

$$R1 \circ R3j(P)$$
$= \{$ definition of $R3j$ $\}$
$$R1\,(\mathbb{I}_D \vartriangleleft wait \vartriangleright P)$$
$= \{$ property of $R1$ $\}$

$(\mathbf{R1}(\mathbb{I}_D) \lhd wait \rhd \mathbf{R1}(P))$

$= \{$ definition of $\mathbb{I}_{rea}$ $\}$

$\quad (\mathbb{I}_{rea} \lhd wait \rhd \mathbf{R1}(P))$

$= \{$ definition of $\mathbf{R3}$ $\}$

$\quad \mathbf{R3} \circ \mathbf{R1}(P)$

The purpose of reformulating $\mathbf{R3}$ is to reduce reactive designs to $\mathbf{R1}$-designs

$$(P \models Q) \;\widehat{=}\; \mathbf{R1}(P \vdash Q)$$

This definition describes three possible behaviours:

- If the program is started in an unstable state, or in a state not satisfying the precondition, then only $\mathbf{R1}$-behaviour is guaranteed:

$$\mathbf{R1}(\neg\, ok \lor \neg\, P)$$

- Otherwise, the program must terminate, and when it does so it will satisfy Q and the trace will be treated properly:

$$\mathbf{R1}(ok' \land Q)$$

The properties of $\mathbf{R1}$-designs are similar to those of standard designs. For example, the space of designs is closed under sequential composition, and a similar result holds for $\mathbf{R1}$-designs:

$$(p \models Q)\,;(s \models T) \;=\; (p \land (\mathbf{R1}(Q)\ \mathbf{wp}_{R1}\ s)) \models (\mathbf{R1}(Q)\,;\mathbf{R1}(T))$$

where the predicate transformer $\mathbf{wp}_{R1}$ is defined to give us:

$$\mathbf{R1}(Q)\ \mathbf{wp}_{R1}\ s \;=\; \neg\,(\mathbf{R1}(Q)\,;\mathbf{R1}(\neg\, s))$$

The term $\mathbf{R1}(Q)\,;\mathbf{R1}(\neg\, s)$ chops the interval in two parts, both of which are $\mathbf{R1}$. In this context, Q fails to establish s.

4   Reactive Design Semantics

[OCW07] gives a denotational semantics for the *Circus* language, essentially imperative CSP, in the form of reactive designs. We present a similar result, but here we use $\mathbf{R1}$-designs. The semantics for *simple prefix* is

$$a \to Skip \;=\; \mathbf{R3}\left(true \models \left(\begin{array}{c} tr' = tr \land a \notin ref' \\ \lhd\ wait'\ \rhd \\ tr' = tr \,^\frown \langle a \rangle \end{array}\right) \land v' = v\right)$$

The postcondition describes two stable states. In one state, the process has terminated ($\neg\ wait'$), and the trace is extended with the occurrence of a; the value of the refusal set *ref'* is irrelevant, since the process has terminated. In the other state, the process is waiting for interaction with its environment (*wait'*). The trace is unchanged, since nothing has happened. Significantly, it is not refusing to perform *a* in this state. In both cases, the program variables *v* are unchanged.

The semantics for the *reactive miracle* is

$$\top_{R1D} \mathrel{\widehat{=}} \mathbf{R3}(\mathbf{true} \models \mathbf{false})$$

This can be simplified somewhat:

$$
\begin{aligned}
&\top_{R1D} \\
={}& \{\, \top_{R1D} \,\} \\
&\mathbf{R3}(\mathbf{true} \models \mathbf{false}) \\
={}& \{\, \mathbf{R1\text{-}design} \,\} \\
&\mathbf{R3} \circ \mathbf{R1}(\mathbf{true} \vdash \mathbf{false}) \\
={}& \{\, \text{above property} \,\} \\
&\mathbf{R1} \circ \mathbf{R3j}(\mathbf{true} \vdash \mathbf{false}) \\
={}& \{\, \mathbf{R3j} \,\} \\
&\mathbf{R1}\,(\mathbb{I}_D \lhd wait \rhd (\mathbf{true} \vdash \mathbf{false})) \\
={}& \{\, \mathbb{I}_D \,\} \\
&\mathbf{R1}\,((\mathbf{true} \vdash \mathbb{I}) \lhd wait \rhd (\mathbf{true} \vdash \mathbf{false})) \\
={}& \{\, \text{conditional design} \,\} \\
&\mathbf{R1}\,((\mathbf{true} \lhd wait \rhd \mathbf{true}) \vdash (\mathbb{I} \lhd wait \rhd \mathbf{false})) \\
={}& \{\, \text{conditional} \,\} \\
&\mathbf{R1}\,(\mathbf{true} \vdash wait \wedge \mathbb{I}) \\
={}& \{\, \mathbf{R1\text{-}design} \,\} \\
&(\mathbf{true} \models wait \wedge \mathbb{I})
\end{aligned}
$$

This is, by definition, **R1**/**R3**-healthy. But it's not **H4**. Let's simplify it one step further:

$$\top_{R1D} = tr \leq tr' \wedge (\neg\, ok \vee (ok' \wedge wait \wedge \mathbb{I}))$$

Now we can see that this is infeasible. Consider the case where the predecessor has terminated cleanly. In this state, the reactive miracle is properly initiated with the *ok* variable true and the *wait* variable false. Clearly,

$$\top_{R1D}[false, true/wait, ok] = \mathbf{false}$$

which is not feasible.

5   Prefixing a Miracle

In the last section we looked at the semantics of the reactive miracle. In this section, we combine the miracle with a simple CSP operator: proper prefixing. The operator constructs a process that engages in an event, say a, and then behaves like another process, say P. It's defined in terms of the simpler prefixing operation $a \rightarrow Skip$.

$$a \rightarrow P \ \widehat{=} \ a \rightarrow Skip \ ; \ P$$

What happens if we perform a and then behave miraculously? Is it a miracle? The following theorem provides an answer:

Theorem 1

$$a \rightarrow \top_{R1D} \ = \ \mathbf{R3}\,(\mathbf{true} \models (tr' = tr \wedge a \notin ref' \wedge wait' \wedge v' = v))$$

Proof

$$a \rightarrow \top_{R1D}$$

$= \{\,\text{compound prefixing}\,\}$

$$a \rightarrow Skip \ ; \ \top_{R1D}$$

$= \{\,\mathbf{R1}\text{-design simple prefix}\,\}$

$$\left(\mathbf{true} \models \mathbf{R3j} \left(\left(\begin{array}{c} tr' = tr \wedge a \notin ref' \\ \lhd\ wait'\ \rhd \\ tr' = tr \frown \langle a \rangle \end{array} \right) \wedge v' = v \right) \right) \ ; (\mathbf{true} \models wait \wedge \mathbb{I})$$

$= \{\,\mathbf{R1}\text{-design sequence}\,\}$

$$\mathbf{true} \models \left(\mathbf{R3j} \left(\left(\begin{array}{c} tr' = tr \wedge a \notin ref' \\ \lhd\ wait'\ \rhd \\ tr' = tr \frown \langle a \rangle \end{array} \right) \wedge v' = v \right) \ ; \ wait \wedge \mathbb{I} \right)$$

$= \{\,\text{property of }\mathbf{R3j}\,\}$

$$\mathbf{true} \models \left(\mathbf{R3j} \left(\left(\begin{array}{c} tr' = tr \wedge a \notin ref' \\ \lhd\ wait'\ \rhd \\ tr' = tr \frown \langle a \rangle \end{array} \right) \wedge v' = v \ ; \ wait \wedge \mathbb{I} \right) \right)$$

$= \{\,\text{relational calculus}\,\}$

$$\mathbf{true} \models \mathbf{R3j}\,(tr' = tr \wedge a \notin ref' \wedge wait' \wedge v' = v)$$

The result is clearly feasible, so it is not a miracle (all the variables are given explicitly, and it's easy to find a value for ref'). But this is a very strange process: it waits for interaction with the environment ($wait'$ is true in every final state), it never refuses to do the event a ($a \notin ref'$ in every final state), but it never actually does a ($tr' = tr$ in every final state)! It violates an axiom of CSP's failures-divergences model, namely:

$$(s, X) \in F \wedge Y \subset A \wedge (\forall a \in Y \bullet (s \frown \langle a \rangle, \emptyset) \notin F) \Rightarrow (s, X \cup Y) \in F$$

We can see that the miracle has pruned the a-transition. Operationally, we could consider that we've backtracked after trying the a and then hitting the miracle. We could control the backtracking to some extent by guarding the miracle with a predicate on the state. That way, we undo the a conditionally.

It's interesting to compare prefixed miracle with prefixed divergence:

$$a \rightarrow Chaos \ = \ \boldsymbol{R3}(\neg (tr \frown \langle a \rangle \leq tr') \models tr' = tr \wedge a \notin ref' \wedge wait')$$

At first sight this is a rather strange process too, since it's made from a design with an unusual precondition: it's a relation on two states, not a condition on just one state. Actually, it fails $\boldsymbol{H3}$, an optional healthiness condition that requires a design $(P \vdash Q)$ to satisfy $(P = P \ ; \ \boldsymbol{true})$ [HoH98, p.82–84]. Our non-$\boldsymbol{H3}$ precondition records the fact that the process can diverge in states other than just the initial state: it can visit a series of stable intermediate states before diverging. This record of interaction is a predicate on traces, in the usual way. In this case it says, "Every interaction that starts with an a-event leads to divergence."

6   External Choice with a Miracle

Now we consider what happens when we offer a choice between a miracle and engaging in some event. Here is the reactive design semantics for external choice:

$$P \square Q \ \hat{=} \ \boldsymbol{R1} \circ \boldsymbol{R3} \left(\neg P_f^f \wedge \neg Q_f^f \vdash \left(\begin{pmatrix} P_f^t \wedge Q_f^t \end{pmatrix} \triangleleft tr' = tr \wedge wait' \triangleright \begin{pmatrix} P_f^t \vee Q_f^t \end{pmatrix} \right) \right)$$

where

- The predicate $\neg P_f^f = \neg P[false, false/wait, ok']$ is P's precondition.
- The predicate $P_f^t = P[false, true/wait, ok']$ is P's postcondition.

The semantics can be recast as an $\boldsymbol{R1}$-design:

$$P \square Q = \begin{pmatrix} \left(\neg wait \Rightarrow \neg P_f^f \wedge \neg Q_f^f \right) \\ \models \\ \left(\mathbb{II} \triangleleft wait \triangleright \left(\left(P_f^t \wedge Q_f^t \right) \triangleleft tr' = tr \wedge wait' \triangleright \left(P_f^t \vee Q_f^t \right) \right) \right) \end{pmatrix}$$

We can now prove the following theorem:

Theorem 2

$$(a \rightarrow Skip) \square \top_{\boldsymbol{R1D}}$$
$$= (\boldsymbol{true} \models (\mathbb{II} \triangleleft wait \triangleright \neg wait' \wedge tr' = tr \frown \langle a \rangle \wedge v' = v))$$

This is another very strange process: it terminates immediately, having performed the event a. There is no state in which the process is waiting for the environment to perform a, it simply happens *instantly*. Intuitively, we can think of this as an *urgent event*. But it violates another important axiom of the standard failures-divergences model of CSP:

- Traces are prefix closed: $(s \frown t, X) \in F \Rightarrow (s, \emptyset) \in F$.

7   Applications

In this section we consider a few applications of miracles.

7.1   Ordered Simultaneity

Burns's timebands model is a way of describing systems whose requirements are structured according to different granularities of time (see [BHB+05]). The model makes use of a notion of simultaneous, but ordered, events, and we can describe such events in CSP using miracles. First, define an operator to make b an urgent event.

$$\underline{b} \rightarrow Skip \; \widehat{=} \; (b \rightarrow Skip) \; \Box \; \top_{\boldsymbol{R1D}}$$

Now we can write a process to require that a and b are simultaneous but ordered:

$$a \rightarrow \underline{b} \rightarrow Skip$$

Clearly a happens before b, but there is no state in which a has occurred without b having occurred. For example, in the 100ms timeband it appears to us that the light is on when we open the fridge door. Of course, we happen to know that opening the door causes the fridge light to come on, but the two events are simultaneous with this granularity of time:

$$open \rightarrow \underline{light.on} \rightarrow Skip$$

We could add a motion sensor to anticipate our opening the fridge. Now, the light will come on simultaneously with opening the door, and we might notice one before the other:

$$sense.motion \rightarrow open \rightarrow \underline{light.on} \rightarrow Skip$$
$$\Box$$
$$light.on \rightarrow \underline{open} \rightarrow Skip$$

7.2   Deadlines

In Timed CSP, the timeout operator $(b \rightarrow Skip) \; \triangleright_{10} \; Skip$ offers the event b for 10 seconds; if it hasn't occurred within this period, then the attempt to synchronise on b is abandoned. A stronger requirement would be to say that b

must occur within 10 seconds. We can model this using miracles in Timed CSP by introducing a deadline operator:

$$(b \ \textbf{deadline} \ 10) \ \widehat{=} \ ((b \rightarrow Skip) \rhd_{10} \top_{\textbf{R1}D})$$

In this process, there is no state 10 seconds from initiation in which b hasn't happened. This is really a very strong requirement in which there is no alternative to meeting the deadline. This may be useful in describing how the real world works. Jackson describes the world according to two moods (in the grammatical sense): *indicative* and *optative* [Jac95, Jac01]. The indicative mood refers to the way the world is—or as Jackson calls it, *the problem context*. The optative mood refers to the way in which we want to change the world—*the requirement*. Our deadline operator could be used to capture indicative models. For example, if today is Friday, then within the next 24 hours it will *change* to being Saturday:

$$(today = Friday) \ \& \ (change \rightarrow today := Saturday) \ \textbf{deadline} \ 24hrs$$

Here, the decision has been taken that the calendar is not within our system, but that it constitutes part of the problem context. And it has physical laws, like the one described here.

Given the wiring and power supply, it may be a physical law of our fridge that the light comes on 10ms after opening the door:

$$open \rightarrow ((light.on \rightarrow Skip) \ \textbf{deadline} \ 10ms)$$

This isn't a requirement, but a reflection of the laws of physics.

Hayes has also used miracles in the timed refinement calculus to describe deadlines for sequential programs [Hay02]. His deadline command takes no time to execute and always guarantees to meet the specified time. If the deadline has been missed, then the command is miraculous.

7.3 External Choice and State

What's the meaning of the following?

$$(x := 0 \ ; \ a \rightarrow Skip) \ \Box \ (x := 1 \ ; \ b \rightarrow Skip)$$

Both sides of the external choice try to update the same variable x. The semantics of the left-hand choice is easily calculated:

$$x := 0 \ ; \ a \rightarrow Skip$$

$$= \{ \textbf{R3j} \ \text{assignment and simple prefix} \}$$

$$\textbf{R3} \ (\textbf{true} \models \neg \ wt' \wedge x' = 0 \wedge tr' = tr) \ ;$$
$$\textbf{R3} \ (\textbf{true} \models (tr' = tr \wedge a \notin ref' \lhd wt' \rhd tr' = tr \cap \langle a \rangle) \wedge x' = x)$$

$$= \{ \textbf{R3j} \ \text{sequence} \}$$

$$\textbf{R3} \left(\begin{array}{l} \textbf{true} \\ \models \\ \neg \ wt' \wedge x' = 0 \wedge tr' = tr \ ; \\ (tr' = tr \wedge a \notin ref' \lhd wt' \rhd tr' = tr \cap \langle a \rangle) \wedge x' = x \end{array} \right)$$

$= \{\text{relational calculus}\}$

$\quad \boldsymbol{R3} \, (\mathbf{true} \models (tr' = tr \wedge a \notin ref' \lhd wt' \rhd tr' = tr ^\frown \langle a \rangle) \wedge x' = 0)$

The right-hand choice has a similar semantics.

$x := 1 \, ; b \to Skip$

$=$

$\quad \boldsymbol{R3} \, (\mathbf{true} \models (tr' = tr \wedge b \notin ref' \lhd wt' \rhd tr' = tr ^\frown \langle b \rangle) \wedge x' = 1)$

In both cases, we see that the state change is observable only after the choice has been made by the environment by synchronising on either a or b. We can prove the following theorem:

Theorem 3

$$(x := 0 \, ; a \to Skip) \, \square \, (x := 1 \, ; b \to Skip)$$

$$= \boldsymbol{R3} \left(\mathbf{true} \models \left(\begin{array}{l} \neg \, wt' \wedge tr' = tr ^\frown \langle a \rangle \wedge x' = 0 \\ \vee \, \neg \, wt' \wedge tr' = tr ^\frown \langle b \rangle \wedge x' = 1 \end{array} \right) \right)$$

This is yet another strange process. Operationally, either side may update the common variable before the choice is made, in which case there will be a conflict between the values of x in the two branches. But the apparent conflict on x's value simply doesn't exist, and in order to make this happen, the choice between the two events has become *urgent*.

8   Conclusions

This is work in progress. We have started to explore the nature of the reactive miracle in UTP, and we've shown how it gives rise to some strange processes. In particular, the presence of miracles leads to violating two of the usual axioms of CSP. In fact, these two axioms are not formulated in UTP: they simply weren't needed for the laws presented in [HoH98]. These laws are rather difficult to express in the UTP point-wise predicative style, but we have shown a connection with miraculous behaviour, and this may lead to a suitable expression of all the axioms of CSP. In the future, we will continue to explore the relationship between miracles and other CSP combinators and study the role of miracles in healthiness conditions.

Finally, we have what seems to be a promising contribution to Burns's time-bands model [BHB+05]. The use of ordered simultaneous events is one way of connecting two timebands where atomic events at the higher level are decomposed into activities at the lower level. But that is a topic for another paper.

Acknowledgements

The following have all made helpful comments and suggestions that are included in this paper: Alan Burns, Andrew Butterfield, Ana Cavalcanti, Jin Song Dong,

Steve Dunne, Leo Freitas, Paweł Gancarski, Ian Hayes, He Jifeng, Tony Hoare, Cliff Jones, and Kun Wei. Andrew and Paweł prompted me to think about the semantics of external choice and updating program state. Most of all, I'd like to thank the MEng4 class at York: the problem of working out the interaction between miracles, prefixing, and external choice was set as the end-of-course take-home assignment for my course on *Unifying Theories* in May 2008. They were all outstanding students.

The anonymous referees made some very helpful suggestions that have made the paper accessible to a wider audience. In particular, I'm grateful to the referee who pointed out Ian Hayes' work on deadlines.

References

[Abr96]   Abrial, J.-R.: The B Book: Assigning Programs to Meanings. Cambridge University Press, Cambridge (1996)

[BHR84]   Brookes, S., Hoare, C.A.R., Roscoe, A.W.: A Theory of Communicating Sequential Processes. Journal of the ACM 31(3), 560–599 (1984)

[Bar93]   Barnes, J.E.: A Mathematical Theory of Synchronous Communication. Programming Research Group Technical Monograph PRG-112 (1993)

[BHB+05] Burns, A., Hayes, I.J., Baxter, G., Fidge, C.J.: Modelling Temporal Behaviour in Complex Socio-Technical Systems. University of York Technical Report YCS-2005-390 (2005)

[CaW04]   Cavalcanti, A., Woodcock, J.: A Tutorial Introduction to CSP in Shape Unifying Theories of Programming. In: Cavalcanti, A., Sampaio, A., Woodcock, J. (eds.) PSSE 2004. LNCS, vol. 3167, pp. 220–268. Springer, Heidelberg (2006)

[Dij76]   Dijkstra, E.W.: A Discipline of Programming. Prentice-Hall Series in Automatic Computation (1976)

[Gri81]   Gries, D.: The Science of Computer Programming. Springer Monographs in Computer Science (1981)

[Hay02]   Hayes, I.J.: The Real-Time Refinement Calculus: A Foundation for Machine-Independent Real-Time Programming. In: Esparza, J., Lakos, C.A. (eds.) ICATPN 2002. LNCS, vol. 2360, pp. 44–58. Springer, Heidelberg (2002)

[HCW08]   Harwood, W., Cavalcanti, A., Woodcock, J.: A Theory of Pointers for the UTP. In: Fitzgerald, J.S., Haxthausen, A.E., Yenigün, H. (eds.) ICTAC 2008. LNCS, vol. 5160, pp. 141–155. Springer, Heidelberg (2008)

[Heh84a] Hehner, E.C.R.: Predicative Programming, Part I. Communications of the ACM 27(2), 134–143 (1984)

[Heh84b] Hehner, E.C.R.: Predicative Programming, Part II. Communications of the ACM 27(2), 144–151 (1984)

[Hoa78]   Hoare, C.A.R.: Communicating Sequential Processes. Communications of the ACM 21(8), 666–677 (1978)

[Hoa85]   Hoare, C.A.R.: Communicating Sequential Processes. Prentice-Hall, Englewood Cliffs (1985)

[HoH98]   Hoare, C.A.R., Jifeng, H.: Unifying Theories of Programming. Prentice-Hall, Englewood Cliffs (1998)

[Jac95]   Jackson, M.J.: Software Requirements & Specifications: a Lexicon of Practice, Principles, and Prejudices. ACM Press, Addison-Wesley (1995)

[Jac01]   Jackson, M.: Problem Frames: Analyzing and Structuring Software Development Problems. Addison-Wesley Publishing Company, Reading (2001)
[Jon90]   Jones, C.B.: Systematic Software Development using VDM. Prentice-Hall, Englewood Cliffs (1990)
[Low93]   Lowe, G.: Probabilities and Priorities in Timed CSP. Programming Research Group Technical Monograph PRG-111 (1993)
[Mor88]   Morgan, C.: Data Refinement by Miracles. Information Processing Letters 26(5), 243–246 (1988)
[Mor90]   Morgan, C.: Programming from Specifications. Prentice-Hall, Englewood Cliffs (1990)
[Mor90]   Morgan, C.C.: Of wp and CSP. In: Dijkstra, E.W. (ed.) Beauty is our Business: a Birthday Salute, Springer, Heidelberg (1990)
[OCW07]   Oliveira, M., Cavalcanti, A., Woodcock, J.: A UTP Semantics for Circus. Formal Aspects of Computing Journal (December 4, 2007), doi:10.1007/s00165-007-0052-5 (Published online)
[RoR88]   Roscoe, A.W., Reed, G.M.: A Timed Model for Communicating Sequential Processes. Theoretical Computer Science 58, 249–261 (1988)
[Ros97]   Roscoe, A.W.: The Theory and Practice of Concurrency. Prentice-Hall, Englewood Cliffs (1997)
[Sch00]   Schneider, S.: Concurrent and Real-time Systems: the CSP approach. Wiley, Chichester (2000)
[Spi88]   Spivey, J.M.: Understanding Z: a Specification Language and its Formal Semantics. Cambridge University Press, Cambridge (1988)
[Spi92]   Spivey, J.M.: The Z Notation: A Reference Manual, 2nd edn. International Series in Computer Science. Prentice-Hall, Englewood Cliffs (1992)
[WoC04]   Woodcock, J., Cavalcanti, A.: A Tutorial Introduction to Designs in Unifying Theories of Programming. In: Boiten, E.A., Derrick, J., Smith, G.P. (eds.) IFM 2004. LNCS, vol. 2999, pp. 40–66. Springer, Heidelberg (2004)
[WoD96]   Woodcock, J., Davies, J.: Using Z—Specification, Refinement, and Proof. Prentice Hall International Series in Computer Science, p. 392 (1996)

Encoding *Circus* Programs in **ProofPower-Z**

Frank Zeyda and Ana Cavalcanti

Department of Computer Science, University of York, U.K.
{zeyda,ana}@cs.york.ac.uk

Abstract. *Circus* combines elements from sequential and reactive programming, and is especially suited for the development and verification of state-rich, reactive systems. In this paper we illustrate, by example, how a mechanisation of the UTP, and of a *Circus* theory, more specifically, can be used to encode particular *Circus* specifications. This complements previous work which focused on using the mechanised UTP semantics to prove general laws. We propose a number of extensions to an existing mechanisation by Oliveira to deal with the problems of type constraints and theory instantiation. We also show what the strategies and practical solutions are for proving refinement conjectures.

Keywords: UTP, semantics, Z, theorem proving, refinement.

1   Introduction

The *Circus* language combines elements from sequential programming and process algebra [4]. Its key notion is that of a process, which encapsulates state and behaviour, defined by actions that operate on the state and communicate with the environment. Actions may be specified as Z operation schemas, Dijkstra's guarded commands, or constructs of the CSP language. *Circus* is particularly suitable for reasoning about state-rich, reactive systems [13,6] using refinement.

In [16] Oliveira presents a semantics for *Circus* based on the UTP, and an extensive encoding of definitions and laws in the ProofPower-Z theorem prover. ProofPower is a versatile and powerful mechanical theorem prover based on HOL that has been successfully used in industry. ProofPower-Z is an extension of ProofPower that additionally embeds the theory of Z. The work involved the creation of a hierarchy of UTP theory encodings, namely for the theories of relations, designs, reactive designs, CSP, and, on top of the hierarchy, *Circus*. Each embedded UTP theory gives rise to a collection of axiomatic Z definitions, and a ProofPower theory is used in each case to hold the definitions.

The motivation for this work was primarily to prove equality and refinement laws which are *generally* valid within the various UTP theories. To this end it has been successfully employed in proving a large repository (≥ 500) of such laws. Little experience has, however, been gained so far in encoding and proving properties of *particular Circus* specifications and programs.

As a motivating example, we consider the process presented in Fig. 1 whose purpose is to compute and output the series of Fibonacci numbers on a channel

A. Butterfield (Ed.): UTP 2008, LNCS 5713, pp. 218–237, 2010.

---

channel *out* : $\mathbb{N}$

process *Fib* $\widehat{=}$ **begin**

    state *FibState* $\widehat{=}$ $[x, y : \mathbb{N}]$

    InitFibState $\widehat{=}$ $[FibState' \mid x' = 1 \wedge y' = 1]$

    InitFib $\widehat{=}$ $out!1 \rightarrow out!1 \rightarrow InitFibState$

    OutFibState $\widehat{=}$
        $[\Delta FibState; \ next! : \mathbb{N} \mid x' = y \wedge y' = x + y \wedge next! = x + y]$

    OutFib $\widehat{=}$ $\mu X \bullet$ **var** *next* : $\mathbb{N} \bullet OutFibState; \ out!next \rightarrow X$

    $\bullet$ *InitFib* ; *OutFib*
end

Fig. 1. Specification of the *Circus* process *Fib*

out. After declaration of the channel in a **channel** paragraph, the process first declares its state components by means of a **state** process paragraph; here, they consist of the variables x and y both of integer type. This is followed by a sequence of actions: first to initialise the state of the process (*InitFibState* and *InitFib*), and further to calculate and communicate the next Fibonacci number (*OutFibState* and *OutFib*). A special action is the main action at the end, following '$\bullet$', which defines the process behaviour.

Initialisation in *InitFibState* is specified by a Z operation that assigns 1 to the state components. *InitFib* outputs the first two Fibonacci numbers prior to initialising the state. *OutFibState*, again defined by a Z schema, computes the next Fibonacci number, stores it in the local variable *next*, and updates the state. The shriek is merely syntactic sugar for output variables in schemas, and when interpreting a schema as an action treated as referring to the after-state variable (here *next'*). The rôle of *OutFib* is then to invoke *OutFibState* and output the calculated number over *out*; it does so repetitively being defined using recursion. The variable block conceals the *next* and *next'* components introduced by *OutFibState* making them local to the action. The main action first calls *InitFib*, and afterwards *OutFib*; it does not terminate.

The encoding of *Fib* in Oliveira's mechanisation of the UTP framework raises a few problems. One of them is that it does not support well the case where predicates of different UTP theories coexist in the same ProofPower scope of definitions. For example, the UTP characterisation of the actions of *Fib* are predicates that belong to a specific *family* of UTP theories that fulfil certain healthiness conditions (those of *Circus*), but at the same time have possibly different alphabets (of programming variables). An example is the variable block that defines *OutFib*, whose body is a predicate including *next* and *next'* in its alphabet, whereas the resulting predicate does not have these variables in the alphabet. In addition, the predicates of Z operation schemas used in the definition of *Fib* actions belong to another family of UTP theories (namely that of relations) with no healthiness conditions, but possibly different variables.

To address this problem, we require a dynamic notion of UTP theory instantiation. In the original work of Oliveira, the closest we get is the by nature static inclusion of the corresponding ProofPower theory. This is problematic mostly since constraints imposed by such 'instantiations' apply globally, and thus affect *all other UTP theories in scope.* Typically, the theory of designs may require the auxiliary variables *okay* and *okay'* to be of boolean type; however, such a constraint would in the existing treatment *a priori* affect instances of all other UTP theories, as, for example, the ones of plain predicative or relational theories. In the *Fib* process this problem equally arises if we assume the local variable *next* is reused somewhere else but with a different type. An illustrating example for this is the construct (**var** *next* • *next* := 1 ; *P*) ⊓ (**var** *next* • *next* := *true* ; *Q*) in which the type of *next* differs in each branch of the choice operator, and for this reason cannot be statically fixed.

In this paper, we first present a revised mechanisation of the UTP *Circus* theory that deals with the problem of instantiation and local type constraints. We then show how the new framework can be used to encode *Circus* processes in a way that the problems mentioned above largely disappear. Finally, we discuss some practical aspects of refinement proofs.

The revisions that we propose follow the approach discussed and justified in detail in [18]. The agenda in this paper is mainly to view them in the light of the *Circus* theory, and apply them to the concrete encoding of a *Circus* specification such as *Fib*. We also address the concern of refinement proofs.

The structure of the paper is as follows. In Section 2 we present the extensions we propose to the original mechanisation of Oliveira. Section 3 explains the embedding of the UTP theory of *Circus* in our modified settings; Section 4 discusses the encoding of *Circus* processes using that embedding; and Section 5 addresses refinement proofs. In Section 6 we draw our conclusions.

2 Extended Mechanised UTP Semantics

In the UTP [9], the fundamental objects are alphabetised predicates representing observable behaviour. We represent them as a set of bindings (functions) that map variable names to values, and a universe, used to define type constraints.

z
$$\mathbf{ALPHA\_PREDICATE} \; \widehat{=} \; \{bs : BINDINGS; \; u : UNIVERSE \mid$$
$$(\forall \, b : bs \bullet dom \; b = Alphabet_U \; u) \land bs \subseteq u\}$$

BINDINGS is the set of all binding sets, and *UNIVERSE* the set of all binding sets which are valid universes. A universe contains all well-typed bindings and so determines the types of the variables in the bindings. Its definition is as follows.

z
$$\mathbf{UNIVERSE} \; \widehat{=} \; \{bs : BINDINGS \mid \varnothing \in bs \land$$
$$(\forall \, b1 : bs; \; b : BINDING \mid b \subseteq b1 \bullet b \in bs) \land$$
$$(\forall \, b1, b2 : bs \bullet b1 \oplus b2 \in bs)\}$$

The empty set of bindings is a valid universe. Additionally, universes have to be subset closed, formalising our intuition that the binding resulting from restricting the domain of a well-typed binding remains well typed. Finally, the type of one variable cannot be sensitive to values taken by another variable, that is type restriction has to be orthogonal to binding (function) overriding.

In the specification of *ALPHA_PREDICATE* we state that the binding set has to be a subset of the universe in order to respect the type constraints imposed by it. Moreover, the universe must not retain information about types of variables outside the alphabet of the predicate. (The alphabet $Alphabet_U$ u of a universe u is the union of the domains of all its bindings.) This avoids anomalies when combining predicates with different universes. In general, this is only possible if the predicates agree on the types of their shared variables, and we do not want variables *irrelevant* to the predicate's meaning to cause clashes. In our model, alphabets are identified with universes; namely, we may conceptually think of universes as alphabets with additional type information attached to them.

A UTP theory is defined by a new schema type as follows.

z
```
┌─ UTP_THEORY ─────────────────────────────────────
│ THEORY_UNIVERSE : UNIVERSE;
│ HEALTH_CONDS : ℙ HEALTH_COND
│
└──────────────────────────────────────────────────
```

UTP theory instances are too associated with universes: the universe of the predicates of the theory. The type *HEALTH_COND* comprises all partial idempotent functions on the set *ALPHA_PREDICATE*, and *HEALTH_CONDS* accordingly records the healthiness conditions of the theory. We have to restrict ourselves to partial functions here since some healthiness conditions may not be applicable to predicates with certain variables or type constraints. For example, applying $\mathbf{H1}(P) = okay \Rightarrow P$ is only sensible if the type of *okay* in P is boolean.

UTP_THEORY does not record the predicates of the theory. We can derive them from the universe and healthiness conditions using the function below.

z
```
│ TheoryPredicates : UTP_THEORY → ℙ ALPHA_PREDICATE
│─────────────────────────────────────────────────
│
│ ∀ th : UTP_THEORY • TheoryPredicates th =
│     {p : ALPHA_PREDICATE | p.2 = th.THEORY_UNIVERSE ∧
│         (∀ h : th.HEALTH_CONDS • p ∈ dom h ∧ h p = p)}
```

As mentioned before, the predicates of a theory share its universe, and are the common fixed points of all the healthiness functions.

The instantiation of UTP theories is simply carried out by constructing a binding of *UTP_THEORY*. To achieve modularity we provide instantiation functions for every encoding of a UTP theory, for example *InstRelTheory u* for the plain theory of relations, *InstDesTheory u* for the theory of designs, and so on. The functions are solely parameterised in terms of a universe since the healthiness conditions for specific UTP theory families are usually fixed.

Our encoding provides further useful functions which allow for modular construction of a UTP theory hierarchy. For example *StrengthenTheory* (*th*, *hs*) enriches an existing theory instance *th* with a set of additional healthiness conditions *hs*. The main benefit of constructing theories in such a manner is that proofs about lower-level predicates and operators can be easily reused in higher-level theories, and moreover interesting properties can be formulated regarding theory dependencies. It is also an approach we will adopt discussing the encoding of the UTP theory of *Circus* in the following section.

3   Semantic Embedding of *Circus*

Our encoding of *Circus* is in essence a recast of Oliveira's *Circus* encoding [16] that takes into account the alterations of the previous section. Our version of the ProofPower-Z theory for *Circus* acts solely as a carrier for the various definitions for instantiating *Circus* theories. When instantiating concrete UTP theories we pursue a uniform approach that suggests a certain *structure* in the definitions. It is mirrored by the order in which definitions are presented here.

We first define the sets *CIRCUS_ALPHABET* and *CIRCUS_UNIVERSE* of possible alphabets and universes of theory instances. Since they are similar to those for reactive designs, we equate them with *REA_ALPHABET* and *REA_UNIVERSE* — the corresponding sets for the theory of reactive processes.

The set *REA_ALPHABET* includes all alphabets that contain the auxiliary variables *okay*, *wait*, *tr* and *ref*, including their primed versions. The variables themselves are introduced as distinct elements of the type *NAME* which represents variable names. Since *REA_ALPHABET* is a restriction of *REL_ALPHABET* (the type of relational alphabets), we only consider alphabets consisting of input (undashed) and output (single dashed) variables.

The set *REA_UNIVERSE* is defined as shown below.

z

$$
\begin{array}{|l}
\textbf{REA\_UNIVERSE} \ \widehat{=} \\
\quad \{u \ : \ DES\_UNIVERSE \ | \\
\qquad Alphabet_U \ u \ \in \ REA\_ALPHABET \ \wedge \\
\qquad typeof \ (wait, \ u) \ = \ BOOL\_VAL \ \wedge \\
\qquad typeof \ (tr, \ u) \ = \ SEQ\_EVENT\_VAL \ \wedge \\
\qquad typeof \ (ref, \ u) \ = \ SET\_EVENT\_VAL\}
\end{array}
$$

The alphabet of the universe of an instance of a reactive process theory has to be in *REA_ALPHABET*, and the types of the auxiliary variables are as we expect. To express the type constraints, we use the function *typeof*.

z

$$
\begin{array}{|l}
\textbf{typeof} \ : \ (NAME \ \times \ UNIVERSE) \ \rightarrow \ \mathbb{P} \ VALUE \\
\hline
\forall \ n \ : \ NAME; \ u \ : \ UNIVERSE \ \bullet \ typeof \ (n, \ u) \ = \ \{b \ : \ u \ | \ n \ \in \ dom \ b \ \bullet \ b \ n\}
\end{array}
$$

It takes a variable name and a universe, and returns the type of the variable: the set of values it can have in the respective universe.

In a $DES\_UNIVERSE$, *okay* has type $BOOL\_VAL$, so we do not need to constrain it. For the primed variables, as $DES\_UNIVERSE$ is a $REL\_UNIVERSE$, a constraint on relational universes ensures that dashed variables, if present, have similar types to their undashed counterparts.

In order to define the instantiation function for *Circus* theories, we need to encode their healthiness conditions. The UTP theory for *Circus* is a restriction of the theory of CSP requiring additional healthiness conditions $C1$, $C2$ and $C3$, which we omit here. Assuming their encoding, the theory instantiation function yielding elements of UTP_THEORY is defined as follows.

z
$$
\begin{array}{l}
\mathbf{InstCircusTheory} : CIRCUS\_UNIVERSE \rightarrow UTP\_THEORY \\
\hline
\forall\ u : CIRCUS\_UNIVERSE\ \bullet \\
\quad InstCircusTheory\ u = \\
\qquad StrengthenTheory\ (InstCSPTheory\ u,\ \{C1,\ C2,\ C3\})
\end{array}
$$

Instantiation is performed by strengthening a corresponding instance of the UTP theory of CSP. Instantiation is defined only if a suitable universe is provided; here, it must be one from the set $CIRCUS\_UNIVERSE$. The instantiation function easily allows us to define the set $CIRCUS\_THEORY$ containing all possible instantiations of *Circus* theories: it is the range of $InstCircusTheory$.

We can now define the subset of alphabetised predicates that characterise valid *Circus* actions and processes: all predicates that belong to some instantiation of a *Circus* theory. They satisfy the healthiness conditions of *Circus* and all subordinate UTP theories i.e. those for CSP, reactive processes, and relations.

z
$$
\begin{array}{l}
\mathbf{CIRCUS\_ACTION} \;\hat{=} \\
\quad \{p : ALPHA\_PREDICATE\ | \\
\qquad (\exists\ th : CIRCUS\_THEORY\ \bullet\ p \in TheoryPredicates\ th)\}
\end{array}
$$

The semantics of a *Circus* process is given by hiding the state components in its main action. Therefore, models of processes are actions whose alphabets include *only* the auxiliary variables *okay*, *wait*, *tr* and *ref*, and their dashed counterparts. The definition is obtained by further restricting $CIRCUS\_ACTION$.

z
$$
\begin{array}{l}
\mathbf{CIRCUS\_PROCESS} \;\hat{=} \\
\quad \{p : CIRCUS\_ACTION\ |\ Alphabet_P\ p = ALPHABET\_OWTR\}
\end{array}
$$

This concludes the presentation of the core definitions that support instantiation of *Circus* theories. In defining the operators on *Circus* actions, we reuse the definitions of [16], but adapt them to take into consideration universes where required. An example is the function that encodes *Skip*, which takes a *universe* as a parameter: the universe of the state components of the process.

z

$Skip_C$: $WF\_Skip_C \rightarrow CIRCUS\_ACTION$

$\forall u$: $WF\_Skip_C \bullet$
  $Skip_C\ u = R\ (True_P\ u \vdash_D TReqTR' \wedge_P (\neg_P WAIT') \wedge_P \Pi_R\ u)$

Skip is defined in terms of applying R, the healthiness condition for reactive processes, to a design that determines the behaviour of the action. The design has a true precondition $True_P\ u$, meaning that it never diverges. The postcondition specifies that *Skip* immediately terminates: the only observable behaviour is that *Skip* is not in an intermediate state ($\neg_P WAIT'$) while the trace is not altered ($TReqTR'$ encodes the predicate $tr = tr'$). The relational *Skip* $\Pi_R\ u$ on the state universe u ensures that the state variables are not changed. The rôle of WF_Skip_C is to restrict the domain of the function as to require homogeneous universes that must only mention state variables but not auxiliary ones.

A second example is the function $\rightarrow_C$ which encodes prefixing of *Circus* actions. Prefixing is used, for example, in the *InitFib* action of the *Fib* process.

z

$\_ \rightarrow_C \_$: $WF\_PREFIXING_C \rightarrow CIRCUS\_ACTION$

$\forall n$: $CHANNEL\_NAME$; e : $EXPRESSION$; p : $CIRCUS\_ACTION \mid$
  $((n,\ e),\ p) \in WF\_PREFIXING_C \bullet$
    $(n,\ e) \rightarrow_C p = R\ (True_P\ p.2 \vdash_D$
      $(do\_C\ (p.2,\ n,\ e)) \wedge_P$
        $(\Pi_R\ (p.2 \ominus_U ALPHABET\_OWTR))) ;_C p$

Prefixing requires a channel name n, an expression e whose value is output on the channel, and the prefixed action predicate p. $WF\_PREFIXING_C$ captures the restriction on the arguments that the free variables in e must be contained in the universe of the predicate to ensures evaluation of e is well-defined. The operator is specified by sequentially composing a reactive process with p that carries out the communication and then terminates. This process as before is specified by applying R to a design. The true precondition of the design indicates again the absence of divergence, and the postcondition makes use of a function $do_C\ (u, n, e)$ being the encoding of the predicate

$$(tr = tr' \wedge (n, e) \notin ref') \triangleleft WAIT' \triangleright tr' = tr \frown \langle (n, e) \rangle.$$

The reactive behaviour is thus to be initially ($tr = tr'$) in a waiting state refusing all events other than (n, e), and to terminate when the process has engaged in the communication event (n, e). The conjunction with *Skip* on the universe of the state components, obtained by removing the auxiliary variables from the universe of p, ensures that values of state variables remain unchanged.

The presence of universes results in many places in additional restrictions on the domains of semantic functions characterising the various UTP theory operators of *Circus* and subordinate theories. In the lower-level theory of alphabetised predicates and relations (utp-alpha and utp-rel), binary operators such as conjunction, disjunction, and so on are defined for predicate pairs whose universes are compatible, but not necessarily the same. This enables us to combine predicates from different theories. In specific theories, we require the arguments of operators in most cases to be of the same theory instance. Consequently, we need new definitions describing such argument restrictions. For example, *WF_CIRCUS_ACTION_PAIR* is the set of all predicate pairs for which there exists a *Circus* theory to which both predicates belong. It is used, for instance, as the domain of action operators modelling internal and external choice.

The amendments to definitions were mainly motivated by the need to prove properties and laws, and, as a minimal requirement, to ensure well-definedness of the underlying function applications. We did not try and identify the strongest condition for sensibly applying operators, but one which is consistent without incurring too heavy a burden on proofs. This is justified by assuming that processes and actions are well typed. If proofs later require stronger restrictions, we will tighten the domain definitions appropriately.

Besides we specify operators in a way that allows us to infer easily that their application yields a predicate within the correct UTP theory: we restrict their range to *CIRCUS_ACTION*. The proof of this is pushed into the consistency theorem for the definition (see Section 5), and closure properties follow trivially from operator definitions and need not be separately formulated as theorems.

4   Encoding of *Circus* Programs

In this section we illustrate how we use the semantic encoding of *Circus* described in the previous section to encode the *Fib* process given in Fig. 1. The ProofPower theory source for all definitions presented here and elsewhere in the paper can be downloaded from `http://www.cs.york.ac.uk/circus/tp/tools.html`.

To accommodate the ProofPower-Z definitions, we create a new ProofPower theory utp-fib as a child of utp-circus. We begin by creating definitions that introduce channel names, state components and local variables. For our example, we use an axiomatic definition to declare a name *out* : *CHANNEL_NAME* for the *out* channel. *CHANNEL_NAME* provides an inexhaustible supply of names (elements from the *NAME* type) to represent channel identifiers. This set is disjoint from *Z_VAR_NAME* which contains names of Z schemas as well as local variables and state components. We declare all the names used in the process description to be of type *Z_VAR_NAME*.

z
$$x,\ x',\ y,\ y'\ :\ Z\_VAR\_NAME$$

$$x' = dash\ x \land y' = dash\ y \land distinct\ \langle x,\ y \rangle$$

When introducing new variables, it is important to ensure they are mutually distinct from any existing ones that may be used in the same predicate. We achieve this by virtue of a predicate *distinct* on sequences of names which holds true for all *injective* sequences. Since the *dash* function modelling decoration is injective too, it is sufficient to enforce uniqueness of the undashed names. By selecting names from Z_VAR_NAME we already ensure that they are distinct from any of the auxiliary variables for *Circus* actions. We introduce the local variables exactly in the same way as illustrated in the above definition.

Next, we instantiate the *Circus* theory for the main and auxiliary actions. To do so we define the universe of the main action. It is as follows in our example.

$$
\begin{array}{l}
\text{z} \\
\hline
\mathbf{\mathit{FIB\_UNIVERSE}} : CIRCUS\_UNIVERSE \\
\hline
\\
\mathit{Alphabet}_U \ FIB\_UNIVERSE = FIB\_ALPHABET \ \wedge \\
\mathit{typeof} \ (x, \ FIB\_UNIVERSE) = INT\_VAL \ \wedge \\
\mathit{typeof} \ (y, \ FIB\_UNIVERSE) = INT\_VAL
\end{array}
$$

$FIB\_ALPHABET$ is the set containing both the auxiliary and state variables. Since universes which are selected from $CIRCUS\_UNIVERSE$ already ensure that auxiliary variables are typed correctly, the only type constraints to be formulated here are the ones restricting the state variables.

We are now able to define the UTP theories for the actions of *Fib*. It is not just one UTP theory that is used to model them, since actions like $OutFibState$ mention extra variables apart from the state components. We need a theory instance for each possible *extension* of $FIB\_UNIVERSE$.

$$
\begin{array}{l}
\text{z} \\
\hline
\mathbf{\mathit{FIB\_THEORY}} \ \widehat{=} \\
\quad \{u : CIRCUS\_UNIVERSE \mid \\
\qquad Compatible_U \ (u, \ FIB\_UNIVERSE) \ \bullet \ InstCircusTheory \ u\}
\end{array}
$$

Intuitively, this definition constructs the family of all instances of the *Circus* theory that have a universe which *at least* contains the state components of *Fib*, and imposes the correct type constraints on them. We recall that two universes are compatible if they agree on the types of their shared variables.

The main benefit of FIB_THEORY is that it permits us to state (or verify) that actions such as $InitFib$, $OutFib$, and so on, are characterised by predicates that belong to one of the *Circus* theories for the *Fib* process, encapsulating healthiness conditions as well as type constraints on the state components. For this we define the set FIB_ACTION which contains all such predicates characterising valid actions in the context of *Fib*.

$$
\begin{array}{l}
\text{z} \\
\hline
\mathbf{\mathit{FIB\_ACTION}} \ \widehat{=} \ \bigcup \ (TheoryPredicates \ (\!| FIB\_THEORY |\!))
\end{array}
$$

It is simply the union of all predicates of UTP theories in FIB_THEORY. A more specific action of *Fib* is its main action, because it only has the auxiliary variables and state components in the universe. We include another definition FIB_MAIN_ACTION, comprising the potential predicates for main actions.

We now turn to encoding the actions actually used in *Fib*. We first look at the ones which are defined through Z operation schemas. Considering, for example, the action *InitFibState*, the corresponding schema $[FibState' \mid x' = 1 \wedge y' = 1]$ has to be lifted to become a *Circus* action, and a valid predicate of a *Circus* theory in *FIB_THEORY*. The schema itself is encoded by a relational predicate over the universe that contains its components x' and y' with the right type.

The semantic function $SchemaExp_C$ performs this lifting; it takes a relational predicate and an instance of *VAR_DECLS* encapsulating the declaration of the schema components. The universe of the predicate has to be compatible with the variable declarations. The latter are encoded by a pair of sequences: the first component listing the variable names, and the second, their types.

z
>
> **Fib_InitFibState_VAR_DECLS** $\widehat{=}$
> $(\langle x,\ y,\ x',\ y' \rangle,\ \langle INT\_TYPE,\ INT\_TYPE,\ INT\_TYPE,\ INT\_TYPE \rangle)$

Types are represented as values (elements of *VALUE*). Here, *INT_TYPE* is the set of integer values. The encoding of *InitFibState* is as follows.

z
>
> **Fib_InitFibState** : *FIB_ACTION*
> $\rule{6cm}{0.4pt}$
>
> $Fib\_InitFibState =$
> $\quad SchemaExp_C\ (Fib\_InitFibState\_VAR\_DECLS,$
> $\qquad (=_P (Create_U\ \{x' \mapsto INT\_VAL\},\ x',\ Val(Int(1)))) \wedge_P$
> $\qquad (=_P (Create_U\ \{y' \mapsto INT\_VAL\},\ y',\ Val(Int(1)))))$

In the above $=_P$ is the semantic function used to construct alphabetised predicates for equalities between variables and expressions. It needs to be provided with a universe, namely that of the resulting relation. For this purpose, $Create_U$ ad-hocly creates a universe from a set of name/type pairs.

Notably, the universe of the schema predicate has x' and y' in its alphabet, since $\wedge_P$ merges the universes of the constituent predicates. The universe of the schema itself comprises x, y, x', and y'. Finally, the predicate defined by $SchemaExp_C$ additionally includes in its universe the auxiliary variables and fulfils the healthiness conditions for *Circus* actions. This illustrates how predicates of different UTP theories coexist in the same definition.

By introducing *Fib_InitFibState* as an element of *FIB_ACTION* we ensure that irrespective of how we define it, that is, using *Circus* operators or plain predicate connectives, it has to characterise a valid action of *Fib*. This is effectively discharged by the consistency proof of the axiomatic definition generated by ProofPower-Z. $Fib\_InitFibState \notin FIB\_ACTION$ would result in a contradiction and hence the existential proof to fail.

The encoding of schemas that include extra components, besides those of the state, like *Fib_OutFibState* for instance, is similar. To simplify the encoding of the schema predicate, we define a universe *Fib_OutFibState_UNIV* (used by all three equalities) containing exactly the variables of the schema. A function

UnivFromVAR_DECLS defines the conversion of a *VAR_DECL* to an element of *UNIVERSE*; we omit its definition and that of *Fib_OutFibState_UNIV* itself.

---
z

Fib_OutFibState : *FIB_ACTION*

Fib_OutFibState =
  SchemaExp$_C$ (*Fib_OutFibState_VAR_DECLS*,
    ($=_P$ (*Fib_OutFibState_UNIV*, x', *Var(y)*)) $\wedge_P$
    ($=_P$ (*Fib_OutFibState_UNIV*, y', *Fun$_2$*(($_- +_V\ {}_-$), *Var(x)*, *Var(y)*)))) $\wedge_P$
    ($=_P$ (*Fib_OutFibState_UNIV*, *next'*, *Fun$_2$*(($_- +_V\ {}_-$), *Var(x)*, *Var(y)*)))))

Terms such as *Var(y)* and *Fun$_2$*(($_- +_V\ {}_-$), *Var(x)*, *Var(y)*) encode expressions in the semantics, here y and $x+y$. The shriek, which introduces an output variable in the operation schema, is generally translated into a corresponding pair of variables to render the alphabet of the action homogeneous. The same applies to input variables decorated with a question mark should they occur.

Not all encoded actions are required to be equipped with an action-specific universe. Examples of actions that do not require a universe are *InitFib* and *OutFib*; the encoding of the latter is given below.

---
z

Fib_OutFib : *FIB_ACTION*

Fib_OutFib =
  μ_C (λ X : *CIRCUS_ACTION* •
    var$_C$ (*next*, *Fib_OutFibState* ;$_C$ (*out*, *Var(next)*) $\rightarrow_C$ X))

Here, the universe of the sequential composition is inferred from its arguments, *Fib_OutFibState* and *out!next* → X. This case again illustrates how predicates of different UTP theories coexist in the same ProofPower definitional scope. The body of the variable block is an action whose universe includes the extra variables *next* and *next'*, which are concealed by the *var$_C$* construct. Hence the universe of *Fib_OutFib* only comprises the auxiliary variables and the state variables.

Crucially, we could indeed have another variable block declaring *next* within the same predicate but *with a different type*. In the original work [15] such would not have been possible since type constraints are *globally* attached to variable names. Above, the types of *next* and *next'* are deduced from the universe of the underlying relation of the body of the variable block. Thus the association of types and variable names takes place upon construction of the predicate and, in fact, is local with respect to the encoded predicate, and thus not static.

---
z

Fib_MainAction : *FIB_MAIN_ACTION*

Fib_MainAction = *Fib_InitFib* ;$_C$ *Fib_OutFib*

Again this action does not require a universe as it is inferred by $;_C$ from those of *Fib_InitFib* and *Fib_OutFib*. Since *Fib_MainAction* is declared to be an element of *FIB_MAIN_ACTION*, that universe has to be *FIB_UNIVERSE*, though.

Fib_MainAction does not truly characterise the process as such since it still contains the state components in its universe. Since these are local to the process they should be hidden it its semantic description. This is achieved by the operator $begin_C$ _ end_C. Utilising it we obtain the following definition for the process *Fib*.

z
| **Fib_Process** : *CIRCUS_PROCESS*
|——————————————————————
| *Fib_Process* = $begin_C$ *Fib_MainAction* end_C

The set *CIRCUS_PROCESS* defined in utp-circus contains all predicates of the *Circus* theory obtained by instantiation with a minimal universe; this is the universe which only comprises auxiliary variables, but no state components.

In this section we have demonstrated how particular *Circus* processes can be encoded using our embedding of the UTP theory of *Circus*. It is possible to automate all steps involved, and that is the next step in our work agenda. The encoding requires that type information is deduced prior to translation and consequently exploited in the construction of universes; this can be easily achieved using the *Circus* type checker [17,7]. In the next section we will examine how properties of the encoded process may be formulated and proved.

5 Reasoning about *Circus* Specifications

In our investigation so far, we have considered two primary possibilities in which mechanical reasoning about *Circus* processes may be exploited. First, the encoding strategy which was informally presented in the previous section gives rise to a number of consistency proof obligations that establish the soundness of the encoding. ProofPower-Z is capable of generating the proof obligations automatically, and more importantly prevents axiomatic definitions from being unconditionally used unless their respective consistency theorem has been discharged. The second possibility is to carry out refinement proofs of actions and processes. We address these two opportunities separately in this section.

5.1 Soundness of Process Encodings
Most of our encoding is based on functions that are defined using Z axiomatic descriptions. In general, an axiomatic description introducing a new global constant *DefName* is of the following form, where S is a set and P a predicate.

z
| *DefName* : S
|——————————————————————
| $P(DefName)$

The notation $P(DefName)$ highlights that *DefName* is assumed to be free in P.

Consistency proofs ensure that there exists some element $DefName \in S$ for which the predicate $P(DefName)$ holds. If this is not true, we would be able to conclude *false* from the axiom of the definition allowing us to prove anything. The corresponding consistency proof obligation hence establishes that $\exists\, DefName : T \bullet DefName \in S \land P$. In Z, arbitrary sets S can be used in declarations (of constants), but their types do not include any constraints embodied in these sets. For example, if we declare a function f of type $A \nrightarrow B$, where A and B are given sets, then the type of f is $\mathbb{P}(A \times B)$; the functional property is a constraint on f, rather than part of its type. A process called normalisation provides axiomatic descriptions whose declarations define types, and all constraints are given in the predicate. Assuming that the axiomatic description initially is not normalised, T, instead of S, is the actual type of $DefName$ after normalisation. The given proof obligation is not exactly how ProofPower expresses the consistency goal when first generated. For brevity we omit the less concise ProofPower goal since it can be easily reduced to this one.

All encoded actions of a process are of the general form below.

z
| $ActionName : PROC\_ACTION$
|
|—————————————————
|
| $ActionName = ActionExpr$

$ActionName$ is the name of the action. $PROC\_ACTION$ is the set of predicates of the instances of the UTP *Circus* theory that have a universe compatible with the state components declaration; for *Fib*, this is FIB_ACTION. Finally, $ActionExpr$ is the alphabetised predicate that models the action defined by applying the functions for *Circus* operators in our encoding. The consistency proof obligations for action encodings are, therefore, always of the following form.

$$\exists\, ActionName : \mathbb{P}\,(NAME \leftrightarrow VALUE) \times \mathbb{P}\,(NAME \leftrightarrow VALUE) \bullet$$
$$ActionName \in PROC\_ACTION \land ActionName = ActionExpr$$

Proving this subgoal is achieved by providing an existential witness for the quantified variable $ActionName$. From the shape of the predicate it is apparent that there can only be one choice of witness that possibly render it true; that is precisely $ActionExpr$ — the right hand side of the action definition. Using $ActionExpr$ as a witness, the consistency proof reduces to merely showing that $ActionExpr \in PROC\_ACTION$ which verifies the encoded action belongs to the set of valid actions for the process; it thus is guaranteed to fulfil the healthiness conditions of *Circus*, and possesses a permissible alphabet that includes the state components and imposes the correct type constraints on them.

To give a concrete example, we consider the consistency proof for *InitFib*.

z
| ***Fib_InitFib*** $: FIB\_ACTION$
|
|—————————————————
|
| $Fib\_InitFib = (out,\ Val(Int(1))) \rightarrow_C (out,\ Val(Int(1))) \rightarrow_C Fib\_InitFibState$

As previously explained, $(c, e) \rightarrow_C p$ encodes the prefixing operator outputting the value of e on channel c, and $Val(Int(1))$ simply encodes the expression 1. *Fib_InitFibState* refers to the encoding of the *InitFibState* action presented in Section 4. The proof obligation which hence needs to be discharged is

$$(out,\ Val(Int(1))) \rightarrow_C (out,\ Val(Int(1))) \rightarrow_C Fib\_InitFibState \in FIB\_ACTION$$

We establish the truth of this goal in essence by exploiting closure properties of the operators. The base case $Fib\_InitFibState \in FIB\_ACTION$ we, notably, get from its definition as it follows from $Fib\_InitFibState : FIB\_ACTION$ in the declaration of the encoding of the *InitFibState* schema action. It is verified by the consistency proof of that definition.

In general, the suggested proof strategy relying on closure laws is symptomatic for *any* consistency proof that arises from the action encodings. (Up to the point where we have to show $ActionExpr \in FIB\_ACTION$ all steps are very easily automated.) The core part of the proof requires nevertheless more sophisticated mechanisms (but we claim that it can be automated too!).

More specifically, after unfolding the definition of FIB_ACTION, another witness needs to be provided to supply the *universe* of the *Circus* theory of which the action is deemed to be a member. $FIB\_UNIVERSE$ can be directly used in this instance since *InitFib* does not include any extra variables. If it did, typing information can be used to determine the right universe. The proof reduces then to showing that the given predicate belongs to the set of predicates of the *Circus* theory *InstCircusTheory FIB_UNIVERSE*. The general closure of *Circus* operators establishes that the defined action is a member of *some Circus* theory instance, and properties of universes of the applied operators establish that it is exactly the theory under consideration.

As a concluding remark, it is worth noting that we are not constrained to use exclusively *Circus* operators in defining actions. For example, we may use plain predicative constructs instead if we desire, reflecting the unified view of any computation being a predicate in the UTP. An advantage of the discussed approach is that soundness is established *irrespective* of the specific way of representing actions, but automation of the proof may only be feasible if closure theorems are available for the underlying operators. If not, the alternative approach is to show membership to the theory of *Circus* by explicitly proving the predicate is a fixed point of the healthiness functions; due to the complexity of this proof in particular for *Circus* theory instances this normally requires human interaction.

5.2   Action and Process Refinement

Refinement is uniformly characterised by (universal) reverse implication in the UTP; consequently it is a property of alphabetised predicates and therefore can be established independently of any particular UTP theory membership. A simple proof approach involves unfolding theory-specific operators in terms of their underlying lower-level relational and predicative operator definitions.

Although in principle feasible, this is not a practical approach which lends itself easily for proof automation, in particular if we deal with more complex operator definitions such as parallelism or interleaving of *Circus* actions. To manage the complexity of refinement proofs involving *Circus* action and process predicates, we have pursued two alternative approaches.

The first approach is to formulate and prove a collection of algebraic refinement and equality laws applying in situations where the predicates are of a certain form. In practice, the provisos that need to be established for application of the laws are (a) memberships to some *Circus* theory, and (b) other restrictions guarding the application of the law which are usually syntactic. The purpose of the provisos in (a) is to guarantee that applications of functions for theory-specific operators are well defined. For example, the following law establishes distribution of *Circus* guarded actions through conjunctions of their guards.

$$\vdash \forall \; g1, \, g2 \, : \, CIRCUS\_CONDITION; \; p \, : \, CIRCUS\_ACTION \; | $$
$$(g1, \, p) \in WF\_Guard_C \land (g2, \, p) \in WF\_Guard_C \; \bullet$$
$$(g1 \lor_P g2) \; \&_C \; p = (g1 \; \&_C \; p) \ominus_C (g2 \; \&_C \; p)$$

WF_Guard_C is the domain of the function that encodes the guarded action construct, namely $(g \; \&_C \; p)$; it is restricted to guards and actions on the same universe. The symbol $\ominus_C$ denotes external choice.

If we apply laws like the above to actions a of *Fib*, we obtain the proof obligation $a \in CIRCUS\_ACTION$ from the stronger condition $a \in FIB\_ACTION$; the definition of the actions allows us to discharge such proof obligations directly. If, however, we apply laws to sub-expressions, membership to $CIRCUS\_ACTION$ has to be shown and depends on the particular sub-expression.

The alphabetised predicates of a UTP theory are not characterised syntactically, but by the healthiness conditions of the corresponding theory, and indeed we do not embed the syntax of the operators in our encoding. Therefore, there is no generic theorem that can be formulated to establish membership of arbitrary predicates to particular theories based on their syntax. Instead, we tackle this problem using specialised, high-level recursive tactics. The tactics selectively apply the closure theorems for the various *Circus* operators, and then proceed recursively on the generated subgoals. Similarly, the definition of laws often require the universes of the involved predicates to be compatible, giving rise to proof obligations asserting compatibility of the underlying universes.

Refinement laws can be equality laws as the above, or genuine refinements. ProofPower facilitates the rewriting of terms through the application of equality laws using its in-built rewrite and conversion mechanisms. On the other hand, we also want to be able to replace sub-expressions of a predicate if the law is not an identity but genuine refinement. In this case, however, we have to justify the application of the law by monotonicity of operators with respect to refinement. This, once again, is a process which cannot be encapsulated by a single theorem but needs to be performed by high-level tactics, guided by the structure of *Circus* actions. Monotonicity also gives rise to a second approach to establish action refinement which in particular exploits the monotonicity of R, the healthiness function for reactive designs.

The underlying idea is to express both actions of a refinement $A_1 \sqsubseteq A_2$ as applications of R, so that the proof reduces to $R(P_1 \vdash Q_1) \sqsubseteq R(P_2 \vdash Q_2)$ which, because of monotonicity, is implied by $P_1 \vdash Q_1 \sqsubseteq P_2 \vdash Q_2$, and in turn can be reduced to $P_1 \Rightarrow P_2$ and $(P_1 \land Q_2) \Rightarrow Q_1$. The semantic definition of the

Circus operators supports this approach by expressing most operators in terms of applying R to some design. The uniformity fosters automation.

To illustrate this approach in the context of *Fib*, we consider the refinement *Fib_InitFibState* $\sqsubseteq$ *Fib_InitFibState_Ref* where *Fib_InitFibState_Ref* is the assignment $x, y := 1, 1$. Its encoding is shown below.

z

Fib_InitFibState_Ref : *FIB_ACTION*

Fib_InitFibState_Ref =
  $Assign_C$ (*FIB_UNIVERSE*, $\langle x, y \rangle$, $\langle Val(Int(1)), Val(Int(1)) \rangle$)

After rewriting the definitions of *Fib_InitFibState* and *Fib_InitFibState_Ref*, the initial refinement goal is expressed as follows.

ProofPower Output

$(* ?\vdash *)$ $_Z SchemaExp_C$ (*Fib_InitFibState_VAR_DECLS*,
  $(=_P$ (*Fib_InitFibState_UNIV*, x', *Val* (*Int* 1))) $\wedge_P$
  $(=_P$ (*Fib_InitFibState_UNIV*, y', *Val* (*Int* 1))))
    $\sqsubseteq Assign_C$ (*FIB_UNIVERSE*, $\langle x, y \rangle$, $\langle Val$ (*Int* 1), *Val* (*Int* 1)$\rangle$)$^\lnot$

Unfolding the semantic functions for *Circus* operators then yields the following.

ProofPower Output

$_Z (* ?\vdash *)$ R ($\exists_P$ (*ran Fib_InitFibState_VAR_DECLS.1* $\cap$ *dashed*,
  $(=_P$ (*Fib_InitFibState_UNIV*, x', *Val* (*Int* 1)) $\wedge_P$
  $=_P$ (*Fib_InitFibState_UNIV*, y', *Val* (*Int* 1))) $\oplus_P$ ...)
    $\vdash_D$
  $((=_P$ (*Fib_InitFibState_UNIV*, x', *Val* (*Int* 1)) $\wedge_P$
  $=_P$ (*Fib_InitFibState_UNIV*, y', *Val* (*Int* 1))) $\oplus_P$ ...) $\wedge_P$
    $TReqTR'$ $\wedge_P$ $\lnot_P$ $WAIT'$ $\wedge_P$ Π_R (...)))
    $\sqsubseteq$
  R (*True_P* *FIB_UNIVERSE*
    $\vdash_D Assign_R$ (*FIB_UNIVERSE*, $\langle x, y \rangle$, $\langle Val$ (*Int* 1), *Val* (*Int* 1)$\rangle$) $\wedge_P$
    $TReqTR'$ $\wedge_P$ $\lnot_P$ $WAIT'$)$^\lnot$

Upon closer inspection we see that both sides of the refinement were rewritten into expressions of the form $R(P \vdash_D Q)$. The precondition of the first design originates from calculating the precondition of the corresponding schema, hence the existential quantification over the dashed variables of the schema corresponding to *ran Fib_InitFibState_VAR_DECLS.1* $\cap$ *dashed*. The postcondition is simply the predicate of the schema with some additional conjuncts to correctly render the behaviour of the defined reactive process.

The formulas in place of the ellipses have been omitted; their purpose is merely to make some adjustments in order to homogenise universes in cases where the universe of the schema predicate is non-homogeneous. The right hand of the refinement corresponds to the definition of *Circus* assignment; the underlying design has a *true* precondition since assignment always terminates, and the postcondition conjoins the relational assignment with the predicates $tr = tr'$ and $\neg\, wait'$, again to appropriately establish the reactive behaviour.

A sketch of the proof first verifies that the precondition of the second design is $True_P\ FIB\_UNIVERSE$. The fact that the preconditions have different universes does not compromise the proof since the universes are compatible. In general, we use laws within the lower-level theories of relations and plain predicates, or otherwise unfold the operators further into the underlying semantic model of alphabetised predicates. Regarding the postcondition, the approach is similar. Here, this requires some rewriting of the $Assign_R$ operator which results in unfolding it into a predicate resembling the postcondition of the first design. A minor simplification is proving that $\Pi_R\ (...)$ above has no effect.

Process Refinement. Process refinement is simply a special case of action refinement where the involved (process) actions only contain auxiliary variables, hence we do not need a special treatment here. An alternative way of establishing process refinement is by reducing it to action refinement of the respective main actions providing their state variables are disjoint; this can be formulated as a theorem and effectively exploited in proofs.

In summary there are at least three different conceptual approaches towards proving *Circus* action refinement which operate on different semantic levels, and vary in terms of the effort that has to be invested. The most convenient is, not surprisingly, to work at the most abstract level — that is the level of high-level algebraic laws. Whether this is possible in specific cases depends on how specialised the conjecture is. The difference between previous work, which encoded *Circus* mostly for the sake of proving general laws, and our present work is that we cannot consider proofs as static entities that have to be established once and for all. Instead we need to provide generic means that automate all aspects of a proof not requiring human interaction so that the user may solely focus on those aspects which are difficult or beyond automation.

6   Conclusions

We have illustrated, by example, how a modified version of Oliveira's mechanisation of the UTP, including its embedding of the *Circus* language can be used to encode particular *Circus* specifications. The encoding is uniform and transparent, and automatically produces consistency proof obligations which guarantee the soundness of encoded programs on a *per case* basis. Although we did not present a formal translation strategy, the principles we outlined are indeed generalisable to semantically encode arbitrary *Circus* specifications using our extension of the mechanised *Circus* semantics. We have also discussed issues regarding the refinement proof of actions and processes, in particular in the light of automation. The latter is important to affirm feasibility for the development of scalable techniques and industrial tools using our extended mechanisation to verify the correctness of realistic, safety-critical systems. A good example of this is the ClawZ system [1] which has been successfully used in the formal verification of non-trivial control systems in the avionics sector.

To solve the problem of predicates from different UTP theories being present in the same ProofPower theory scope (or even in the same definition), we formalised and integrated the notions of UTP theory and typing universes in the semantic model. Revisiting one of the motivating examples given in the introduction, the following predicate

$$(\mathbf{var}\ next \bullet next := 1\,;P)\ \sqcap\ (\mathbf{var}\ next \bullet next := true\,;Q)$$

declares different types for *next* in the branches of the choice, namely $\mathbb{N}$ and $\mathbb{B}$. Whereas in the original work such predicates could not be represented since the type of *next* would have to be statically (and globally) identified with either $\mathbb{N}$ or $\mathbb{B}$, our encoding of the predicate creates a suitable universe for each of the bodies of the variable blocks in which the type of *next* is dynamically bound. The type information for *next* is erased by the **var** blocks, which hide *next* by contracting the universes; thus no clashes arise in the overall encoding.

An alternative approach to solve the above problem is to eliminate conflicting uses of variables with clashing types through renaming. This would, however, still require the facility to constrain the type of the variable. A main restriction of the original encoding is the inability to take into account typing constraints in the general theory of relations. Constraints introduced *a posteriori* are, unlike our definitions, not automatically checked in ProofPower-Z for consistency. In addition, elimination of naming clashes would complicate the translation of *Circus* syntax into its semantic characterisation making it more susceptible to errors, and produce less readable and tractable encodings. Another challenge with this approach is to ensure uniqueness of names across separate translations in order to be able to combine them without interference on a semantic level. Even more generally, we could think of a shallow embedding of alphabetised predicates themselves. This, however, could be problematic because they do not naturally map to predicates of the host logic (HOL) carrying *more* information, namely, an alphabet and associated types.

What became clear though in attempting proofs for particular refinements is that even for simple conjectures as the one considered in Section 5, the theorems incidentally become very large to a point where they are not manageable anymore. Our experience suggests that it is crucial to interleave certain simplification steps for alphabets and universes with steps performing a deeper unfolding (rewriting) of functions representing operators. The simplifications can in many cases eliminate operator invocations exploiting certain theorems. As an example, the alphabet of a conjunction may be rewritten as the union of the alphabets of the conjuncts. We are currently experimenting with the development of simplification tactics for automating the rewrite of semantic functions.

Related Work. Closely related work is Nuka's mechanisation of the alphabetised relation calculus and UTP [11,12]. It presents a deep semantic embedding of alphabetised predicates and core operators mechanised in ProofPower-Z. Nuka's semantic model shares commonalities with ours in that predicates are represented as sets of bindings which themselves are partial functions from names to values. It mostly differs in that no type information is attached to predicates. The lack of type information prevents it, for example, from proving type-dependant properties such as $\neg\,(okay = TRUE) \Leftrightarrow okay = FALSE$[1]. Furthermore, to our knowledge Nuka's embedding has not been used so far in proving properties of particular UTP specifications; doing so would be interesting, in particular to investigate possible ramifications of its untyped view.

In [3,2] Camilleri reports on a mechanisation of the CSP traces and failure-divergence model in HOL. Its primary focus is on proving standard CSP laws that are valid within the two semantic models, and another concern is to deeply encode the syntax of CSP. In these publications, however, similarly no account is given on how the mechanisation performs in proving particular CSP process refinements. An alternative embedding of the CSP traces model into PVS is presented in [5] where the authors additionally illustrate its application in verifying robustness properties of an authentication protocol. In doing so they realise the need for specific proof tactics (strategies in PVS) to conduct the proof at a more abstract level, and the scope for proof automation via tactics driven by the structure of proof goals. This coincides with our experience.

In [8] Groves et al. report on a tactic-driven tool implemented in Prolog that aids in performing program derivation in Morgan's refinement calculus [10]. The tool is illustrated by applying it to the example of a simple sorting algorithm. Interestingly, the authors postulate a hierarchy of refinement tactics which categorises them into "derived rules", "goal-directed rules" and high-level "strategies", corresponding to different levels of automation at which subsequent refinements are constructed. We currently do not consider the automation of refinement proofs at a comparably high level, but the experience gained in this work could ultimately be useful when tackling similar goals in the future.

Future Work. Future work will focus on two primary aspects. First, the translation of *Circus* processes such as *Fib* into the semantic encoding shall be automated. There is no fundamental reason why this may not be possible, however the automation would need to type check the specification in order to infer the necessary information to construct universes of predicates and actions where needed. In [13] a step into this direction is made by defining a set of formal translation rules. The aim will be to extend and recast these in the light of the informal strategy we propose, and thereby formalise the translation.

A second important area for future work is the development of tools assisting refinement proofs. We already explained the usefulness of powerful ProofPower tactics for this purpose, but in certain cases a proof mostly consists of the application of high-level algebraic refinement laws. In this case, the ArcAngelC tactic language provides a more abstract and expressive notation for specifying tactics for *Circus* refinements [14]. It is a tactic language that supports backtracking through angelic choice, and is in this aspect superior to ProofPower's tactic language which does not entail backtracking. We have already developed a prototype implementation of ArcAngelC in ProofPower-Z giving some encouraging results; subsequent publications will report on this work.

---

[1] Note that this does not invalidate the law of the excluded middle in the relational algebra of Nuka's encoding; $okay = TRUE \vee \neg\,(okay = TRUE)$ is still provable.

Acknowledgements. We would like to thank Marcel Oliveira for useful discussions and feedback on our revisions to his original mechanisation of the UTP, as well as the anonymous referees for their suggestions. We also is acknowledge EPSRC for funding this work under research grant EP/E025366/1.

References

1. Adams, M., Clayton, P.: ClawZ: Cost-Effective Formal Verification of Control Systems. In: Lau, K.-K., Banach, R. (eds.) ICFEM 2005. LNCS, vol. 3785, pp. 465–479. Springer, Heidelberg (2005)
2. Camilleri, A.: A Higher Order Logic Mechanisation of the CSP Failure-Divergence Semantics. Technical Report HPL-90-194, HP Laboratories (September 1990)
3. Camilleri, A.: Mechanizing csp trace theory in higher order logic. IEEE Transactions on Software Engeneering 16(9), 993–1004 (1990)
4. Cavalcanti, A., Sampaio, A., Woodcock, J.: A Refinement Strategy for *Circus*. Formal Aspects of Computing 15(2-3), 146–181 (2003)
5. Dutertre, B., Schneider, S.: Using a PVS embedding of CSP to verify authentication protocols. In: Gunter, E.L., Felty, A.P. (eds.) TPHOLs 1997. LNCS, vol. 1275, pp. 121–136. Springer, Heidelberg (1997)
6. Freitas, L., Cavalcanti, A., Woodcock, J.: Taking Our Own Medicine: Applying the Refinement Calculus to State-Rich Refinement Model Checking. In: Liu, Z., He, J. (eds.) ICFEM 2006. LNCS, vol. 4260, pp. 697–716. Springer, Heidelberg (2006)
7. Freitas, L., Woodcock, J., Cavalcanti, A.: An Architecture for *Circus* Tools. In: SBMF 2007: Brazilian Symp. on Formal Methods, August 2007, pp. 6–21 (2007)
8. Groves, L., Nickson, R., Utting, M.: A Tactic Driven Refinement Tool. In: 5th Refinement Workshop, January 1992, pp. 272–297. Springer, Heidelberg (1992)
9. Hoare, C.A.R., Jifeng, H.: Unifying Theories of Programming. Prentice Hall Series in Computer Science. Prentice Hall, Englewood Cliffs (1998)
10. Morgan, C.: Programming from Specifications. Prentice-Hall International Series In Computer Science. Prentice Hall, Englewood Cliffs (1998)
11. Nuka, G., Woodcock, J.: Mechanising the Alphabetised Relational Calculus. Electronic Notes in Theoretical Computer Science 95, 209–225 (2004)
12. Nuka, G., Woodcock, J.: Mechanising a Unifying Theory. In: Dunne, S., Stoddart, B. (eds.) UTP 2006. LNCS, vol. 4010, pp. 217–235. Springer, Heidelberg (2006)
13. Oliveira, M.: Formal Derivation of State-Rich Reactive Programs using *Circus*. PhD thesis, Department of Computer Science, University of York, UK (2005)
14. Oliveira, M., Cavalcanti, A.: ArcAngelC: a Refinement Tactic Language for *Circus*. Electronic Notes in Theoretical Computer Science 214, 203–229 (2008)
15. Oliveira, M., Cavalcanti, A., Woodcock, J.: Unifying Theories in ProofPower-Z. In: Dunne, S., Stoddart, B. (eds.) UTP 2006. LNCS, vol. 4010, pp. 123–140. Springer, Heidelberg (2006)
16. Oliveira, M., Cavalcanti, A., Woodcock, J.: A UTP semantics for *Circus*. Formal Aspects of Computing (2007) (Online First)
17. Xavier, M., Cavalcanti, A., Sampaio, A.: Type Checking *Circus* Specifications. In: SBMF 2006: Brazilian Symposium on Formal Methods, pp. 105–120 (2006)
18. Zeyda, F., Cavalcanti, A.: Mechanical Reasoning about Families of UTP Theories. In: SBMF 2008: Brazilian Symp. on Formal Methods, pp. 145–160 (2008)

Component Publications and Compositions[*]

Naijun Zhan[1], Eun Young Kang[2], and Zhiming Liu[2]

[1] State Key Lab. of Computer Science, Institute of Software, CAS, Beijing, China
znj@ios.ac.cn
[2] International Institute for Software Technology, United Nations University, Macau
{kang,lzm}@iist.unu.edu

Abstract. One of the major issues in component-based design is how to use a component correctly in different applications according to the given interface specification, called the *publication*, of the component. In this paper we formulate this as the problem of component publication composition and refinement. We define the notion of publications of components that describes how a component can be used by a third party in building their own components or in writing their applications without access to the design or the code of the component. It is desirable that different users of the components can be given different publications according to their need. The first contribution of this paper is to provide a procedure, which calculates a weakest contract of the required interface of a component from the contract of its provided interface and its code. The other contribution, that is more significant from a component-based designer's point of view, is to define composition on publications so that the publication of a composite component can be calculated from those of its subcomponents. For this we define a set of primitive composition operators over components, including *renaming, hiding, internalizing, plugging* and *feedback*. This theory is presented based on the semantic model of rCOS, a refinement calculus of component and object systems.

Keywords: Contracts, Components, Component Publications, and Composition.

1 Introduction

The widespread tendency in software and system engineering is towards component-based design [12] by which systems are designed by combining small components into bigger ones. The component-based technique allows a complex design problem to be decomposed by separation of functionality into simpler design problems. It thus helps to decrease the degree of coupling among components and reduce the probability of major accidents caused by combinations of independent component failures [8].

rCOS [5,4,1] provides the notions of *interfaces, contracts, components* and *component publications*. A component is explicitly specified in terms of the contracts of its *provided interface* and *required interface*.

---

[*] Naijun Zhan is supported in part by the projects NKBRPC-2002cb312200, NSFC-60493200, NSFC-60721061, NSFC-60573007, NSFC-90718041, and NSFC-60736017, and the other authors are partially supported by the projects HighQSoftD and HTTS funded Macao S&T Fund, STCSM No.08510700300 and NSFC-90718014.

A. Butterfield (Ed.): UTP 2008, LNCS 5713, pp. 238–257, 2010.

In rCOS, a contract of an interface is a specification of the reactive behavior of the component, including the *interaction protocol* that the environment is assumed to follow, and the data and functionality of each method of the interface [1]. This extends the concept of Meyer's "Design-by-contract" [10], which started out specific to the Eiffel programming language, but is now also used in other languages such as Java and JML [9].

In [3], de Alfaro and Henzinger presented a general theory of composition and refinement of interfaces and components. They also developed a concrete interface theory based on the *interface automata* in [2]. An rCOS contract can be understood as an interface automaton, and a closed rCOS component (i.e. one that does not require services) can be regarded as an I/O automaton of the component. However, a general open component in rCOS has a *provided interface* and a *required interface* and each has a specified contract, meaning that with the *assumption* of the contract for the required interface the component *guarantees* to deliver the specified by the contract of the provided interface. Furthermore, rCOS adopts a declarative approach and denotational semantics. The rCOS contracts also specify rich data structures and functionality of the interface operations in terms of pre- and postconditions in an OO setting. It thus directly supports OO design and implementation of component.

In [1], a procedure is given for an assumed contract of the required interface to calculate a contract of the provided interface. Obviously, it is the *strongest contract of the provided interface* for the given contract of the required interface. However, it is often the case that a component is developed from a specification of its provided services, i.e. a contract of its provided interface. Thus, for a given contract of the provided interface of the component, we need to calculate from the code a contract of its required interface such that the component guarantees the contract of the provided interface. The first contribution in this paper is to give a procedure that for the code of a component and a contract of its provided interface calculates the *weakest contract* of the required interface of the component.

A component vendor normally only provides users with a specification of part of the functionality (i.e. services) according to the users' needs and budgets instead of source code. Such a specification is called a *publication* and is an abstraction of the contracts of the provided and required interfaces. A publication only states the static data functionality of the provided and required methods and an interaction protocol with the environment and it is written in a descriptive style as to serve as a manual for a user to use and for an assembler to assemble it with other components. An assembler composes several simpler components to form a composite component according to their publications. However, a publication of the composite component has to be provided. The other contribution of this paper is to define a set of composition operators on publications. For this, we change the definition of a publication of a component given in [4] such that a publication $(\mathcal{G}, \mathcal{A}, C)$ consists of specifications $\mathcal{G}$ and $\mathcal{A}$ of the data functionality of the provided and required interfaces and an interaction protocol C. The protocol C specifies the interactions with the environments as well as invocation relation of the required methods by the provided methods. In [4], the interactions are separated as provided protocol and the required protocol without the invocation dependency. An invocation dependency oriented protocol C can be represented in different formalisms such as a transition graph, a set of traces, a temporal formula, and a CSP process. In this paper, we use a set of traces of the provided and required methods. In fact, if the set is a regular language, it can also be represented by an automaton [2]. The composition operators we are to define include *renaming, hiding, internalizing , plugging* and *feedback*. We then show that they are consistent with the corresponding operators on components defined in [4,1] in the sense that the composite publication is indeed a correct publication for the corresponding composite component if the operand publications are correct for the operand components.

Section 2 briefly introduces the unifying theories of programming (UTP) [7] and some basic notions of traces. Section 3 presents the main modeling elements of component based design in rCOS. Section 4 defines the notion of publications. Section 5 introduces an algorithm for calculating the weakest contract of the required interface of a component from its provided contract and source code. Section 6 reviews the composition operators on components and define their counterparts for publications. We will also investigate the correctness of the compositions on publications with respect to the compositions of components. Section 7 discusses future work and concludes the paper.

2   Preliminaries

In UTP, a *sequential program* (but possibly nondeterministic) is represented by a *design* $D = (\alpha, P)$, where

- α denotes the set of state variables (called observables). Each state variable comes in an unprimed and a primed version, denoting respectively the pre- and the post-state value of the execution of the program. In addition to the program variables and their primed versions such as x and x', the set of observables includes two designated Boolean variables, ok and ok', that denotes termination or stability of the program.
- P is a predicate, denoted by $p(x) \vdash R(x, x')$, and defined as $(ok \wedge p(x)) \Rightarrow (ok' \wedge R(x, x'))$. It means that if the program is activated in a stable state, ok, where the *precondition* $p(x)$ holds, the execution will terminate, ok', in a state where the postcondition R holds; thus the post-state x' and the initial state x are related by relation R. We use *pre.D* and *post.D* to denote the pre- and post-conditions of D, respectively. If $p(x)$ is *true*, then P is shortened as $\vdash R(x, x')$.

Definition 1. *Let $D_1 = (\alpha, P_1)$ and $D_2 = (\alpha, P_2)$ be two designs with the same alphabet. D_2 is a* refinement *of D_1, denoted by $D_1 \sqsubseteq D_2$, if the following closed implication holds $\forall x, x', ok, ok' \cdot (P_2 \Rightarrow P_1)$. Let $D_1 = (\alpha_1, P_1)$ and $D_2 = (\alpha_2, P_2)$ be two designs with possible different alphabets $\alpha_1 = \{x, x'\}$ and $\alpha_2 = \{y, y'\}$. D_2 is a* data refinement *of D_1 over $\alpha_1 \times \alpha_2$, denoted by $D_1 \sqsubseteq_d D_2$, if there is a relation $\rho(y, x')$ s.t. $\rho(y, x'); D_1 \sqsubseteq D_2; \rho(y, x')$.*

It is proven in UTP that the domain of designs forms a complete lattice with the refinement partial order, and *true* is the smallest (*worst*) element of the lattice. Furthermore, this lattice is closed under the classical programming constructs, and these constructs are *monotonic operations* on the lattice. These fundamental mathematical properties ensure that the domain of designs is a proper semantic domain for sequential programming languages. There is a nice link from the theory of designs to the theory of predicate transformers with the definition $\mathbf{wp}(p \vdash R, q) \mathrel{\widehat{=}} p \wedge \neg(R; \neg q)$ that defines the *weakest precondition* of a design for a post condition q.

Semantics of *concurrent and reactive programs* is defined by the notion of *reactive designs* with an additional Boolean observable *wait* that denotes suspension of a program. A design P is a *reactive design* if it is a fixed point of $\mathcal{H}$, i.e. $\mathcal{H}(P) = P$, where $\mathcal{H}(p \vdash R) \mathrel{\widehat{=}} (\mathit{true} \vdash \mathit{wait}') \lhd \mathit{wait} \rhd (p \vdash R)$. Here, $P_1 \lhd b \rhd P_2$ is a conditional statement, which means if b holds then P_1 else P_2, where b is a Boolean expression and P_1 and P_2 are designs. We define a *guarded design* $D = (\alpha, g \& P)$, where P is a design, to specify the reactive behavior $\mathcal{H}(P) \lhd g \rhd (\mathit{true} \vdash \mathit{wait}')$, meaning that if the guard g is false, the program stays suspended, otherwise it behaves like $\mathcal{H}(P)$. We use *guard.D* to denote the guard g and *func.D* to denote its functionality P. A reactive design is to ensure that a synchronization of a method invocation by the environment and the execution of the method can only occur when the guard is true and *wait* is false. The domain of reactive designs enjoys the same closure properties as the domain of sequential designs, and also refinement is defined as logical implication. This allows us reactive designs to define the semantics of concurrent programming languages of guarded commands of the form $g \& c$. For details, we refer the reader to our earlier work in [6].

2.1 Notations for Traces

Given a set Σ of events, we use Σ^* to denote the set of all finite traces generated out of Σ in which $\langle \rangle$ is a special one, i.e. the empty trace, and Σ^∞ the set of all infinite traces generated from Σ. For a trace $s_1 \in \Sigma^*$ and a trace $s_2 \in \Sigma^* \cup \Sigma^\infty$, $s_1 {}^\smallfrown s_2$ is the conventional concatenation operation. We use s^k to denote the concatenation of s k times, where $k \in \mathbb{N} \wedge k \geq 0$. If $k = 0$, then s^k is denoted by $\langle \rangle$. s^* denotes $\exists k \in \mathbb{N}.k \geq 0 \wedge s^* = s^k$, whereas s^+ denotes $\exists k \in \mathbb{N}.k > 0 \wedge s^+ = s^k$. This operation is also conventionally overloaded to operate on sets $T_1 T_2$ and $E^\smallfrown T_2$, where T_1 is a subset of Σ^*, T_2 a subset of $\Sigma^* \cup \Sigma^\infty$, and E a subset of Σ. A trace s_1 is a *prefix* of s_2, denoted by $s_1 \leq s_2$, if there exists a trace s such that $s_2 = s_1 {}^\smallfrown s$, and s is called a *suffix* of s_2. We use $\mathbf{tail}(s)$ and $\mathbf{head}(s)$ to stand for the tail and the head of s, respectively. We use $s[b/a]$ to denote the trace obtained from s by replacing all occurrences of a with b, and $T[b/a]$ the set of traces obtained from T by replacing a with b in each trace of T. The *projection* of a trace s on a set E of events, denoted by $s \downharpoonright E$, is the trace obtained from s by removing from it all events that are not in E, and we write $s \downharpoonright a$ when E contains only one element a. We also overload this operation and extend it to define the projection of a set T of traces on a set E of events $T \downharpoonright E$. The *restriction* of a trace set T on a set of events M, denoted by $T \backslash M$, is defined by $\{s \mid s \downharpoonright M = \langle \rangle \wedge (\exists t \in T \exists a \in M.s {}^\smallfrown \langle a \rangle \leq t \vee s \in T)\}$. If M is a singleton $\{m\}$, $T \backslash M$ is shortened by $T \backslash m$. For simplicity, we denote $s_1 + s_2$ as $\{s_1\} \cup \{s_2\}$, and $T_1 + T_2$ as $T_1 \cup T_2$. We now define the synchronization between s_1 and s_2 via a set E of events, denoted $s_1 \|_E s_2$, as follows:

$$
s_1 \|_E s_2 = \begin{cases}
\langle \rangle & \text{if } (s_1 = \langle \rangle \wedge s_2 = \langle \rangle) \vee (s_1 = \langle \rangle \wedge s_2 = \langle a \rangle {}^\smallfrown s_2' \wedge a \in E) \vee \\
& \quad (s_2 = \langle \rangle \wedge s_1 = \langle a \rangle {}^\smallfrown s_1' \wedge a \in E), \\
\langle a \rangle {}^\smallfrown (s_1' \|_E s_2) & \text{if } s_1 = \langle a \rangle {}^\smallfrown s_1' \wedge a \notin E \\
\langle a \rangle {}^\smallfrown (s_1 \|_E s_2') & \text{if } s_2 = \langle a \rangle {}^\smallfrown s_2' \wedge a \notin E \\
\langle a \rangle {}^\smallfrown (s_1' \|_E s_2') & \text{if } s_1 = \langle a \rangle {}^\smallfrown s_1' \wedge s_2 = \langle a \rangle {}^\smallfrown s_2' \wedge a \in E
\end{cases}
$$

When E is empty, $s_1 \|_E s_2$ represents the interleaving of s_1 and s_2, shortened by $s_1 \| \| s_2$.

3   Contract and Component

We provide models of components at different levels of abstraction. A *component* is a unit of software that *implements* a functionality via its *provided interface*. The functionality is specified as a *contract* of the provided interface. A component, to implement the specified contract, may also *require* or *assume* services from other components. The *required services* are specified by a contract of the *required interface* of the component.

3.1   Contract

An interface $I = \langle F, M \rangle$ provides the syntactic declarations of a set of *fields* and a set of *signatures of operations* (or methods). Each field is declared with type $x : T$, and a signature of an operation is given by a method name, some input and output parameters. For theoretical treatment, we assume one operation has only one input parameter and at most one output parameter and is written as $m(in; out)$, where each of *in* and *out* declares a variable with a type. We use *field.I* and *Meth.I* to refer to the fields and operations of interface I.

A contract of an interface specifies the functionality of the methods declared in the interface, the protocol of the interaction with the environment, and the reactive behavior of the component.

Definition 2. *A contract is a tuple $C = (I, \theta, S, \mathcal{T})$, where*

- *I is an interface, denoted by IF.C; and we use Meth.C for Meth.IF.C and field.C for field.IF.C,*
- *θ, denoted by init.C, is a design $\vdash R \wedge \neg wait'$ that initializes the values of field.C, i.e. defines the initial states,*
- *S, denoted by spec.C, specifies each method $m(in; out)$ in IF.C by a guarded design $S(m)$,*
- *$\mathcal{T}$ is called the protocol and denoted by prot.C, which is a set of traces of the events over Meth.C[1].*

Example 1. A contract of one-place buffer $B_1 = (I, \theta, S, \mathcal{T})$ is described as follows:

$$I \; \widehat{=} \; \langle \{buff:int^*\}, \{put(in\, x:int), get(out\, y:int)\} \rangle$$
$$\theta \; \widehat{=} \; \vdash buff' = \langle \rangle$$
$$S(put(in\, x:int)) \; \widehat{=} \; buff = \langle \rangle \& (\vdash buff' = \langle x \rangle ^\frown buff)$$
$$S(get(out\, y:int)) \; \widehat{=} \; buff \neq \langle \rangle \& (\vdash buff' = \mathbf{tail}(buff) \wedge y' = \mathbf{head}(buff))$$
$$\mathcal{T} \; \widehat{=} \; (\langle put \rangle ^\frown \langle get \rangle)^* + (\langle put \rangle ^\frown (\langle get \rangle ^\frown \langle put \rangle)^*)$$

Given a contract $C = (I, \theta, S, \mathcal{T})$, let $Meth.C^+ \; \widehat{=} \; \{m(u; v) \mid m(x : T_1; y : T_2) \in Meth.I \wedge u \in T_1 \wedge v \in T_2\}$. The dynamic semantics of C is given by a divergence set $\mathcal{D}(C)$ and a failure set $\mathcal{F}(C)$. $\mathcal{D}(C)$ is the set of all traces $m_1(u_1; v_1), \ldots, m_k(u_k; v_k)$ over $Meth.C^+$ such that the execution of these invocations of a prefix of the trace in consecution from the initial state enters a diverging state. Also, the *failure set* of C is the set of pairs $\langle s, X \rangle$ such that either after the execution of the trace s over $Meth.C^+$, all the events in $X \subseteq Meth.C^+$ are

---

[1] Notice that this is an abstract version of the protocol in our earlier versions [6,1].

not enabled, i.e their guards are disabled, or s is a divergence. The failure-divergence semantics of contracts allows us to use the CSP failure-divergence partial order [11] as a refinement relation between contracts [1], denoted by $C_1 \sqsubseteq C_2$. C_1 and C_2 are equivalent, denoted $C_1 \equiv C_2$, if $C_1 \sqsubseteq C_2 \wedge C_2 \sqsubseteq C_1$. It is noted that this refinement relation requires that the interfaces $Meth.IF.C_1$ and $Meth.IF.C_2$ have exactly the same set of methods.

A contract C has to be *consistent* in the sense that no execution of a trace in the protocol from an initial state may enter a *blocking state* in which *wait* is *true* or a *diverging state* in which ok' is false. The notion of consistency is defined in [1] and a theorem of *separation of concerns* is proven there that allows the refinement of a design *func.spec.C(m)* without violating the consistency, and $C = (I, \theta, S, \mathcal{T}_1 + \mathcal{T}_2)$ is consistent iff $C_i = (I, \theta, S, \mathcal{T}_i)$ are both consistent, $i = 1, 2$. Furthermore, for a triple (I, θ, S) there exists a *largest protocol* $\mathcal{T}$ such that contract $C = (I, \theta, S, \mathcal{T})$ is consistent, and called a *complete contract*. A complete contract can be simply written as $C = (I, \theta, S)$ by omitting its protocol, and we use *trace.C* to denote the largest protocol of C.

For a trace *tr* over $Meth.C^+$, we define an *abstraction* tr^-, that is a trace over the events $Meth.C^+$: $\langle\rangle^- = \langle\rangle$, and $(\langle(m(u; v)\rangle^{\frown}tr)^- = \langle m\rangle^{\frown}tr^-$. Thus, we have the following theorem of the relation between the traces and the failure set for a complete contract.

Theorem 1. *For a complete contract C, $trace.C = \{tr^- \mid (tr, X) \in \mathcal{F}(C) \wedge tr \notin \mathcal{D}(C)\}$.*

Example 2. For the one-place buffer in Example 1, we can further give the following two contracts $B_2 = (IF.B_1, init.B_1, S_2, \mathcal{T}_2)$ and $B_3 = (IF.B_1, init.B_1, S_3, \mathcal{T}_3)$, where

$$S_2(put(\text{in } x{:}int)) \mathrel{\widehat{=}} (\vdash buff'{=}\langle x\rangle^{\frown}buff) \lhd buff = \langle\rangle \rhd (\vdash buff'{=}buff)$$
$$S_2(get(\text{out } y{:}int)) \mathrel{\widehat{=}} buff \neq \langle\rangle \& (\vdash buff' = \mathbf{tail}(buff) \wedge y' = \mathbf{head}(buff))$$
$$\mathcal{T}_2 \mathrel{\widehat{=}} (\langle put\rangle^{\frown}\langle put\rangle^* \,{}^{\frown}\langle get\rangle)^*$$

$$S_3(put(\text{in } x{:}int)) \mathrel{\widehat{=}} buff = \langle\rangle \& (\vdash buff'{=}\langle x\rangle^{\frown}buff)$$
$$S_3(get(\text{out } y{:}int)) \mathrel{\widehat{=}} (\vdash buff' = \mathbf{tail}(buff) \wedge y' = \mathbf{head}(buff)) \lhd buff \neq \langle\rangle \rhd$$
$$(\vdash \exists c \in int.buff'{=}buff \wedge y' = c)$$
$$\mathcal{T}_3 \mathrel{\widehat{=}} (\langle get\rangle{+}(\langle put\rangle^{\frown}\langle get\rangle))^*$$

We see that B_1, B_2 and B_3 are complete contracts satisfying $B_1 \sqsubseteq B_2 \wedge B_1 \sqsubseteq B_3$, but $B_2 \not\sqsubseteq B_3$ and $B_3 \not\sqsubseteq B_2$.   □

The following theorem indicates that any contract is equivalent to a complete contract.

Theorem 2. *Given a contract $C = (I, \theta, S, \mathcal{T})$, let C' be $(\langle field.C \cup \{tr : Meth.C^*\}, Meth.C\rangle$, $init.C \wedge tr' = \langle\rangle, S', \mathcal{T})$, where $S'(m) = (\exists s \in \mathcal{T}.tr^{\frown}\langle m\rangle \leq s \wedge guard.S(m))\&(pre.S(m) \vdash post.S(m) \wedge tr' = tr^{\frown}\langle m\rangle)$. Then, C' is complete, and $trace.C' = \mathcal{T} \wedge C' \equiv C$.*

Based on this theorem, in what follows, we will only focus on complete contracts, and therefore all contracts are referred to as complete contracts, if not otherwise stated.

3.2 Component

A component K is an *implementation* of a contract of an interface that provides services to other components. This interface is called the *provided interface*. In order to implement the provided services, K may *use* services provided by other components via an interface, called the *required interface*.

244 N. Zhan, E.Y. Kang, and Z. Liu

Definition 3. *A* component *is a tuple* $K = (I, M, c_0, \mathbb{C}, J)$, *where*

- *I is an interface, called the* provided interface *of K and denoted by pIF.K. We also write pMeth.K for Meth.pIF.K and pfield.K for field.pIF.K.*
- *M is a set of method signatures, called the* private methods *of K and denoted by priMeth.K.*
- c_0 *is the initialization statement of the component, denoted by init.K, that initializes the set of states of the component.*
- $\mathbb{C}$ *is called the* coding function *and denoted as code.K that maps each method in pMeth.K ∪ priMeth.K to a guarded command.*
- *J is an interface, called the* required interface *of K and denoted by rIF.K. We also write rMeth.K for Meth.rIF.K and rfield.K for field.rIF.K. It is required that rMeth.K contains all the methods that occur in the code of the methods given by code.K, but not declared in pMeth.K ∪ priMeth.K.*

The code in guarded command of each method can be defined as a *reactive design*. For a given contract C_r of the required interface *rIF.K* of K, a contract C_p of the provided interface *pIF.K* can be calculated from the code of the methods given by *code.K*. This determines a function $\lambda C_r \cdot spec.K$ such that for a complete contract C_r of *rIF.K*, $spec.K.C_r$ is a complete contract of *pIF.K*. We take the function *spec.K* as the semantics of component K[6]. This semantics enjoys the following property that for two contracts C_1 and C_2 of *rIF.K*, if $C_1 \sqsubseteq C_2$ then $spec.K.C_1 \sqsubseteq spec.K.C_2$.

We say that a component K *implements* a contract C_p of its provided interface *pIF.K* with a contract C_r of its provided interface *rIF.K* if $C_p \sqsubseteq spec.K.C_r$, and K *implements* C_p if there exists such a contract C_r. Obviously, $spec.K.C_r$ is the *strongest contract* that K implements with C_r.

Example 3. The following three components K_1, K_2 and K_3 respectively implement the contracts B_1 in Example 1 and B_2 and B_2 in Example 2. For convenience, we shall rename some method and field in the interface.

$$
\begin{aligned}
pIF.K_1 \quad &= IF.B_1, \\
priMeth.K_1 \quad &= \emptyset, \\
init.K_1 \quad &= buff := \langle\,\rangle, \\
code.K_1(put) \quad &= buff = \langle\,\rangle \rightarrow (buff := \langle x \rangle), \\
code.K_1(get) \quad &= buff \neq \langle\,\rangle \rightarrow (y := \mathbf{head}(buff); buff := \langle\,\rangle) \\
rIF.K_1 \quad &= \emptyset
\end{aligned}
$$

$$
\begin{aligned}
pIF.K_2 \quad &= IF.B_2[buff_1/buff, get_1/get], \\
priMeth.K_2 \quad &= \emptyset, \\
init.K_2 \quad &= buff_1 := \langle\,\rangle, \\
code.K_2(put) \quad &= buff_1 := \langle x \rangle \lhd buff_1 = \langle\,\rangle \rhd put_1(\mathbf{head}(buff_1)); buff_1 := \langle x \rangle \\
code.K_2(get_1) \quad &= buff_1 \neq \langle\,\rangle \rightarrow (y := \mathbf{head}(buff_1); buff_1 := \langle\,\rangle) \\
rIF.K_2 \quad &= \langle \{put_1(in\ x:int)\} \rangle \\
pIF.K_3 \quad &= IF.B_3[buff_2/buff, put_1/put], \\
priMeth.K_3 \quad &= \emptyset,
\end{aligned}
$$

$$init.K_3 \qquad = buff_2 := \langle \ \rangle,$$
$$code.K_3(put_1) = buff_2 = \langle \rangle \rightarrow buff_2 := \langle x \rangle$$
$$code.K_3(get) \ = (y := \mathbf{head}(buff_2); buff_2 := \langle \rangle) \lhd buff_2 \neq \langle \rangle \rhd get_1(y)$$
$$rIF.K_3 \qquad = \langle \{get_1(out\ y:int)\} \rangle$$

4   Publications of Components

To compose components and use components to write applications, one does not need to know their code or even their design. However, one needs a specification to some extent about what services are provided and what services are required and the protocol that describes the interactions with the environments. The idea is that the less details specified the better. In this section we define such as specification, called a *publication* of a component. For a generic representation, we first define the notion of a *specification* of a component.

Definition 4. *A* specification *of a component K is a triple S = $(\mathcal{P}, \mathcal{R}, C)$, where*

- *$\mathcal{P}$ is a complete contract of pIF.K, denoted by pCtr.S ;*
- *$\mathcal{R}$ is a complete contract of rIF.K, denoted by rCtr.S ;*
- *$C \subseteq (pMeth.K + rMeth.K)^*$, denoted by causal.S, is a protocol that specifies the interactions with the environments as well as invocation relation of the required methods by the provided methods of K, called the* invocation dependency oriented protocol *of S,*

such that the following conditions are satisfied

1. *$\mathcal{P} \sqsubseteq spec.K.\mathcal{R}$; and*
2. *causal.S $\downarrow$ pMeth.K $\supseteq$ trace.pCtr.S $\land$ causal.S $\downarrow$ rMeth.K $\subseteq$ trace.rCtr.S.*

The first condition indicates that with K's required contract, K implements its provided contract, while the second condition says that projecting the invocation dependency oriented protocol onto the provided methods results in a protocol of the provided contract that is consistent with the specification of the methods; but projecting the invocation dependency oriented protocol onto the required methods results in a protocol that is a subset of the largest protocol of the required contract. This is just an analog of the law of strengthening the postcondition and weakening the precondition in Hoare logic of programs. Verifying the two conditions can be done by checking a design document of the component that contains the verification of the refinement relation, by verification of the source code [2]. The refinement relation between specifications of component can be defined from the refinement of contracts.

Definition 5. *For two specifications S $_1$ and S $_2$ of K, S $_1 \sqsubseteq S_2$, if*

1. *pCtr.S $_2$ is a refinement of pCtr.S $_1$;*
2. *rCtr.S $_1$ is a refinement of rCtr.S $_2$; and*
3. *$\forall c \in C_2.c \downarrow Meth.\mathcal{P}_2 \in prot.\mathcal{P}_1 \Rightarrow c \in C_1$.*

---

[2] Such a verification should be part of the *certification* of the component.

The conditions 1&2 say a refined specification should have a stronger provided contract and a weaker required contract. Condition 3 indicates that a refined specification provides more services to and requires less services from the environment and it is equivalent to

$$causal.S_1 \mid pMeth.K \subseteq causal.S_2 \mid pMeth.K \wedge causal.S_1 \mid rMeth.K \supseteq causal.S_2 \mid rMeth.K.$$

The complete contracts in a specification are given in terms of reactive designs. Therefore, they are not easy to be used for checking their compatibility with the specifications of other components. Further, the guards in the method specification and the protocol provide duplicated information to the user. Therefore, one does not need to have both when they compose and use components. We thus define the notion of *publication* by removing the guards in the method specification. We first define each part of a component publication as *publication contract*.

Definition 6. *A publication contract C is a tuple $(I, \theta, \mathcal{D}, \mathcal{T})$, where*

- *I is an interface and θ is an initialization design,*
- *$\mathcal{D}$ is a function, denoted by spec.C that defines each method m of I with a design (no guard) $\mathcal{D}(m)$,*
- *$\mathcal{T}$ is a set of traces over the Meth.I, denoted by prot.C.*

Definition 7. *A publication of component K is $U = (\mathcal{G}, \mathcal{A}, C)$ where*

- *$\mathcal{G}$ is a publication contract of an interface I such that $Meth.I \subseteq pMeth.K$,*
- *$\mathcal{A}$ is a publication contract of an interface J such that $Meth.J \supseteq rMeth.K$, and*
- *C is a causal relation over $Meth.I + Meth.J$, denoted by causal.U, such that*

$$causal.U \mid Meth.I = prot.\mathcal{G} \wedge causal.U \mid Meth.J = prot.\mathcal{A}.$$

Definition 7 allows the component vendor to give different publications to different component users. This is characterized by the refinement relation between publications.

Definition 8. *For a component K, let $U_1 = (\mathcal{G}_1, \mathcal{A}_1, C_1)$ and $U_2 = (\mathcal{G}_2, \mathcal{A}_2, C_2)$ be publications of K. U_2 is a refinement of U_1, $U_1 \sqsubseteq U_2$, if*

1. *$Meth.pCtr.U_1 \subseteq Meth.pCtr.U_2, Meth.rCtr.U_1 \supseteq Meth.rCtr.U_2$,*
2. *$init.pCtr.U_1 \sqsubseteq init.pCtr.U_2$, and $init.rCtr.U_1 \sqsupseteq init.rCtr.U_2$,*
3. *$\forall m \in Meth.pCtr.U_1.spec.pCtr.U_2(m) \sqsubseteq spec.pCtr.U_2(m)$, and $\forall n \in Meth.rCtr.U_2.spec.rCtr.U_1(n) \sqsupseteq spec.rCtr.U_2(n)$,*
4. *$prot.pCtr.U_1 \subseteq prot.pCtr.U_2$, and $prot.rCtr.U_1 \supseteq prot.rCtr.U_2$,*
5. *$\forall c \in C_2.c \mid Meth.\mathcal{G}_2 \in prot.\mathcal{G}_1 \Rightarrow c \in C_1$.*

Condition 1 says that a refined publication has more provided methods and less required methods; Condition 2 indicates that a refined publication has a stronger initial condition on the provided fields and a weaker initial condition on the required fields; Condition 3 expresses that a refined publication assigns a stronger specification (design) to each provided method, while a weaker specification (design) to each required method; Conditions 4&5 indicate that a refined publication is more likely to provide services to its environment, but less likely to invoke services provided by environment.

4.1 Specification vs. Publication

A publication of a component has to be certified and this is done by the verification of the validity of a specification of the component. This is done by relating a contract and a publication contract.

Definition 9. *We define a mapping $\mathcal{M}$ from the domain of complete contracts to that of publication contracts as: for a given complete contract $C = (I, \theta, S)$, $\mathcal{M}(C)$ is a publication contract defined by*

1. *IF.$\mathcal{M}(C)$ = IF.C = I;*
2. *init.$\mathcal{M}(C)$ = init.$C[false/wait, false/wait'] = \theta[false/wait, false/wait']$;*
3. *spec.$\mathcal{M}(C))(m) = P[false/wait, false/wait']$, if spec.$C(m) = g\&P$, for any $m \in$ Meth.C;*
4. *prot.$\mathcal{M}(C)$ = trace.C.*

Then we have the following equivalence relation in terms of contracts.

Theorem 3. *For any complete contract C, we have $C \equiv \mathcal{M}(C)$.*

This theorem indicates that we can use a protocol instead of the guards of the provided methods of a component to control the interaction between the component and its environment.

Definition 10. *Conversely, we define a mapping $\mathcal{L}$ from the domain of publication contracts to the domain of complete contracts as: for a given publication contract $C = (I, \theta, \mathcal{D}, \mathcal{T})$, $\mathcal{L}(C)$ is a complete contract defined by*

1. *IF.$\mathcal{L}(C) = \langle field.I \cup \{tr : Meth.C^*\}, Meth.I \rangle$;*
2. *init.$\mathcal{L}(C)$ = init.$C \wedge tr' = \langle \rangle \wedge \neg wait' = \theta \wedge tr' = \langle \rangle \wedge \neg wait'$;*
3. *spec.$\mathcal{L}(C))(m) = (\exists s \in \mathcal{T}.tr^\frown \langle m \rangle \le s)\&\mathcal{D}(m) \wedge tr' = tr^\frown \langle m \rangle$, for any $m \in$ Meth.C.*

Note that the idea of this definition is similar to Theorem 2 by strengthening the guard of each method to obtain a complete contract. We also have

Theorem 4. *For any publication contract C, we have $C \equiv \mathcal{L}(C)$.*

This theorem indicates that we can add a guard to each of the provided methods of a component instead of its protocol to control the interaction between the component and its environment.

Theorem 3 and Theorem 4 indicate that $\mathcal{M}$ and $\mathcal{L}$ form a Galois connection, and imply that interaction between a component and its environment can be done either decentralizedly by the guards of its provided methods or centralizedly by a protocol.

Corollary 1. (Contract and Publication Contract)

1. *$\mathcal{L}(\mathcal{M}(C))$ is a complete contract for any complete contract C, and $C \equiv \mathcal{L}(\mathcal{M}(C))$; and*
2. *$\mathcal{M}(\mathcal{L}(C))$ is a publication contract for any publication contract C, and $C \equiv \mathcal{M}(\mathcal{L}(C))$.*

The connection between specification and publication of component is expressed as follows:

Theorem 5. *(Specification vs. Publication)*

1. *If $S = (\mathcal{P}, \mathcal{R}, C)$ is a specification of K, then $U = (\mathcal{M}(\mathcal{P}), \mathcal{M}(\mathcal{R}), C)$ is its publication;*
2. *If $U = (\mathcal{G}, \mathcal{A}, C)$ is a publication of K, then $P = (\mathcal{L}(\mathcal{G}), \mathcal{L}(\mathcal{A}), C)$ is a specification of $K[IF.\mathcal{G}/IF.K, IF.\mathcal{A}/rIF.K]$, where $K[IF.\mathcal{G}/IF.K, IF.\mathcal{A}/rIF.K]$ is the component derived from K by restricting its provided methods to $IF.\mathcal{G}$ and extending its required methods to $IF.\mathcal{A}$.*

5   Calculate Weakest Required Contract and Publication

To calculate the weakest required contract, $wrc.K.pCtr$ for a component K to implement a given provided contract $pCtr$, we first calculate the invocation dependency oriented protocol $ioprot.K.pCtr$ of K from its code and the protocol of $pCtr$. We then derive from this protocol and the functionality specification of the methods in $pCtr$ the weakest required contract.

5.1   Calculating Invocation Dependency Oriented Protocol

Let K be a component and assume $pMeth.K = \{m_1, \cdots, m_k\}$, $priMeth.K = \{n_1, \cdots, n_\ell\}$ and $rMeth.K = \{r_1, \cdots, r_e\}$. For any method $m \in pMeth.K$, we calculate the set X_m of sequences of invocations to methods in $rMeth.K$ which are the possible invocation sequences to required methods in the execution of the code $code.K(m)$ of m. We define a function that for a program command c computes the set $\mathcal{T}r(c)$ of invocation sequences in the execution of c:

$$
\mathcal{T}r(c) \; \widehat{=} \;
\begin{cases}
\langle m \rangle & \text{if } c = m(x,y) \text{ or } c = z := m(x,y), \text{ where } m \in rMeth.K \\
X_m & \text{if } c = m(x,y) \text{ or } c = z := m(x,y), \\
& \text{where } m \in pMeth.K \cup priMeth.K \\
\mathcal{T}r(c_1)\widehat{\ }\mathcal{T}r(c_2) & \text{if } c = c_1; c_2 \\
\mathcal{T}r(B)\widehat{\ }(\mathcal{T}r(c_1) + \mathcal{T}r(c_2)) & \text{if } c = \textbf{if } B \textbf{ then } c_1 \textbf{ else } c_2 \\
(\mathcal{T}r(B)\widehat{\ }\mathcal{T}r(c_1))^* & \text{if } c = \textbf{while } B \textbf{ do } c_1 \\
\langle \rangle & \text{otherwise}
\end{cases}
$$

Using function $\mathcal{T}r$, we define the following $k + \ell$ trace equations for the provided and private methods of component K:

$$
X_{m_1} = \mathcal{T}r(code.K(m_1)), \ldots, X_{m_k} = \mathcal{T}r(code.K(m_k)),
$$
$$
X_{n_1} = \mathcal{T}r(code.K(n_1)), \ldots, X_{n_\ell} = \mathcal{T}r(code.K(n_\ell)).
$$

Note that since a provided method could call required methods implicitly via calling private methods of K, we have to consider the provided methods together with the private methods in the trace equations (1). It is easy to see that these trace equations contain recursion because a provided or a private method can call any other provided or private methods, including themselves. Since all trace operations used in $\mathcal{T}r$ are monotonic w.r.t the set containment. The least fixed points of the above trace equations exist and are taken to be the solutions to the variables X_{m_i} and X_{n_j} for $1 \leq i \leq k$ and $1 \leq j \leq l$, and each of them is a subset of $(rMeth.K)^*$.

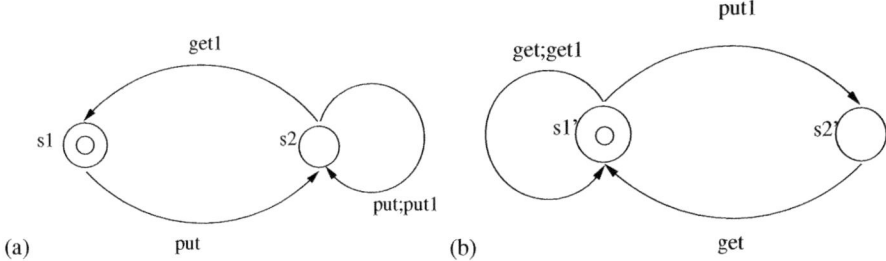

Fig. 1. (a) Transition Graph of *code*.K_2, (b) Transition Graph of *code*.K_3

For example, for K_2 and K_3 in Example 3, we have $X_{put} = \langle\rangle + put_1$, $X_{get_1} = \langle\rangle$ for K_2 and $X_{get} = \langle\rangle + get_1$, $X_{put_1} = \langle\rangle$ for K_3.

For each provided method m, the solution to X_m contains all possible sequences of the invocations to the methods in *rMeth.K* in the code of m. However, in an invocation sequence of the provided methods, each execution (occurrence) of a provided method m might contain only part of the invocation sequences in X_m. This is due to, for instance, a conditional. Thus, we have to calculate this subset X_m^i of X_m for each occurrence m^i of each provided method m in *prot.pCtr* according to the transition graph of the component. The invocation dependency oriented protocol *ioprot.K.pCtr* can be obtained by replacing each occurrence of a provided method m in *prot.pCtr* with $m^{\wedge}X_m^i$ that is the event m concatenated with the invocation sequences of this occurrence of m.

Example 4. According to the code of *put*, we know the fact that if $buff_1 = \langle\rangle$ then *put* does not invoke put_1, otherwise it indeed invokes put_1. On the other hand, we have $X_{put} = \langle\rangle + \langle put_1 \rangle$ and if we directly replace *put* in *prot.B_2* with $\langle put \rangle^{\wedge}X_{put}$, the resulting execution trace $prot.B_2[\langle put \rangle / X_{put}]$ will violate the above fact.

The transition graphs for *code*.K_2 and *code*.K_3 in Example 3 are given in Fig.1. According to Fig.1. (a), we know in the cases of its first execution and each execution following get_1, *put* does not invoke put_1, and in other cases it invokes put_1. Therefore, we have to replace the first occurrence of *put* by *put*, and any other occurrences of *put* with $put; put_1$ in the subexpression $\langle put \rangle; \langle put \rangle^{*}; \langle get_1 \rangle$ of *prot.B_2*. This derives *ioprot.K.B_2* as $(\langle put \rangle^{\wedge} \langle put; put_1 \rangle)^{*}{}^{\wedge} \langle get_1 \rangle)^{*}$, written as C_{B_2}. Similarly, the invocation dependent protocol *ioprot.K_3.B_3* of K_3 for B_3 is $(((\langle put_1 \rangle^{\wedge} \langle get \rangle) + (\langle get; get_1 \rangle)^{*})^{*}$. □

5.2   Calculating Weakest Required Contract

After calculating the invocation dependency oriented protocol *ioprot.K.pCtr*, we can easily obtain the protocol of the required contract *wrc.K.pCtr* by projecting it onto the required methods: $prot.wrc.K.pCtr \,\widehat{=}\, ioprot.K.pCtr \,|\, rMeth.K$. With this protocol and Theorem 2, we only need to calculate the specification of the data functionality of the required methods. In other words, if we obtain the unguarded designs of the required methods in *rMeth.K*, together with *ioprot.K.pCtr* we form a publication contract, and then *wrc.K.pCtr* is the contract of the required interface obtained from Theorem 2.

Let $rMeth.K = \{r_1, \ldots, r_t\}$, and for each $r \in rMeth.K$ let D_r represent the design for r. Then, $D_{r_1}, \ldots, D_{r_t}$ are calculated as the weakest solution to the following equation family.

$$[[n_1]] \equiv [[code.K(n_1)]][D_{r_1}, \cdots, D_{r_t}/r_1, \cdots, r_k],$$

$$\vdots$$

$$[[n_\ell]] \equiv [[code.K(n_\ell)]][D_{r_1}, \cdots, D_{r_t}/r_1, \cdots, r_t],$$
$$spec.pCtr(m_1) \sqsubseteq [[code.K(m_1)]][D_{r_1}, \cdots, D_{r_t}/r_1, \cdots, r_t], \qquad (1)$$

$$\vdots$$

$$spec.pCtr(m_k) \sqsubseteq [[code.K]](m_k)[D_{r_1}, \cdots, D_{r_t}/r_1, \cdots, r_t]$$

Solving the equations (1) is essentially equivalent to the problem of decomposition of sequential programs in the denotational setting. In general, the equations are not solvable. Nevertheless under some special restrictions, such as each occurrence of D_{r_i}, $i = 1, \cdots, t$ is linear, the equations can be solvable. The initial condition of $rCtr$ can be derived from $init.pCtr$ and $init.K$.

Example 5. We apply the above calculation procedure to Example 4. First from Theorem 2, $IF.wrc.K_2.B_2 = \langle\{tr : put_1^*\}, \{put_1(in\,x{:}int)\}\rangle$, and the protocol $prot.wrc.K_2.B_2 = put_1^*$, the design of the method put_1 is $\vdash tr' = tr^\frown\langle put_1\rangle$, and the initial condition is $tr = \langle\rangle$.

Similarly, for K_3 and B_3, the interface $IF.wrc.K_3.B_3 = \langle\{tr : get_1^*\}, \{get_1(out\,y{:}int)\}\rangle$, the initial condition $init.wrc.K_3.B_3 = tr = \langle\rangle$, the design of get_1 is $\vdash tr' = tr^\frown\langle get_1\rangle$, and protocol $prot.wrc.K_3.B_3 = get_1^*$. $\qquad\square$

6   Compositions of Components and Their Publications

Composing a composite component from existing simpler ones via connectors plays a key role in component-based methods. In this section, we first review and revise the compositions on component given in [4,1]. However, the main contribution in this section is to define composition on component publications and present their relation to the compositions of components.

6.1   Compositions of Components

We define the basic operators of components including *renaming*, *hiding*, *internalizing*, *plugging* and *feedback*.

Renaming. Renaming an interface method of a component is a simple connector defined as follows.

Definition 11. *Let K be a component and $m(x : T_1; y : T_2)$ a method signature that does not occur in $priMeth.K$.*

1. *Renaming a provided $n(u : T_1, v : T_2)$ in $pMeth.K$ gives a component $K[m/n]$ such that*
   - *$pIF.K[m/n] = \langle field.pIF.K, Meth.pIF.K + \{m\} - \{n\}\rangle, priMeth.K[m/n] = priMeth.K$ and $rIF.K[m/n] = rIF.K$;*
   - *$init.K[m/n] = (init.K)[m/n]$;*

- $code.K[m/n](m) = (code.K(n))[m/n]$, and $code.K[m/n](op) = (code.K(op))[m/n]$ for any other op in $pMeth.K[m/n] \cup priMeth.K[m/n]$.

2. *Renaming a required method $n(u : T_1, v : T_2)$ in rMeth.K gives the component $K[m/n]$ such that*
   - $pIF.K[m/n] = pIF.K$, $priMeth.K[m/n] = priMeth.K$ and $rIF.K[m/n] = \langle field.rIF.K,$
     $Meth.rIF.K - \{n\} + \{m\}\rangle$;
   - $init.K[m/n] = (init.K)[m/n]$;
   - $code.K[m/n](op) = code.K(op)[m/n]$ for any op in $pMeth.K[m/n] \cup priMeth.K[m/n]$.

Where $c[m/n]$ is the command obtained from c by replacing each occurrence of n with m.

Notice that in the above definition, the code of a provided method, a private method, or the initiation statement may contain some invocations to n, so we have to rename n to m in the corresponding code of the renamed component. Besides, $K[m/n] = K$ if n does not occur in K.

A renamed component $K[m/n]$ can be easily implemented by using a connector, which is a component that provides the method with the fresh name m and the body of m calls the provided method n of K.

Hiding. We sometimes restrict a user from using some provided methods of a component by hiding these methods $(K\backslash m)$. Hiding is semantically the same as moving the hidden methods from the provided interface to the set of private methods of the component. Formally,

Definition 12. *Let $K = (I, M, c_0, \mathbb{C}, J)$ be a component, $m \in Meth.I$. Hiding m in K is denoted by $K\backslash m$ and defined as $(\langle Meth.I - \{m\}, field.I\rangle, M \cup \{m\}, c_0, \mathbb{C}, J)$.*

The hiding operator is associative. Therefore hiding a set of provided methods is same as hiding them one by one. Notice that hiding should be used carefully as hiding a method may result in a dead component. E.g. in Example 3, $K_1\backslash put$ results in a deadlock.

$K\backslash m$ can be implemented by renaming each provided method n of K to a fresh method n_1, and by adding a connector component that provides all the methods n that K provides except for m, and each n calls its code, which is the renamed method n_1 of the renamed component.

Internalizing. Similar to hiding, *internalizing* a method m in a component K is to remove it from the provided interface of K and add it into the private method set, denoted by $K\diagup m$. However, unlike hiding, internalizing just changes all explicit invocations to the internalized method to implicit invocations to the method. For example, in Example 3, internalizing get in K_1 results in a new component that provides only put, but every execution of put will implicitly be followed by an execution of get, therefore it allows any number of put operations on consecution. Formally,

Definition 13. *For a component K and a set of methods M in its provided interface, we define the component $K\diagup M$ as*

- $pIF.K\diagup M = (pIF.K)\backslash M$, $priMeth.K\diagup M = priMeth.K + M$, $rIF.K\diagup M = rIF.K$,

- $init.K \diagup M = init.K$,
- $(code.K \diagup M)(n)$ can be defined in different ways:
  - $(code.K \diagup M)(n) = \sqcap_{s \in M^*} code.K(s); code.K(n); \sqcap_{s \in M^*} code.K(s)$ for $n \in pMeth.K \diagup M$, where $code.K(s)$ stands for the sequential execution of the methods in sequence s and $\sqcap$ is the nondeterministic choice operator in the program language,
  - $(code.K \diagup M)(n) = code.K(n)$ for $n \in priMeth.K$
  - $(code.K \diagup M)(m) = code.K(m)$ for $m \in M$

The above definition indicates internalizing essentially changes all explicit invocations to the internalized methods to implicit invocations. This is semantically equivalent to reprogramming all provided methods in $pMeth.K - M$ by adding possible sequences of invocations to M before and after the code of n, i.e. $code.K(n)$, for each $n \in pMeth.K - M$. However, instead of changing the code, the internalizing connector is implemented by programming a scheduling processes that synchronizes with the component on the internalized methods.

In most cases, the number of invocations to these internalized methods before and after a noninternalized method should be finite; otherwise internalizing must give rise to an divergence, i.e. livelock. We can see this by further investigating the example given in the above. After internalizing get in K_1, it is clear that put can execute infinite many times. Thus, internalizing put in $K_1 \diagup \{get\}$ will cause a divergence.

Plugging. The most often used composition in component construction is to plug the provided interface of a component K_1 into the required interface of another K_2, denoted by $K_1 \bowtie K_2$. A component can plug into another component only if they have no name conflicts.

Definition 14. *A component K_1 is pluggable to a component K_2 if the following conditions hold:*

1. $(field.pIF.K_1 \cap field.pIF.K_2) = \emptyset$, and $(pMeth.K_1 \cap pMeth.K_2) = \emptyset$;
2. $(priMeth.K_1 \cap priMeth.K_2) = \emptyset$;
3. $(field.rIF.K_1 \cap field.rIF.K_2) = \emptyset$, and $(rMeth.K_1 \cap rMeth.K_2) = \emptyset$;
4. $priMeth.K_i \cap (pMeth.K_j + rMeth.K_j + priMeth.K_j) = \emptyset$, where $i \neq j$ and $i, j = 1, 2$.

Notice that the above conditions can always be guaranteed by renaming conflicting names.

Definition 15. *Let K_1 be a component that is pluggable to a component K_2. Then plugging K_1 to K_2, denoted $K = K_1 \bowtie K_2$, is defined as follows:*

- $filed.pIF.K = filed.pIF.K_1 + field.pIF.K_2$;
- $pMeth.K = pMeth.K_1 + pMeth.K_2 - rMeth.K_1 - rMeth.K_2$;
- $priMeth.K = priMeth.K_1 + priMeth.K_2 + (pMeth.K_1 \cap rMeth.K_2) + (rMeth.K_1 \cap pMeth.K_2)$;
- $filed.rIF.K = filed.rIF.K_1 + field.rIF.K_2$;
- $rMeth.K = rMeth.K_1 + rMeth.K_2 - pMeth.K_1 - pMeth.K_2$;
- $init.K = init.K_1 \wedge init.K_2$; and
- $code.K(m) = (code.K_1 \oplus code.K_2)(m)$ for each $m \in \sum_{i=1}^{2} pMeth.K_i + priMeth.K_i$, where $\oplus$ is the union of two functions.

Notice that we do not allow calling circles in the above definition.

The above definition indicates that the provided methods of K_1 that are plugged to the required methods of K_2 become private and not available to the environment anymore, and vice versa.

Example 6. From the above definition, we know that the components K_2 and K_3 in Example 3 are pluggable, $K_2 \bowtie K_3$ can be defined as:

$$
\begin{aligned}
pIF.K_2 \bowtie K_3 &= \langle \{buff_1, buff_2 : int^*\}, \{put(in\, x{:}int), get(out\, y{:}int)\} \rangle \\
priMeth.K_2 \bowtie K_3 &= \{put_1(in\, x{:}int), get_1(out, y{:}int)\} \\
init.K_2 \bowtie K_3 &= buff_1 := \langle\,\rangle; buff_2 := \langle\,\rangle \\
code.K_2 \bowtie K_3(put) &= (buff_1 := \langle x \rangle) \triangleleft buff_1 = \langle\rangle \triangleright (put_1(\mathbf{head}(buff_1))) \\
code.K_2 \bowtie K_3(get) &= (y := \mathbf{head}(buff_2); buff_2 := \langle\rangle) \triangleleft buff_2 \neq \langle\rangle \triangleright get_1(y) \\
code.K_2 \bowtie K_3(get_1) &= (buff_1 \neq \langle\rangle) \rightarrow (y := \mathbf{head}(buff_1); buff_1 := \langle\,\rangle) \\
code.K_2 \bowtie K_3(put_1) &= (buff_2 = \langle\rangle) \rightarrow buff_2 := \langle x \rangle \\
rIF.K_2 \bowtie K_3 &= \emptyset.
\end{aligned}
$$

The transition graph of $K_2 \bowtie K_3$ is given in Fig.2, which is a two-place buffer.   □

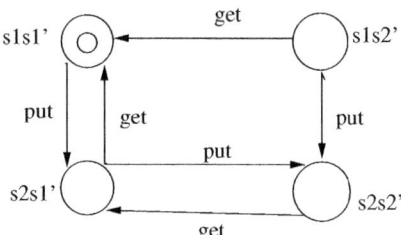

Fig. 2. Transition Graph of $K_2 \bowtie K_3$

Feedback. Let K be a component, suppose its provided method m has the same signature as the required method n. We use the notion $K[m \hookrightarrow n]$ to represent the component which feeds back its provided service m to the required one n such that whenever n is invoked in K, m is invoked in $K[m \hookrightarrow n]$. This *feedback* can be defined by using the plugging operator. Let F be the component, which only provides n, and the code of n be $n()\{m()\}$, i.e. F only requires m. Then $K[m \hookrightarrow n] \cong K \bowtie F$.

6.2   Composition of Publications

In this subsection, we investigate these operators at the level of publications from the user's point of view.

Renaming. Since a publication contains two publication contracts, renaming a method in a publication definitely involves renaming a method in a publication contract. So, we first define renaming in (publication) contract.

Definition 16. *Given a contract C and $n \in Meth.C$, renaming n to m in C, denoted $C[m/n]$, is defined as*

- $IF.C[m/n] = (IF.C)[m/n];$
- $init.C[m/n] = init.C;$
- $spec.C[m/n](n) = spec.C(n)$, and $spec.C[m/n](op) = spec.C(op)$ for any other method of the interface;
- $prot.C[m/n] = (prot.C)[m/n]$,

where m is a fresh method name, with the parameter type as n.

Definition 17. Let $U = \langle \mathcal{G}, \mathcal{A}, C \rangle$. Renaming a method $n \in Meth.\mathcal{G} \cup Meth.\mathcal{A}$ gives the publication $U[m/n] = \langle \mathcal{G}[m/n], \mathcal{A}[m/n], C[m/n] \rangle$.

Hiding.   Hiding a provided method in a publication is semantically equivalent to removing this method from its provided interface. Formally,

Definition 18. Let $U = (\mathcal{G}, \mathcal{A}, C)$ be a publication, and $m \in Meth.\mathcal{G}$. Hiding m in U, denoted $U \backslash m$, is defined by $U \backslash m = \langle \mathcal{G} \backslash m, \mathcal{A}, C \backslash m) \rangle$, where $\mathcal{G} \backslash m$ is defined by

- $IF.\mathcal{G} \backslash m = \langle field.\mathcal{G}, Meth.\mathcal{G} - \{m\} \rangle$,
- $init.\mathcal{G} \backslash m = init.\mathcal{G}$,
- $spec.\mathcal{G} \backslash m(n) = spec.\mathcal{G}(n)$ for each method n in $Meth.\mathcal{G} - \{m\}$, and
- $prot.\mathcal{G} \backslash m = (prot.\mathcal{G}) \backslash m$.

Note that hiding required methods in a component or publication does not make sense as required methods can be looked as bound variables (names) from a logical point of view.

Internalizing.   Internalizing a set of methods in a publication is via internalizing these methods in its provided contract and hiding them in its invocation dependency oriented protocol. Internalizing methods in a publication contract is quite similar to internalizing methods in a component by changing all explicit invocations to these internalized methods to implicitly invocations. Thus, from outside, these methods are invisible, but their impacts are still there.

Given a publication contract $C = (I, \theta, D, \mathcal{T})$, let $M \subseteq Meth.I$ be internalized in C and $m \in Meth.I - M$. Then, all possible sequences of invocations to these internalized methods in M before and after each execution of m can be calculated according to $\mathcal{T}$ as follows:

$$maxT(\mathcal{T}, m, M) \widehat{=} \{\ell \hat{~} e \hat{~} r \mid \ell \in M^* \wedge r \in M^* \wedge \exists tr_1, tr_2 \in Meth.I^*.tr_1 \hat{~} (\ell \hat{~} e \hat{~} r) \hat{~} tr_2 \in \mathcal{T}\}$$

Definition 19. Let $\mathcal{G}$ be a publication contract and $M \subseteq Meth.\mathcal{G}$. Internalizing M in $\mathcal{G}$, denoted $\mathcal{G} \diagup M$, is the publication such that

- $IF.\mathcal{G} \diagup M = (IF.\mathcal{G}) \backslash M$,
- $init.\mathcal{G} \diagup M = init.\mathcal{G}$,
- $spec.\mathcal{G} \diagup M(n) = \sqcap_{s \in maxT(prot.\mathcal{G}, n, M)} spec.\mathcal{G}(s)$ for each method n in $Meth.\mathcal{G} - M$, and
- $prot.\mathcal{G} \diagup M = prot.\mathcal{G} \mid (Meth.\mathcal{G} - M)$

Then, internalizing on a publication can be defined

Definition 20. For a publication $U = (\mathcal{G}, \mathcal{A}, C)$, $U \diagup M = (\mathcal{G} \diagup M, \mathcal{A}, C \mid (Meth.\mathcal{G} - M))$.

Plugging. We now define the plugging operator on publications. A publication U_1 can plug into another publication U_2 only if on one hand, U_1 and U_2 have no naming conflicts; on the other hand, if a method m is respectively specified in U_1's provided contract and U_2's required contract, then the former must be a refinement of the latter, and vice versa. Formally,

Definition 21. *Let U_i, $i = 1, 2$, be publications. U_1 and U_2 are pluggable if*

1. *$(field.pCtr.U_1 \cap field.pCtr.U_2) = \emptyset$, and $(Meth.pCtr.U_1 \cap Meth.pCtr.U_2) = \emptyset$;*
2. *$(field.rCtr.U_1 \cap field.rCtr.U_2) = \emptyset$, and $(Meth.rCtr.U_1 \cap Meth.rCtr.U_2) = \emptyset$;*
3. *$spec.pCtr.U_i(m) \sqsupseteq spec.rCtr.U_j(m)$, for each $m \in pMeth.U_i \cap rMeth.U_j$, where $i, j = 1, 2$ and $j \neq i$.*

Definition 22. *Given two publications U_1 and U_2, which are pluggable. Then plug U_1 to U_2 is denoted by $U_1 \bowtie U_2$, and defined as $U_1 \bowtie U_2 = \langle \mathcal{G}, \mathcal{A}, C \rangle$, where*

- *$field.\mathcal{G} = filed.pCtr.U_1 + field.pCtr.U_2$,*
- *$Meth.\mathcal{G} = pMeth.U_1 + pMeth.U_2 - rMeth.U_1 - rMeth.U_2$,*
- *$Meth.\mathcal{A} = rMeth.U_1 + rMeth.U_2 - pMeth.U_1 - pMeth.U_2$,*
- *$spec.\mathcal{G}(m) = spec.pCtr.U_1(m) \oplus spec.pCtr.U_2(m)$, for $m \in Meth.\mathcal{G}$,*
- *$spec.\mathcal{A}(m) = spec.rCtr.U_1(m) \oplus spec.rCtr.U_1(m)$, for $m \in Meth.\mathcal{A}$,*
- *$prot.\mathcal{G} = causal.U_1 \bowtie U_2 \downarrow (pMeth.U_1 - rMeth.U_2)$,*
- *$prot.\mathcal{A} = causal.U_1 \bowtie U_2 \downarrow (rMeth.U_1 - pMeth.U_2)$,*
- *$causal.U_1 \bowtie U_2 = causal.U_1 \parallel_{(rMeth.U_1 \cap pMeth.U_2) \cup (pMeth.U_1 \cap rMeth.U_2)} causal.U_2$.*

From the above definition, you can see that once a required method of a publication is provided by another publication, then the method does not appear in the plugging of the two publications. This is consistent with plugging two components makes a method required by one and provided by the other private to the composite component.

Example 7. From the above definition, we know that the publications U_{B_2} and U_{B_3} in Example 5 are pluggable, and $U_{B_2} \bowtie U_{B_3}$ is:

$$pIF.U_{B_2} \bowtie U_{B_3} = \langle \{buff_1, buff_2 : int^*\}, \{put(in\ x : int), get(out\ y : int)\} \rangle$$
$$rIF.U_{B_2} \bowtie U_{B_3} = \emptyset,$$
$$spec.pCtr.U_{B_2} \bowtie U_{B_3}(put(in\ x : int)) = (\vdash buff_1' = \langle x \rangle ^\frown buff_1) \lhd buff_1 = \langle \rangle \rhd (\vdash buff_1' = buff_1)$$
$$spec.pCtr.U_{B_2} \bowtie U_{B_3}(get(out\ y : int)) = (\vdash buff_2' = \mathbf{tail}(buff_2) \wedge y' = \mathbf{head}(buff_2)) \lhd buff_2 \neq \langle \rangle \rhd$$
$$(\vdash buff_2' = buff_2 \wedge \exists c \in int.y' = c)$$
$$causal.U_{B_2} \bowtie U_{B_3} = C_{B_2} \parallel_{\{get_1; put_1\}} C_{B_3}$$
$$= [(\langle put; get \rangle)^* ^\frown(\varepsilon + \langle put \rangle ^\frown(\langle put; get \rangle)^* +$$
$$\langle put \rangle ^\frown(\langle put; get \rangle)^* ^\frown \langle get \rangle)]^*.$$

We can see $U_{B_2} \bowtie U_{B_3}$ is exactly a publication of $K_2 \bowtie K_3$.   □

Feedback. Feedback for publications can be defined similarly to the definition for components.

A publication of a component tells the user what component does and how to use it. Therefore, it must be certified that the component does indeed do what is said in its publication. The following theorem shows that if the subcomponents conform to their publications, a composition of them will conform to the composition of their publications.

Theorem 6. *(Certification of Publication) All the operators defined above are compositional. That is,*

1. *if U is a publication of K, then U[m/n] is a publication of K[m/n];*
2. *if U is a publication of K, then U\m is a publication of K\m;*
3. *if U is a publication of K, U⤢M is a publication of K⤢M;*
4. *if U_1 is a publication of K_1 and U_2 is a publication of K_2, then $U_1 \bowtie U_2$ is a publication of $K_1 \bowtie K_2$;*
5. *if U is a publication of K, then U[m ↪ n] is a publication of K[m ↪ n].*

7   Conclusion and Future Work

This paper presents our further investigation on component publications and compositions of rCOS. We proposed a general approach on how to calculate the weakest required contract of a component according for a given provided contract. Then, we defined a set of composition operators on components and on their publications, and we studied the relation between compositions of components and their publications.

We hope the definitions and theorems in this paper set up the foundation for our ongoing research on the following problems

- **Decomposition.** The semantic equation (1) in Section 5 is in general unsolvable (undecidable). We have shown that the equations is solvable under some special cases. We will study further conditions under which it is solvable. This is significant to the general problem of program decomposition.
- **Refinement Theories.** The refinement relation between contracts and components in rCOS [5,1] is essentially the *failure/divergence* partial order of CSP [11]. The disadvantages of such a refinement relation include: 1) it can only be used to compare two components with the same interface; 2) it mainly concerns safety property, but in component-based methods, we have to consider the reactivity to invocations of services from the environment, which is liveness property. To illustrate the second disadvantage, consider the example: let m_1 and m_2 be two simple stateless methods, without divergence and deadlock. Let $C_1 = \{false\&m_1, false\&m_2\}$, $C_2 = \{true\&m_1, false\&m_2\}$, $C_3 = \{true\&m_1, true\&m_2\}$ be complete contracts. Then, $prot.C_1 = \emptyset$, $prot.C_2 = \{m_1\}^*$, and $prot.C_3 = \{m_1, m_2\}^*$. It is easy to get $\mathcal{D}(C_1) = \mathcal{D}(C_2) = \mathcal{D}(C_3) = \emptyset$, and $\mathcal{F}(C_1) = \{(\langle\rangle, \{m_1, m_2\})\} \wedge \mathcal{F}(C_2) = \{(\langle m_1^n \rangle, \{m_2\}) \mid n \geq 0\} \wedge \mathcal{F}(C_3) = \emptyset$. According to the definition, obviously, $C_1 \sqsubseteq C_3$ and $C_2 \sqsubseteq C_3$, but C_1 cannot be compared with C_2. But from a user's point of view, C_2 should be better than C_1.

  We often need to support incremental design by extending a component to provide more services. Therefore, we are currently studying a more general refinement theory with the concepts of *strongest provided contracts* and *weakest required contracts*.
- **Glue Theory.** We are interested in developing a coordination model for specification and verification of glue code in the framework of rCOS.

Acknowledgments

We thank Prof. Jifeng He for so much fruitful discussions on the topic with him and his useful comments on early version of this paper. We are also grateful to the anonymous referees for their criticisms and constructive comments that has led to substantial improvements of the presentation of this paper.

References

1. Chen, X., He, J., Liu, Z., Zhan, N.: A model of component-based programming. In: Arbab, F., Sirjani, M. (eds.) FSEN 2007. LNCS, vol. 4767, pp. 191–206. Springer, Heidelberg (2007)
2. de Alfaro, L., Henzinger, T.: Interface automata. In: Proceedings of the Ninth Annual Symposium on Foundations of Software Engineering (FSE'01), January 2001. ACM Press, New York (2001)
3. de Alfaro, L., Henzinger, T.: Interface theories for component-based design. In: Henzinger, T.A., Kirsch, C.M. (eds.) EMSOFT 2001. LNCS, vol. 2211, pp. 148–165. Springer, Heidelberg (2001)
4. He, J., Li, X., Liu, Z.: Component-based software engineering. In: Van Hung, D., Wirsing, M. (eds.) ICTAC 2005. LNCS, vol. 3722, pp. 70–95. Springer, Heidelberg (2005)
5. He, J., Li, X., Liu, Z.: rCOS: a refinement calculus of object systems. Theor. Comput. Sci. 365(1-2), 109–142 (2006)
6. He, J., Li, X., Liu, Z.: A theory of reactive components. Electr. Notes Theor. Comput. Sci. 160, 173–195 (2006)
7. Hoare, C.A.R., He, J.: Unifying Theories of Programming. Prentice-Hall, Englewood Cliffs (1998)
8. Holzmann, G.J.: Conquering complxity. Software technology, pp. 111–113 (December 2007)
9. Leavens, G.T., Leino, K.R.M., Poll, E., Ruby, C., Jacobs, B.: JML: notations and tools supporting detailed design in Java. In: OOPSLA 2000, pp. 105–106. ACM Press, New York (2000)
10. Mandrioli, D., Meyer, B.: Design by Contract. Prentice-Hall, Englewood Cliffs (1991)
11. Roscoe, A.W.: The Theory and Practice of Concurrency. Prentice Hall, Englewood Cliffs (1997)
12. Szyperski, C.: Component Software: Beyond Object-Oriented Programming. Addison-Wesley, Reading (1998)

Denotational Approach to an Event-Driven System-Level Language[*]

Huibiao Zhu, Jifeng He, Xiaoqing Peng, and Naiyong Jin

Shanghai Key Laboratory of Trustworthy Computing
Software Engineering Institute
East China Normal University
3663 Zhongshan Road (North), Shanghai, China, 200062
{hbzhu,jifeng,xqpeng,nyjin}@sei.ecnu.edu.cn

Abstract. As a system-level modelling language, SystemC possesses several novel features such as delayed notifications, notification cancelling, notification overriding and delta-cycle. It is challenging to formalise SystemC. In this paper, we study the denotational semantics for SystemC using *Unifying Theories of Programming* (abbreviated as UTP) [6]. Two trace variables are introduced, one is to record the state behaviours and another is to record the event behaviours. The timed model is formalised in a three-dimensional structure. A set of algebraic laws is explored, which can be proved via the achieved denotational semantics.

1 Introduction

SystemC is a system-level modelling language, which can be used to model a system at different abstract levels. Modelling and simulation in SystemC gives the designers early insights about the potential design problems that could arise. Compared with traditional hardware description languages, SystemC possesses several new and interesting features, including delayed notifications, notification cancelling, notification overriding and delta-cycle.

In SystemC, processes can trigger events actively while in Verilog [7] events are generated based on the changes of states. In SystemC, events represent some general condition during the execution of the program. An event can be notified on many separate occasions. There are three kinds of event notifications: immediate event notifications, delta-cycle delayed notifications and timed notifications. Delayed notifications can be cancelled via cancel statements before they are triggered. Delayed notifications on the same event override each other and only one delayed notification survives.

Although SystemC comes with a user manual ([9,10]), a formal semantics of SystemC is mandatory for various applications in simulation, synthesis, and

---

[*] This work is partially supported by the National Basic Research Program of China (No. 2005CB321904), the National High Technology Research and Development Program of China (No. 2007AA010302), the National Natural Science Foundation of China (No. 90718004), Shanghai STCSM project (No. 06JC14022 and No. 067062017) and Shanghai Leading Academic Discipline Project (No. B412).

A. Butterfield (Ed.): UTP 2008, LNCS 5713, pp. 258–278, 2010.

formal verification. Müller et al presented an ASM-based SystemC simulation semantics [12]. That semantics covers method, thread, and clocked thread behaviour as well as their interactions with the simulation kernel process. Gawanmeh et al extended the work in [12] to deal with more complex components of SystemC [2]. Habibi and Tahar presented a semantics of the main part of SystemC in terms of fixed points [3]. We have also provided an operational semantics for SystemC [11], where a set of algebraic laws has been explored via the concept of bisimulation [8].

This paper considers the denotational semantics of SystemC, where our approach is based on *Unifying Theories of Programming* (abbreviated as *UTP*) [6]. *UTP* was developed by Hoare and He in 1998 [6] and has been successfully applied in studying the semantics of programming languages and their algebraic laws, as well as the refinement calculus of different level programs. The new features of SystemC make it worthwhile to formalise its denotational semantics via *UTP* approach.

The rest of this paper is organized as follows. In section 2 we select a kernel subset of SystemC and present an introduction for the language. We also provide the denotational semantic model in this section. The timed model of SystemC is considered in a three-dimensional structure. A set of healthiness conditions is explored in order to achieve the denotational semantics. Section 3 is devoted to the denotational semantics using the *UTP* approach. Two traces are applied for the formalization, one is to record the state behaviour and another is to record the event behaviour. Section 4 explores the algebraic laws of SystemC, which can be proved via the achieved denotational semantics. A set of algebraic laws is studied, including the algebraic laws concerning the distinct features for SystemC. Section 5 concludes the paper.

2   The Semantic Model of SystemC

2.1   The Syntax of SystemC

In this paper we select a kernel subset of SystemC for exploring its semantics. Although it is a subset of SystemC, it still covers the interesting and main features, such as delay notifications, notification cancelling, notification overriding, channel, concurrent processes and delta-cycle. In this section, we present the syntax of the selected subset and give a brief introduction of its interesting features.

For simplicity, we omit the syntactic elements for representing the architecture of a SystemC program. The subset language adopts a C-like syntax:

$$PP ::= P \mid PP \parallel PP$$
$$P ::= \textbf{Skip} \mid v := exp \mid chan\_stmt \mid event\_stmt \mid wait\_stmt$$
$$\mid P; P \mid \textbf{if } b \textbf{ then } P \textbf{ else } P \mid \textbf{while } b \textbf{ do } P$$
$$chan\_stmt ::= ch??v \mid ch!!exp$$
$$event\_stmt ::= notify(e_{\Delta 0}) \mid notify(e_{\Delta 1}) \mid notify(e_{\sharp T}) \mid cancel(e)$$

$$wait\_stmt ::= wait(\Delta 1) \mid wait(\sharp T) \mid wait(e\_list)$$
$$e\_list ::= single\_e \mid \mathbf{or}_{i \in I}\{single\_e_i\}$$
$$single\_e ::= e \mid pe(ch) \mid ne(ch)$$

For statements such as **Skip**, assignment statement ($v := exp$), sequential composition ($P; Q$), conditional statement (**if** b **then** P **else** Q) and iteration statement (**while** b **do** P), their meanings are similar to the conventional programming language.

Channel output statement $ch!!exp$ is executed in evaluation phase, which generates a request to update the channel. These update requests will be carried out in the following update phase. Channel input statement $ch??v$ assigns the current value of channel ch to variable v.

An event is notified by statement $notify$. An event can be notified immediately (i.e., $notify(e_{\Delta 0})$) or after a period of time (i.e., $notify(e_{\Delta 1})$) or $notify(e_{\sharp T})$). Statement $cancel(e)$ cancels the delayed notifications on event e.

A process may wait for the arriving or firing of an event. These events can be classified into two types; i.e., single events or complex events. Single events can have three forms; i.e., e, $pe(ch)$ and $ne(ch)$, where event e can be generated by event notifications. $wait(pe(ch))$ is fired only when the current value of channel ch is greater than its previous value, whereas $wait(ne(ch))$ stands for the opposite firing case. Complex events can be of the form $\mathbf{or}_{i \in I}\{single\_e_i\}$. For the waiting of complex events, if anyone is fired or becomes active, the whole waiting behaviour becomes fired or active.

Different from traditional hardware description language, time delay has two types; i.e., micro time advance and macro time advance. $wait(\Delta 1)$ stands for one unit micro time advancing, whereas $wait(\#T)$ stands for T units macro time advancing.

$P \parallel Q$ means P runs in parallel with Q. Their communication is through channels and variables. Further, their synchronization is based on events.

If there exist branch processes of a parallel process ready to run, one branch will be selected to be executed. The selection is nondeterministic. Channels will be updated when a waiting command is encountered during the current execution. If all branch processes are still waiting, then time will be advanced. Micro time (Delta-cycle) will be advanced first. If that does not activate any processes, then macro time will be advanced. The executed is proceeded by the following steps.

(1) Evaluation Phase. Select a ready process to execute. The order of the selection is nondeterministic. The selected process does its execution until a waiting command is encountered. This sequence of instantaneous commands form an atomic action, which is uninterrupted.

   The execution of a process may cause immediate event notifications to occur. It may also generate pending requests to update channels in the following update phase.

(2) Update Phase. Carry out all pending channel update requests generated in last evaluation phase, which may generate some events $pe(ch)$ or $ne(ch)$. Then go to step (1).

(3) Micro Time (Delta-cycle) Advancing Phase. If there are no processes ready to run and no pending channel update requests, but there exist pending delta-cycle notifications or delta-cycle timeouts, advance the delta-cycle. Then determine which processes are ready to run and go to step (1).

(4) Macro Time Advancing Phase. If there are no processes ready to run, no pending channel update requests, no pending delta-cycle notifications and no delta-cycle timeouts, advance the current macro time by one time unit. And determine which processes become ready to run due to events or timeouts that are triggered at the current time. If there exist processes ready to run, then go to step 1, otherwise advance the current macro time by one time unit again.

2.2   The Denotational Semantics Model

SystemC possesses the feature of shared-variable concurrency. In order to deal with this feature, we introduce a sequence type variable $tr1$ for recording the behaviour of state change of a program. Moreover, SystemC not only has the feature of traditional time delay, it also contains the feature of Δ time delay (i.e., micro time delay). Therefore, the structure of $tr1$ can be depicted as Figure 1.

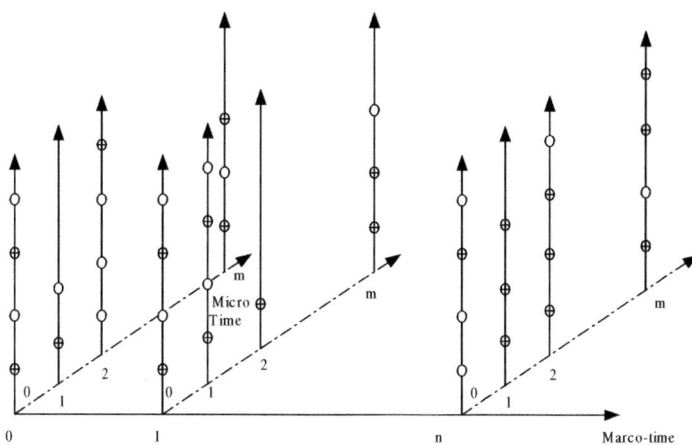

Fig. 1.

At the relative macro time "i" point, time may also advance in Δ time step, standing for the micro-time advancing. Therefore, a sequence of behaviours may be recorded at each Δ time point. These behaviours can be classified into two types; i.e., contributed by the process itself or its environment. In Figure 1, the symbol "$\oplus$" and "$\circ$" stand for the contribution by the process itself and its environment respectively.

In order to record these behaviours, the concept of snapshot is introduced, expressed as (σ, f), where σ stands for the contribution of the behaviour and

f stands for the flag. "$f = 1$" indicates that the behaviour is contributed by the process itself and "$f = 0$" indicates that the behaviour is contributed by its environment. Below is the formal structure of trace $tr1$.

$$Element1 = \{(\sigma, f) | \sigma \in State \wedge f \in \{0, 1\}\},$$

$$tr1 \in \textbf{seq}(\textbf{seq}(\textbf{seq}(Element1)))$$

Here, $\textbf{seq}(T)$ stands for a sequence type, where each sequence is composed of elements from type T.

We select the components of a snapshot using projections.

$$\pi_1((\sigma, f)) =_{df} \sigma \quad \text{and} \quad \pi_2((\sigma, f)) =_{df} f$$

In SystemC, waiting guards can be triggered by events, which can be generated by the process itself or its environment. We use the trace variable $tr2$ to record all the events generated by the process or its environment. $tr2$ has the same time structure, as shown in the above Figure 1. It can be defined as below.

$$Element2 = \{(e, f) | e \in Event \wedge f \in \{0, 1\}\}$$

$$tr2 \in \textbf{seq}(\textbf{seq}(\textbf{seq}(Element2)))$$

For any $tr1$ (or $tr2$) type trace s, $len(s)$ stands for the length of sequence s; i.e., it stands for the length of macro-time advancing. $s[0]$ and $s[len(s) - 1]$ stand for traces of the start point and end point of the current macro-time observation interval. Furthermore, $s[i][j]$ stands for the trace behaviour at the point of macro-time i and micro-time j.

Example 2.1. Let $P_i = notify(e_{i\Delta0})$; $notify(f_{i\Delta0})$; $u_i := u_i + 1$; $v_i := v_i + 2$ $(i = 1, 2)$. Assume that the initial states for the above four shared variables are 0. Consider the traces $tr1$, $tr2$ for process P_1, P_2 and $P_1 \parallel P_2$.

As the four statements in P_1 and P_2 form an atomic action respectively. Either $notify(e_{1\Delta0})$ or $notify(e_{2\Delta0})$ can be scheduled first. For all these considered traces, their lengths are 0, and their lengths at the current macro time point are also 0.

If $notify(e_{1\Delta0})$ is scheduled first, below are the three $tr1$ traces at the point of macro time 0 and micro time 0 for P_1, P_2 and $P_1 \parallel P_2$ respectively.

$$\langle(\sigma_1, 1)\rangle^\frown\langle(\sigma_2, 0)\rangle, \qquad \langle(\sigma_1, 0)\rangle^\frown\langle(\sigma_2, 1)\rangle, \qquad \langle(\sigma_1, 1)\rangle^\frown\langle(\sigma_2, 1)\rangle$$

where, $\sigma_1 = \{u_1 \mapsto 1, \ v_1 \mapsto 2, \ u_2 \mapsto 0, \ v_2 \mapsto 0\}$,

$\quad\quad\ \sigma_2 = \{u_1 \mapsto 1, \ v_1 \mapsto 2, \ u_2 \mapsto 1, \ v_2 \mapsto 2\}$

At this case, three $tr2$ traces at the point of macro time 0 and micro time 0 for P_1, P_2 and $P_1 \parallel P_2$ are shown below respectively.

$$\langle(e_1, 1)\rangle^\frown\langle(f_1, 1)\rangle^\frown\langle(e_2, 0)\rangle^\frown\langle(f_2, 0)\rangle, \qquad \langle(e_1, 0)\rangle^\frown\langle(f_1, 0)\rangle^\frown\langle(e_2, 1)\rangle^\frown\langle(f_2, 1)\rangle$$

$$\langle(e_1, 1)\rangle^\frown\langle(f_1, 1)\rangle^\frown\langle(e_2, 1)\rangle^\frown\langle(f_2, 1)\rangle$$

On the other hand, if $notify(e_{2\Delta0})$ is scheduled first, the analysis is similar. $\square$

As $tr1$ and $tr2$ have three dimensional structure, now we introduce the prefix definition between two $tr1$ (or $tr2$) type traces, denoted as $\preceq_1$.

Definition 2.2

$$s \preceq_1 t =_{df} \exists m, n \bullet \left(\begin{array}{l} m = len(s) \wedge n = len(t) \wedge m \leq n \wedge \\ \forall i \in \{0..m-2\} \bullet s[i] = t[i] \wedge \\ \exists k \bullet \left(\begin{array}{l} k = len(s[m-1]) \wedge \\ \forall l \in \{0..k-2\} \bullet s[m-1][l] = t[m-1][l] \wedge \\ s[m-1][k-1] \preceq t[m-1][k-1] \end{array} \right) \end{array} \right)$$

For traditional sequences s and t, $t - s$ stands for the sequence that subtracts sequence s from t with respect to the traditional prefix structure $\preceq$. On the other hand, if s and t are the sequences of $tr1$ (or $tr2$) type structure, $t - s$ has the similar meaning with respect to the new $\preceq_1$ prefix structure.

The execution of an atomic action is represented by a single snapshot. In order to describe the behaviour of individual shared variable assignment, we introduce a variable ttr to model the accumulated change made by the statements of the atomic action. An assignment is simply formulated as storing the result in variable ttr. Meanwhile, the current value of channel ch is also stored in variable ttr. On the completion of an atomic action, the corresponding snapshot is attached to the end of the trace to record its behaviour.

The event generated by channel receiving will not be immediately attached to the end of the trace variable $tr2$. After all the behaviours in an atomic action complete, the process enters into the update phase. Hence we use a trace variable RQ to record new channel states due to the channel receiving.

Three kinds of event notifications are introduced in SystemC for generating events. $notify(e_{\Delta 0})$ is used to generate event e, which will be active immediately. For $notify(e_{\Delta 1})$, it can generate event e that will be active in one micro time unit. Moreover, $notify(e_{\#T})$ also generates event e. However, it can only be active in T macro time units. For recording the events contributed by the above last two notification commands, we introduce two set type variables, $EN2$ and $EN3$. Here, $EN2$ records the generated events, which will be active in one micro time unit. $EN3$ contains the pairs (e, T), which indicates that event e will be active in T macro time units.

Example 2.3

Let $P = notify(e_{1\,\Delta 0})$; $notify(e_{2\,\Delta 1})$; $notify(e_{3\,\#2})$; $notify(f_{1\,\#4})$. Assume that $EN2 = \{e_1\}$ and $EN3 = \{(e_3, 1), (f_1, 5)\}$. Here e_1, e_2, e_3 and f_1 are all events. Now we consider new $EN2$ and $EN3$ after the execution of all these notifications.

The first immediate notification will record event e_1 in the trace variable $tr2$, which may fire the environment's waiting command immediately. Moreover, event e_1 should also be removed from $EN2$, while $EN3$ remains unchanged. The execution of the second notification command will add event e_2 to $EN2$ and also keep $EN3$ unchanged.

As $(e_3, 1)$ has already belonged to $EN3$, the execution of the third command will not add anything to $EN3$. Furthermore, the fourth command will remove pair $(f_1, 5)$ from $EN3$ and add $(f_1, 4)$ to $EN3$ because the time stamp in $(f_1, 4)$

is smaller than the time stamp in $(f_1, 5)$. Therefore, the final values of $EN2$ and $EN3$ are:

$$EN2 = \{e_2\} \quad \text{and} \quad EN3 = \{(e_3, 1), (f_1, 4)\} \qquad \square$$

The execution of a SystemC process can never undo an atomic action that has already been performed. A formula P which identifies a program must therefore imply this fact; i.e., it has to meet the following healthiness condition:

$(H1)\ P\ =\ P \wedge Inv(tr1, tr2)$

where, $Inv(tr) =_{df} (tr1 \preceq_1 tr1') \wedge (tr2 \preceq_1 tr2')$

Here $Inv(tr1, tr2)$ indicates $tr1$ and $tr2$ are the prefix of $tr1'$ and $tr2'$ respectively, which indicates that trace can only get longer. As in relational calculus, for any denotational variable u, we use u and u' to stand for the initial value and final value for the current execution respectively.

A SystemC process may perform an infinite computation and enter a *divergent state*. To distinguish its chaotic behaviour from the stable ones we introduce the variables $ok, ok' : Bool$ into the semantical model, where $ok = true$ indicates that the process has been started, and $ok' = true$ states that the process is *stable* currently. $ok = false$ means that the program has never started and even the initial values are unobservable.

Definition 2.4. Let Q and R be formulae not containing ok and ok'. Define

$$Q \vdash R =_{df} \neg ok \wedge Inv(tr1, tr2) \vee \neg Q \vee (ok' \wedge R)$$

A *design* is a formula that is expressed in this form. $\qquad \square$

A timing controlled statement cannot start its execution before its guard is triggered. To distinguish its waiting behaviour from terminating one, we introduce another pair of variables $wait, wait' : Bool$. When $wait$ is true the program is started in an intermediate state, and when $wait'$ is true the program is idle. Therefore, for sequential composition "$R\ ;\ P$", all the intermediate observations of R are also the intermediate observations of "$R\ ;\ P$". Control can pass from R to P only when R is in its terminating state, distinguished by the fact that $wait'$ is false. If program P is asked to start in a waiting state of R, it leaves the state unchanged.

$(H2)\ P\ =\ II \lhd wait \rhd P$, where

$$II =_{df} \textbf{true} \vdash (\bigwedge_{s \in \{tr1, tr2, ttr, X, RQ, EN2, EN3, wait\}} s' = s)$$

and $\ P \lhd b \rhd Q =_{df} (P \wedge b) \vee (\neg b \wedge Q)$

Here, X stands for the vector containing all the local variables for the current program. $X' = X$ indicates that all the local variables remain unchanged.

Definition 2.5. Formula P is healthy iff there exists a design $D = (Q \vdash (W \lhd wait' \rhd T))$ such that $P = \textbf{H}(D)$, where

$$\textbf{H}(Y) =_{df} (II \lhd wait \rhd (Y \wedge Inv(tr1, tr2))) \qquad \square$$

Theorem 2.6. $\textbf{H}(Y)$ satisfies healthiness condition $(H1)$ and $(H2)$. $\qquad \square$

Now we give the definition for sequential composition.

Definition 2.7. Let P_1 and P_2 be formulae. Define

$$P1 \; ; \; P2 \; =_{df} \; \exists S \; \bullet \; (P1[S/V'] \wedge P2[S/V])$$

where, V stands for the list of all denotational variables in our model; i.e., ok, $tr1$, $tr2$, ttr, X, RQ, $EN2$,$EN3$, $wait$.   □

Now we provide a simple refinement calculus for healthy formulae and show that they are closed under sequential composition, conditional choice, disjunction and conjunction.

Theorem 2.8.   If $\neg Q_i = \neg Q_i \wedge Inv(tr1, tr2)$, $W_i = W_i \wedge Inv(tr1, tr2)$, $T_i = T_i \wedge Inv(tr1, tr2)$ for $i = 1$, 2, then

(1) $\mathbf{H}(Q_1 \vdash W_1 \lhd wait' \rhd T_1) \; ; \; \mathbf{H}(Q_2 \vdash W_2 \lhd wait' \rhd T_2)$

$= \; \mathbf{H}(\neg(\neg Q_1 \; ; \; Inv(tr1, tr2)) \wedge \neg(T_1 \; ; \; \neg Q_2) \vdash (W_1 \vee (T_1 \; ; \; W_2)) \lhd wait' \rhd (T_1 \; ; \; T_2))$

(2) $\mathbf{H}(Q_1 \vdash W_1 \lhd wait' \rhd T_1) \lhd b \rhd \mathbf{H}(Q_2 \vdash W_2 \lhd wait' \rhd T_2)$

$= \; \mathbf{H}((Q_1 \lhd b \rhd Q_2) \vdash (W_1 \lhd b \rhd W_2) \lhd wait' \rhd (T_1 \lhd b \rhd T_2))$

(3) $\mathbf{H}(Q_1 \vdash W_1 \lhd wait' \rhd T_1) \; \vee \; \mathbf{H}(Q_2 \vdash W_2 \lhd wait' \rhd T_2)$

$= \; \mathbf{H}((Q_1 \wedge Q_2) \vdash (W_1 \vee W_2) \lhd wait' \rhd (T_1 \vee T_2))$

(4) $\mathbf{H}(Q_1 \vdash W_1 \lhd wait' \rhd T_1) \; \wedge \; \mathbf{H}(Q_2 \vdash W_2 \lhd wait' \rhd T_2)$

$= \; \mathbf{H}((Q_1 \vee Q_2) \vdash ((Q_1 \Rightarrow W_1) \wedge (Q_2 \Rightarrow W_2)) \lhd wait' \rhd ((Q_1 \Rightarrow T_1) \wedge (Q_2 \Rightarrow T_2)))$□

The laws for disjunction and conjunction can be generalised to the union and intersection of arbitrary set. This indicates that healthy formulae form a complete lattice under the implication order. We use HF to denote the set of all healthy formulae. The weakest fixed point of a monotonic function Φ on HF can be defined by

$$\mu_{HF} X \bullet \Phi(X) \; =_{df} \; \sqcap\{F \mid F \Rightarrow \Phi(F) \text{ and } F \in HF\}$$

In the subsequent sections we will formalize a SystemC process P as a healthy formula of the form

$$\mathbf{H}(\neg div(P) \vdash wait(P) \lhd wait' \rhd ter(P))$$

where, $div(P)$, $wait(P)$ and $ter(P)$ stand for the divergent behaviour, waiting behaviour and termination behaviour of P respectively.

3   The Denotational Semantics for SystemC

3.1   Sequential Constructs

Program variables can be classified into two types; i.e., shared variable assignment and local variable assignment.

Let

$$Env(s) =_{df} \forall i, j \bullet ((0 \leq i \leq len(s)) \wedge (0 \leq j \leq len(s[i]))) \Rightarrow \pi_2(s[i][j]) \in 0^*$$

$$Instenv(s) =_{df} len(s) = 0 \wedge len(s[0]) = 0 \wedge Env(s)$$

$Env(s)$ is used to describe the phenomena that the new states (or new events) are generated by the environment. $Instenv(s)$ behaves like $Env(s)$, and the macro time and micro time do not advance.

$$InstEnv =_{df} \mathbf{H} \left(\mathbf{true} \vdash \left(\begin{array}{c} \neg wait' \wedge \bigwedge_{t \in \{tr1, tr2\}} Instenv(t' - t) \\ \wedge\, ttr' = \pi_1(last(last(last(tr1')))) \\ \wedge\, same(\{X, RQ, EN2, EN3\}) \end{array} \right) \right)$$

where, $same(A) =_{df} \bigwedge_{x \in A} (x' = x)$. Here $last(s)$ stands for the last element of sequence s.

Formula $InstEnv$ indicates that the trace behaviours of $tr1$ and $tr2$ should all satisfy a condition expressed in the function $Instenv$ and the state of the last snapshot of trace $tr1$ is assigned to variable ttr. All other variables remain unchanged.

Now we consider the behaviour of **Skip**. If it is the first statement of an atomic action, its behaviour can be formalised using formula $InstEnv$. Otherwise, it behaves like II.

$$\mathbf{Skip} =_{df} InstEnv \lhd ttr = null \rhd II$$

Next we consider the definition of shared variable assignment. Let

$$sassign(v, e) =_{df} \mathbf{H} \left(\mathbf{true} \vdash \left(\begin{array}{c} \neg wait' \wedge ttr' = ttr[e/v] \wedge \\ same(\{tr1, tr2, X, RQ, EN2, EN3\}) \end{array} \right) \right)$$

Formula $sassign(v, e)$ indicates that the value of expression e is assigned to v via the state variable ttr. Based on this, we can have the definition of shared-variable assignment $v := e$.

$$v := e =_{df} \mathbf{Skip} \,;\, sassign(v, e)$$

For considering the definition of local variable assignment, we introduce function $lassign(x, f)$.

$$lassign(x, f) =_{df} \mathbf{H} \left(\mathbf{true} \vdash \left(\begin{array}{c} \neg wait' \wedge x' = f \wedge \\ same(\{tr1, tr2, ttr, X \backslash \{x\}, \\ RQ, EN2, EN3\}) \end{array} \right) \right)$$

The definition of local variable assignment $x := f$ can be described as:

$$x := f =_{df} \mathbf{Skip} \,;\, lassign(x, f)$$

$(P \,;\, Q)$ behaves like P before P terminates, and then behaves like Q afterwards.

$$(P \,;\, Q) =_{df} (P) \,;\, (Q)$$

The definition of conditional can be defined based on **Skip**.

$$\mathbf{if}\ b\ \mathbf{then}\ P\ \mathbf{else}\ Q =_{df} \mathbf{Skip} \,;\, (P \lhd b \rhd Q)$$

The iteration construct is defined in the same way as its counterpart in conventional programming languages

$$\mathbf{while}\ b\ \mathbf{do}\ P =_{df} \mu_{HF} X \bullet \mathbf{if}\ b\ \mathbf{then}\ (P; X)\ \mathbf{else}\ \mathbf{Skip}$$

where the notation $\mu_{HF} X \bullet F(X)$ denotes the weakest fixed point of the monotonic function F over the set of healthy formulae.

3.2 Channel Communication

Firstly, we consider the message output via channel. Let

$$RqUpdate1(ch, exp)$$

$$=_{df} \mathbf{H} \left(\text{true} \vdash \left(\begin{array}{c} \neg wait' \wedge \bigwedge_{x\in\{tr1,tr2\}} Instenv(x'-x) \\ \wedge \, same(\{ttr, X, EN2, EN3\}) \\ \wedge RQ' = RQ\backslash(ch, -)^\frown \langle(ch, exp(y))\rangle \end{array} \right) \right)$$

$$RqUpdate2(ch, exp)$$

$$=_{df} \mathbf{H} \left(\text{true} \vdash \left(\begin{array}{c} \neg wait' \wedge \, same(\{tr1, tr2, ttr, X, EN2, EN3\}) \\ \wedge RQ' = RQ\backslash(ch, -)^\frown \langle(ch, exp(y))\rangle \end{array} \right) \right)$$

where:

(1) y in the above two formulae stands for expression $\pi_1(last(last(last(tr1))))$.

(2) $^\frown$ stands for the concatenation of two traditional sequences.

(3) "$\backslash$" is used to remove the pairs from the update sequence. It can be defined as below:

$$\langle\rangle\backslash(ch, m) =_{df} \langle\rangle$$

$$(\langle(ch, -)\rangle^\frown t)\backslash(ch, m) =_{df} t\backslash(ch, m)$$

$$(\langle(ch1, n)\rangle^\frown t)\backslash(ch, m) =_{df} \langle(ch1, n)\rangle^\frown(t\backslash(ch, m))$$

Here, $ch1 \neq ch$ and "$-$" matches to any elements.

For channel output command, its execution can be classified into two cases. One is the case that the channel is in the first statement of an atomic action, while another stands for the opposite. Formulae $RqUpdate1(ch, exp)$ and $RqUpdate2(ch, exp)$ stand for the above two cases respectively.

The last line in the above two formulae indicates that, before appending the value and its associate channel ch to the trace variable, the snapshots concerned with the corresponding channel need to be removed because of the recording of the new value of the channel. Furthermore, if channel output command is the first statement of an atomic action, the environment can have the chance to do variables update and events generating. This is reflected via function "$Instenv(\ )$". Based on the above definitions, we can have the definition of channel output.

$$ch!!exp =_{df} RqUpdate1(ch, exp) \lhd ttr = null \rhd RqUpdate2(ch, exp)$$

Next we can consider the message input via a specific channel $ch??w$, which can be considered as assigning the value on channel.

If w is the shared variable, then

$$ch??w =_{df} \mathbf{Skip} \ ; \ sassign(w, ch)$$

If w is the local variable, then

$$ch??w =_{df} \mathbf{Skip} \ ; \ lassign(w, ch)$$

3.3   Event Notification

In order to define the semantics of event notifications, we first define formula $InstEnv1$ as below. Compared with formulae $InstEnv$, the formula below does not concern the issue about assigning a value to variable ttr. It keeps the value of ttr unchanged.

$$InstEnv1 =_{df} \mathbf{H} \left(\mathbf{true} \vdash \left(\begin{array}{c} \neg wait' \wedge \bigwedge_{t \in \{tr1,tr2\}} Instenv(t'-t) \\ \wedge\, same(\{ttr, X, RQ, EN2, EN3\}) \end{array} \right) \right)$$

Then we can define a formula **Skip1** as below, which can be used to define the semantics of event notifications.

$$\mathbf{Skip1} =_{df} InstEnv1 \lhd ttr = null \rhd II$$

Now we consider the immediate event notification $notify(e_{\Delta 0})$.

$$InstEApp(e) =_{df} \mathbf{H} \left(\mathbf{true} \vdash \left(\begin{array}{c} \neg wait' \wedge len(tr2'-tr2) = 0 \wedge \\ len((tr2'-tr2)[0]) = 0 \wedge \\ (tr2'-tr2)[0][0] = \langle (e,1) \rangle \wedge \\ same(tr1, ttr, X, RQ, EN2, EN3) \end{array} \right) \right)$$

Formula $InstEApp(e)$ indicates that event e is attached to the end of trace variable $tr2$ without macro and micro time advancing.

$$EveUpd0(e) =_{df} \mathbf{H} \left(\mathbf{true} \vdash \left(\begin{array}{c} \neg wait' \wedge same(tr1, tr2, ttr, X, RQ) \\ \wedge\, EN2' = f1(EN2, e) \\ \wedge\, EN3' = g1(EN3, e) \end{array} \right) \right)$$

where, $f1(A, e) =_{df} \{x \mid x \in A \wedge x \neq e\}$
$g1(A, e) =_{df} \{(x, T) \mid (x, T) \in A \wedge x \neq e\}$

Formula $EveUpd0(e)$ models the case below. For the immediate event notification $notify(e_{\Delta 0})$, after event e is attached to the end of the trace variable, two set type variables $EN2$ and $EN3$ need to be modified due to the attachment of event e to trace variable $tr2$. This modification is reflected from the above two functions $f1(A, e)$ and $g1(A, e)$.

Then $notify(e_{\Delta 0})$ can be defined as below:

$$notify(e_{\Delta 0}) =_{df} \mathbf{Skip1} \;;\; InstEApp(e) \;;\; EveUpd0(e)$$

Now we consider the definition of $notify(e_{\Delta 1})$. Firstly we can give the definition for function $EveUpd\Delta(e)$. It models the behaviour that event e needs to be added to $EN2$, while removing the event e related pairs from $EN3$.

$$EveUpd\Delta(e) =_{df} \mathbf{H} \left(\mathbf{true} \vdash \left(\begin{array}{c} \neg wait' \wedge same(tr1, tr2, ttr, X, RQ) \\ \wedge\, EN2' = f2(EN2, e) \\ \wedge\, EN3' = g2(EN3, e) \end{array} \right) \right)$$

where, $f2(A, e) =_{df} A \cup \{e\}$
$g2(A, e) =_{df} \{(x, T) \mid (x, T) \in A \wedge x \neq e\}$

Different from $notify(e_{\Delta 0})$, the execution of $notify(e_{\Delta 1})$ only makes the changes for variable $EN2$ and $EN3$, while leaving other variables unchanged. Then $notify(e_{\Delta 1})$ can be defined as below:

$$notify(e_{\Delta 1}) =_{df} \mathbf{Skip1} \;;\; EveUpd\Delta(e)$$

For considering the definition of $notify(e_{\#T})$, we first give the definition for function $EveUpd\#((e, T))$ below.

$$EveUpd\#((e,T))=_{df} \mathbf{H}\left(\mathbf{true} \vdash \begin{pmatrix} \neg wait' \wedge \ same(tr1,tr2,ttr,X,RQ) \\ \wedge EN2' = f3(EN2,e,T) \\ \wedge EN3' = g3(EN2,EN3,e,T) \end{pmatrix}\right)$$

where:

$$f3(A,e,T) =_{df} A$$

$$g3(A,B,e,T)$$

$$=_{df} \begin{cases} B \cup \{(e,T)\} & \text{if } e \notin A \wedge \forall T1 \in N \bullet (e,T1) \notin B \\ B & \text{if } e \in A \ \text{ or } \ \exists T1 \in N \bullet T1 \leq T \wedge (e,T1) \in B \\ B \backslash \{(e,T3) \mid \exists T3 \in N\bullet & \text{if } \exists T2 \in N \bullet T2 > T \wedge (e,T2) \in B \\ \quad (e,T3) \in B\} \cup \{(e,T)\} \end{cases}$$

The behaviour of macro time event notification $notify(e_{\#T})$ is mainly represented by the above two functions ($f3$ and $g3$) via formula $EveUpd\#((e,T))$. Macro time event notification does not affect set variable $EN2$. However, it affects the set variable $EN3$, which can be dealt with in several cases shown above.

For function $g3(EN2,EN3,e,T)$, its behaviour can be classified into three cases. The first one expresses the case that $EN2$ does not contain event e and $EN3$ does not contain event e related pairs. Then the result of this macro time event notification simply adds the pair (e,T) to $EN3$. The second expresses the case that either e is already in $EN2$ or there exist event e related pairs whose macro time stamp is not greater than T in $EN3$. For this case, $EN3$ remains unchanged. Furthermore, if there exist event e related pairs whose macro time stamp is greater than T, then $EN3$ needs to be modified. For this case, event e related pairs need to be removed from $EN3$, and the considered pair (e,T) needs to be added.

Then $notify(e_{\#T})$ can be defined as below:

$$notify(e_{\#T}) =_{df} \mathbf{Skip1} \ ; \ EveUpd\#((e,T))$$

Finally we consider the event cancel statement $cancel(e)$. The cancellation is mainly represented by formula $EveUpd0(e)$.

$$cancel(e) =_{df} \mathbf{Skip1} \ ; \ EveUpd0(e)$$

3.4 Event Waiting

This section considers the semantics of event waiting statement. Firstly, we give some preliminary definitions.

$$attach$$

$$=_{df} \mathbf{H}\left(\mathbf{true} \vdash \begin{pmatrix} \neg wait' \wedge ttr = null \wedge \\ same(tr2,X,RQ,EN2,EN3) \wedge \\ tr1' = tr1 \lhd ttr = null \ \vee \ last(y) = ttr \rhd \\ \begin{pmatrix} y' = y^\frown \langle(ttr,1)\rangle \wedge \\ len(tr' - tr) = 0 \wedge \\ len((tr' - tr)[0]) = 0 \end{pmatrix} \end{pmatrix}\right)$$

where, $y = last(last(tr))$ and $y' = last(last(tr'))$ in the above formula. The purpose of the behaviour of $attach$ is to append the contribution stored in ttr to the end of trace variable $tr1$.

Next we define $update(RQ)$, which is used to generate events from sequence RQ. The generated events will be appended to the end of trace variable $tr2$. $update(s)$ can be defined as:

if $s = \langle \rangle$,   then $update(s) =_{df} II$

otherwise,

$$update(s) =_{df} \mathbf{H} \left(\mathbf{true} \vdash \left(\begin{array}{c} \neg wait' \wedge s' = tail(s) \wedge \\ (\bigvee_{i \in \{1,2,3\}} CompAtt(s, i)) \wedge \\ same(tr1, ttr, X, EN2, EN3) \end{array} \right) \right) ; \; update(s)$$

where, $tail(s)$ stands for the sequence s but the first element.

Here, $CompAtt(s, op)$ can be defined as:

(1) if $op = 1$,   then
$CompAtt(s, op)$
$=_{df} ttr(\pi_1(head(s))) < \pi_2(head(s)) \wedge y' = y^\frown \langle (pe(\pi_1(head(s))), 1) \rangle \wedge$
$ttr' = ttr[\pi_2(head(s))/\pi_1(head(s))]$

(2) if $op = 2$,   then
$CompAtt(s, op)$
$=_{df} ttr(\pi_1(head(s))) > \pi_2(head(s)) \wedge y' = y^\frown \langle (ne(\pi_1(head(s))), 1) \rangle \wedge$
$ttr' = ttr[\pi_2(head(s))/\pi_1(head(s))]$

(3) if $op = 3$,   then
$CompAtt(s, op)$
$=_{df} ttr(\pi_1(head(s))) = \pi_2(head(s)) \wedge (tr2' = tr2) \wedge (ttr' = ttr)$

where, $y' = last(last(tr2'))$ and $y = last(last(tr2))$ in the above definition. Here $head(s)$ stands for the first element of sequence s.

The behaviour of $ComAtt(s, op)$ is to generate the exact event based on the two values recorded in ttr and the first element of trace s for the corresponding channel. If the first value is less than the second, positive edge event on the channel will be generated. Inversely, negative edge event will be generated. Further, if the two values are the same, no event will be generated.

Now we consider the semantics for the triggering for single event $wait(et)$. There are two event triggering cases. The first case is the self-triggering case; i.e., the event is triggered by the process itself, which indicates that the event is generated by the most recent completed atomic actions. We use formula $selftrig(et)$ to represent this case. In this case, the update based on sequence RQ needs to be executed, as well as attaching the result of the recent completed atomic action. It should also need to be judged whether the current situation belongs to the self-triggering case.

$$selftrig(et) =_{df} \textbf{Skip2} \; ; \; update(RQ) \; ; \; (ttr \neq null) \wedge attach \; ; \; selfjudge(et)$$

where:

$$\textbf{Skip2} =_{df} InstEnv2 \lhd ttr = null \rhd II$$

and

$$InstEnv2$$
$$=_{df} \textbf{H}\left(\textbf{true} \vdash \left(\begin{array}{c} \neg wait' \wedge ttr' = \pi_1(last(last(last(tr1)))) \\ \wedge \, same(\{tr1, tr2, X, RQ, EN2, EN3\}) \end{array}\right)\right)$$

and

$$selfjudge(et)$$
$$=_{df} \textbf{H}\left(\textbf{true} \vdash \left(\begin{array}{c} \neg wait' \wedge last(last(last(tr2))) = (et, 1) \\ \wedge \, same(tr1, ttr, X, RQ, EN2, EN3) \end{array}\right)\right)$$

The second case is the environment triggering case; i.e., an event is generated by the environment and this event triggers the waiting behaviour. For this case, the update based on sequence RQ and the attachment for the recent atomic action need to be executed. Then the process waits for the environment to generate the event which can trigger the current waiting command. The whole behaviour can be partitioned into two phases. One is the waiting period, during which the environment can generate events and these events can not trigger our waiting command. The second phase is the triggering behaviour.

$$await(et)$$
$$=_{df} \textbf{Skip2} \; ; \; update(RQ) \; ;$$
$$(ttr = null \vee last(last(last(tr2))) \neq (et, 1)) \wedge attach \; ; \; aawait(et)$$

and

$$aawait(et) =_{df} \textbf{H}\left(\textbf{true} \vdash \left(\begin{array}{c} \forall i, j \bullet et \notin \pi_1((tr2' - tr2)[i][j]) \wedge \\ \bigwedge_{x \in \{tr1, tr2\}} Env(x' - x) \wedge \\ same(RQ, X, ttr, EN2, EN3) \end{array}\right)\right)$$

$$trig(et) =_{df} \textbf{H}\left(\textbf{true} \vdash \left(\begin{array}{c} Instenv(tr2' - tr2) \wedge \\ last(last(last(tr2' - tr2))) = \langle(et, 0)\rangle \wedge \\ same(tr1, ttr, RQ, EN2, EN3) \end{array}\right)\right)$$

Therefore, we can have:

$$wait(et) =_{df} selftrig(et) \vee (await(et) \; ; \; trig(et))$$

Next we consider the semantics of compound event "or". Let

$$selfjudge(\textbf{or}_{i \in I}\{et_i\})$$
$$=_{df} \textbf{H}\left(\textbf{true} \vdash \left(\begin{array}{c} \neg wait' \wedge same(tr1, X, ttr, EN2, EN3) \\ \wedge (\bigvee_{i \in I} last(last(last(tr2))) = (et_i, 1)) \end{array}\right)\right)$$

$$aawait(\textbf{or}_{i \in I}\{et_i\})$$

$$=_{df} \mathbf{H} \left(\mathbf{true} \vdash \left(\begin{array}{c} \forall i,j,k \bullet et_i \notin \pi_1((tr2'-tr2)[j][k]) \wedge \\ \bigwedge_{x \in \{tr1,tr2\}} Env(x'-x) \wedge \\ same(RQ,X,ttr,EN2,EN3) \end{array} \right) \right)$$

$$trig(\mathbf{or}_{i \in I}\{et_i\})$$

$$=_{df} \mathbf{H} \left(\mathbf{true} \vdash \left(\begin{array}{c} Instenv(tr2'-tr2) \wedge \\ \bigvee_{i \in I}(last(last(last(tr2'-tr2))) = \langle(et_i,0)\rangle) \wedge \\ same(tr1,ttr,RQ,EN2,EN3) \end{array} \right) \right)$$

Therefore, we can have:

$$wait(\mathbf{or}_{i \in I}\{et_i\})$$
$$=_{df} selftrig(\mathbf{or}_{i \in I}\{et_i\}) \vee (await(\mathbf{or}_{i \in I}\{et_i\}) ; trig(\mathbf{or}_{i \in I}\{et_i\}))$$

For time delay statements, we first consider the Δ delay (micro time delay).

$$hold\Delta(1) =_{df} \mathbf{H} \left(\mathbf{true} \vdash \left(\begin{array}{c} wait' \wedge \bigwedge_{x \in \{tr1,tr2\}} Instenv(x'-x) \wedge \\ same(ttr,X,RQ,EN2,EN3) \quad \vee \\ \neg wait' \wedge same(ttr,X,RQ,EN2,EN3) \\ \wedge \bigwedge_{x \in \{tr1,tr2\}}(len(x'-x) = 0 \wedge \\ len((x'-x)[0]) = 1 \wedge Env(x'-x)) \end{array} \right) \right)$$

$hold\Delta(1)$ stands for the behaviours of one unit micro time advancing. Before the advancing, the environment can generate new states and new events at the current micro time point. After the advancing, the environment can also do similar behaviours at the new micro time point.

$$W upd\Delta =_{df} \mathbf{H} \left(\mathbf{true} \left(\begin{array}{c} \neg wait' \wedge len(tr2'-tr2) = 0 \wedge \\ len((tr2'-tr2)[0]) = 0 \wedge \\ \pi_1((tr2'-tr2)[0][0]) \in permu(EN2) \wedge \\ \pi_2((tr2'-tr2)[0][0]) \in 1^* \wedge \\ same(ttr,tr1,X,RQ,EN3) \wedge EN2' = \emptyset \end{array} \right) \right)$$

where, $permu(A)$ stands for the set containing all permutations of set A.

$W upd\Delta$ indicates that a sequence of events will be attached to the end of trace $tr2$ at the current time point. These sequences are the permutations of all the events recorded in $EN2$.

Hence, $wait(\Delta1) =_{df} UpdAtt ; hold\Delta(1) ; W upd\Delta$

where, $UpdAtt =_{df} \mathbf{Skip2} ; update(RQ) ; attach$

Next we consider the semantics of macro-time delay. Firstly, we introduce formula $hold\#(n)$. $hold\#(n)$ models the behaviour that macro time can advance n time units. If time has not advanced n units, the process is still at the waiting state. Otherwise, the process is at the terminating state. During the time advancing period, only the environment can generate new states or new events.

$hold\#(n) =_{df}$

$$\mathbf{H} \left| \; true \vdash \left(\begin{array}{c} \left(\begin{array}{c} wait' \wedge len(tr1' - tr1) < n \wedge Env(tr1' - tr1) \wedge \\ len(tr2' - tr2) < n \wedge Env(tr2' - tr2) \wedge \\ same(ttr, X, RQ, EN2, EN3) \\ \vee \\ \neg wait' \wedge len(tr1' - tr1) = n \wedge Env(tr1' - tr1) \wedge \\ len(tr2' - tr2) = n \wedge Env(tr2' - tr2) \wedge \\ same(ttr, X, RQ, EN2, EN3) \end{array} \right) \end{array} \right) \right.$$

After n macro time units elapse, new events need to be attached to the end of trace $tr2$ at the current micro time point. These events are taken from the pairs in $EN3$ whose time stamp is n. We use $Wupd\#(n)$ to model these behaviours.

$$Wupd\#(n) =_{df} \mathbf{H} \left| \; true \vdash \left(\begin{array}{c} \left(\begin{array}{c} len(tr2' - tr2) = 0 \wedge \\ len((tr2' - tr2)[0]) = 0 \wedge \\ (\; \pi_1((tr2' - tr2)[0][0]) \in \\ permu(\{e \mid (e, n) \in EN3\}) \;) \wedge \\ \pi_2((tr2' - tr2)[0][0]) \in 1^* \wedge \\ EN3' = \{(e, T) \mid (e, n + T) \in EN3\} \wedge \\ same(tr1, ttr, X, RQ, EN2) \end{array} \right) \end{array} \right) \right.$$

Based on the above definitions, we can define macro-time delay.

$$wait(n) =_{df} UpdAtt \; ; \; hold\#(n) \; ; \; Wupd\#(n)$$

3.5 Parallel Composition

For defining parallel composition, we first provide several merge functions.

$$pmerge(s, t, u) =_{df} \left(\begin{array}{c} \pi_1(s[0..len(t) - 1]) = \pi_1(t[0..len(t) - 1]) \wedge \\ \pi_1(s[0..len(t) - 1]) = \pi_1(u[0..len(t) - 1]) \wedge \\ (\; \pi_2(u[0..len(t) - 1]) = \pi_2(s[0..len(t) - 1]) + \\ \pi_2(t[0..len(t) - 1]) \;) \wedge \\ 2 \notin \pi_2(u[0..len(t) - 1]) \wedge len(u) = len(s) \end{array} \right)$$

where, $\langle i_1, ..., i_n \rangle + \langle j_1, ..., j_n \rangle =_{df} \langle (i_1 + j_1), ..., (i_n + j_n) \rangle$

A snapshot is expressed as a pair (σ, f). The first two lines indicate that the sequence of the states (or events) for a parallel process is the same as the sequence of states (or events) for its two components. The third and fourth lines inform that any state contributed by a parallel process is actually the contribution by one of its components. These two lines also indicate that any state (or event) contributed by the environment of a parallel process cannot be the contribution of either of its components. The fifth line means that any state contributed by a parallel process cannot be contributed by both of its components.

$pmerge(s, t, u)$ is to merge two sequences s and t, the result is stored in sequence u. Here, s and t are one dimensional sequences; i.e., the sequence of type $tr1$ (or $tr2$) at some micro time points. For $pmerge(s, t, u)$, the length of sequence s is greater than or equal to the length of sequence t.

Next we introduce $merge(s, t, u)$, which merges two sequences s and t into one single sequecne. Its definition is based on the above $pmerge$ function. For $merge(s, t, u)$, there are no length restrictions on sequence s and t.

$merge(s, t, u)$

$$=_{df} \left(\begin{array}{l} len(s) > len(t) \Rightarrow \left(\begin{array}{l} pmerge(s, t, u) \wedge \\ u[len(t)..len(s) - 1] = s[len(t)..len(s) - 1] \end{array} \right) \wedge \\ len(s) = len(t) \Rightarrow pmerge(s, t, u) \wedge \\ len(s) < len(t) \Rightarrow \left(\begin{array}{l} pmerge(t, s, u) \wedge \\ u[len(s)..len(t) - 1] = t[len(s)..len(t) - 1] \end{array} \right) \end{array} \right)$$

Now we introduce the merge behaviour further. $Pmerge(s, t, u)$ is to merge two sequences s and t into one single sequence u, where the types of these sequences are of $tr1$ and $tr2$. Similarly, the length of s is also greater than or equal to the length of t.

$Pmerge(s, t, u)$

$=_{df} \forall i \bullet 0 \leq i \leq len(t) - 1 \Rightarrow$

$$\left(\begin{array}{l} len(s[i]) > len(t[i]) \Rightarrow \left(\begin{array}{l} \forall j \bullet 0 \leq j \leq len(t[i]) - 1 \Rightarrow \\ merge(s[i][j], t[i][j], u[i][j]) \wedge \\ u[i][len(t[i])..len(s[i]) - 1] = \\ s[i][len(t[i])..len(s[i]) - 1] \end{array} \right) \wedge \\ len(s[i]) = len(t[i]) \Rightarrow \left(\begin{array}{l} \forall j \bullet 0 \leq j \leq len(t[i]) - 1 \Rightarrow \\ merge(s[i][j], t[i][j], u[i][j]) \end{array} \right) \wedge \\ len(s[i]) < len(t[i]) \Rightarrow \left(\begin{array}{l} \forall j \bullet 0 \leq j \leq len(s[i]) - 1 \Rightarrow \\ merge(t[i][j], s[i][j], u[i][j]) \wedge \\ u[i][len(s[i])..len(t[i]) - 1] = \\ t[i][len(s[i])..len(t[i]) - 1] \end{array} \right) \end{array} \right)$$

Based on the above "$Pmerge()$" function, we introduce merge function $Merge(s, t, u)$. It has similar behaviours as function $merge(s, t, u)$. The difference is that the types of sequence s and t here are of $tr1$ and $tr2$.

$Merge(s, t, u)$

$$=_{df} \left(\begin{array}{l} len(s) > len(t) \Rightarrow \left(\begin{array}{l} PMerge(s, t, u) \wedge \\ u[len(t)..len(s) - 1] = s[len(t)..len(s) - 1] \end{array} \right) \wedge \\ len(s) = len(t) \Rightarrow PMerge(s, t, u) \wedge \\ len(s) < len(t) \Rightarrow \left(\begin{array}{l} PMerge(t, s, u) \wedge \\ u[len(s)..len(t) - 1] = t[len(s)..len(t) - 1] \end{array} \right) \end{array} \right)$$

Finally we introduce the merge operator $\otimes$ for two behaviours P and Q. Its definition is based on the above $Merge$ function.

$P \otimes Q$

$=_{df} \exists \ tr1_P, tr2_P, tr1_Q, tr2_Q, ttr_P, ttr_Q,$
$\qquad EN2_P, EN3_P, EN2_Q, EN3_Q, RQ_P, RQ_Q \quad \bullet$

$$\begin{pmatrix} P[tr1_P, tr2_P, ttr_P, RQ_P, EN2_P, EN3_P / \\ \quad tr1, tr2, ttr, RQ, EN2, EN3] \qquad\qquad \wedge \\ Q[tr1_Q, tr2_Q, ttr_Q, RQ_Q, EN2_Q, EN3_Q / \\ \quad tr1, tr2, ttr, RQ, EN2, EN3] \qquad\qquad \wedge \\ Merge(tr1_P, tr1_Q, tr1) \qquad\qquad\qquad \wedge \\ Merge(tr2_P, tr2_Q, tr2) \qquad\qquad\qquad \wedge \\ RQ' = \langle\rangle \wedge EN2' = \emptyset \qquad\qquad\qquad \wedge \\ EN3' = EN3_P \cup EN3_Q \end{pmatrix}$$

We are now ready to define the denotational semantics for program P and Q. This can be proceeded by considering the divergent, waiting and terminating behaviours of $P \parallel Q$.

- It stays at a waiting state if either component does so.

$$wait(P \parallel Q)) =_{df} (\ wait(P) \otimes wait(Q) \ \vee \ wait(P) \otimes ter(Q) \ \vee \\ ter(P) \otimes wait(Q)\ )$$

- It terminates when both components complete their execution.

$$ter(P \parallel Q) =_{df} (\ ter(P) \otimes ter(Q)\ )$$

- It behaves chaotically when either component is divergent.

$$div(P \parallel Q) \\ =_{df} (\ div(P) \otimes div(Q) \ \vee \ div(P) \otimes wait(Q) \ \vee \ div(P) \otimes ter(Q) \ \vee \\ div(Q) \otimes wait(P) \ \vee \ div(Q) \otimes ter(P)\ )$$

4   Algebraic Laws

Algebra is well-suited for direct use by engineers in symbolic calculation of parameters and the structure of an optimal design [5,6]. This section aims to explore a set of algebraic laws for SystemC. These laws can be verified with respect to the semantics given in the above section.

For assignment, conditional, iteration, nondeterministic choice and sequential composition, our language enjoys similar algebraic properties as those reported in [4,6]. Moreover, parallel composition can have similar expansion laws as those in [13] by introducing an extra operator named "*guarded choice*". In what follows, we shall only focus on novel algebraic properties for SystemC.

4.1   Channel Statements

The behaviour of channel input statement $ch??v$ is to assign the current value of ch to variable v, which does no effect on channel ch. So the algebraic laws associated with channel input statements are similar to those associated with assignments.

Channel output statement is executed during the evaluation phase of a delta-cycle. The new value will not be available to be read until the next delta-cycle.

L1. $ch!!exp$; $S = S$; $ch!!exp$

where, $S \in \{$ **Skip**, $x := exp$, $ch??x$, $notify(e_{\Delta 0})$,
$\qquad\qquad\quad notify(e_{\Delta 1})$, $notify(e_{\sharp T})$, $cancel(e)\}$

If multiple channel output statements occur to the same channel, the last statement executed determines the new value of the channel.

L2. $ch!!exp$; $ch1!!exp1$; $ch!!exp' = ch1!!exp1$; $ch!!exp'$

where, $ch \neq ch1$.

From L1 and L2, we can have:

- For each channel, at most one output statement takes its effect in an atomic action.

4.2   Event Statements

Events are used to synchronize concurrent processes. Therefore, the execution order between statements dealing with events and statements dealing with variables and channels can be swapped in an atomic action.

L1 $S1; S2 = S2; S1$, where,

$S1 \in \{notify(e_{\Delta 0}), notify(e_{\Delta 1}), notify(e_{\sharp T}), cancel(e)\}$,
$S2 \in \{$ **Skip**, $x := exp$, $ch??x$, $ch!!exp\}$

The effect of delayed notifications does not occur immediately, so the order of delayed notifications on different events can be changed in an atomic action.

L2 $notify(e_{DT1})$; $notify(f_{DT2}) = notify(f_{DT2}); notify(e_{DT1})$

where, $DT1 \in \{\Delta 0, \Delta 1, \sharp T\}$, $DT2 \in \{\Delta 1, \sharp T\}$

An immediate notification can override the pending notification on the same event.

L3 $notify(e_{DT}); notify(e_{\Delta 0}) = notify(e_{\Delta 0})$,   where $DT \in \{\Delta 1, \sharp T\}$

Only pending notifications can be cancelled. And at any moment, for one event at most one pending notification can exist.

L4 (1) $notify(e_{\Delta 0}); cancel(e) = notify(e_{\Delta 0})$

$\qquad$ (2) $notify(e_{DT}); cancel(e) = cancel(e)$

$\qquad$ (3) $cancel(e); cancel(e) = cancel(e)$

where, $DT \in \{\Delta 1, \sharp T\}$

More than one delayed notification on the same event override each other and the one scheduled to occur earlier overrides that scheduled to occur later. Delta-cycle delayed notifications are scheduled to occur earlier than timed notifications.

L5 (1) $notify(e_{DT1}); notify(e_{DT2})$ $\qquad$ (2) $notify(e_{\sharp T1}); notify(e_{\sharp T2})$

$\qquad\quad = notify(e_{DT2}); notify(e_{DT1})$ $\qquad\qquad = notify(e_{\sharp T2}); notify(e_{\sharp T1})$

$\qquad\quad = notify(e_{\Delta 1})$ $\qquad\qquad\qquad\qquad\quad = notify(e_{\sharp T1})$

where, $T1 \leq T2$, $DT1, DT2 \in \{\Delta1, \sharp T\}$ and $(DT1 = \Delta1) \vee DT2 = \{\Delta1\}$.

From the above laws, we can have:

- For each event, at most one delta-cycle delayed notification takes effect during one delta-cycle.
- For each event, at most one timed delayed notification takes effect during one simulation time unit.

5   Conclusion

Compared with traditional programming language, SystemC possesses several novel features, including delayed notifications, notification cancelling, notification overriding and delta-cycle. In this paper we studied its denotational semantics via the concept of *Unifying Theories of Programming* [6]. The timed model was formalised in a three dimensional structure. A refinement calculus was designed for this three dimensional denotational model. A set of algebraic laws has been studied, especially those which can represent the novel features of SystemC. These laws can be verified via our denotational model.

For the future, we are continuing to work on the semantics for SystemC, especially the further unifying theories [1,6,13] for the various semantics of SystemC. Further, program verification based on our achieved model for SystemC is also an interesting topic to be explored.

References

1. Brookes, S.D.: Full abstraction for a shared-variable parallel language. Information and Computation 127(2), 145–163 (1996)
2. Gawanmeh, A., Habibi, A., Tahar, S.: An executable operational semantics for SystemC using abstract state machines. Technical report, Department of Electrical and Computer Engineering, Concordia University Montreal (March 2004)
3. Habibi, A., Tahar, S.: SystemC fixpoint semantics. Technical report, Department of Electrical and Computer Engineering, Concordia University Montreal (January 2005)
4. He, J.: Provably Correct Systems: Modelling of Communication Languages and Design of Optimized Compilers. McGraw-Hill International Series in Software Engineering (1994)
5. Hoare, C.A.R., Hayes, I.J., He, J., Morgan, C., Roscoe, A.W., Sanders, J.W., Sorensen, I.H., Spivey, J.M., Sufrin, B.: Laws of programming. Communications of the ACM 38(8), 672–686 (1987)
6. Hoare, C.A.R., He, J.: Unifying Theories of Programming. Prentice Hall International Series in Computer Science (1998)
7. IEEE. IEEE Standard Hardware Description Language based on the Verilog Hardware Description Language, vol. IEEE Standard 1364-2001. IEEE, Los Alamitos (2001)
8. Milner, R.: Communication and Mobile System: π-calculus. Cambridge University Press, Cambridge (1999)

9. Open SystemC Initiative (OSCI). Functional Specification for SystemC 2.0 (October 2001)
10. Open SystemC Initiative (OSCI). SystemC 2.0.1 Language Reference Manual (2003)
11. Peng, X., Zhu, H., He, J., Jin, N.: An operational semantics of an event-driven system-level simulator. In: Proc. SEW-30: The 30th IEEE/NASA Software Engineering Workshop, Columbia, Maryland, USA, April 2006, pp. 190–200. IEEE Computer Society Press, Los Alamitos (2006)
12. Ruf, J., Hoffmann, D.W., Gerlach, J., Kropf, T., Rosenstiel, W., Müller, W.: The simulation semantics of systemc. In: DATE '01: Proceedings of the conference on Design, automation and test in Europe, Piscataway, NJ, USA, March 2001, pp. 64–70. IEEE Press, Los Alamitos (2001)
13. Zhu, H.: Linking the Semantics of a Multithreaded Discrete Event Simulation Language. PhD thesis, London South Bank University (February 2005)

Author Index

GPSR Compliance

*The European Union's (EU) General Product Safety Regulation (GPSR)
is a set of rules that requires consumer products to be safe and our
obligations to ensure this.*

*If you have any concerns about our products, you can contact us on
ProductSafety@springernature.com*

In case Publisher is established outside the EU, the EU authorized
representative is:

Springer Nature Customer Service Center GmbH
Europaplatz 3
69115 Heidelberg, Germany

Batch number: 09490872

Printed by Printforce, the Netherlands